The Development of the British Welfare State

The Development of the British Welfare State

MICHAEL SULLIVAN

Department of Social Policy
University of Wales, Swansea

PRENTICE HALL
HARVESTER WHEATSHEAF

London   New York   Toronto   Sydney   Tokyo   Singapore
Madrid   Mexico City   Munich

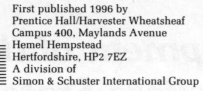

First published 1996 by
Prentice Hall/Harvester Wheatsheaf
Campus 400, Maylands Avenue
Hemel Hempstead
Hertfordshire, HP2 7EZ
A division of
Simon & Schuster International Group

© Michael Sullivan 1996

All rights reserved. No part of this publication may be reproduced,
stored in a retrieval system, or transmitted, in any form, or by any
means, electronic, mechanical, photocopying, recording or otherwise,
without prior permission, in writing, from the publisher.
For permission within the United States of America
contact Prentice Hall Inc., Englewood Cliffs, NJ 07632

Typeset in 9½/12pt Melior by
Keyword Publishing Services Ltd, Barking

Printed and bound in Great Britain by
T. J. Press (Padstow) Ltd

Library of Congress Cataloging-in-Publication Data

Available from the publisher

British Library Cataloguing in Publication Data

A catalogue record for this book is available from
the British Library

ISBN 0–13–518184–4

1 2 3 4 5   00 99 98 97 96

Library
University of Texas
at San Antonio

For Sue

and for the medical staff of the breast-care service at Ysbyty Tysog Philip (Prince Philip Hospital), Llanelli, who reminded us again of the importance of a national health service free at the point of use

Contents

Acknowledgements

Writing a book such as this while managing a social policy department would have been impossible without the decision of University of Wales, Swansea, to grant me five months sabbatical leave. My first debt is therefore to my university though, with the 1996 Research Assessment Exercise looming and with the Department's Teaching Quality Assessment successfully negotiated, they no doubt thought it was time to grant me my first sabbatical leave in fourteen years. I am also indebted to my social policy colleagues in Swansea for picking up my summer workload and especially to Ken Blakemore who wisely resisted the temptation to be me during my leave but who nonetheless ended up dealing with many of the things that usually find their way to my desk.

Clare Grist has, as usual, seen the project through with a mixture of tact, astuteness, encouragement and firmness. My thanks go to her. Without her talents, neither this nor my two most recent books would have been so smoothly negotiated. I am also indebted to Alison Stanford at Prentice Hall/ Harvester Wheatsheaf who moved heaven and earth to ensure the publication of this book by the magic date of 31 March 1996 at which point the Funding Council's time for publication of research to be counted in the 1996 Research Assessment ran out!

I am also indebted to the anonymous readers of the manuscript. They drew my attention to issues which I was in danger of overlooking. I hope that I have dealt successfully with some of these issues at least.

Though sabbatical leave has allowed me to complete this book, other matters have also borne in on me. It has been written in the period immediately following Sue Sullivan's recent brush with cancer. I mention this not to elicit the sympathy of reviewers but because, once more, I have been struck by the preciousness of the National Health Service and of those doctors committed to performing an effective and patient-centred service. The service offered to Sue was second to none. In writing the chapter on the NHS, the importance of a public health service struck me even more forcefully than it had previously done. I also mention this episode because it helps to explain the book's dedication.

Numerous colleagues and students have contributed to my understanding of the welfare state. I thank them, while reserving for myself responsibility for all that is deficient or mistaken about this book.

My final thanks must go to Sue Sullivan who, despite the tumult going on in her (and my) life, encouraged the completion of this project and insisted on its importance. Other, more disinterested, critics may question her judgement. Nobody will question the unselfishness of her support.

Michael Sullivan
Swansea

Introduction

This is a book about the British welfare state. It attempts to plot a political and social history of the development of the welfare state. It describes and asks questions about welfare without the state and about the road to comprehensive state involvement in welfare with the advent of the welfare state. It analyses the emergence of the classic welfare state in the early post-war period and considers its rise, and alleged fall. It reflects on the emergence of markets in welfare in the recent period and on an apparent re-emphasis of the individual in social policy. These reflections take place on two levels: first, in Part One, we consider these issues in relation to the welfare state in general before moving on in Part Two to develop the arguments at the level of individual welfare state services.

Viewed from the mid-1990s, the heyday of the 'classic welfare state' appears to have passed (Lowe, 1993).

Following the election of the post-war Labour government, a package of state sponsored services was introduced. Taken together, those services made up the welfare state. A national health service (NHS) was created, which was intended to provide universal health care free at the point of use for all citizens. Compulsory secondary education, a key element of the 1944 Education Act, was introduced with the stated purpose of equalising the educational opportunities of children from different social classes. A system of social security, drawing largely on the philosophy outlined in the Beveridge Report (HMSO, 1942), replaced the less significant social insurance schemes of the early twentieth century Liberal governments, and was seen by many as the instrument by which poverty would be eradicated. The state replaced private charities as the main provider of personal social services and intervened in the provision of housing in a way undreamed of before the Second World War.

By the 1990s much seems to have changed. At the surface level, the NHS continues to provide services free at the point of use to those that need them. However, recent reforms have emphasised the need to ration services and have created an internal market within the service (Sullivan, 1992). Markets have also been introduced into the provision of personal social services. In the 1980s and 1990s state social services departments, while retaining the responsibility for purchasing all services, have been required to contract out elements of service provision to the charitable and private sectors of welfare. Momentous changes have occurred in relation to housing policy, key among them being the decision in the early 1980s to allow council tenants to buy the council houses in which they lived. This aspect of 'peoples' capitalism' (Thatcher, 1983) had the twin effect of increasing the proportion of people owning their own homes and of seriously depleting the council house stock. Secondary education remains free and compulsory but changes in the funding of higher education have introduced a loan element into the student grant as well as encouraging universities to increase student numbers without proportionate increases in fee income. The meaning and implications of these changes and others will be analysed in greater detail later in the book. Suffice it to say here that, on the surface at least, significant changes have occurred in both the provision of welfare and in the principles underpinning that provision. Much of this change is seen, by some at least, as springing from an understanding of society promoted by New Right thinkers and acted upon, however imperfectly, by three 1980s governments headed by Margaret Thatcher. Thatcherite social policy is seen as differing from the classic welfare state not only in its emphasis on efficiency but, more importantly, in its emphasis on *individualistic* rather than *collectivist* assumptions. In this apparently new order, individuals should be responsible, at least in part, for financing their own welfare and a greater proportion of the population should be freed from the shackles of the 'nanny state' and allowed to satisfy the *natural* inclination to own property rather than rent it from the local state.

Of course, the ideas which nurtured the classic welfare state – as well as the practices which stemmed from those ideas – were also at some distance from earlier welfare principles and practices. Nineteenth and early twentieth century welfare provision, from the Victorian Poor Law to self-help and philanthropy, rested on individualistic assumptions. Those in need of welfare had, likely as not, placed themselves in that position. They should therefore be encouraged to find their own solutions to self-imposed misery or, if the recipients of state or philanthropic help, should receive it under conditions of 'less eligibility' (Pimlott, 1988; Digby, 1989).

The ideology of the Victorian Poor Law divided the poor into deserving, and therefore worthy of philanthropic action, and undeserving, to be punished for their feckless behaviour. Some commentators see the roots of this individualistic and punitive approach to welfare provision and the growth of private charity organisations like the Charity Organisation Society as emerging, in part at least, from particular religious ideologies. According to this approach, the Christian revival of the mid-nineteenth century nourished the seeds of individualism from which social action grew and flourished (Parry *et al.*, 1979). Evangelical Christianity, with its emphasis on personal salvation, is seen here as leading to philanthropic work with an emphasis on rescuing the immoral or preventing immorality. Poverty is, in these accounts, ignored as a possible cause of need. Instead, its individual manifestations, from theft to prostitution, are taken as the problem and an attempt is made to 'save' fallen *individuals*.

Others see the origins of nineteenth century welfare as rooted in quite a different morality. For Steadman Jones (1971) the ancestry of nineteenth century philanthropic and social welfare action are better seen in the need for a well-socialised proletariat in order to integrate all sections of the population into the structure, culture, norms and values of capitalist society and prevent social revolution. He reminds his readers of the philanthropist Samuel Smith's caution that:

> *I am deeply convinced that the time is approaching when this seething mass of human misery will shake the social fabric, unless we grapple more earnestly with it than we have done . . . The proletariat may strangle us unless we teach it the same virtues which have elevated the other classes of society. (Smith, cited in Steadman Jones, 1971, p. 291)*

On the face of it then, the circle has been squared: individualism as the motor of economic and social policy in the nineteenth and early twentieth centuries gave way to the collectivism of the classic welfare state only to re-emerge in the late twentieth century.

This is the conclusion of some at least (Digby, 1989). One of the major tasks of this book is to subject the claim of the demise of welfare statism to critical scrutiny. To do so we will use the history of twentieth century social policy as an intellectual vehicle. The passengers in this vehicle are a set of critical questions which will be returned to at appropriate junctures:

- How do we understand the coming of the welfare state?
- Did the move to comprehensive state welfare arise from stirrings of collectivism or is it better understood as a ransom paid for security and stability?
- Did the emergence of the welfare state mark a break with pre-war capitalism or is continuity more obvious than change?
- What have been the major policy developments during the welfare state years and what political processes can we discern behind them?
- Can we discern major changes in the philosophies underpinning social policy over time?

These passengers, or – to change the metaphor – intellectual anchors will prompt us throughout the book to construct plausible accounts of the development of social policy in mid to late twentieth century Britain.

The shape of the book

The book is divided into three parts. Part One, *The development of the British welfare state*, comprises four chapters which look at the evolution of social policy in general during the present century.

Chapter 1 concentrates on social policy debates and developments in the early decades of the twentieth century. Particularly, it looks at the tentative welfarism of the Liberal governments of the early century and the conversion of the Labour Party from hostility to welfare to a welfarist party. In other words, it acts as a bridge leading us from that period where welfare was most often provided outside the state, or by a patchwork of minimal state services and private welfare agencies.

Chapter 2 considers war-time developments in social policy and their influence on the growth of a post-war welfare state. It analyses the immediate pre-war search by some Conservatives for a 'middle way' (Macmillan, 1938) between capitalism and socialism and its effect on erstwhile dominant ideas about the legitimacy of state intervention in economic and social policy. It suggests that this re-orientation of political principle, together with the growth of collectivism and the experience of war, created a fertile seed-bed for the development of new ideas and policies in welfare and were rooted in a *de facto* political consensus on post-war aims between the major political parties. The chapter discusses the extent to which the earlier emergence of Keynesianism and the social ideas of Beveridge, and particularly of the Beveridge Report, created a social and economic legitimacy for comprehensive state involvement in welfare. The extent to which these pre-welfare state policies reflected the will of the British public is considered. The chapter closes by looking forward to the immediate post-war years and to the Labour government's plans for a welfare state.

Chapter 3 falls into three sections. The first documents and comments on the emergence of a contribution-based, full-employment-reliant welfare state in the immediate post-war period. It considers the economic, social and political contexts of welfare state emergence and the principles on which a supposedly comprehensive welfare state were based. It deliberates the extent to which the institutions that appeared can be regarded as Labour's political property alone and draws attention to the apparent political consensus at its establishment. It looks at the way in which questions about the extent of welfare funding were, in fact, questions about political and social priorities. The second section reflects on the growth of the welfare state, as measured by both the scope of services and expenditure, through to the early 1970s. The final section of the chapter introduces the reader to increasingly strong objections to welfare marshalled towards the end of this period. These objections, questioning both the fiscal and political legitimacy of welfare statism, were, it will be argued, forerunners of attacks on the welfare state made in the late 1970s and the 1980s.

Chapter 4, the final chapter in this part of the book, covers the last twenty years. It argues that significant changes have occurred in provision and that these changes stem from a transformation in dominant political ideologies married to changed economic conditions. Using policy examples, the chapter will consider whether it is legitimate to see these changes as 'granny footsteps' on the way to strategically-planned radical change or whether it is more appropriate to see the changes as reflecting pragmatic responses to changed economic and social climates.

Part Two of the book, *Welfare state services*, moves the analysis from the macro-level of the welfare state as social institution to the intermediate level of individual social policy areas. Each chapter presents a chronological account of major policy developments in the area and analyses their significance. Major case studies, using original as well as secondary material, are constructed in the areas of education and health. This reflects the importance attached to these services by, and the support they garner from, the population at large. This extended treatment is also aimed at exposing the political processes involved in the emergence and implementation of policy which are clearer in these services than in the others. These case studies are followed by chapters on personal social services, housing and social security which possess the virtue of relative brevity because they make use of general principles and understandings developed in the previous chapters.

In Chapters 5 and 6 we look at education policy. Following a broadly chronological structure these chapters are organised around the following themes:

Schooling

- The Butler Act and the introduction of universal secondary education.
- The campaign for comprehensive education.
- Comprehensivisation and the standards debate.
- The great debate on education.
- The introduction and development of a national curriculum.
- The marketisation of schooling: the example of the grant-maintained option.

Higher education

- Higher education before Robbins.
- The Robbins 'revolution': widening access to higher education.
- The development of higher education policy in the 1970s.
- Contraction in higher education in the 1980s.

In Chapter 7 we look at health policy. We argue that the development of post-war health policy is best seen as falling into five stages, each reflecting important considerations of the time in which they emerge. It will consider, *inter alia*, the extent to which such changes have been driven by external factors and factors internal to the National Health Service. The chapter is organised around the following five stages:

1. The establishment of the National Health Service. Here we document the establishment of the NHS by the post-war Labour government and the major

features of the service. We analyse the extent to which the shape and nature of the service that emerged was pre-figured by war-time plans for health. We consider the role played by the medical profession in modifying some of Bevan's original plans and, given the alleged political consensus of the time, we enquire whether the early NHS can be regarded as solely Labour's political property.

2. Consolidationism, conflict and health policy. In this part of the chapter we cover the period starting with economic crisis in the late 1940s and stretching throughout the 1950s. The effects on health policy and the NHS of the political consolidationism of the Labour government will be closely examined.

   Part of this task will involve considering the roots, nature and extent of the intra-party dispute about political priorities in the context of the economic problems of the late 1940s. The chapter will proceed by looking carefully at the effect on the NHS of cuts in public expenditure and introduction of charges by that government and by tracing the health policy trajectories of the Conservative government throughout the 1950s. Though it is argued that consolidationism and rationing were elements common to both government's development of health policy, this part of the chapter will also consider the scope and nature of conflict over health policy during this period. This means paying attention not only to the opposition to welfare statism from some Conservative politicians but also the critique of public health services emerging in the late 1950s from the new Institute of Economic Affairs.

3. Health policy and rational planning. This section of the chapter concentrates on the effects on health policy of the adoption of rational planning processes in the 1960s and early 1970s. It considers the extent to which this development within the NHS should be seen simply as a service-specific manifestation of the emerging faith in economic planning.

4. Health policy and economic crisis. This section looks at the effect on health policy and health-care provision of the economic crisis of the mid-1970s. It goes on to analyse the policy prescriptions being made by both major political parties at this time and assesses the extent to which these unfolding policies were consistent with original NHS principles. The section concludes by detailing the early health policy of the Conservative government elected in 1979.

5. Health policy transformed. The final section of the chapter is devoted to considering the major changes in health policy during the 1980s and early 1990s: the introduction of general management; efficiency strategies; quasi-privatisation, and the introduction of internal markets.

Chapter 8 covers personal social services policy. Following the pattern set for the organisation of material in the previous two chapters, this 'service' chapter looks at major developments in PSS and housing policy since the war.

It considers the following:

- The post-war establishment of a tripartite model for service delivery.
- The failure of this model and the drive for preventative social work.
- The pressure for reorganisation of social services.
- The Seebohm process and the Seebohm report.
- The Local Authority Social Services Act and the reorganisation of PSS.
- Economic changes and social work in the 1970s.
- The Barclay Report and the myth of 'community social work'.
- Internal markets and the marketisation of PSS.
- Back to the future: unitary local authorities and the break-up of social services.

Chapter 9 looks at housing policy and is particularly concerned with the following:

- Housing policy before 1945 – a prelude.
- Welfare statism and housing 1945–79.
- The re-orientation of housing policy since 1979.

The first section of the chapter will act as a prelude to the more extensive sections which follow. It will trace the development of a housing policy based on quality, quantity and price during the inter-war period and the relationship between central and local government in policy implementation. The second section will follow the changing emphases of housing policy in the post-war period. It will document the transition from an early preoccupation with output, through efforts to replace unfit housing, to a 1970s emphasis on rehabilitation. The final section of the chapter will be concerned with the re-orientation of policy in the 1980s and 1990s. This section will deal, *inter alia*, with the introduction of the 'right to buy' scheme, with the shrinking council housing programme and with later changes as a result of the Housing Act (1988).

As with the earlier chapters, internal and external processes associated with policy change and development are analysed. Here, as in earlier chapters, we attempt to trace general patterns of social and economic development, seeking to determine how, if at all, these relate to this specific area of policy.

The final chapter in this section of the book is concerned with social security policy. It will trace the development of social security policy since the Second World War. It starts with a discussion of the Beveridge principles and the policies and ideology adopted by the post-war Labour government. It proceeds by considering how this approach was affected by the so-called rediscovery of poverty in the early 1960s and goes on to consider the factors associated with the abandonment of Beveridgism in the 1980s and the targeting of benefits in the 1980s and 1990s. This treatment will integrate description and analysis and will introduce, *inter alia*, key theoretical debates around the provision of anti-poverty policies: for example, the culture of poverty, cycle of disadvantage and underclass debates.

The final part of the book, Part Three, *From the cradle to the grave?*, comprises the concluding chapter of the book, which reviews the evidence presented in earlier chapters and suggests how we should understand the progress of social policy from workhouse, through welfare statism, to residualism and marketisation. It proposes that part of the reason for the present state of welfare is that the principles of welfare statism were never firmly established in British political culture and that the earlier welfare consensus was therefore fragile and susceptible to disintegration in the context of economic crisis and ideological turbulence. In reaching this conclusion, attention is drawn to threats to welfare statism and the welfare consensus throughout the post-war period. The final pages of this chapter pose, though they do not answer, the question of whether British social policy has now turned almost full circle? In other words, we will ask whether welfare policy is now driven more by the principles of individualism, consumerism, selectivity and of the market than by those of welfarism.

PART ONE

The development
of the
British welfare state

CHAPTER ONE

Before the welfare state

Chronology   **Before the welfare state**

1886	Birth of the Fabian Society
1906	Liberal government Labour Party formed
1908	The first old age pensions
1909	The 'people's budget' House of Lords blocks Finance Bill
1910	Liberals win elections fought on the Budget and the powers of the House of Lords
1921	First Labour government Tawney's 'secondary education for all'
1929	Second Labour government
1931	National government Hunger marches
1938	Macmillan's *The Middle Way* published
1939	Commencement of the Second World War

It is tempting in a book such as this to start the story of the welfare state at the end of the Second World War. For, at that point, with the election of a Labour government, Britain appeared to move into an era of welfare capitalism in which the state took responsibility for funding, co-ordinating and providing a wide range of social services (see Chapter 3). If we wish to understand the factors that precipitated the development of a welfare state, then there is an argument for moving the starting point back to the commencement of that war. For war and war-related issues certainly contributed to the establishment of a post-war welfare state (see Chapter 2). However, there are compelling reasons to start this story near the start of this century. Chief among these is that, with the election of a Liberal government in 1906, we witness the first stirrings of a welfare collectivism and with it the embryo of the welfare state.

Liberal social policy

In January 1906, after almost twenty years of Conservative rule, the Liberals under Campbell-Bannerman won a landslide election victory, giving them a majority of 356 seats over all other parties. Though the idea of social reform was not at the forefront of the Liberal election campaign, it was one of the main beneficiaries of the victory. This was in part because of the disproportionate influence of 53 Labour MPs in the House of Commons. This group, though numerically insignificant, was symbolically powerful. They represented the aspirations of working men and women who believed that the two-party system failed to represent their interests (Thane, 1984; Sullivan, 1991). They were therefore a reminder to the Liberals that in order to maintain their new-found strength they would have to satisfy the major needs of working people; or, put another way:

> *The emergence of a strong Labour element in the House of Commons has been generally welcomed as the most significant outcome of the present election. It lifts the occasion out of the ordinary groove of domestic politics and will have a far wider influence than any mere turnover of party voters. (The Times, 30 January 1906)*

In fact, it was a Labour MP who introduced one of the early pieces of welfare legislation in the Commons requiring local authorities to provide school meals for needy children. Labour, then, acted as a conscience for the Liberal majority and, as we shall see, witnessed the first stirrings of welfarism.

The embryonic welfare state

The first old age pensions

In 1908 the Government introduced old age pensions but not before being prodded into action by the back benches and by events outside of the House. Despite a clear majority in the House for the introduction of pensions, the government had dragged its feet perhaps fearing that the Conservative-dominated House of Lords would overturn the legislation. A series of bad by-election results in which the Labour Party won seats previously held by Liberals seems to have propelled Asquith, who became Prime Minister on Campbell-Bannerman's death, into action. At the same time the President of the Board of Trade, David Lloyd George, was having similar ideas as he confided to his brother: 'It is about time that we did something that appealed straight to the people; it will I think stop the electoral rot and that is most necessary' (George, 1958, p. 220).

It was Lloyd George, as Chancellor in Asquith's new administration, who took the legislation through the Commons. The Bill proposed that old age pensions be non-contributory and argued for their necessity on the grounds that they would offer relief to aged paupers and thus relieve the strain on the Poor Law, whose future was under consideration by a Royal Commission. Though many had wished for the pensionable age to be 65, the economics of the situation led Lloyd George to propose 70 years, at which point a single person would receive five shillings per week and a married couple, seven shillings and sixpence. These rates were removed from the Bill on its passage through the Commons during an exercise in which the principles of the Bill found almost universal support. Pensions thus commenced being paid on 1 January 1909.

Lloyd George and Lord Richard Cecil on old age pensions, 1908

Mr Lloyd-George The first general criticism is that this is a non-contributory scheme. So long as you have taxes imposed upon commodities which are consumed practically by every family in the country there is no such thing as a non-contributory scheme. A workman who has contributed health and strength, vigour and skill, to the creation of the wealth by which taxation is borne has made his contribution already to the fund which is to give him a pension when he is no longer fit to create that wealth. Therefore, I object altogether to the general division of these schemes into contributory and non-contributory schemes. There is, however, a class of scheme which is known as a contributory one. There is the German scheme, in which the workmen pay into a fund. It is rather a remarkable fact that most social reformers who have taken up this question have at first favoured contributory schemes, but a closer examination has almost invariably led them to abandon them on the ground that they are unequal in their treatment of the working classes, cumbersome, and very expensive, and in a country like ours hopelessly impracticable. Let me give now two or three considerations why, in my judgement, a contributory scheme is impossible in this country. In the first place, it would practically exclude women from its benefits. Out of the millions of members of friendly societies there is but a small proportion, comparatively, of women. Another consideration is that the vast majority are not earning anything and cannot pay their contributions. The second reason is that the majority of working men are unable to deflect from their weekly earnings a sufficient sum of money to make adequate provision for old age in addition to that which they are now making for sickness, infirmity, and unemployment. I do not know what the average weekly wage in this country is; we have not had a wages census since 1886 . . . The average weekly wage in 1886 was 24s. 9d., and 57 per cent. of the working classes in this country were then earning 25s. or less. It is quite clear, therefore, that out of such wages they cannot make provision for sickness, for all the accidents and expenses of life, and also set aside a sufficient sum to provide a competence for old age as well . . .

I find that some of the friendly societies which have superannuation benefits demand that if you fail in your subscriptions you either make it up afterwards, sometimes with interest, or you forfeit **your** benefit altogether. Now it is obviously impossible that that could be done with the great majority of workmen. The friendly societies of this country have a membership of about 12 000 000. So far from the number being over 12 000 000 **it** would very likely be under, because a good many members of trade unions are also members of benefit societies. It is very gratifying that such a large number of workmen should have the **prudence**, foresight, and restraint to enable them to set aside out of earnings money which they might have spent on necessaries or the comforts of the moment. I point that out for this reason, that the House may depend upon it that, if it were within the compass of the means of the working classes to make provision for old age, the fact that they had provided for sickness, that a good many have provided against unemployment and accidents of that kind, would in itself be a proof that they would have provided superannuation for old age if they could have done it. Besides that, I do not think the State has a right to invite the workman earning from 15s. to 20s. or 25s. a week to make the sacrifice which is necessary the sacrifice, really, of some of the absolute necessaries of life as far as he and his children are concerned, in order to make provision for old age, but that the State itself ought to make it.

Lord R. Cecil He did not wish to attempt to define socialism and individualism, but there were two very distinct principles on which they might proceed in approaching this question of old-age pensions. There was the principle that primarily it was the duty of everybody to provide for his own old-age, and provide for himself generally. That was the principle that he himself held, and he quite admitted that they were entitled to add to that that where for some reason or another the individual was unable to provide for himself, it was reasonable for the State to come in and give assistance to that individual. That was the principle on which the contributory system rested. The Chancellor of the Exchequer had a very strange view of what was meant by the contributory scheme. He said that all schemes of old-age pensions were contributory because everybody paid taxes. Of course it was quite true that every expenditure was to some extent contributed to by the general body of taxpayers, but nobody knew better than the Chancellor of the Exchequer that that was not what was intended by a contributory scheme at all. The essential theory upon which the contributory scheme was based that there was to be no out and out gift of money by the State class, but that there was to be a subvention to thrift and a gift of money which was to be in return for some contribution made by recipient. The contrary was that the State was bound to provide all who required assistance. It might well be said that that was socialistic theory, that it was the business of the State to step in take upon itself the duty which ordinarily lay upon the individual. That appeared to him to be the true definition of socialism. They looked at this measure and asked upon which of those principles it was based, could anyone doubt that it was based the second?

From *Hansard, Parliamentary Debates*, House of Commons, 4th Series, vol. 140, Cols 565–586, June 1908

So started what was in contemporary and future years to be referred to as the 'Lord George' for – or so many thought – only a Lord could afford to make such resources available. Because pensions were to be paid as a matter of right, the stigma associated with Poor Law relief was removed. As a result the numbers who applied for pension were far in excess of the Government's estimates, suggesting, in Lloyd George's phrase: 'a mass of poverty and destitution which is too proud to wear the badge of pauperism'. Thus was taken what might be seen in retrospect as the first twentieth century step in the growth of social rights.

A people's budget

The co-existence of destitution and wealth was a theme which had run through Lloyd George's political speeches as an MP since 1890 and its demand for social justice was to mark his first Budget. He was faced in 1909 with a huge projected budget deficit of £16 million. He decided to raise the revenue not only through increasing duty on tobacco and alcohol, which the whole population consumed, but also in ways which earned it the epithet 'the people's budget'. He increased duty on petrol and on the use of motor cars, which hit the better-off disproportionately and introduced a progressive form of income tax. In other words, the Budget was overtly redistributive of wealth through taxation; in David Lloyd George's words:

> *This is a War Budget. It is for raising money to wage implacable warfare against poverty and squalidness. I cannot help hoping that before this generation has passed away we shall have advanced a great step towards that good time when poverty and wretchedness and human degradation which always follow in its camp will be as remote to the people of this country as the wolves which once infested the forests. (Hansard, 29 April 1909)*

So radical were these proposals in the context of the time that the House of Lords rejected them. Lloyd George warned the Lords that, in his words, 'five hundred men chosen accidentally from among the unemployed' would not frustrate the will of a democratically elected government. But the Lords was in no mood for compromise. The Liberals fought two elections in 1910: one on the budget and one on the constitutional powers of the House of Lords. The 'people's budget' was passed in 1910 and the rights of the House of Lords to delay finance bills, or to do more than delay other Bills coming from the Commons, were abolished by statute in 1911.

Liberal social insurance

The battle with the Lords had delayed the introduction of another piece of social legislation. This time it was social insurance to cover interruptions in earnings. Drawing on his experience of Bismarckian Germany he favoured an insurance-based scheme in order to extend pensions to a wider constituency of needy groups than the elderly:

> *... Provisions against the accidents of life which bring so much undeserved poverty to hundreds of thousands of homes, accidents which are quite inevitable such as the death of the breadwinner or his premature breakdown in health. I have always thought that the poverty which was brought upon families owing to these causes presents a much more urgent demand upon the practical sympathy of the community than even old age pensions. With old age the suffering is confined to the individual alone; but in these other cases it extends to the whole family of the victim of circumstances. (Lloyd George, 1910)*

Finally, and after a delicate balancing act intended to keep the trade unions, the finance houses and his colleagues on board, Lloyd George introduced a Bill into the Commons in May 1911. Part I of the Bill was a health insurance scheme made up of contributions of fourpence from the insured, threepence from the employer and twopence from the state (the famous 'ninepence for fourpence' scheme). The scheme had many shortcomings (as we see later in greater detail): it did not cover wives unless they were in employment or families; it did not cover hospital treatment except that some free access to hospital was possible in the case of tuberculosis sufferers, and it did not cover diagnostic tests. Nonetheless it was a significant step and laid the insurance principle on which Beveridge, who had been involved in planning the scheme as a civil servant, was to build thirty years later.

The creation of an embryonic welfare state by the Liberals was an important factor in the development of welfare policy in the next thirty years. With the eclipse of the Liberals after the First World War, however, policy development was sporadic. Conservative and national governments throughout the 1920s and 1930s relied on harsh economic policies to negotiate Britain's way through economic slump. Labour's two minority administrations were too short to see any significant policy input. But despite this, Labour was, through the years leading down to 1945, gradually moving from a party suspicious of state intervention to one associated with social reform.

Viewed from the 1990s, Labour can be seen quintessentially as a party of social reform. That is to say, its political *raison d'être* is often described as the redistribution of resources and life chances by means of the introduction of economic and social policies aimed to achieve those ends (Foote, 1986; Sullivan, 1991). That perception is based largely, however, on the introduction and implementation of a package of social policies in the late 1940s, following the party's election to government in 1945. Yet the road to social reformism was a difficult one for it to follow.

Social democracy: the political source of reformism?

From its inception in 1906, Labour was more indebted to social democratic political traditions (see Sullivan, 1992, 1994) than to any other apparently more radical socialist traditions. Instead of adopting the class-war strategies of some of its European counterparts in the early part of this century, it appeared then – as it appears now – to have opted for social democracy as a political means and for moderate, rather than extensive, egalitarianism as a political goal, with its attendant concern with the gradual reform of state structures and the introduction of social and economic strategies to 'civilise capitalism' (Crossman, 1952). It is tempting, therefore, to see the Labour Party as having moved in a linear and consistent political direction towards the goal of welfare statism. That temptation ought, of course, to be resisted because the assumptions on which it rests constitute a rewriting of history.

Initially, at least, two particular strands of thought and action in the Labour Party posed threats to any ideas of Labour as the party of social democratic welfarism.

Marxism and Labourism: twin threats to welfare statism

Towards the end of the last century, the dominance of the labour movement by social democratic and welfarist approaches seemed less likely than the adoption of a Marxist understanding of politics and the social world.

In the 30 years before the formation of the Labour Party in 1906, the Marxism of the – for our purposes confusingly named – Social Democratic Federation (SDF) had the potential to influence nascent leaders of the Labour Party. The Federation, perhaps the most important of the multiplicity of socialist societies in late nineteenth century Britain, had adopted classical Marxist understandings of economics and politics. Specifically, it thought that as a social, economic and political system, capitalism was seriously flawed. Following Marx, the SDF believed that the ultimate fate of capitalist organisation was that it would implode as a result of the tensions existing between capitalist values on the one hand and the operation of democracy on the other. The road to its final demise would be littered with political and economic crises, each of which would leave capitalism in a more vulnerable state than it had been before (see Marx, 1974, for Marx's own formulation of the nature and future of capitalism).

The SDF's early adaptation of Marxist political theory to the British situation contained elements which both linked it to, and separated it from, the later social democratic traditions. Under the leadership of Hyndman, an amateur cricketer turned Marxist, it developed a crude and dogmatic approach. It rejected co-operation with the trade unions on the basis that they were simply reactionary labourist organisations (Hyndman, 1881) and believed that capitalism would be overthrown and socialism installed, as it must inevitably be, through a process of class warfare. This sort of political trajectory, of course, proved to be unacceptable to later social democrats within the Labour Party. The link between nineteenth century SDF Marxism and twentieth century social democratic approaches in the Labour Party was that Hyndman, at least, believed, despite his commitment to class warfare, that the British state could be inclined to the job of administering socialism once it had been won by the proletarian class (Hyndman, 1881). Had the SDF become an influential forerunner of the Labour Party, then the latter's development as a reformist party, both in its wider reformation of Marxism and in its association with social reform, is unlikely to have progressed beyond still birth (see Sullivan, 1991, Ch. 2).

A number of factors, however, contributed to the SDF's relative unimportance as an influence on the political direction of the Labour Party. In the first place, the SDF's militant programme and its autocratic leadership by H. M. Hyndman contributed to it remaining, in Friedrich Engels' words, 'purely a sect. It has ossified Marxism into a dogma and, by rejecting every labour movement which is not orthodox Marxism . . . it renders itself incapable of becoming anything else but a sect' (Marx and Engels, 1968). Engels's words were, as we now know, prophetic. The SDF was to withdraw from the Labour Party just one year after the party had been formed in exasperation at its failure to present itself as a class party. It was also to fail to win support in the wider reaches of the labour movement. In essence, the SDF came, with the encouragement of Hyndman, to see British trade unionism as a reactionary political force incapable of playing its part in a socialist revolution (see, for instance, Hyndman, 1883; Sullivan, 1991). It was so because, during the last decades of the nineteenth century it appeared more concerned with allegedly defensive battles in support of better working conditions of its members and self-help strategies, such as the support of friendly societies, to provide some security for trades union members during times of income interruption (see Thane, 1982). Such strategies could not, for the SDF at least, replace the positive and socialist strategy of direct action by the labour movement to bring the British capitalist system to its knees. Accordingly, the Federation garnered for itself decreasing influence in the labour movement and appeared to become a political anachronism within its lifetime. Its influence on the political direction of a nascent Labour Party was hardly increased by its expulsion of future Labour Marxists, particularly William Morris and Tom Mann (Foote, 1986, pp. 22–3). If the torch of Marxism was to be carried into the emerging Labour Party, the SDF ensured, by its sectarian approach to individuals and organisations within the labour movement, that it would not be the torch bearer.

One of the effects of the demise of the SDF was to minimise the potential authority that Marxism might have developed in the early Labour Party. Though Morris and Mann attempted to develop a Labour Marxist approach in the early Labour Party, the experience of the sectarianism of the SDF proved to be a dead-weight around the Labour Marxists' necks (Pelling, 1984; Foote, 1986; Laybourn, 1988).

Despite the hostility it engendered among the SDF Marxists, the other early threat to the development of Labour as a welfarist party was the wider labour movement itself. Indeed, the best evidence suggests that at the beginning of this century welfarism was seen by working class people and their representatives in the labour movement as a threat to their attempts to create a better quality of life for themselves (Pelling, 1968; 1984; Thane, 1984). The labourist response to the extension of state powers under the reforming Liberal government was to oppose the development of an embryonic welfare state (Pelling, 1968; Laybourn and Reynolds, 1984). Part of that hostility appears to have stemmed from experience of state institutions which had been the expression of national social policy in the nineteenth century. Pelling produces clear evidence that the responses of ordinary people to the idea of expanded state welfare was to fear an extension of the workhouse solution to poverty (Pelling, 1968, p. 2). Indeed when the Royal Commission on the Poor Law (1905–9) invited the diocesan bishops of the Church of England to collect evidence about popular feeling in respect of the Poor Law the clerics concluded that it was almost universally loathed. They found that the idea and experience of indoor relief were repugnant to the poor who had experienced its operation as meaning the loss of home and liberty. As a consequence, the bishops found 'a great reluctance on the part of the poor to enter the [Poor Law] union' (cited in Pelling, 1968, p. 3). Though outdoor relief did not involve the loss of either home or liberty, the bishops found it was resented by ordinary people, because of the loss of respect and the sense of social stigma perceived by its recipients.

It was not only the experience of poverty policies that led, in the years each side of the beginning of the century, to a suspicion among ordinary working people about, and a general hostility towards, the idea of extended welfare. Their experience of intervention in the housing and education fields reinforced the view that welfarism could prove an additional burden rather than a boon.

In the late nineteenth century increasing attention had been paid to the housing problem which existed in many of the major British cities. In 1875 Parliament gave borough councils permissive powers to remove slum properties and provide alternative accommodation for slum-dwellers. The experience of those who had lived in slum conditions was that a great many slum properties were, in fact, pulled down but that precious little alternative accommodation was provided (see Pelling, 1968; Thane, 1984). Where new housing was provided, it was almost always as a result of charitable intervention and led to the provision of accommodation in buildings like the Peabody Buildings in London. Even when this was the case, poor people often found the results of charitable intervention to be of dubious benefit. More often than not, this new accommodation boasted large well-ventilated rooms, which were more congenial to the health and comfort of large families living in limited space but which became impossibly expensive to heat. More than this, tenancy in one of these charitable buildings often involved adherence to a set of rules and regulations about behaviour which were found to be an incursion into people's liberty and life-style.

In the education field, the story was a similar one. Compulsory education to the end of elementary school engendered feelings of hostility or indifference among many of the working people who would be the future constituency of the Labour Party. One of the major grounds for objection was that compulsory state education involved loss of earnings for many families, some or all of whose children became wage-earners long before they would now leave school

(Simon, 1974). Despite the view expressed in the report of the Royal
Commission on the Elementary Education Acts that:

> the indifference of parents to education for its own sake must, we fear, be reckoned as
> an obstacle which has perhaps been aggravated by compulsion, and has presumably not
> yet reached its worst. (Royal Commission on Elementary Education, 1888)

the reality was that many families were dependent on the earnings of their
school-aged children as a bulwark against starvation.

One concrete example of this opposition to state welfare policy was
resistance to the abolition of the half-time system in the textile industries. As
late as 1909, a plebiscite of the members of the Cotton Operatives Amalga-
mation resulted in a four-to-one vote against the proposal to raise the school-
leaving age to 13 years (Sullivan, 1991). Though general opposition to state
education had moderated after the abolition of fees for schooling in 1891, this
particular area of social reform, like the drive for an 8-hour working day,
remained substantially unsupported by ordinary working people in the late
nineteenth century (on this, see Pelling, 1968, pp. 3–5).

In Pelling's view, this late nineteenth century labourist hostility to welfare,
notwithstanding official trade union support for an extension in state
education barely a generation later was grounded in an anti-statist philosophy:
a belief that the state was run by and for the wealthy (Pelling, 1968, p. 5).
Though the empirical reality of working class opposition to state welfare seems
incontrovertible, Pelling's interpretation of the sources of hostility are
questioned, or at least refined, by Thane (1984). Whereas Pelling appears to
emphasise the sources of working class hostility as a desire for independence
and a suspicion of the complex and interweaving institutions of the state,
Thane is more inclined to see the origins of hostility, or indifference, as
stemming from other factors. Chief among these is, according to Thane, the fact
that the working class had already created an alternative form of welfare
provision. This alternative to state welfare was built on the solid foundation
of Friendly Society activity. These societies, which had a membership of over
five million people at the turn of the century, were centrally concerned with
mutual insurance against sickness and old age. Opposition to state social
security plans seems, according to Thane, to have originated from the belief
that self-help was socially and morally preferable to redistributive provision
implemented by state functionaries whose activities would, no doubt, involve
intrusion into the private lives of recipients (Thane, 1984, p. 879).

Be that as it may, one thing seemed obvious. A clearly welfarist party,
appealing for the votes of working people in the early years of this century,
might have faced extinction shortly after birth. Indeed, psephological
evidence, such as it is, suggests that neither Labour nor the Liberals (who were
responsible for the early century reforms in income maintenance) attempted
to foster their electoral fortunes by appealing to an overtly 'welfare vote'
(Pelling, 1968; Thane, 1984; Lloyd, 1986). Indeed, a fairly respectable argument

can be mounted to suggest that the Liberal social reforms were exceptional pieces of legislation rather than reflecting the general political direction of that party in government (Lloyd, 1986, pp. 1–25).

How, then, do we explain the apparent conversion of the Labour Party to welfarism by the middle of the century?

Fabianism, ethical socialism and social democracy

A straightforward answer to the question posed above is that, like SDF Marxism before it, labourism failed to achieve dominance as a strategic political position within the Labour Party. The eclipse of labourism was associated temporally, and possibly in more direct ways, with the development of Fabian and ethical socialist strands of thinking within the party.

Fabianism: its appeal for Labour

Marx's belief had been that social revolution in Europe would follow the formation of revolutionary parties of the working class (Marx, 1974). Those parties, though made up largely of working class people, would attract sections of the middle class and the intelligentsia. That analysis, though valid in many European countries, reckoned without the pragmatic traditions of the British! Instead, in the 1880s, a number of progressive intellectuals established the Fabian Society, a think-tank before the days of think-tanks, to reform or revise the socialist ideas that were starting to make an impression in Continental Europe (see Clarke, 1978; Foote, 1986; Sullivan, 1991). The Society, formed in 1884, is said to have been named after the Roman general Fabius Maximus, whom some wags credit as having never lost a battle simply because he refused to engage in any. The political purpose and influence of the Fabian Society over the 60 years between its inception and the coming of the welfare state was, however, rather more complex than the apocryphal inaction of its ancient patron.

The Society, though initially attracting quasi-Marxists like George Bernard Shaw, soon came to be dominated by the political and social ideas emanating from a circle around Sidney Webb and his future wife, Beatrice Potter. Sidney, a one-time civil servant, who was to become a Labour MP, had been fascinated in his early life by positivist philosophical thought. Positivism's belief in a well-ordered and harmonious society guided by an educated elite appealed to this lower middle-class civil servant manqué. The philosophical approach offered by positivism was supplemented by his own belief in the importance of collectivist politics which would inform a political ethic based on the idea that the individual must submit to the common good. As he was to write, his theory of life was 'to feel at every moment that I am acting as a member of a committee . . . I aspire never to act alone or for myself' (cited in Woolfe, 1975, p. 276; Sullivan, 1991, p. 36). This secular Protestantism was never allowed to ossify into dogma as Marxism had been in the SDF. Shaw, Besant, Oliver and other leading Fabians acted as counterbalances to Webb's cranial and rather joyless political creed. Nonetheless, Webb's emphasis on collectivism was to permeate the Society's thinking and that of the Labour Party for much of the following century.

Fabianism's contribution to Labour thinking

Fabianism's major contributions were as follows. First, and in contrast to the Labour Marxists, Fabians argued that socialism was entirely compatible with political institutions and modes of behaviour which were peculiarly British. Socialism could be and should be achieved through a parliamentary route and, once this had been realised, a politically neutral civil service could be left to administer it. Marx and Marxists had called for the abolition of the capitalist state if socialism was to be achieved. Fabians, on the other hand, saw in socialism an extension of the existing British state (including parliament, the military and the monarch). Socialism for the Fabians was a sort of collectivism, the rules of which would be guaranteed, and if necessary enforced, by a set of neutral umpires, who would include state functionaries, the law and the Royals. In Shaw's words, 'the socialism advocated by the Fabian Society is state socialism exclusively' (Shaw, 1896). Fabian political thought diverged fundamentally from orthodox Marxism in this respect. For Fabians, unlike their Marxist half-siblings, the capitalist state was not, in itself, a hindrance to the achievement of socialism. Early Fabians saw it as controlled, pro tempore, by the bourgeoisie but as capable of transformation. The state was, in other words, essentially neutral.

The problem with the state was merely a problem of which class was to control its functions. This problem would be resolved if the class composition of the House of Commons, seen by Fabians as the source of state authority, was changed. Put crudely, the election of a Labour government would, or so Fabians believed, resolve the problem of the state. Some of the Fabian rhetoric, especially that flowing from the pen of Shaw, had a distinctly revolutionary flavour '. . . [The state] will continue to be used against the people by the classes until it is used by the people against the classes with equal ability and equal resolution' (Shaw, 1893, p. 27). The reality was, however, that Fabian state socialism was based on the idea of Labour's control of Westminster and, via Westminster, of Whitehall. Webb was to describe this view thus:

> For the Labour Party, it must be plain. Socialism is rooted in political democracy; which necessarily compels us to recognise that every step towards our goal is dependent on gaining the assent and support of at least a numerical majority of the whole people. (Labour Party, 1923)

This is an excerpt of a speech made by Webb to the annual Labour Party Conference. In it we see not only Fabianism's constitutional road to socialism but also a hint of what such a road might require in policy terms. Essentially, Webb and the Fabians were to argue that, in order to get the parliamentary power necessary to take over the state and use it for the people, Labour would need to promote policies that appealed to a wider audience than its 'natural' working class constituency. This claim prefigured later arguments between the right of the party, which was to adopt an essentially Fabian position in this respect, especially over nationalisation and welfare state proposals, and the party's left wing, who were less than completely convinced.

The second major contribution to Labour thinking is one which seems to have etched itself into the fabric of Labour policy-making procedures. The Society, while concerned to theorise the ways in which the state could be captured for the people, seems to have had a low estimation of the people for whom the state was to be captured. Though Labour socialism was to be based on parliamentary democracy, Fabians appeared to hope that democracy would permeate little further than parliament. In Fabian eyes, representative democracy appeared to rule out the direct participation in policy making by the producer, consumer or welfare recipient:

> the utmost function that can be allotted to a mass meeting in the machinery of democracy is the ratification or rejection of a policy already prepared for it, and the publication of decisions to those concerned. (Fabian Society, 1896, p. 35)

Fabianism's faith in the expert administrator as the guarantor of British socialism was an early part of its programme. The civil service was to be the guiding hand of socialism with the elected parliament acting as a check on its activities. If the parliament could also be well-endowed with experts, then so much the better: 'a body of expert representatives is the only way of coping with expert administrators. The only way to choose expert representatives is popular election, but that is just the worst way to obtain expert administrators' (Fabian Society, 1896, p. 43).

The contribution of Fabianism considered

Fabian thinking, then, might be summarised in the following way. Socialism, or more accurately social democracy, required not that the state be smashed but that it be fashioned into an instrument of social change. This would be possible because the state *per se* was not the creature of any particular social class but the politically neutral administrative arm of government. Nonetheless, the expertise possessed by state personnel made them ideally placed to be guarantors of a socialism won through the ballot box. As we shall see later, Fabian political theory, if it can be graced with that description, had a not insignificant effect on the Labour Party in the 1940s and 1950s. That it was able to develop such a position of influence was in no small part because it was able to square a circle which the SDF had preferred to leave circular.

Though fundamentally anti-labourist in their inclinations '. . . the working classes [seem to us] stupid, and in large sections sottish, with no interest except in racing odds' (Webb and Webb, 1948), Fabians developed a way of separating out personal prejudice from practical politics. For the Webbs, trade unionism had a vital part to play in any well-ordered and humane society. It was concerned with the 'regulation of conditions of employment in such a way as to ward off from the manual working producers the evil effects of industrial competition' (Webb and Webb, 1909). The beauty of this formulation, of course, was that it avoided the dismissive attitude of the SDF to the trade unions, though many senior Fabians appeared to hold their members in equal contempt, while constructing a role for trade unionism compatible with capitalist or socialist government – an equally important consideration as turn-of-the-century Fabians were unclear as to whether they should throw their lot in with the Labour Party or allow their opinions to permeate all of the major political parties.

What the Fabians gave the early Labour Party, particularly after their decision to affiliate to it, was an intellectual framework which was congruent with, and sometimes supplemented, the labourist structure of the party. The idea of gradual progress towards collectivist social and economic policies is one which has remained with the party. Fabianism, particularly in this period, was, however, a pretty cranial business. Though it might have provided the Labour Party with a theoretical rationale for social reformism, it hardly guaranteed the future of Labour as a popular political force.

Ethical socialism: the heart of Labour social reformism

If Fabianism was the head of Labour during this period, then it seems that ethical socialism was its heart. Ethical socialism is here defined as that strand within the Labour Party for which the social deprivation experienced by large sections of the working class before the Second World War was seen as reason enough to support a movement for social reform. At the centre of this reform coalition was the Independent Labour Party (formed in 1893 and later to affiliate to the Labour Party) but its adherents included many individuals driven by a sense of Christian obligation or moral outrage at the appalling conditions of many citizens' lives. Though many so-called ethical socialists were committed, like the Independent Labour Party, to the collective ownership of the means of production, distribution and exchange, that commitment was often fired by a non-conformist notion of social morality rather than a Marxist passion for class conflict. These notions, of course, have a longer history than the history of the Labour Party and were visible in the outreach and welfare concerns of Hobhouse (Dennis and Halsey, 1988), in

Christian socialism (*op.cit.*, pp. 171–9) and in the New Liberalism of Hobson and Hobhouse. In the modern period, thinkers like Tawney, author of the now famous *Religion and the Rise of Capitalism* (1977, first published in 1922), can be categorised as belonging to this grouping. He, like other ethical socialists, was clear that morality lay at the base of political and social action and that the raison d'être of the Labour Party was the achievement of a more equal society. Like many Labour politicians who followed him, Tawney was concerned not only with the achievement of greater equality but also with the development of a philosophy to underpin this egalitarian drive. For him, as for many social reformers, socialism was merely the expression of a Christian or quasi-Christian morality.

In *The Acquisitive Society* (1921), Tawney saw the sources of poverty and inequality as the capitalist emphasis on individual rights to the exclusion of individual obligation. Such an emphasis allowed the wealthy to exercise rights under law in order to accrue wealth. Its corollary was that it under-emphasised the responsibility persons should feel to act in ways which ensured that the acquisition of wealth for some did not lead to the immiseration of others. Capitalist societies like Britain in the twenties 'may be called *acquisitive societies* because their whole tendency and interest and preoccupation is to promote the acquisition of wealth' (cited in Winter and Joslin, 1972, p. 32). Driven by the development of an ethical socialist morality which saw Labour's justification for social reform as the abolition of the mean-mindedness of capitalism, Tawney looked for vehicles capable of carrying this morality forward into practical politics. One of these vehicles was Fabian political economy and especially the Webbian formulation of the relationship between the individual and the collective. The marriage of an ethical socialist morality with Fabian political theory led Tawney to call for a functional society based on the performance of duties rather than the maintenance of rights. This is particularly clear in his *Equality* (1952, originally published in 1931). This book, rightly seen as presenting a philosophy for Labour socialism, mounted a blistering attack on the inequalities seemingly inherent in an unbridled capitalist system. Within its pages we find an attack on the British upper classes for practising a form of class war by their determination to amass wealth through the exploitation of a labouring class. Rather than regard such inequalities as natural or inevitable, Tawney believed them to be grotesque and barbarous (Tawney, 1952, p. 38). This led him to promote a notion of equality which emphasised equality of esteem and dignity based on common humanity, a definition of equality which allowed for disparities in income and wealth which were not the result of crude exploitation and which placed him at the head of a tradition of thought later expanded by the Labour politician Crosland (1956) and the sociologist Marshall (1963).

This idea was the rationale for a Labour Party committed to a package of social reform that would eliminate the most blatant excesses of inequality. It was, if you will, a manifesto for the principle and practice of equality of opportunity. While accepting that it was unrealistic to conceive of a society characterised by equality of outcome, Tawney believed that the touchstone for Labour policy should be that:

> . . . *men are men, social institutions – property rights and the organisation of industry, and the system of public health and education – should be planned . . . to emphasise and strengthen, not the class differences which divide but the common humanity which unites them. (Tawney, 1952, p. 38)*

Tawney's aspirations were not for total equality but for as much equality as was consistent with individual differences and economic growth. He accepted that differences in education, health and background would be the hallmarks of any conceivable society but believed that Labour should be committed to a society in which such differences were not perceived as distinguishing features of social superiority or inferiority. More than this, his philosophy for Labour was that it should develop economic and social policies (especially relating to education, employment and health) which would lead to the diminution of artificially created differences (1952, pp. 86–7).

Tawney's ethical socialism: Labour and social policy

Of most concern to Tawney were inequalities in education and health where he found them to be all too present. Ill-health and high rates of morbidity and mortality were concentrated in working class areas. Public schooling ensured that privilege was passed on from one generation to another and, as a corollary, social deprivation appeared to take on an hereditary nature. His argument was that the remedy lay in greater collective action to end or minimise inequalities in education and health. This would result in the creation of a health service free at the point of use and in high-quality free state education for all. The vehicle to carry these aspirations would be a welfare state introduced by a Labour government.

Throughout the 50-year period before the Second World War, then, the labour movement, the emerging Labour Party and leading Labour members had been nourished by Fabian politics and the political philosophy of the ethical socialists, and particularly of Tawney. It is one of the arguments of this book that Labour's social reform policies in the period following the Second World War are heirs to the pre-war marriage of Fabianism and ethical socialism. What remains to be considered here are the factors associated with the transformation of this strand of social democracy into a political form capable of winning electoral support.

Labour social democracy: social reformism comes of age?

By 1945 when Labour gained a landslide general election victory, the hostility of the labour movement to state social welfare appears to have evaporated.

In part, this appears to have been the result of workers' experience of the protracted slump in the 1920s and 1930s. During that period, privilege and privation existed side by side: on the one hand, the continued drive for profit by entrepreneurial and corporate capitalists, on the other, the crushing poverty for the many during the inter-war years. During this period the hostility of ordinary people to state intervention to improve living conditions understandably diminished (Cronin, 1984). Trade union opposition to the imposition of a social wage became less strident as many trade union members found themselves without a real wage to be increased by trade union activity. In these circumstances Labour plans like those for a national health service, originating from the Socialist Medical Association in 1930 but becoming party policy by 1934, looked increasingly attractive (see Sullivan, 1992). The calls by Keynes, Beveridge and others for a full-employment policy and a welfare state (see Harris, 1981; Thane, 1982; Sullivan, 1992) were similarly attractive. Labour's plans during the 1930s to administer a planned economy should it be returned to government and its emerging championing of a welfare state package made it identifiable with the crucial social issues of the day and was responsible, according to one commentator, for it reaching its zenith as a working class party (Cronin, 1984). It was, however, undoubtedly the experience of war which set the seal on Labour as a social reformist party and on social reformism as an electoral advantage.

CHAPTER TWO

The road to 1945: war, welfare and the people's will

Chronology	War and social policy
1939	Outbreak of Second World War Establishment of emergency health service Coalition Government formed
1941	Beveridge commissioned to chair committee on workmen's compensation
1941	Beveridge circulates his *Heads of Scheme* to committee
1942	Beveridge Report submitted Government resists publication Report published
1943	Government forced to accept Beveridge as a blueprint for post-war reconstruction
1944	'Butler' Education Act Health White Paper suggesting establishment of comprehensive national health system
1945	War ends Election of first majority Labour government committed to establishment of a welfare state, full employment and a mixed economy

As we have already seen, state involvement in social policy has a history that goes back much further than the Second World War and includes early twentieth century legislation. For many, however, the second war is seen as a, or even the, significant factor in the emergence of the British welfare state (see, for instance, Titmuss, 1950; Addison, 1975; Barnett, 1987; Marquand, 1988;

Jones, 1991). In what senses, then, is the Second World War regarded as the
seed-bed of post-war social policy?

Many accounts of this period (Morgan, 1990, Williamson, 1990, Timmins,
1995) see the figure of Sir William Beveridge striding the historical landscape
like a colossus, changing the direction of British social policy unaided.

Just William?

Beveridge before the Beveridge Report

For many, then, it has seemed that the key to understanding the effect of war-
time is, in fact, to understand the contribution to post-war social policy made,
during war-time by Sir William Beveridge. The son of a senior official on the
Indian Civil Service and a friend of the Webbs, Beveridge had already made a
significant contribution to the development of British social policy. On the
recommendation of the Master of Balliol College, Oxford, his college as an
undergraduate, Beveridge had found himself in 1905, at the age of twenty six,
as a leader writer on the right-leaning *Morning Post*. There he wrote on social
policy issues and came into contact with Winston Churchill, seven years his
senior and since 1901 a Liberal. In 1908, Churchill persuaded the young
Beveridge to become a civil servant in the Board of Trade. During the next three
years, he played a significant part in the creation of a network of labour
exchanges, of which he became the first director, and in the formation of the
Liberal social insurance scheme, introduced by David Lloyd George. This
experience and his observation of the introduction of old age pensions by Lloyd
George played no mean part in ensuring that Beveridge became and remained
a Liberal throughout the rest of his life. It was also to have a significant
influence on his views about social policy. He would also have been party to
discussions about the first tentative steps towards state health provision, Lloyd
George's famous 'ninepence for fourpence' scheme. This was an insurance
scheme by which workers contributed fourpence, the employer contributed
threepence and the state added twopence. This scheme, administered by
approved societies, provided to the insured the services of a 'panel' doctor and
sick pay at the rate of ten shillings a week. It did not, however, provide for
hospital treatment, nor did it provide any cover for the families of insured
workers save for a maternity grant.

Before he left Whitehall in 1919, Beveridge had also served in the Ministry
of Munitions, where he had drawn up policies on the movement of labour –
much resented by the trade union movement – and in the Ministry of Food,
where he was involved in developing price controls and rationing.

With peace, he moved out of government service and became director of the
London School of Economics, a post he held until 1937 when he returned to
Oxford as Master of University College. During his career up to this point, he

had become acquainted with both Clem Attlee, who was to become Labour's post-war Prime Minister, and with Hugh Dalton, who was to be Labour's first post-war Chancellor of the Exchequer. They were both lecturers at the London School of Economics (LSE), as was Lionel Robbins, who was to make his own sizeable contribution to British social policy as the chairman of the Robbins Committee. At Oxford he was to employ a future Labour Prime Minister, Harold Wilson, as a research assistant on a project about unemployment. His other notable connections were his friendship with John Maynard Keynes and his familial relationship with Tawney by his sister's marriage to him.

Beveridge gets a job, but not the one he wants

One might expect that, with the coming of the Second World War and the importation of other academics, like Keynes, into government service, Beveridge would also have received the call. This was also Beveridge's expectation. Put at its kindest, Beveridge never underestimated his importance and the failure to get a government job, especially given his work during the First World War, left him frustrated and bitter (Harris, 1977). He deluged government departments with suggestions about how the war should be negotiated and offered himself for service. Finally, in the summer of 1940, Bevin – the Minister of Labour and leader of the Transport and General Workers' Union who had been brought into the government on Churchill's insistence – came, unwillingly, to his rescue. He offered Beveridge work undertaking a brief survey of war-time manpower requirements. This completed, he became once more a full time civil servant in Bevin's ministry at the end of the year. It is clear, however, that the two were far from soul mates. They were both possessed of arrogance and autocratic ways of working, added to which Bevin was never to trust with significant responsibility a man who he associated with the coercion of labour during the previous war. Bevin really wanted to be rid of this troublesome mandarin (Harris, 1977, p. 376). The opportunity was soon to present itself.

In February 1941, a delegation of trade unionists had put pressure on the coalition government to tidy up the mess that surrounded sickness and un-employment benefits for workers: seven ministries were directly or indirectly involved in the administration of benefits and confusion reigned. In an April meeting of Cabinet the idea of an inter-departmental committee to review this problem was mooted. Initially, Bevin resisted this idea but when the possibility of getting rid of Beveridge occurred to him he became one of its staunchest supporters. As a consequence, and with Bevin's encouragement, Anthony Greenwood (the Labour Minister of Reconstruction) offered Beveridge the chair of this committee in June 1941. The latter, who had really wanted the director of manpower job in the Ministry of Labour which had been offered to someone else, accepted with bad grace (Harris, 1977, p. 376). Beveridge was being sidelined and he knew it: '[Bevin] pushed me as Chairman of the Social Insurance Committee by way of parting with me . . . my removal from the Ministry of Labour was a kicking upstairs' (Harris, 1977).

It is also clear that Bevin, and perhaps the rest of the Cabinet, saw the job as merely bureaucratic. Bevin's parting shot to the less than enthusiastic Beveridge was that the enquiry should be essentially administrative in character. Little did they anticipate what was to emerge! Beveridge was to come to see his new post as an opportunity to change the course of British social policy. In this he was abetted, wittingly or otherwise, by Greenwood, who had ensured that the press saw the committee as one of prime importance to post-war social reconstruction. As a result the newspapers billed the committee as a wide-ranging and comprehensive investigation into social conditions aimed at establishing economic and social security for the whole population (Addison, 1992, p. 169).

Beveridge goes for broke

The first signal that this was exactly what Beveridge intended was sent in July when he produced a memorandum for his committee titled *Social Insurance: General Considerations*. In it he argued:

> The time has now come to consider social insurance as a whole, as a contribution to a better new world after the war. How would one plan social insurance now if one had a clear field, without being hampered by vested interests of any kind? The first step is to outline the ideal scheme, the next step to consider the practical possibilities of realising the ideal, and then the changes of existing machinery that would be required. (Beveridge, 1941)

The other members of Beveridge's committee were all civil servants from the ministries involved in the administration of benefits and from the Ministry of Reconstruction. They met throughout the summer of 1941 without Beveridge, whose mind was still largely focused on the study of skills in the armed forces that he was completing for the Ministry of Labour. They called for written evidence to the committee and arranged sessions for verbal evidence to be brought before it. However, in December 1941, when only one piece of written evidence had been submitted, Beveridge produced another memorandum, *Heads of Scheme*, which was the Beveridge Report in microcosm. It recommended bringing the existing insurance schemes together, paying a flat-rate benefit yielded by a flat-rate contribution from the insured, a contribution from the employer and a contribution from the state – shades of Lloyd George's 'ninepence for fourpence' health insurance scheme. It was his first point, however, that was to take the government's breath away. That point outlined key assumptions and signalled in banner headlines that Beveridge intended not to be constrained by the committee's terms of reference. Far from carrying out a tidying-up job, Beveridge had embarked on planning the post-war welfare state. Or so it seemed. His notion was that a social security system could not be devised without making three assumptions:

1. The creation of a national service providing free and comprehensive treatment to the whole population.
2. The provision of child allowances to the families of all children under 14 years or, if in full-time education, under 16 years.
3. The guarantee of full employment by the state.

In order to make social security work, Beveridge was arguing, governments would have to intervene in civil society on a wider scale than had ever been the case. It would need to create a national health service, introduce family allowances and intervene economically to ensure that unemployment was reduced to minimum levels.

His reliance on insurance was, no doubt, an attempt to recreate in a wide-ranging social security scheme what he had helped plan in relation to the narrower Liberal social insurance schemes earlier in the century. The insurance principle also appealed to him because it presented benefits as a social right. In guaranteeing benefits during earnings interruptions as a right bought by previous contributions, Beveridge was moving away from the means test method of benefit administration. This approach, hated by British workers, especially during the 'hungry thirties' when its use was enormous and harsh, was an anathema to Beveridge and he hoped to do his bit to bury it as the principle by which assistance was given.

Once *Heads of Scheme* had been produced, Beveridge saw much of the real work as having been done:

> *Once the memorandum had been circulated, the committee had their objectives settled for them and discussion was reduced to consideration of the means of attaining that objective. (Beveridge, 1968, p. 298)*

As one might expect, the other members of the committee were more than a little unhappy at Beveridge's presumption in reducing their contribution to that of bit players. The Cabinet, on the other hand, were outraged. After conversations with Sir Kingsley Wood, Greenwood was required to write to Beveridge to change the constitution of the committee. Henceforth, he told Beveridge, the civil service members of the committee would be regarded by government not as participants but as advisers only. The final report would be signed by Beveridge alone and the civil servants would not be associated with any of its proposals or recommendations. In other words, the Government told Beveridge that the report was to be his and his alone. The Government was distancing itself from what it already suspected would emerge (Sullivan, 1992; Timmins, 1995). It is difficult to imagine that Sir William lost any sleep over this!

Throughout 1942 the work of the committee went on apace, no doubt helped by the pretence that Beveridge should listen to its other members having been removed. Evidence was taken, much of it in line with Beveridge's own views (Sullivan, 1992) and the report, with the uninspiring title *Social Insurance and Allied Services*, was published in December 1942 (HMSO, 1942). The public reception to its publication was ecstatic. On the eve of issue, queues of would-be purchasers formed outside HMSO offices as if it were the Harrods sale or as if they were queuing for seats at a Wimbledon final. Sales topped 100 000 within a month and reached 200 000 by the end of 1944. The report, based on Beveridge's three assumptions, called for the provision of an insurance-based social security system which would, he hoped, abolish poverty. That system should be contribution based, should yield flat-rate benefits from flat-rate contributions and should be based on co-operation between the individual and the state. But the report ranged wider. It presented as the state's business the slaying of five giants: apart from want, these were disease, ignorance, squalor and idleness. Though Beveridge provided little detail, he was arguing for a post-war welfare state. No wonder that they queued throughout the night! For, like all good publicists, Beveridge had ensured that his public were given early warning of what was to come. The report's author, like many others, saw his recommendations as radical. Referring to the special conditions that had been created by war, he argued, 'a revolutionary moment in the world's history is a time for revolutions not patching'.

His proposals were, he believed, part of the process of 'using the powers of the state, so far as may be necessary without any limit whatever, in order to abolish the five giant evils' (Beveridge, 1943). Later, he was to argue 'there are vital things needing to be done to raise the standard of health and happiness in Britain which can only be done by common action' (Beveridge, 1945) and that 'we cannot overcome social evils without an extension of the responsibilities of the state' (Beveridge, 1944).

Consensus with the major stake-holders

Revolutionary as his ideas may have seemed, they also tapped into a *de facto* political consensus. Despite Bevin's hostility, the trade unions appear to have agreed with Beveridge on almost all major issues (Harris, 1981, pp. 250–1). There was an absence of the antagonism to social security in particular, and state welfare in general, which had been the position of the labour movement at the turn of the century (Pelling, 1968; Sullivan, 1991; Thane, 1984). In this earlier period, as we have hinted in Chapter 1, opposition had taken a number of forms.

The first was adherence to a sort of 'servile state' theory of welfare in which the state, and therefore its welfare functions, was seen as occupying a handmaiden role to the owners of capital (Thane, 1982, p. 251; Thane, 1984).

This was certainly a popularly held view in the Social Democratic Federation at the turn of the century. While accepting that outright opposition to social reform was counterproductive, the SDF saw capitalist reforms as capable only of benefiting capitalists (Thane, 1984, pp. 880–2). Another element of hostility had its roots in the principles and practice of the Friendly Societies. These bodies were centrally concerned with mutual insurance against sickness and old age and consequently were less than enthusiastic about the Liberal social insurance reforms in the early twentieth century. This opposition was rationalised in philosophical or political terms which were quintessentially liberal or libertarian in their nature: self-help was socially and morally preferable to redistributive provision implemented through a state which was excessively intrusive and powerful (Thane 1984, p. 878). The resulting strategy was for the SDF to commit itself to 'measures to palliate the evils of our society' (housing at low rents, free compulsory education, an 8-hour working day, and so on). These measures were seen as consistent with the SDF's revolutionary socialism in that they were measures which redistributed resources, improved the material conditions of the working class and so helped to create a proletariat stronger and more active in the class struggle.

By the Second World War, however, the position of the labour movement had matured, some would say degenerated, into support for collectivism. This may have been made easier by Beveridge's apparent deviation from the mainstream Liberalism to which he had been a pre-war adherent. In order to slay the 'five giants' it would be necessary to take land and housing into public ownership, to institute the public control of investment, to expand secondary and adult education massively, to phase out private ownership of the means of production and to maintain full employment – all this in addition to the implementation of his plans on social insurance and health services. This, at least, was the argument he mounted in discussions with a sub-committee of the Ministry of Reconstruction, the Advisory Panel on Home Affairs. He expressed this graphically as 'making up our minds to becoming a community in which undertakers' profit as a guide to production disappears permanently over a large part of the whole field of economic activity'. This, of course, was the sweetest music in the ears of the trade union movement. What one would expect to have chimed less harmoniously with the labour movement was his view that these strategies would need to be supplemented by the imposition of permanent statutory control over wages and prices and the abolition of free collective bargaining. These strictures were, if not popular, at least tolerated by the movement's leaders.

Though there was a sharp difference of opinion with Beveridge over workmen's compensation, the financing of which the unions believed should continue to be solely borne by the employers, there was substantial agreement on the need for comprehensive systems of health care and social insurance and for full employment strategies. This overall agreement did mask some relatively minor dissension. For instance, there was some opposition to the principle of universal insurance from trade unions like the National Union of Railwaymen with traditionally low vulnerability to unemployment or existing favourable insurance schemes. In general, however, the views of the unions were in accord with Beveridge's own views (Hill, 1990).

More surprising perhaps were the views expressed in other quarters. The major insurance companies expressed support for the idea of a statutory insurance system, particularly if they were retained as collection agencies by government (HMSO, 1942; Harris, 1981, p. 251).

Alternative practical strategies were suggested of course but even these were made within the framework of principle outlined by Beveridge. This was the case with the recommendation from the research institute, Political and Economic Planning (PEP), that social insurance should be financed from a surcharge on income tax as it was with the advice of the International Labour Organisation and the Association of Approved Societies that social insurance should be introduced as a progressively graduated scheme like those in many other European countries (Beveridge, 1941; HMSO, 1942; Harris, 1981).

The Government reaction

Even before the Beveridge Report was published, the Government was seeking ways to minimise the impact of his anticipated proposals. Brendan Bracken, the Minister of Information, had warned Churchill as early as October that 'I have good reason to believe that Beveridge and his friends are playing politics and that when the report appears there will be an immense amount of ballyhoo about the importance of implementing the report without delay' (Addison, 1992, p. 216). The Chancellor of the Exchequer took the view that the plan involved a commitment to make resources available that was economically and politically impractical and told Churchill as much in the month preceding publication. He believed that in order to finance the plan, income tax would have to be raised significantly. Rather than abolish want, the plan would, he believed, give benefits to many who did not need them: 'The weekly progress of the millionaire to the post office for his old age pension would have an element of farce but for the fact that it is provided in large measure by the general taxpayer' (Kingsley Wood, cited in Addison, 1975, p. 220). He added, coming to his main point, that:

> *Many have persuaded themselves that the cessation of hostilities will mark the coming of the Golden Age – many were so persuaded last time also. However this may be, the time for declaring a dividend on the profits of the Golden Age is the time when those profits have been realised in fact, not merely in the imagination. (Cited in Addison, 1975, p. 220)*

Churchill, however, took the view that, while government facilities should not be made available for press conferences and the like, 'once it [the report] is out he can bark to his heart's content' (Addison, 1992, p. 217).

Once it was published the Government was faced with the sticky question of what to do about it, especially as Keynes appeared to believe that the plan was workable. Indeed Beveridge, who had been in constant touch with Keynes during the report's preparation, had scaled down some of his recommendations on the latter's advice (Harris, 1977). One of Churchill's closest advisers, Lord Cherwell, also weighed in to support Beveridge. His advice was that the report, while altruistic, was worth supporting, particularly as he believed that it was unlikely to worsen the economic position (Timmins, 1995). His only concern was that the ideas contained in the report might lead to an estrangement with the American government which was payrolling the war effort. The result of this contradictory advice was that the Government played for time. First, it referred the report to a committee of civil servants chaired by Sir Thomas Phillips, one of Beveridge's old adversaries at the Board of Trade earlier in the century. This committee accepted Beveridge's proposals for universality and for a comprehensive health system. It remained unconvinced, however, about key aspects of the recommendations on social security. While accepting the outline of the proposals, the committee attempted to neutralise its most significant and radical elements: the principle of subsistence benefits was rejected; the need for family allowances questioned, and the importance of retaining a deterrent system of means-tested poor relief in order to control an 'irreducible class of hopeless, feckless persons' was emphasised, though it had been clearly rejected by the Beveridge Committee. A further reconstruction committee continued this process of attempted policy erosion when it was set up to consider the practical implementation of Beveridge and produce the White Paper on Social Security in 1944 (HMSO, 1944). A more faithful policy response than this had to await the election of a Labour government in 1945.

More than this, when the Beveridge proposal on full employment had been discussed by a panel of experts looking at the Beveridge Report before publication, one of the senior civil servants protested that 'before making revolutionary changes in our pre-war economic system it is desirable to examine the possibilities of improvement'. This view was supported by both the Conservative Party representative, Willink, and by the Liberal social reformer, Seebohm Rowntree. The latter complained that 'once it was begun there was no stopping place before a complete system on Russian lines had been achieved and with it total sacrifice of freedom'.

The Government forced to debate Beveridge: Cabinet disagreement

It therefore fell to Sir William Jowitt, who had succeeded Greenwood as Minister of Reconstruction, to play for more time and tell the House of Commons that the Government, having studied the report, would formulate its own proposals. This strategy was not, however, without its difficulties. Chief among them was that it risked splitting the coalition. For, unsurprisingly, most of the Labour ministers in the Government were broadly in favour of the plan. While Bevin took against it, either in principle or because it had been produced by Beveridge, claiming erroneously that the unions opposed it, Attlee and Dalton were in favour of it. Their reservation was not about the plan itself but resided in the fact that they were fearful that Churchill might call an election to test support for Beveridge (he had written a minute that could be interpreted in this way) and that he would win it. Notwithstanding these tactical difficulties, Herbert Morrison, who had joined the War Cabinet, argued with passion and in great financial detail for its immediate implementation. His argument was that the social gains of the plan were great and that, 'we should be able to bear the financial burden of the plan, except on the basis of a number of very gloomy assumptions' (Donoughue and Jones, 1973, pp. 314–5). Though the Treasury opposed the implementation of the plan, to accept their view would, he argued, 'be a surrender to idiocy in advance' (Donoughue and Jones, 1973, p. 315). Though Morrison was unable to move the Cabinet to support, he appears to have struck a chord in Churchill who agreed that the Government should undertake to prepare the legislation for implementing the Beveridge report on the understanding that it would require a new House of Commons to vote the necessary expenditure (Hill, 1990).

Parliament gives the Government a bloody nose

In the ferment that surrounded the publication of Beveridge, it was a vain hope – if hope the Government did – that Parliament would not wish to debate it. So, two months after publication and responding to parliamentary pressure, the Government succumbed and a debate took place. Misjudging the atmosphere of the House, the Lord President of the Council, Sir John Anderson, who led off for the Government, made his distaste for the proposals clear. This inflamed opinion not only on the Labour benches but also among back-bench Conservatives. Quintin Hogg, later to become, unbecome and become again Lord Hailsham, who played a large role in the creation of a group of reform-minded, war-time Conservatives and who saw Beveridge as a relatively Conservative document, tabled a motion seeking the immediate creation of a Ministry of Social Security. He was supported by some forty Conservative MPs. He was, much later, to recall that, 'what brought us together was a feeling that the attitude of our leaders in the corridors of power as exemplified by their pussyfooting over the Beveridge Report was unduly unconstructive and unimaginative' (Hailsham, 1990, p. 216). Jim Griffiths, the Labour MP who was to become Minister of National Insurance in the post-war government, went one better and called for the immediate implementation of the Beveridge plan. Morrison had, perhaps with malice aforethought, been lined up to wind up for the Government. He could not bring himself to be negative and so ended up drawing attention to the 16 (out of 23) Beveridge proposals with which the Government agreed. The result of the debate was that while Conservative critics of the Government reluctantly voted with it, 121 MPs from Labour, Liberal and Communist Parties voted against it. Among them was David Lloyd George, registering his last Commons vote.

Churchill forced to accept Beveridge

Consistent pressure through the following month saw Churchill broadcasting to the nation on 21 March 1943 and acknowledging the need to 'peer through the mists of the future to the end of the war' (cited in Timmins, 1995, p.48). He promised to work for changes in five or six practical areas once the war was over. Though Churchill could not bring himself to mention Beveridge's name, the meaning was clear and within a further month a committee was established to consider the implementation of the Beveridge Report. Out of this emerged in 1944 a White Paper on social security.

Just William?

To some, then, it has seemed that almost single-handedly Beveridge created the conditions and the blueprint for post-war social policy and the welfare state and that he is rightly credited as the founding father of the welfare state. Others, as we will see later in this chapter, regard this sort of account as one of the enduring myths of the welfare state (Glennerster, 1995). Be that as it may, the story so far presents a sort of 'just William' approach to social policy. But Beveridge, and his proposals, had in fact been influenced by a range of social, political and economic factors.

In the first place, experience of the inter-war recessions appears to have played a part. Beveridge himself, had, for a greater part of this period, been committed to a neo-liberal stance on the relationship between state and civil society. He had been less than convinced of the efficacy and morality of governments intervening in economic and social policy (Harris, 1981). In this he reflected the dominant attitude of the policy-making establishment. But in the later years of this period, all this was to change. The influences on Beveridge, as on others, seem to have included the development of Keynesian economic principles and of Keynes's views on the relationship between the economic and the social. Keynes had been sharply aware of the privations suffered by the unemployed and many of the employed during the inter-war years. The general principles of Keynesian economics were intended in part to act as guidelines for macro-economic management which would even out the cyclical movements of the British economy. But Keynes also supported more specific economic proposals which would affect the social. Initially, he sought to tackle the problem of poverty by recommending a *de facto* national minimum wage. The mechanism he suggested was a highly progressive direct taxation system with an exempt minimum. This suggestion that the state should directly intervene to alter the distribution of income was, in its day, a radical proposal which had its effects on Beveridge (Harris, 1977; Sullivan, 1992). By the early war years, Keynes had, in fact, moved closer to a position to be taken up by Beveridge: that of support for a family allowance which would ameliorate child and family poverty (Thane, 1982, p. 240). Indeed, as we have seen, the Beveridge proposals as a whole were discussed with, and largely supported by, Keynes (George and Wilding, 1985).

More than this, it was accepted, by the Labour Party at least, that the creation and sustenance of a comprehensive post-war welfare state was possible only if the economy was managed in a way that maintained full employment. In this regard, Keynesian support for Beveridge was vital and was ably promoted not only by Keynes himself but also by three groups of civil servants advising the war-time government. The first group was made up of three temporary civil servants working under the patronage of Dalton at the Board of Trade. They were the Labour academics Evan Durbin, Douglas Jay and Hugh Gaitskell, who was later to become a Labour minister and leader of the party. Convinced Keynesians, they gave Keynesian economics a social democratic slant. The second group of economists were temporary civil servants who made up the Prime Minister's Statistical Section. They had been recruited by Lord Cherwell, who advised Churchill on economic and scientific affairs. The head of the section, Donald MacDougall, was a convinced disciple of Keynes and converted Cherwell to the gospel of full employment. In turn, Cherwell was to advise Churchill and the Cabinet of the efficacy of Keynesianism. Writing to Churchill in early 1944 he strongly supported the idea of high public spending during economic recession:

It is, I think, generally agreed that if money could be put into circulation when a depression began, and if the very natural reaction of government and people to cut down expenditure because the times were bad could be overcome, we should have gone a long way to solving the problem. (Cited in Sullivan, 1992, p. 203)

The third and most important group were members of the Economic Section of the War Cabinet. The section, headed by Lionel Robbins, from the LSE were Keynesians who shared the view that inflationary risks were worth taking in order to maintain full employment and to increase public spending. Both welfarism and the economic means to sustain it were, then, promoted by a sort of Beveridge–Keynes axis.

Second, it seems likely that interest groups outside the policy-making elite influenced the development of policy. As we have seen, the Beveridge Committee was established to consider ways of responding to labour movement pressure for reform of workmen's compensation schemes. Its proposals were clearly in line with, if not stemming from, the evidence provided to the committee by the trade unions. Additionally, the awakening of many professional people to the poverty of ordinary citizens lives in the early years of the war bolstered, if it did not shape, the direction of the Beveridge Report (Marwick, 1974; Calder, 1965). Here there seems evidence that agreements that emerged between the Labour Party and the population over the Beveridge proposals were in part the result of political struggle, a point not missed in Marshall's later analysis of citizenship and social policy (Marshall, 1963). The expansion of social rights explicit in Beveridge's proposals was, at best, greeted without enthusiasm by most senior government ministers. That the proposals became consensually accepted and later largely implemented had much to do with a strategic alliance between key actors in the policy-making elite (Beveridge, Keynes and so on), professional opinion, enlightened by the experience of war, and the interests of the trade union and labour movement.

Beveridge, then, though proposing a very British revolution, had tapped into a consensus on ideas for change and had been influenced by movements in inter-war opinion on social security and welfare. During war time, his contribution to creating the policy context for a welfare state was significant. But, whatever the extent of Beveridge's contribution to the creation of the welfare state, it is clear that other war-time movements were afoot. Among these was a more general collectivist impulse, of which Beveridge was a part and a reflection, but which went much wider.

A collectivist impulse?

In fact, for those who couple the creation of the welfare state with the experience of the Second World War, the notion that war-time experience triggered a collectivist impulse is as significant, if not more significant, than the titanic and individualistic efforts of 'the people's William' (Addison, 1975). For example, this sort of understanding draws attention to the egalitarian effect of social planning on the domestic front in order to promote the war effort. That war effort demanded a degree of equality and shared misery. From the Royal Family to the munitions worker, rationing was introduced on food, clothing and other basic commodities. As Eleanor Roosevelt recorded 20 years later, her visit to Buckingham Palace in 1942 left a lasting impression of equality English-style:

> When we arrived at the Palace [the King and Queen] took me to my rooms explaining that I could only have a small fire in my sitting room and one the outer waiting room . . . Everything in Great Britain was done as one would expect it to be. The restrictions on heat and water were observed as carefully in the royal household as in any home in England. There was a clearly marked black line in my bathtub above which I was not supposed to run the water. We were served on gold and silver plates, but our bread was

the same kind of war bread every other family had to eat and, except for the fact that occasionally game from one of the royal preserves appeared on the table, nothing was served . . . that was not served in any of the war canteens. (Cited in Barnett, 1987, p. 64)

So even in one of the richest households of the land, at least for Mrs Roosevelt's visit, the appearance of equality of suffering was held to be important. Indeed, as the war progressed, some economic levelling did appear to be taking place. This was the result of the interaction of the following factors: first, personal income was taxed at a high level; second, by 1943 the wage rates of wage-earners had overtaken inflation; third, war had abolished unemployment, as the unemployed of the 1930s became service men and women or worked on the home front producing weapons and other equipment necessary for the war effort (Addison, 1975; Addison, 1992; Jones, 1991). Thus, the social and economic planning of war-time led to real and apparent redistribution of resources and is often seen as a sort of 'dry run' for (or prototype for) post-war welfare state planning (Titmuss, 1950, 1958).

This collectivist thrust was also obvious, or so it is claimed by some, in war-time social policy. One of the clearest examples of this was said by Titmuss (1950) to have been the creation of the Emergency Hospital Service (EHS). The EHS had been established in the expectation that air-raid injuries would be more extensive than they actually turned out to be. Nonetheless, war had required a wider geographical and social distribution of health care than the pre-war years because casualties were expected to be widely distributed geographically. This led to a number of interesting consequences. First, doctors who had spent their time in major hospitals, including teaching hospitals, and who were usually from the professional middle class, experienced living and practising medicine in areas of high social deprivation. Shock at the poverty and paucity of adequate medical care in many provincial hospitals acted as a politically educative experience for these personnel, or so it is sometimes claimed. A further consequence of the establishment of the EHS and the relatively light casualties associated with air raids was that the service treated a substantial number of people for ailments unrelated to war. As a result, the EHS gave citizens experience of and access to a health system based on collective planning and free at the point of use. Such experience and access had not hitherto been enjoyed and may be seen in some ways as prefiguring the plans introduced later by Bevan (see Sullivan, 1992).

It is sometimes claimed that these factors, together with the shared danger of war-time, created a greater sense of social solidarity in British society than had hitherto, or indeed has since, been the case. Conscripts from different walks of life and social classes were thrown together in the armed forces and formed bonds of comradeship born out of fellow-feeling and imminent danger. Docker and doctor and their families shared the security of air-raid shelters in the major cities. And rural, often middle class, families provided new homes for evacuees from the major cities. For one influential commentator, this war experience of social cohesion and egalitarianism was the nearest that British society came to socialism (Foot, 1983). For another (Titmuss, 1950; 1958), it formed the bed-rock of the 1945 welfare settlement.

In a semi-official history of the war and social policy (1950) and in a collection of academic essays (1958), that second commentator argued that a moral-rational consensus emerged out of the experience of war, war-time egalitarianism and social solidarity.

His analysis suggested that the influence of war was discernible at three levels: popular attitudes; information about social problems and government response (see, inter alia, Harris, 1981, pp. 247–8; Thane, 1982, pp. 223–4; Sullivan, 1992, as well as Titmuss, 1950, p. 508, 1958, pp. 75–87).

At the level of popular attitudes, the war provided a step on the road to acceptance of egalitarian social and economic policies, or so Titmuss believed. War had also exposed the nature of social problems and their scope. It had revealed social disadvantage and social ills that had previously remained hidden, at least to governments and to the relatively advantaged. Problems of family poverty, malnutrition and the unequal geographical distribution of health services were stripped bare, in large part as a result of evidence that a large number of armed forces recruits proved to be unfit for war duty (Addison, 1975, pp. 171–4). Similarly, the failure of the pre-war education system to provide opportunities to working class children was uncovered by war. Again, as in the Boer and First World Wars, the war recruitment process revealed high levels of illiteracy and innumeracy in the population (Addison, 1975, pp. 237–9).

More than this, the combination of changed public attitudes and new information led to changes at a third level: government response. Attitudes and information combined to convince government of the moral desirability and strategic necessity of intervention to provide welfare services which would meet the social needs exposed by the war.

What we have here, then, is what has become the orthodox Fabian under-standing of policy development applied to a specific set of circumstances. A moral-rational consensus on the creation of a welfare state was built, or at least its foundations laid, by the provision of hitherto unavailable information about social conditions and changes in public attitudes to social and political issues. Titmuss himself expressed the approach thus:

> for five years of war the pressures for a higher standard of welfare and a deeper comprehension of social justice steadily gained in strength . . . the mood of the people changed and, in sympathetic response, values changed as well (Titmuss, 1950, p. 508).

This interpretation found echoes in many contemporary accounts. Aca-demics, adult educators and political activists seemed to have witnessed, at first hand, welfare capitalism's birth: the translation of one kind of social system into another as a result of changed attitudes and shared experience. This evidence arises not only from retrospective reports of an imagined golden age, like Foot's record of war-time 'socialism'. It also emerges in comments made and written at the time.

Public interest in a more collective post-war future is evidenced by first-hand accounts of war-time experience. The late Barbara (Baroness) Wooton, for instance, commented on adult education classes she led during the war. The classes were concerned with a large number of social issues but 'post-war reconstruction played a considerable part in those that I took because it was all that seemed important at the time' (Harrington and Young, 1978, p. 120). The Communist Party leader, Harry Pollitt, pointed to a sort of equality of esteem relating to all sections of the population that accompanied a call to equality of sacrifice in war time.

Further evidence is volunteered by Mass Observation surveys of public opinion during war-time (Addison, 1975, pp. 206–7; 250; Marwick, 1982, p. 127) which found that the majority of the population were concerned that post-war society should be characterised by greater economic and social security and that they favoured collectivist means to achieve this end. Marwick goes further and suggests, like Titmuss, that the experience of war was the experience of collective organisation (1982, p. 180) and that a majority consensus for social reform emerged (1982, pp. 181–6). Certainly this appearance is reinforced by the growth of opinion in the armed services that radical reform was necessary and desirable, an opinion encouraged by the Army Bureau for Current Affairs. This organisation had, in the eyes of one critic, a tendency 'towards the soft life and total reliance on the State to provide everything from the womb to the tomb' (cited in Marwick, 1982, p. 127).

Clearly, this is one interpretation of the rise of welfare statism. It presents a particular view of history. In it, the history of the post-war welfare state can be traced back to the war, the provenance of welfarism was the war itself, the nature of that welfarism was that individual needs should be met through a process of collective responsibility.

A rather different gloss is put on this interpretation by the right-wing historian Corelli Barnett in both his *Audit of War* (1987) and his *The Lost Victory* (1995). His 'audit of war' is nowhere near as positive as Titmuss' account, although, and most importantly, the forward march of collectivism is not doubted. For Barnett, political decisions made during the process of war set the pattern for peace. Woefully, he charts the progress of the campaign for a 'New Jerusalem'. Landmarks on the journey are the decision to practice central planning in war-time Britain, the emergence and impact of the Beveridge Report and the establishment and recommendations of reconstruction committees. Pilgrims on the road to this New Jerusalem were led by a left-leaning intellectual elite both within and without Parliament: Attlee, William Temple – the socialist Archbishop of Canterbury. The Conservative education minister, R. A. Butler, and numerous broadcasters marked the contours of this millenarian post-war society. It was to be a secular Kingdom of Heaven with the state concerning itself with economic planning and social welfare. This 'welfare state' would translate pre-war selfish greed, the moral legacy of Victorian capitalism, into a community of people motivated to work for the good of all (1987, p. 11). With the coming of war, left-wing social millenarians snatched the home-front initiative from the political right and developed a campaign of propaganda for political change. The nature of this transformation is nowhere more graphically set out than by E. H. Carr in an article in The Times in the summer of 1940:

> If we speak of democracy, we do not mean a democracy which maintains the right to vote but forgets the right to work and the right to live. If we speak of freedom, we do not mean a rugged individualism which excludes social organisation and economic planning. If we speak of equality, we do not mean a political equality nullified by social and economic privilege. If we speak of economic reconstruction, we think less of maximum production (though this too will be required) than of equitable distribution.
> (Carr, cited in Titmuss, 1950, p. 508)

The outcome of this search for the New Jerusalem was the creation of a comprehensive welfare state and, for Barnett at least, 'a lost victory' and a financial Dunkirk (Barnett, 1995). Resources that should, after the war was over, have been invested in industrial infrastructure, as it was in Germany and France, was invested in welfare. The result was the end of Britain as a significant player in the world economy.

For both the left (represented by Titmuss) and the right (represented by Barnett) the reality of the war years is the same. Though they view the rise of collectivism from different political vantage points, they are agreed on its vitality in war-time Britain and beyond. For the former, this is a cause for celebration. For the latter it is the source of post-war ills.

The idea that the welfare state arose out of the collectivist impulse of war had, and still has, considerable currency. Many have regarded the Second World War as, in more senses than one, a 'people's war' (Calder, 1965) leading, at its close, to a 'people's peace' (Morgan, 1990). In Titmuss's words, the welfare state emerged out of the 'war warmed impulse to generosity'. Though it is undoubtedly the case that the collective planning of war time created senses of belonging which were invisible in the pre-war years, caution needs to be adopted in swallowing this sort of approach whole. Though it is indisputable that the experience of war wrought substantial social change, the development of a comprehensive welfare state made as much sense for the entrepreneur as for the altruist, for it would create the social conditions in which industry would flourish. And for left-radical critics of the welfare state, the welfare state was simply a new phase of capitalism (Saville, 1957).

Social policy intervention is seen here as having arisen not out of a war-warmed collectivist instinct but from the requirements of post-war capitalism. It marked neither the end of capitalism, as some on the political right had feared (Powell, 1969), nor its transformation as some social democrats had hoped and believed (Crosland, 1952). Rather, it strengthened the power and wealth of the powerful and wealthy. The welfare state, far from being an informed, moral and rational response to the exposure of need is, in this reading of history, simply an institution of late capitalism (Sullivan, 1987, 1992).

It is left to others from the 'political economy' wing of Marxism to remind us that the welfare state probably emerged from both the desire to meet need and the desire to protect profit and maintain social stability (Ginsburg, 1979; Gough, 1979).

The emergence of Labour

Another factor which is said to be associated with the move towards welfarism was the emergence, during the war, of the Labour Party as a party of government.

Most histories of social policy (see particularly, Jones, 1991; Addison, 1975) see the emergence of the Labour Party as part of the war-time coalition government as a major impetus to the creation of a welfare state. The 'emergence of Labour' thesis is based on the following reading of history.

The appointment of Churchill as Prime Minister, following Chamberlain's inglorious fall, is important on two counts. In the first place, the Labour Party's National Executive Committee had hastened Chamberlain's fall and Churchill's ascendancy by refusing to serve in a national unity government headed by the former and by indicating that any request to serve in a government headed by the latter might well elicit a different response. Of more importance, however, was Churchill's decision to appoint Labour politicians to head many, though not all, of the home ministries while he and a maverick band of Churchillian Conservatives and political independents saw to the execution of war policy (Addison, 1992; Hill, 1993). Labour's Cabinet Ministers – Attlee, Bevin, Dalton, Greenwood and, later, Morrison – are seen as having played critical roles in shifting the coalition government towards collectivist and welfarist policies during the war as well as pressing successfully for post-war reconstruction to be high on the political agenda of the war-time government.

At particular and crucial points of the war, Labour stole the initiative from Conservative members of the government and argued that the prize for a people's war and the defeat of Nazi Germany should be a people's peace in which ordinary working people gained extensive citizens' rights and a more equal share of Britain's prosperity. For instance, Ernest Bevin, Labour's Minister of Labour, seeking trade union support on the eve of Dunkirk for a more energetic war effort, told an emergency conference of trade union executives:

> *If our Movement and our class rise with all their energy now and save the people of this country from disaster, the country will always turn with confidence forever to the people who saved them. They will pay more attention to an act of that kind than to theoretical arguments or any particular philosophy. (Cited in Sullivan, 1992, p. 63)*

He, as much as any Labour leader, saw the importance of enthusiastic working class participation in the war effort. For that involvement would make it difficult for any post-war government to deny the extension of peace time rights to ordinary people. Chief among these rights was full employment. Bevin, according to his biographer, had calculated the price for Labour's collaboration with the Conservatives. He was resolved not only to increase wage rates during the war but also to demand the creation of a full employment post-war society, guaranteed by state intervention (Bullock, 1967, pp. 190–1).

At another key point, Bevin, if accidentally, and Greenwood (as Minister without Portfolio, in charge of post-war problems of reconstruction) acted, as we have seen, as political midwives to one of the most significant founding documents of the welfare state. Had it not been for them, and a fair dose of political accident, the Beveridge Report might never have emerged. The beginnings of this propitious war-time episode were, as we have already seen, inauspicious.

Labour was also responsible, in the early war years, for the provision of free milk to all children; abolition of the household means test; for the decision to pay, through the Assistance Board (which had replaced the Unemployment Assistance Board in 1940), hardship grants to families whose homes had been bombed, and for the payment of supplementary pensions to needy pensioners.

Labour MPs, if not their representatives in the Cabinet, also played a part in pressing for the Government to accept the recommendations of the Beveridge Report as we have seen above.

Labour's activity in the home front ministries is also seen by some as being responsible, in part at least, for a swing to the left among the war-time population. According to these accounts, Labour proved itself during war-time to be the party most likely to introduce sweeping welfare reforms once peace had returned and the war-time population, having experienced collectivist policies, were hungry for change. In other words, Labour appeared to be the political beneficiaries of war. By 1943, a *Gallup* poll estimated that Labour was ahead of the Conservatives by between 7 and 11 per cent. In the same year *Mass-Observation* carried out a study of attitudes to demobilisation. That study found that most people, remembering the broken promises following the First World War, were anxious that this war should not be followed by heavy unemployment and mass poverty. Instead, the population wished for a peace-time government that would bring jobs, housing and social security (Mass Observation, 1944). Labour were the clear beneficiaries of the population's anxieties and aspirations as Table 2.1 shows.

The swing to the left was also demonstrated during the last two years of the war by a series of by-elections. On entering the war-time coalition government, Labour had agreed to an electoral truce whereby when seats fell vacant they would be filled by an MP of the party which had held the seat previously. However, during these two years, a number of seats were contested by Labour proxies: by the Independent Labour Party, by Independent Labour candidates

Table 2.1 Voting intentions 1943–5 (%)

		Con	Lab	Lib
1943	June	31	38	9
	July	29	39	9
	December	27	40	10
1944	February	23	37	10
1945	February	24	42	11
	April	24	40	12

Source: Addison, 1975

and by the left-wing Common Wealth Party. In all but one of 14 contests there were swings to the non-Conservative party contesting the election and four Conservatives loyal to the government were unseated. These figures are all the more significant because the elections were fought on the outdated electoral register of 1939, thus disenfranchising significant numbers of mostly younger voters who might be expected to have been more left-wing in their inclinations than the population at large (Addison, 1975, pp. 166–8).

To summarise, then, the war years saw the rehabilitation of Labour as a potential party of government. More than that, the evidence appears to suggest that a population saw Labour as the more likely of the major parties to carry out significant social reform as a peace-time government. Labour's war-time emphasis on the social and economic changes necessary for reconstruction and their preference for universalistic social policies resonated with the anxieties and aspirations of the population at large.

Social policy in war time

The experience of war is also seen as leading to the creation of the British welfare state in another way. War-time social policy is understood in this perception as the forerunner of a peace-time welfare state based on the ideas of universalism and citizen rights. It is generally agreed that political practices, and maybe political philosophies, prominent in war time differed markedly from those which operated in the inter-war peace. Plans for a national health system, hardly on the political agenda in the inter-war years, emerged – apparently as the political property of all shades of political opinion – during this time (Willcocks, 1968; Leathard, 1991). A compulsory and free secondary school system was planned by a Board of Education headed by the Conservative minister, R. A. Butler, and Chuter Ede his Labour deputy, though it had been promoted almost exclusively by the political left before the war (Parkinson, 1970; Rubinstein and Simon, 1973; Godsen, 1976; Weeks, 1986; Reynolds and Sullivan, 1987) and so on. Was war then the cradle of the welfare state?

Certainly, it was the case that the war-time coalition was active in the social policy field. In some areas, particularly in relation to health policy, this activity was encouraged by Conservatives in the Government as well as by Labour politicians and their Liberal counterparts.

Health policy

As suggested above, the idea of a comprehensive health system was one which gained widespread support during the war years. After the war, Attlee's Labour government introduced a national health service which offered treatment free at the point of use to all citizens.

Discussions about the reform of British health care had, in fact, occurred between the National Government and interested parties during the 1930s (Abel-Smith, 1964, pp. 424–7). The starting point for these discussions was the extension of health insurance rather than the position adopted by the Socialist Medical Association (SMA) in the early 1930s. These latter proposals, which became Labour Party policy in 1934, included the provision of free services to patients, the establishment of a corps of full-time salaried doctors and the introduction of local health centres which would be the hubs of the health care system. The discussions between doctors and government had emphasised the need to cater for the British Medical Association's preference for the retention of a large private sector in health and the extension of health insurance to cover hitherto uninsured groups (Leathard, 1991, p. 24).

During the early war years the departmental civil service encouraged the continuation of these discussions and received deputations from the medical profession and the Trades Union Congress. Events, however, overtook these discussions. The formation of the Emergency Hospital Service had, as we have noted earlier, the effect of providing a planned health service, albeit in the conditions of war.

By 1941, civil servants in the Ministry of Health, perhaps influenced by the running of the EHS, suggested a comprehensive national health system in which general practitioners would be grouped in health centres associated with local hospitals. In October of the same year, the Minister of Health, the Liberal, Ernest Brown, announced that some sort of comprehensive service would be introduced after the war. The organisational and funding arrangements of the service remained unclear, though the minister did suggest that patients 'would be called on to make a reasonable payment towards cost, whether through contributory schemes or otherwise' (Hansard, 10 October 1941). At this time, a survey of hospital provision was also set under way.

At the same time, professional interests were attempting to influence the shape of any future national health system. First, the voluntary hospitals, which had been in financial difficulties before the war, started to plan to avoid the return of financial ill-health after the war. Their suggested framework for a national health system included a closer co-operation between the two existing hospital systems in which local authority hospitals might buy services from the voluntary sector, a call echoed of course in the late 1980s, if in a slightly different form and from a different source!

The British Medical Association and the Royal Colleges were also active. Charles Hill, better known to a generation earlier than that of the author's as 'the radio doctor', and later to become a Conservative Minister of Health, argued that 'those who planned first would be more likely to influence the final form [of the health service]'. That planning initially included an acceptance of the ideas emerging about General Practitioner (GP) health centres, as well as those of central planning and of a universal and free service.

By the following year, however, the doctors' prescription for health services appears to have changed. Now the British Medical Association (BMA) resisted the idea of local or central government control and reverted to a preference for a system financed from health insurance rather than from the Exchequer. This new turn by the BMA did, in fact, mask differences of opinion within the doctors' ranks: medical officers of health remained enthusiastic supporters of a free, universal and salaried service; general practitioners working in practices in deprived areas were clearly more accepting of such a service than were other general practitioners or hospital consultants. In reality divided, the doctors' formal opposition to previously accepted principles deepened after the publication of the war-time government's health White Paper (Ministry of Health, 1944).

The White Paper, introduced by the then (Conservative) health minister, Henry Willink, conceded very little to the doctors and the voluntary hospitals. Indeed it was, at first sight, almost as radical in intent as the National Health Service came to be seen. Under this plan, a national health service was to be comprehensive and free and financed out of general taxation and local rates. A closer look at the White Paper reveals acknowledgement of some of the doctors concerns, however. The planned service would, as far as the ministry was concerned, be free and comprehensive. There would, nonetheless, be no compulsion for doctors or patients to use the planned public service but doctors who opted into the system would be offered the opportunity to become salaried employees of the central or local state. This latter offer, of course, flew in the face of the formal position adopted by the BMA.

But in making this opposition clear, as it did, the leadership of the BMA were at odds with many 'rank and file' doctors. A questionnaire of all BMA members showed a significant minority (around 40 per cent) in favour of the White Paper proposals *in toto* and a large majority in favour of a free and comprehensive service. The response of the BMA leadership to this survey was breath-taking. They suggested that the Socialist Medical Association might have stuffed the ballot boxes (Eckstein, 1959) and that already salaried doctors, usually medical administrators who had voted heavily in favour of a salaried service which was both free and comprehensive, should have been excluded from the survey because they had no understanding of private medical practice (Eckstein, 1959).

In the succeeding months, political lobbying was intense. BMA leaders engaged in secret negotiations with Willink and appeared to have achieved a large degree of success. It seems that the minister colluded with the BMA in dismembering the proposals contained in the White Paper. First the idea of a Central Medical Board was dropped to be followed by the demise of plans for a salaried service organised around health centres. Local authorities, it was now decided, could build health centres, but not control them. Instead GPs would rent the buildings, would be remunerated by capitation fee and be entirely free to engage in private practice.

What then is the significance for post-war social policy of this war-time policy-making?

First, the principle of a comprehensive health system had been won. Though the White Paper's proposals were watered down in the light of the BMA's resistance, government and the profession had conceded that the post-war world must be one in which health care was a citizen right.

In war time, citizens had experienced easier access to health services in part as a result of the EHS. Emergency Hospital Service doctors had experienced the health needs of Britain's working class population. War, then, seems to have affected both the attitudes of the population and, perhaps of equal importance, the attitudes of influential medical practitioners.

These professionals were in a position to facilitate the dissemination of information about health problems. This, along with the groundswell of desire for change among the general population, seems to have been a vital factor which influenced the Government's commitment to develop plans for a comprehensive national health system.

This, though, is not the whole story. The war cannot sensibly be regarded as the midwife of the NHS. Some account must also be taken of pressure for change in health policy during the inter-war years.

As we have already seen, the SMA were successful in placing their recommendations for a national health service on the political agenda during the 1930s. These proposals for a free and comprehensive service with a salaried staff formed the basis of Labour Party policy as early as 1934. The proposals put forward during this decade by the BMA were, of course, less radical but acknowledged that there were fundamental weaknesses in available medical cover. On two occasions in the 1930s, it published reports which recommended that each citizen should have access to a family doctor and to the services of appropriate specialists. These recommendations, like later proposals from the BMA, fell short of a national, or nationalised, health service; the financing of the service was seen as best achieved through a system of health insurance. The BMA were even unwilling to accept the recommendations of its own Medical Planning Commission about the scope of a health insurance scheme (Sullivan, 1992). Nonetheless, the BMA, during the 1930s, was ready to concede that co-ordination of any post-war service was most satisfactorily located at the national level.

There had, of course, been an even earlier call for a national health service. In 1926 the report of the Royal Commission on National Health Insurance was published. It acknowledged that the insurance system established in 1911 by a reforming Liberal government had become an accepted part of national life. It suggested, however, that '. . . the ultimate solution will lie we think in the direction of divorcing the medical service entirely from the insurance system and recognising it, along with all other public health activities, as a service to be supplied from the general public funds' (HMSO, 1926).

While it is undoubtedly the case that the experience of war played some part in promoting ideas about changes in the principles and practices of health care (ultimately represented in the 1944 White Paper), it is far from clear that this process represented a new beginning. War may simply have achieved the acceleration of an already established process of policy movement.

Nor should we fall into the trap of seeing the development of war-time health policy as consensual, leaving a Labour government only to decide on the best way to implement agreed policy frameworks. Though many doctors, even in war time, supported the idea of a health system funded from general funds and including a salaried service, there was critical resistance to some of the measures outlined in Willink's White Paper. That resistance, from the BMA leadership and, it must be said, from a small majority of doctors responding to a BMA survey, included resistance to the idea of doctors as public servants and, sometimes, to the idea of a comprehensive health system itself.

Even among those medical and other interests favouring the establishment of a comprehensive system, there were conflicts about other issues. While the SMA, the Labour Party and Service doctors supported the idea of financing the service from the national Exchequer, most other doctors and certain elements in the Conservative Party favoured a system of health insurance, either publicly or privately administered. While the former grouping favoured control of the health service by central or local government, many doctors opposed government activity that went beyond central planning functions. While the SMA, Service doctors and local medical officers, the Labour Party and some ministers in the coalition government favoured a salaried service, this found very little support in the wider ranks of the medical profession.

By the end of the war there was agreement of only a limited nature, which masked a wide divergence of opinion amongst interested parties in the health field and in the wider social politics of health.

War-time health policy seems, then, to be of less significance than some claim in defining post-war health policy. Though limited agreement on the need for a comprehensive system had emerged, conflict remained over the nature of that system. More than this, inter-war factors seem to be not insignificant in the growth of pressure for a comprehensive health system. War undoubtedly accelerated the acceptance as orthodoxy hitherto contested arguments. Nevertheless, as Aneurin Bevan was to find out, that orthodoxy was still some way short of a national health service.

Education policy

One approach to policy-making in this area sees the 'Butler' Education Act (1944) as the beginning proper of a state system of secondary education in the United Kingdom and the Second World War as fertile ground which nourished the seeds of education policy-making. As is often the case, the reality is more complex than this simple analysis suggests. The war years appear to have accelerated change rather than being its engine. When Churchill appointed Butler to the Board of Education in 1941, he had anticipated that no major reforms would emerge during the war. That the Act was placed on the statute book is in large part because of the energy and foresight of Butler and of Chuter Ede, his Labour deputy. However, the process that led to the Education Act had a considerably longer history than the span of the war.

The first point to be made is that the social politics of education had been concerned with the issue of state-provided secondary education for at least two decades before the publication of the 1943 White Paper on Education and the subsequent 1944 Education Act. Indeed, earlier struggles for state secondary education can be dated as far back as the early nineteenth century (Simon, 1974, pp. 72–170). Certainly by 1897 the trade union movement was mobilising support not only for free secondary education for all children but also for that education to take place in a 'common school' (Simon, 1974, p. 202). In the context of the twentieth century, there had been quite substantial political activity in the education field in the inter-war years.

As early as 1920, attempts were being made at a parliamentary level to move beyond elementary education for all to secondary education for all (for a description of the state system existing at this time, see Griffiths, 1971; Rubinstein and Simon, 1973, pp. 1–18). A Departmental Committee of the Board of Education, reporting in this year, argued that the sole relevant criteria for entry to secondary education should be ability (an argument to be echoed more than forty years later in relation to higher education by the Robbins Committee (HMSO, 1963)). This is of course a position which was not inconsistent with the Labour Party's plans for secondary education (Labour Party, 1922), written for the minority Labour government by R. H. Tawney.

That document argued that secondary education should be provided free for all children between the ages of 11 and 16. It further claimed that an education system divided into superior secondary schools and inferior elementary schools was 'educationally unsound and socially obnoxious' (Labour Party, 1922).

In fact what emerged from the policy process at this time was the development of different sorts of post-primary schooling and academic streaming. In 1926, the so-called Hadow Report, the report of a consultative committee of the Board of Education on the Education of the Adolescent, made recommendations for education up to the age of 15 years. It suggested that there should be one type of primary school for children aged up to 11 years and a variety of types of post-primary education. Post-primary schooling would include the high prestige secondary schools following a literary or scientific curriculum. It would also take place in central schools which would offer a 4-year practical course, modern schools for the bulk of those pupils not catered for in secondary or central schools, and junior technical and trade schools.

In other words what happened in the early part of the inter-war period was the development of ideas, within the Board of Education and outside it, about policy change followed by the report of a consultative committee which significantly diluted those ideas. Even if Hadow's stated aim of establishing equality of educational opportunity through this structure is taken seriously, it ran against the status consciousness of the British educational establishment.

War seems to have played a not insignificant but relatively minor part in the development of policy in this area. It is certainly possible to argue that a political consensus on policies for schooling emerged during the war years. But the process leading to political agreement over secondary education appears to have had less to do with the experience of war than with a range of political activities which took place later in the inter-war period.

The inter-war movement for secondary education seems to have been driven by a *de facto* 'triple alliance' made up of the Labour Party, the teaching unions and the wider trade union movement. Although individual actors in this alliance presented, at particular conjunctures, policy plans differing in emphasis and recommendations, the common ground in their approaches is, as we will see below, clear. What we will see emerge is a process whereby the political and professional activities of these organisations, while failing to achieve a wider consensus on all of their goals, accomplished agreement among opinion-formers and policy-makers on the key issue of secondary education.

Between the publication and acceptance of the Hadow Report and the commencement of the Second World War, each of these organisations acted in ways that put compulsory secondary education on the political agenda and kept it there. A critical moment in this process is represented by the publication of plans for education by the Labour Party at the end of the 1920s.

In a major policy statement issued on May Day 1929, a month before the party's election as a minority government, it had noted that the party 'has always been committed to securing equal educational opportunity for every child' (Labour Party, 1929). A key part of the process of achieving this goal was to introduce 'facilities for free secondary education at once'. In fact, since 1907 no pupil of suitable ability was debarred from a grammar school place as a result of the introduction of a 'free places quota'. That, at least, was the theory. In reality numerous working class children failed to take up places for which they were qualified because their parents were unable to afford the obligatory school uniform. It was to this reality that the phrase 'facilities for free secondary education' was addressed. In the event, of course, the short-lived Government was unable to do any such thing but these policy commitments represented a benchmark for further developments.

A similar position had already been adopted by some of the teacher unions. In 1925, anticipating the emphasis on differentiation that the Hadow Report would subscribe to, the Association of Assistant Masters (AMA) had called for the establishment of secondary education for all. Though the sort of school that the AMA had in mind was one with multiple biases catered for on one site, rather than the separation of secondary age pupils into different schools, it was in the forefront of educational and political thinking on this policy issue.

In the late 1920s both the National Union of Teachers (NUT) and the National Association of Labour Teachers contributed to this process of setting the policy agenda. Both of these organisations made recommendations that the provision of post-primary education should be in secondary schools for all pupils. Their preference, like that of the AMA, was for multilateral or multibias schools but the policy principle was clear. Secondary schooling should be provided as a compulsory and free part of a state education system (see Rubinstein and Simon, 1973; Reynolds and Sullivan, 1987; Sullivan, 1991). This principle was made clear by the teacher unions in evidence they gave to government enquiries into education in the 1930s.

The first of these, carried out by the Consultative Committee of the Board of Education and chaired by Sir William Spens, had been asked to report on secondary education in general and the matter of technical high schools in particular. The evidence given to the committee by the NUT underlined the union's previous policy decision. National Union of Teachers witnesses made clear to the Spens Committee its views, increasingly supported by educational research, that the sharp differentiation of pupils into diverse forms of post-primary education was neither justified nor justifiable on educational or social grounds. They repeated their view that the most appropriate organisational form for secondary education was one centred around multilateral schools which would offer academic, technical and vocational education on one site and questioned the evidence provided by other witnesses that a child's ability was immutably fixed by the age of 11 years. In so doing, the NUT was contributing to the development of a later political consensus in favour of equality of educational opportunity. The union's view became the orthodoxy of the labour movement in the 1930s and was echoed by the Trades Union Congress (TUC) in its evidence to Spens.

The Spens Report, when it was published in 1938, in some senses at least, marked the success of the consensus-building exercise. It recommended that all post-primary education should be provided in secondary schools. It did demur from the labour movement's views on the unified secondary school, preferring to accept psychological evidence that children's varying abilities were fixed by the age of 11 years (Spens, 1938, pp. 123–5). This part of the report was challenged, particularly by the TUC and the teacher unions. The TUC insisted that so long as social stratification of children into social and industrial strata remained at the age of 11 years, it was meaningless to talk about parity of education. The report did, nonetheless, argue for the need for parity of esteem between the different types of school, the grammar, the technical and the modern, which it recommended should be established.

By the beginning of the war, then, the views of the Labour Party, the TUC and the teacher unions had started to hold sway among opinion-formers and policy advisers. The push for secondary education had succeeded in influencing opinion-formers even if the progress of policy ideas on multilateral schooling had been limited. War-time experience seems to have achieved a rapid translation of this political agenda on education into implemented policy and a jelling of the educational consensus.

Under Butler's stewardship of education policy, the limited consensus on education was entrenched and finally became statute. For the first two years, he was pre-occupied by the question of what might constitute an appropriate relationship between Church schools and the rest of the future state system. But there seemed to be no question about whether a state secondary education system should be established (for an interesting account of this period, see Howard, 1987).

In July 1943, the Government published a White Paper on education as a prelude to legislation (Board of Education, 1943). It reflected the limited consensus on education in a number of ways. First, it claimed that there was little to justify a system which sharply differentiated between children on social and educational bases at an early age. Second, it suggested that a state system of secondary education be established which would provide education, free of charge, to children between the ages of 11 and 15 years. Third, while adopting the recommendation of the Spens Committee for different types of secondary school as the norm, it allowed the possibility of multilateralism in some circumstances. This last point was underlined by Butler when he addressed Parliament on the issue.

I would say to those idealists who want to see more than one form of secondary education in the same school – sometimes called multilateral schools – that I hope that more than one type of secondary education may, from time to time, be amalgamated under one roof. (Hansard, 29 July 1943)

The passage of the 1944 Education Act saw these principles enshrined in statute. It also marked the end of one moment in the policy-making process in relation to secondary education. The Act represented the end of a process which had started with conflicting political attitudes to state provision of educational services and the beginning of a new process to take the issue of state secondary education beyond the principles of 1944.

In this area of policy development, then, it is not at all clear that war, of itself, was the cradle of reform. Rather, the movement for policy change, eventuating in consensual policy proposals and implementation, was the result of a longer term set of pressures. It is possible to argue that the levels of illiteracy and innumeracy that war-time recruitment exposed might have been a significant factor in government decisions to legislate on compulsory secondary schooling.

Coming to conclusions

There can be little doubt that, in one way or another, the Second World War acted as a catalyst to social policy development. Preparations for war had, for example, created the EHS. Not only did the almost accidental treatment of disadvantaged people by the EHS raise consciousness about poverty and deprivation. Not only did that knowledge permeate the policy elites of the political parties. But the EHS also demonstrated the viability and effectiveness of a centrally-organised and controlled health service, a point not lost on Aneurin Bevan as post-war Minister of Health. Similarly, Butler used the social dynamic of war time to draw the church authorities into a wider educational agreement which was to lead, before the end of the war, to legislation guaranteeing secondary schooling to all British children. Social policy in war certainly acted as a foundation on which the architects of the welfare state built.

In this they were aided by the political and public consensus reflected in and facilitated by Beveridge. Though it would be unwise to characterise the post-war welfare state as the progeny of just William, the Beveridge episode played, or so I believe, a major part in legitimising state welfare. Governments, said Beveridge, supported in large part by Keynes, had an obligation in the modern world to intervene to banish social evils. That Beveridge's plan was supported not only by the trade unions but also by the insurance industry, no doubt improved its chances. But Beveridge had tapped into something much deeper. He had caught the beat of a collectivist impulse that punctuated the lives of ordinary, and not so ordinary, war-time citizens. That impulse, present also in the Labour Party, had the effect of sweeping away Conservative resistance to Beveridge's proposals. Those proposals are significant for us as much because of Beveridge's vision of a welfare state as for his detailed plan for social security. Britain at war, it seemed, was capable of producing revolutionary plans. This radical edge was reinforced by Labour in Parliament, for which it was rewarded with stewardship of immediate post-war Britain. But, as we have already noted, the war-time revolution was very British in character. The Beveridge proposals, for example, with their emphasis on the insurance principle, emphasised individual responsibility to meet need as well as governments' obligations. Social rights were to be conferred only as partners to social responsibilities. In any event, or so Beveridge seems to have believed, the British citizen would not wish to receive something for nothing.

In fact, social insurance can easily be seen as conservative in its approach. It was to provide *minimum* standards of income based on a principle of *contribution*. The state was to take on responsibilities, as were employers, but the Beveridge proposals were a sort of 'you gets what you pay for' approach to social policy. This conservatism is said by Glennerster (1995) to be the result of Beveridge's 'contradictory struggle between his deep desire to cover everything and everybody and his choice of method. Contributory insurance through employment'. Though any other road would probably have been impossible, and would certainly have risked the hostility of the unions, Beveridge's British revolution was based not on citizenship rights but on labour market participation. Though insurance removed stigma, it also narrowed eligibility. Women, for example, were to be covered predominantly by their husband's contributions. Which brings us on to a final issue. Despite claims that the social insurance schemes, dreamed by Beveridge, and earlier by David Lloyd George, were attempts to postpone a Labour government by conceding some social security, they were never intended to address issues of equality. Social security was to provide a floor beneath which no-one should fall. Plans to build an egalitarian New Jerusalem (Barnett, 1987, 1995) were the dreams of others, not of Beveridge.

Indeed, although it is almost certain that a post-war welfare state would have emerged even if the Conservatives had won the general election in 1945, it is less likely that issues of equalisation and equity would have been as thoroughly addressed, even if Labour, having addressed the issues, appeared to forget about them.

CHAPTER THREE

The emergence and growth of the welfare state

Chronology	The post-war period
1945–	Labour's council housing drive
1946	National Health Services Act
	National Insurance Act
	Curtis Report on the care of children
1948	Birth of the National Health Service
	Social security system inaugurated
1949–	The first comprehensive schools
1950	Labour narrowly wins second post-war general election
1951	Charges introduced for some health service treatments
	Aneurin Bevan, Harold Wilson and John Freeman resign from
	Government over health charges and rearmament for the
	Korean War
	Conservatives win general election
1951–64	Growth of the welfare state under Conservative governments
	but right-wing opposition to welfarism
Early 1960s	Rediscovery of poverty
1963	Robbins Report on Higher Education
1964	Labour government elected
1965	Labour introduces comprehensive school policy

In the last chapter we looked at emerging social and economic policy during the war years and considered the extent to which war-time social policy could be considered the harbinger of the welfare state. We concluded that, though war had created a more collectivist social and political ethos than was obvious in the inter-war years, it had often simply accelerated inter-war policy processes. More than this, it seemed that the war-time policy outcomes were sometimes, though not always, at some distance from what we now regard as the principles of the post-war welfare state.

In this chapter, we move on to chart the emergence and growth of the welfare state in the 30 or so years after the end of hostilities.

The emergence of the welfare state

In July 1945 the Labour Party won a landslide general election victory. The new Parliament was made up of 393 Labour Members of Parliament (MPs), 213 Conservatives and 34 MPs from other parties. It got close to attracting a majority of the votes cast with nearly 48 per cent of the vote, compared to the Conservatives' share of just under 40 per cent. Labour became the electoral beneficiaries of war-time radicalism. During that war, working people had sacrificed much and now elected a government which it expected to deliver economic and social change. At the very least, there was an expectation that the Beveridge proposals would be implemented without delay. The Labour victory had in fact been won on a manifesto that committed it to significant nationalisation of key industries and to the introduction of a comprehensive welfare system (Labour Party, 1945). Accepting the challenge of government, Attlee had also accepted the challenge to implement policies consistent with the twin goals of economic recovery and social justice. The experience of war-time government had convinced Labour of the possibility of transforming British capitalism from the individualistic political creed of the pre-war years into a collectivist social democracy.

The economic context

Throughout the years of the 1945–51 Labour governments, social and economic policy-making was to be influenced, though not determined, by economic difficulties and the challenge presented by a war-torn economy.

Whichever party had won the election in 1945 would have been faced with economic difficulties of serious proportions. Britain's overseas liabilities (excluding the Land-Lease scheme by which the UK had borrowed from the United States during the war) had increased from £542 million in June 1939 to £3,354 million in June 1945, while its reserves of gold and US and Canadian dollars had risen by only £121 million to £624 million between August 1939 and June 1945 (Peden, 1991). And further borrowing would be necessary to finance imports as the Land-Lease scheme ended with the coming of peace. The diversion of British industry to war production meant that in 1945 exports were only 46 per cent of their 1938 volume. The sale of assets overseas to help finance the war had reduced income from other countries from £168 million before war to £50 million in 1945. Like much of the rest of the world, Britain was critically short of dollars to pay for goods from North America. The first priority for the new Labour government was therefore to secure further loans in order to pay for raw materials while Britain built up its export industries. One of the first acts of the Government was therefore to send Keynes to the USA to try to negotiate fresh credit. As a result of his efforts, the United States granted Britain credit of $3,750 million and Canada made $1,250 million available. However, the terms of the former loan were harsh. Britain was required to make sterling convertible for current transactions a year after the loan had been ratified by the US Congress. The British government was also required to recommend to Parliament a policy of adherence to the Bretton Woods agreement of 1944 to maintain stable exchange rates. It is not clear how Britain was expected to maintain currency stability once convertibility had been achieved, unless the demand for dollars was not such as to lead to a greater conversion of sterling into dollars than its meagre reserves of gold and dollars would bear. But part of the agreement prevented the British government from any actions which would reduce the demand for dollars (tariffs, surcharges, quotas, etc.) and discriminate against American imports. A reduction in dollar expenditure therefore necessitated a cut in all imports and as a consequence war-time controls over imports were retained.

However, the economic context proved to be even more inauspicious. Post-war inflation in the United States proved to be higher than anticipated. This had the effect of cutting the real value of the credit by around one quarter by July 1947 when the United Kingdom was to make sterling available. Moreover, the United Kingdom's trade balance deteriorated in the immediate post-war years with the cost of imports rising markedly and outstripping rises in the value of exports. Because the Attlee government was reluctant to limit imports before 1947, the dollar credit was exhausted more quickly than had been anticipated. When convertibility was attempted, it was quickly abandoned because it gave other countries the opportunity to exchange sterling for scarce dollars and provoked a sterling crisis. In response to this, the Labour government felt driven to cut imports, including food, to the minimum consistent with the maintenance of the health and morale of the British population. At the same time the Government encouraged an export drive, though this was at the expense of home consumption (Cairncross, 1992, ch. 6). Economic problems were to dog the post-war Labour governments through to 1951, despite the provision by the United States of Marshall Aid to underwrite the European Recovery Programme.

Industrial production was held back by shortages of coal, steel and labour. The downward trend of coal production during the war carried on in the peace. Industry was brought to a standstill in early 1947 by a coal crisis which reduced exports from the United Kingdom by at least £100 million (about one quarter of the balance of payments deficit that year (Cairncross, 1992, ch. 13)). Industrial labour power was in short supply because, even after demobilisation, the Government retained conscription into the armed forces.

These gathering economic crises were accompanied, in the late 1940s, by an economic recession in the United States which reduced export earnings in dollars and caused a drain on UK reserves. This forced the hand of the Labour government and led Cripps to devalue sterling.

The economic conditions of the mid to late 1940s were then inauspicious. This was hardly, one would think, the ideal context for the emergence of a comprehensive welfare state. Indeed, as we have seen, Labour was worried on coming to power that the extent of national indebtedness would inhibit its ability to implement its social policy pledges. However, despite the problem of external debt and a sluggish economy, the Government managed to create a budget surplus during its tenure of office that paid for social policy expansion. This was possible because Labour kept tax rates at high war-time levels and because, at least in the immediate post-war years, defence expenditure was reduced:

> As demobilisation proceeded, defence expenditure dropped from £4.4 billion to £0.85 billion . . . between 1945–6 and 1947–8 and changed little thereafter until rearmament in 1951–2. Expenditure on other supply services trebled over those two years . . . absorbing roughly one third of the purchasing power released by the fall in defence expenditure. (Cairncross, 1992, p. 420)

In other words, the establishment of the welfare state was, in part at least, guaranteed by a 'peace dividend' which freed sufficient finance to make increased expenditure on social policy possible, even during unfavourable economic circumstances. Cairncross's arguments have, of course, recently been subjected to criticism. In *The Lost Victory: British Dreams, British Realities* (1995), Correlli Barnett develops arguments which first appeared in his *Audit of War* (1987). Specifically, he argues that the Labour government's insistence on continuing to see Britain as a world power and its introduction of a welfare state bankrupted the economy. It had put 'parlours before plant' (1995, p. 63) and welfare before re-building Britain's defunct industrial infrastructure:

> The truth is that the Labour government, advised by its resident economic pundits, freely chose not to make the re-equipping of Britain as an industrial society the Schwerpunkt of her use of Marshall Aid. Instead, the government saw Marshall Aid . . . primarily as a wad of greenbacks stuffed by a kindly Uncle Sam into the breeches pocket of a nearly bankrupt John Bull who, though diligently seeking future solvency, nevertheless wished in the meantime to go on playing the squire, beneficent to his family and the poor and grand among his neighbours (1995, p. 365).

Labour was concerned to build the New Jerusalem but was doing it on tick (1995, pp. 135–7).

Of course, as Glennerster (1995) clearly sees, the problem with the Barnett line is that it simply cannot hold. In fact, greater demands were placed on continental economies by welfare development than the welfare state placed on Britain's and yet those economies still managed to outperform ours (Harris, 1990). If post-war Britain was bankrupt, it was a state of affairs caused by factors outside of the welfare state.

Be that as it may, and readers might find Barnett more secure on ideology than economics, a welfare state was established.

The post-war welfare state

Against, and to some extent constrained by, a sometimes unfavourable economic backdrop, the post-war Labour government introduced and developed major social policies which we have come to see as the welfare state. Introduced by a government programmatically committed to social reform, these policies can be seen both as a radical break with the past and as a manifestation of contemporary political and social conservatism.

The most obvious break with the past was the Labour government's commitment to the principle of universalism in service provision. For most Labour policy makers, this universalist assumption was rooted in experience of the inter-war years. During this period, high unemployment cast many families into abject poverty as the bread-winner exhausted (usually) his rights to unemployment insurance. More than this, the 'means test', which had to be undergone before extended and uncovenanted insurance benefits could be granted, was an abomination to Labour politicians, as was the humiliation of second-class medical care by 'panel doctors' while the financially better-off got apparently superior service from private medicine. In response, Labour's social policy thrust was a universalistic impulse. That impetus was important for two reasons. First, or so it was believed, universalism was the only way of guaranteeing that best quality services could be made available to all who needed them. Second, only universal services would remove the stigma associated, as a result of inter-war experience, with state services.

Universalism, then, became one of the totems of Labour's post-war policy makers. It is nowhere more clearly demonstrated than in Labour's social security policies. But, as we shall see, the constraints of the past and the present are also obvious in Labour's post-war approach to income maintenance.

Developing social security

As readers will recall, the Beveridge Report had recommended a national insurance scheme which was based on a contributory principle: citizens would receive benefits during time of earnings interruption because they had made contributions as workers before sickness or unemployment had befallen them.

Labour was determined to introduce universal social security provision, as had been Beveridge, but was mindful of the harsh economic winds blowing in the post-war world. Though many had been unhappy with the insurance principle lying at the heart of Beveridge, it was seen as the most viable way forward if universal social security was to be introduced in an inauspicious economic context. The contributory principle had one other advantage of course. A system based on contribution could not be presented as a 'dole' or unearned handout. The memories of Labour politicians and ministers were long and scarred. As a consequence, what emerged was a scheme in which the idea of universality was married with the Beveridgian and Liberal tradition of national insurance. Introducing the National Insurance Bill in 1946, James Griffiths, the Labour social security minister, presented it as the introduction of a national minimum standard. Though this safety net was unlikely to be needed by the financially comfortable, Labour's universalism made it as available to them as to poorer citizens. Contributions to the scheme were registered as stamps on each citizen's national insurance card. Thus contributions were to be not only real but also visible!

Though based on an insurance principle, Labour's plan for social security stood little chance of being truly self-financing. This was largely the case because the Labour government decided that old-age pensions should be paid at full rate immediately (Beveridge had recommended that there should be a 20-year phasing-in period before maximum pension rates were achieved). Labour's decision, though more politically astute than Beveridge's counsel, meant that pensions would take up two thirds of all social security expenditure at once. These decisions were recorded in the National Insurance Act (1948).

Notwithstanding the insurance principle at the heart of national insurance, Labour also wished to safeguard the interests of those citizens who, for whatever reasons, found themselves ineligible for receipt of national insurance benefits. The Government therefore retained elements of the Poor Law, while officially abolishing it in the National Insurance Act. This was achieved by introducing a national assistance scheme in parallel with national insurance. The National Assistance Act (1948) retained the Assistance Board (Unemployment Assistance Board before 1940) and re-titled it the National Assistance Board. The Board was to deal with those ineligible for national insurance and those who received national insurance benefits but found them inadequate to their needs. National Assistance, the ancestor of both Supplementary Benefit, Income Support and the Social Fund, was to be paid out only after the administration of a personal needs test. Labour's social security policies were then created with an eye to the future and an eye to the past, or at least to contemporary orthodoxies. The governing party wished the future to be one substantially free of the selectivism of previous policy but felt compelled to adhere to a Beveridge-type insurance scheme and to retain elements of means-testing in national assistance.

Introducing a national health service

As we have seen in the previous chapter, discussions about a comprehensive health system had taken place under the tenure of the war-time coalition government. Its introduction has been one of the most studied social policy innovations (Eckstein, 1959). In the hearts of the British public, it has come to be seen as the central achievement of the Attlee government (Sullivan, 1992; Glennerster, 1995). It has also recently been seen as a clear example of the capture of a welfare state service by dominant professionals and of the exclusion of users from that service. Or, at least, this seems to have been the case until recent years.

As we have already seen, calls for a national health system have had a reasonably long history. As early as 1920, the government-commissioned Dawson Report called for the establishment of a comprehensive health system and proposals of differing political complexion emerged from the Socialist Health Association (SHA), the BMA and the centre-left of the Conservative Party during the 1930s (Sullivan, 1992; Hill, 1993). However, attempts to develop a consensual health policy during the war years were ultimately dashed on the rocks of BMA resistance. It was left to the Labour Party to develop and implement policy for a national health service. The challenge facing Labour's Minister of Health, Aneurin Bevan, was large and complex. In the first place, he was, like his colleague James Griffiths, limited to some extent by the general political consensus over health policy contained in the Health White Paper in 1944. Additionally, though a national health system had not previously existed, estimates needed to be made about the extent of health need and an attempt made to quantify the range of services required to maintain the nation's health. More than this, health policy proved to be an area strewn with political landmines primed to explode. For controversy was to dog every political step on the road to the National Health Services Bill (1946) and beyond this to the establishment of the NHS in 1948.

The first controversy related to whether the NHS should be accountable to local or central government? Bevan finally came down in favour of central control with 14 regional health boards reporting directly to the Minister of Health. This decision completely overturned the immediate past in which local authorities, along with a voluntary sector, had controlled hospitals. Instead, it was proposed that there should be 'a complete take-over – into one national service – of both voluntary and municipal hospitals' (Public Records Office, 1945a, cited in Klein, 1989). In essence, the minister was to argue that the only way to achieve a truly national service with universal standards was to run it from the centre with some powers delegated to Regional Hospital Boards whose members would be appointed by the Minister of Health. This, of course, flew in the face of the 1944 White Paper and also led to conflict within the Government. The major antagonist against Bevan's centralising tendency was the Lord President of the Council, Herbert Morrison. Morrison had been a member and leader of the London County Council for many years before his entry to Parliament and he bridled against this element of Bevan's plan. He argued in a memorandum to Cabinet that the Minister of Health was:

> on the horns off a dilemma. If the Regional Boards and District Committees are to be subject to the Minister's directions on all matters of policy, they will be mere creatures of the Ministry of Health with little vitality of their own . . . yet it is difficult under a state system to envisage the alternative situation in which, in order to give them vitality, they are left free to spend Exchequer money without the Minister's approval and to pursue policies which at any rate in detail might not be the Minister's, but for which he would presumably be answerable. (Public Records Office, 1945, cited in Klein, 1989)

However, the Bevan plan would weaken local government:

> It is possible to argue that almost any local government function, taken by itself, could be administered more efficiently in the technical sense under a national system, but if we wish local government to thrive . . . we must consider the effect on local government of each particular proposal. It would be disastrous if we allowed local government to languish by whittling away its most constructive and interesting functions. (Public Records Office, 1945, cited in Klein, 1989)

In essence, while conceding that central control might be administratively superior, Morrison thought that this was outweighed by the political effect on local government. Here, then, is an ideological fissure which centres on the relationship between local and central government. Morrison's arguments are couched in explicitly political terms: the NHS should be locally administered because local administration would provide local authorities with opportunities to become schools of political education. Bevan's arguments were considerably harder-headed. Central control was to be preferred: because local government was not yet ready to administer a major social policy initiative; because central administration was the only clear way to achieve near universalisation of standards (the minister's fear was that left to their own devices rich areas would develop good services while poor areas would receive and inferior service), and because public control should follow public money. Bevan's arguments were for rationality, efficiency and accountability.

Bevan won the support of the Labour Cabinet over this issue. However this victory was not without a policy cost. One of Morrison's arguments for the retention of local control was that it would mean that hospital and personal health services were unified under local government. Now the services would be fragmented. Aware of this problem Bevan thought about moving the responsibility for personal health services – child welfare, district nursing, dental services, etc. – from local to central government control (Klein, 1989). However, as the policy process unfolded, Morrison appears to have successfully protected these services from the clutches of central control.

The major concessions in Bevan's legislation were, however, reserved for the medical profession. Determined to split the profession, which was threatening to prevent the establishment of the NHS, Bevan adopted the strategy of buying off the prestigious medical specialists in the Royal Colleges.

This was achieved by a five-pronged approach. First, teaching hospitals, in which these specialists often worked, were given special status with governing bodies of their own directly under the Minister of Health, instead of being integrated into the administrative structure of the hospital service. Second, the regional hospital boards were given executive status rather than the advisory status envisaged in the Conservative caretaker government's proposals in 1945. Third, Bevan enshrined the right for doctors to engage in private practice in NHS pay beds, much to the discomfort of Labour backbenchers. Bevan's fourth concession was to introduce the idea of merit awards for hospital specialists. Originally the brain-child of Lord Moran of the Royal College of Physicians, merit awards over and above basic salary were to be made to doctors whose performance was regarded as meritorious by their peers. Finally, Bevan opened the door for doctors to serve on health and hospital authorities by abandoning the principle that representatives should be elected by local government. In doing this he went further than the 1944 White Paper was prepared to go and opened the way for doctors to remain prominent in the management of health services as well as in the provision of health care. In his own words: 'The full principle of direct public responsibility must of course be maintained, but we can – and must – afford to bring the voice of the expert right into direct participation in the planning and the running of the service'. Foot (1982) also attributes to him the earthier assessment that 'I choked the doctors' throats with gold'. (This claim is more often reproduced as 'I choked the doctors' mouths with gold'. Foot's version is, I think, nearer to the truth, for Bevan saw this gilt sword as double edged: the doctors' reward was pecuniary but they might have been expected, on reflection, to gag on what he saw as a pyrrhic victory.)

Health policy making then involved negotiating not only the tension between central and local government, as we have already seen, but also a politics of acquiescence or – at the very least – compromise with the traditional self interest of the medical profession. Implicit in the legislation establishing the NHS is the idea of medical prominence, if not dominance, in the planning and running of the service. This dubious inheritance is one passed on by Bevan to succeeding governments and was only challenged by the Thatcher governments of the 1980s. Professional prominence was, as we shall see later, also a feature of other post-war Labour social policies.

Interesting here is the fact that Bevan's enthusiasm for professional influence in the NHS was limited. In response to the TUC's claim for other health professionals to be members of health authorities, Bevan closed the door firmly:

I attach great importance to the principle that these bodies shall consist of members appointed for their individual suitability and experience, and not as representatives or delegates of particular, and possibly conflicting, interests. This means that the members of the Regional Boards and Management Committees could not be appointed to 'represent' the health workers, and I could not agree to the alternative suggestion that has been put forward – that a proportion of members of these authorities should be appointed after consultation with health workers. The difficulty here would be to draw any line which would keep membership ... down to a reasonable number. If the nurses were to be consulted, why not also the hospital domestics, the radiotherapists, the physiotherapists and so on? (Public Records Office, 1946, cited in Klein, 1989)

Hospital doctors were, then, to be members of these bodies, not representing the medical profession, but because of their 'health expertise'. This was a distinction that required hair-splitting but allowed Bevan to exclude other health workers from participation in the management of the service. Given the Minister of Health's generosity to the Royal Colleges, it is no surprise that their resistance to the establishment of the NHS melted like April snow. General Practitioners were, however, to prove another matter. For it was Bevan's arrangements for general practice that provoked the fiercest antagonism from the profession and from the Conservative Opposition.

The most striking feature of Bevan's policy in relation to GPs was his acceptance of the 1945 Conservative plan to reincarnate Insurance Committees as Local Executive Committees. GPs would contract with this body, thus removing the threat that they would become central government employees, as envisaged by the 1944 White Paper, or local authority employees. This then was a major retreat by the Labour minister but GP suspicions were not easily allayed. They feared the implications of other elements of Bevan's plans. These were: that health centres would be provided by local authorities, thus fulfilling a long-standing Labour commitment and forming a bridge between local authority services and centrally controlled ones; that GPs would be remunerated on the basis of part-salary part-capitation fee; that a central Medical Practices Committee would be established to oversee the equitable distribution of GP practices, and that Labour would prohibit the sale of practices. These proposals made discussions with the BMA tinder-box-like in their intensity. The flames of medical paranoia were fanned by sometimes fantastical interpretations of the Minister's intentions. In order to facilitate a settlement with the GPs, Bevan established a 'negotiating committee' on which the Royal Colleges and the BMA were represented. As we have seen, consultant interests were in the process of being satisfied but the BMA, claiming to represent the whole profession but dominated by GPs, were the dominant force. Between 1945–8 Bevan was involved in pitched battle with the BMA, to such an extent that it was unclear whether the planned vesting day for the NHS (July 1948) would be viable until barely a month before it. The issues described above, along with others, appeared to convince the BMA that Labour intended to create a GP service in which the freedom of patients to choose their own doctors and the freedom of doctors to practice their profession free of interference would be compromised. The BMA Council, often driven by a vociferous minority who were hostile to the idea of state medicine, came out strongly against Bevan's plans (Foot, 1975, pp. 113–16).

Early in 1948, BMA opposition to the NHS appeared to be implacable. A plebiscite of doctors showed a nine-to-one majority against serving in a national health service. In these circumstances the Government took the unusual step of staging a parliamentary debate reaffirming support for the establishment of the NHS. Notwithstanding this, it looked as if the majority of doctors might refuse to become part of the service. In April 1948, when it appeared because of medical hostility that the NHS would not emerge on its appointed vesting day, the Minister made an apparently breathtaking concession to the BMA. Advised by Moran, he promised to introduce amending legislation which would make it clear that he did not intend to create a whole-time, salaried GP service. GPs would continue to be paid on the basis of capitation fees and part-time salaries would be introduced only for new entrants to the profession and then only for three years. Though this commitment had the desired effect on the doctors – against BMA opposition, doctors returned only a small majority against the NHS in a further plebiscite – it caused difficulties for the Minister with his own backbenchers, many of whom were in favour of a salaried service. This prompted Bevan to tell them during the second reading of the National Health Services Bill that the medical profession was not yet 'ripe for this'. 'There is', he added, 'all the difference between plucking fruit when it is ripe and plucking it when it is green' (cited in Foot, 1975, p. 151).

In the end, the BMA lost control of the situation. Despite threats to the contrary, it failed to advise GPs against becoming part of the NHS, and in these circumstances they started to enrol in large numbers. The BMA then capitulated.

The BMA leadership had proved to be a consistent thorn in Bevan's side. It is clear, however, that throughout the struggle, GPs were split among themselves and that the wider medical profession was far from homogeneous. The constitution of the BMA had required that all decisions were referred back to its Council and that its officers could take no unilateral action. This led throughout the period to sharp changes in strategy. Commenting 25 years later, Charles (Lord) Hill (its general secretary in the mid to late 1940s) wrote:

It is undeniable that emotional outbursts in public at critical times, inevitable on a large body at times of crisis, did sometimes embarrass the profession's spokesmen by the headlines they stimulated and the somersaults of policy they encouraged. . . . Furthermore, the Representative Body did declare itself, in advance of any government plans, in favour of many features of a health service which it subsequently rejected. It did sometimes tend to ignore such gains as its representatives had secured and immediately to switch its intention to the points on which it had not won, however important or unimportant they were. Balance sheets of gain and loss are not always judged dispassionately in large assemblies. . . . Tactics are better devised in private by the few than publicly by the many. (Hill, 1973)

On 5 July 1948, the NHS was established. Given the hostility of the BMA, its creation must be regarded as a policy victory for the Government. More than this, Bevan had managed to create a more unified service than had been hitherto envisaged. Nonetheless, the victory was won at a substantial cost and the conflicts aroused by the proposals for an NHS were significant. In the end, the service which was established reinforced the power and influence of the medical profession. The governing structure of the service allowed, as we have seen, for medical interests to be represented at all levels, including the Ministry of Health itself. Other, apparently more democratic structures, were rejected, particularly the control of the NHS by local government. Though there is good reason to accept Bevan's judgement that the United Kingdom local authority structure was unsuitable for managing the new service, central control may have created a democratic deficit. This seems particularly to have been the case in relation to user influence on the planning and management of services, where the centralised NHS has proved to be much more impervious than local government could have afforded to have been.

The structure of the NHS that emerged from Bevan's political negotiation was tripartite, comprising hospital services, family practitioner services and local authority public health services (see Figure 3.1).

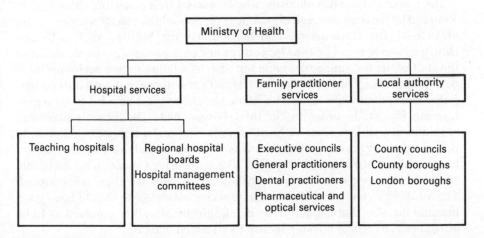

Figure 3.1   The structure of the emergent NHS

Labour's housing policy

Nor was Labour's housing policy an unproblematic area. Housing was, until 1951, the responsibility of the Ministry of Health and post-war housing policy bore the stamp of Bevan's convictions. Labour had promised in its manifesto:

Housing will be one of the greatest and one of the earliest tests of a government's real determination to put the nation first. Labour's pledge is firm and direct – it will proceed with a housing programme with the maximum practical speed until every family in this island has a good standard of accommodation. (Labour Party, 1945)

As it turned out, this apparently uncomplicated aspiration proved very difficult to realise.

Though there was agreement by both major political parties on the need to initiate a substantial house-building programme after decades of neglect and the ravages of the war, Bevan and his officials appear to have underestimated the size of the problem. The Ministry's target of 750 000 houses turned out to be woefully inadequate and the speed with which the programme could be carried out was affected first by a shortage of skilled personnel to build the houses and second by a shortage of appropriate materials. The former problem was the result of the Government's insistence on an orderly demobilisation process. This meant that, in the early years of the programme, many skilled building workers were still in the armed forces. The latter problem was the result both of the rundown of domestic production and of the balance of payments difficulties referred to above which made imported materials expensive.

The Government's discomfiture was increased by a squatting campaign in 1946 and by the economic and climactic problems which emerged in the winter of 1946–7. The Government, and particularly the Minister of Health and Housing, was savaged by the Opposition not only because of the slowness of the start of the housing programme but also in relation to two socio–political decisions made by him. The first was Bevan's insistence that local authorities, rather than private, speculative builders, should be the dominant providers of housing for let. In order to do this, Bevan made significantly-increased subsidies available to local authorities; an action certain, if not calculated, to provoke Opposition hostility. Bevan was also determined that the new council housing should be of a high standard. Consequently, a space standard of 900 square feet, as opposed to the pre-war standard of 750 square feet, was adopted. The Minister's view was not only that working class people should have good housing but also that council housing should be of such a standard as to be attractive as a form of housing tenure to all social classes:

We should try to introduce in our modern villages and towns what was always the lovely feature of English and Welsh villages, where the doctor, the grocer, the butcher and the farm labourer all lived in the same street. I believe that it is essential for the full life of a citizen . . . to see the living tapestry of a mixed community. (Cited in Foot, 1975, p.76)

The Minister's values and the decisions associated with them had some, though not a significant, effect on the speed of the post-war housing programme. Where it is more important is that it opened up an ideological gulf between the Government and the Conservative Opposition. Churchill's parliamentary troops could neither understand nor appreciate Bevan's allergic political reaction to private speculative building. Nor could they support his insistence on high-quality builds. The Opposition determined therefore to make the Minister's housing programme one of its most frequent targets. It also resolved to make housing one of its own priorities in preparation for government.

Bevan's values also opened up a rift within his own party. Prime among his critics was Dalton, who was to become the minister in charge of housing in 1951. He accused Bevan of being 'a tremendous Tory' for insisting on high standards of housing rather than going for building volume and initiated reduced standards in 1952 which were taken up by his Conservative successor (Seldon, 1981, p. 254).

The post-war Labour government managed, then, in austere economic circumstances to give birth to a welfare state. The social policies that it was composed of were both signals of a new future and moulded by the political past. Labour's commitment to universalism acted as a strange bed-fellow to the Government's adherence to an insurance principle in social security. In health, universal health care was bought only at the price of buttressing professional power and excluding consumers of health care from influencing the development of the NHS. Labour's welfare state appears, then, to have been the child of both radical and conservative impulses.

The mosaic of reform and conservatism

Morgan has described Labour's welfare state as a 'mosaic of reform and conservatism' (1985, p. 179). This judgement is based not only on his view that radical departures in health and housing policy were counterbalanced by rather less extensive change in education and social security. It is an acknowledgement of a number of other features of the post-war welfare state.

He argues that, on one level at least, Labour's post-war social policy maintained the *status quo ante*. This argument, alluded to also by Marwick, sees post-war social reform as deviating little from the ground rules set by the war-time coalition government (Morgan, 1985; Marwick, 1990). While it is true, for instance, to argue that Bevan's insistence that the NHS should be centrally and politically accountable represented a break with the wartime consensus, the establishment of the NHS did not constitute any radical departure from a widespread political agreement to establish a comprehensive national health system in the post-war period. Indeed, at one point, central control was regarded, even by the leaders of the BMA, as preferable to control by local authorities (Morgan, 1985, pp. 179–89; Marwick, 1990, pp. 51–3; Leathard, 1991, p. 26).

In a similar vein, there is an argument that Labour's social insurance reform was an inevitable result of war-time public support for Beveridge, rather than a bold piece of political radicalism (Marwick, 1990, pp. 48–9). Second, there is, or so it is argued, a sense in which Labour's social reforms, indeed the whole of Labour's social politics, can be seen as resting on a conservative rather than a radical notion of citizen rights. This interpretation is clearly one important element of Williamson's analysis of class and welfare (Williamson, 1990). Here the argument is that Labour's social policy reforms were based on an understanding of citizenship more limited and less dynamic than that presented later by Marshall (1963). The social rights (to employment, education, social security and health) conferred by early welfare state policies seemed less the outcome of political struggle than benefits bestowed by the Labour Party on its supporters, working class people (Williamson, 1990, p. 76).

Labour social policy, and the framework in which it developed, are seen as reinforcing conservative values. Thus, the granting of welfare state benefits reinforced social stability rather than social change. Welfare state policies were not intended nor understood as radical departures from a previous political and social order or as steps in a fundamental change in the class structure (Williamson, 1990, p. 76). Rather, they were intended and understood as 'a support for the more effective realisation of . . . private ambitions' (Williamson, 1990, p. 81).

Moreover, Labour social politics in this period implied the values of deference and clientism over those of participation and consumerism. The model of political and social organisation implied is one in which the populace as a whole, and the working class in particular, receive what experts, be they political or professional, deem appropriate benefits. Thus the notion of clinical judgement in determining the precise nature of the delivery of health services to patients seems never to have been an issue of controversy between the minister and the BMA and the Royal Colleges prior to or after the establishment of the NHS; in Williamson's words, 'governments offer advantages and guarantee entitlements' (1990, p. 81). They were to be received or rejected by the clients of government or state services. Those clients were not to become active consumers or joint planners of services given as rights. Or not at least until the 'Thatcher years' but that is another story to which we return.

But not conservative enough?

Notwithstanding the apparent conservatism of key elements of the post-war welfare state, it would be a mistake to see it as sufficient to placate those on the political right. Though at the level of leadership politics both the major political parties declared themselves in favour of state welfare, there was significant, if not serious, opposition to the welfare state from within Conservative ranks. These objections, usually from the free-market right of the party, fall into three major groupings.

The first category saw the welfare state as an attempt to impose social equality and to thus transform the British class structure which was itself regarded as a 'natural' and immutable part of the social order. So that one right-wing Conservative could argue in 1946 that 'every society has its divisions between leaders and the led' (Jones, cited in Eccleshall, 1977, p. 74). The justification for the argument ran thus:

> Such a division is one of the inescapable facts of life. The capacity to guide and inspire is rare; the ability to follow under guidance, to do the humdrum tasks necessary for the realisation of a project inspired by another, is much more common. It is inevitable, therefore that the rarer quality should be granted a priority status. . . . (Eccleshall, 1977, p. 74)

In any event, and this should have been of some comfort to the Conservative right, the quest for equality was doomed: 'Within a very short space of time this new equality will have vanished into the mist. Some men will be rich, some will be poor. Some will be masters, some will be servants. A few will lead. The rest will follow' (Braine, cited in Eccleshall, 1977, p. 74).

The argument from the right was that welfare state policies were misplaced, if not perverse. More than this, social policies not only aimed to achieve equality but their implementation also posed an egalitarian threat. State services, especially those which were universal in their coverage like health, education and social security, presumed higher levels of taxation. The result of this would be more equality through a process of levelling down:

> The upper-middle classes can scarcely secure . . . the good and comfortable homes they set their hearts on – let alone the weekend cottages which were so passionately sought between the wars. Education other than that provided in state-aided schools becomes more costly, while some politicians would abolish it altogether. Medical attention is being 'equalised' and those who wish to obtain it outside the National Health Service have to pay twice. . . . Finally, not only are legacies taxed, but keen Socialists broadcast their longing to abolish completely the transmission of wealth in any form. (Lewis and Maude, 1949, p. 221)

This opens up a second category of criticism: namely, that Labour's post-war social policies constituted a threat to freedom of choice. Taxation levied in order to pay for welfare state policies removed from individuals, to some extent at least, the right to choose how they wished to dispose of their income. The objection here is two-fold. First, it is an objection that the state interferes in what ought to be private choices about the expenditure of income by top-slicing a proportion of earnings and wealth. Second, it is an objection that the purposes to which those taxes are put might include purposes actively disapproved of by the individual tax payer. Here, of course, the Conservative right were giving practical illustration to the theoretical objections to welfare statism expressed by Hayek (1944). Welfare state policies, and the economic interventionism which accompanied them, reduced the status of the individual citizen to that of serf or slave. This was so because government took away the right to make decisions in crucial economic areas (how to spend income) and imposed policies, the effects of which would be to create a dependency culture.

The third class of objection concerns the effects of both domestic and foreign policy on the status of the United Kingdom as a great nation. Here the argument seems to be that the combination of spendthrift social policies eating up an ever-increasing proportion of gross national product (GNP) and anti-colonialist foreign policies were having the effect of damaging the British identity as an imperial power and making her a debtor to the United States. Despite its appearance as a national issue, what really seemed at stake here was the traditional Conservative concept of 'nation'. Those who held such a concept seemed incapable of conceptualising a post-imperial United Kingdom. Braine draws attention to the depth of the right-wing critique here:

> We are an imperial power or we are nothing . . . Under a spiritless socialism, which has succeeded only in dampening down the fires of our native genius, we have become dependent for our very existence on foreign aid. (Cited in Gamble, 1987, p. 167)

Braine's objection was not only that the imperial experience was almost past, and with it a particular way of experiencing 'Britishness', but also that one of the contributory elements in the retreat from empire – the development of a welfare state – had required that the United Kingdom seek and accept Marshall Aid from the United States. Britain now was in danger of becoming colonised.

The welfare statism of the immediate post-war period was seen by this group of Conservatives as regretable and to be resisted. For them, the policies of the post-war Labour government were the betrayal of a great past and should be unacceptable to all Conservatives. These views were to become fashionable orthodoxies three decades later but were regarded as outside the Conservative mainstream in the late 1940s.

The conventional Conservative stance during this period was one of critical support for the Government, in its social policy developments at least. Dissent was, as a consequence, relatively easily channelled and diverted. The right of the Conservative Party was appeased by occasional rhetorical attacks on the evils of socialism, though none quite as outrageous as Churchill's claim in 1945 that the election of a Labour government would involve the creation of a British Gestapo and the end of freedom. Meanwhile the policy establishment in the Conservative Party worked to share the centre ground of politics with the Government.

Consolidationists versus radicals: controversy in government

Of more surprise were political controversies within the Government itself. The first three years of government had been a period of sometimes heady political reform. Labour had established the foundations of a modern welfare state with the establishment of the NHS and of a social security system and had taken a number of key industries into public ownership. From 1948, the unity of purpose that had characterised the earlier years gave way to a political contest within the party and government about the way forward. The debate was, explicitly at least, between those who wished to consolidate the policy developments of the immediate post-war period and those who wished to keep up the impetus for reform. Of course, influences outside the party, notably the economic and fuel crises of the previous year (see Morgan, 1990, pp. 66–70), had their impact on the debate. Morrison, Labour's Lord President of the Council, argued that, because of the economic problems besetting government and country, the most prudent course for the Government was to consolidate and wait for more auspicious times (Donoughue and Jones, 1973, pp. 442–51). He urged an approach which combined idealism and realism and took note of the grievances expressed by the middle classes. Particularly, he engaged in a successful debate in Labour's Home Policy Committee for an end to nationalisation measures.

There were, however, those on the left of the party and the Government for whom consolidationism heralded the end of the Labour government as a radical force. Bevan, for instance, took the view that the Government should take the swiftest possible route to the pre-eminence of the public sector of the economy (Foot, 1982, p. 255). For the time being, however, battle was to be postponed. The left seemed as aware as the supporters of Morrison that the Government's nationalisation programme was unpopular with industrial workers and that there was a need for better public relations in the presentation of this policy to the electorate. As a consequence, Morrison's consolidationism won the day, particularly as the welfare state policies already established seemed safe.

That apparent security was, however, thrown into question the very next year. Again, economic crisis threatened the course of government policy. Early in 1949, the balance of payments went seriously awry and sterling came under pressure. Rumours about the need for devaluation began to surface and later became a reality. In this unfavourable economic context, Cripps, the Labour Chancellor of the Exchequer, with the encouragement of the future leader of the party, Gaitskell, mooted the idea of introducing charges for certain NHS services. It is from this point onwards that agreement within the party and between the government and party came under considerable strain.

The decisions by Government to levy charges for prescriptions in 1949, and for dental and ophthalmic services in 1950, though not implemented at this point, and the further decision to limit NHS expenditure, exposed tensions and contradictions within post-war social democracy and its political partner, consensus politics. To some in the party, the willingness to diverge from the principle of medical services which were free at the point of use made absolute sense. The United Kingdom was in the grip of economic crisis and economic prudence dictated that cuts in expenditure needed to be found somewhere. The Conservatives, who had on the whole supported the welfare state reforms, were calling for economies in line with the economic needs of the time. Free services had been used profligately and some form of control through monetary charge was no bad thing.

Many on the left of the party and Government saw things in an altogether different way. Bevan, talking of his membership of a subcommittee established to look at these issues and the issue of industrial insurance, is recorded as saying:

> *It is a form of torture unknown to the ancients, to be compelled on the last Wednesday of every month to convert the leaders of the Labour party afresh to the most elementary principles of the party; to be compelled to fight every inch of the way to recapture territory occupied by Beveridge . . . [and then with his stutter returning]. Now I can sympathise with that fellow S-S-Sisyphus and his bl-bl-bloody boulder. (Cited in Foot, 1982, p. 259)*

For him, and for many on the left, these attempts to bring in charges for services introduced as free services marked a move away from the principles behind the establishment of the welfare state. At the 1949 Labour Party Conference he drew attention to what the left saw as an emerging rift between the priorities and values of Beveridge and the newly elected Labour government, on the one hand, and the consolidationist wing, on the other:

> *'Suffer the little children to come unto me' is not now something which is said only from the pulpit. We have woven it into the warp and woof of our national life . . . What is national planning but an insistence that human beings shall make ethical choices on a national scale? . . . The language of priorities is the religion of socialism. We have accepted over the last four years that the first claims on the national product shall be decided nationally and they have been those of the women, the children and the old people. What is that except using economic planning to serve a moral purpose? (Cited in Foot, 1982, p. 261, my emphasis)*

The challenge from the left, then, was an ideological and political challenge. Implicit in it was a theme that was to become explicit in 1951: that the first claim on the national product should be welfare rather than perceived defence requirements.

Here, then, was a serious tension in post-war Labour welfarism. The centre and right of the Labour Party, represented by senior figures like Morrison and rising political stars like Gaitskell, took one view of how the welfare state should develop. Consolidation and, where necessary, the modification of original welfare state principles would, according to this view, encourage bipartisan support – or at least tolerance – of the Government's management of the mixed economy. Labour would therefore demonstrate itself to be economically prudent and committed to the political mainstream.

From this point of view, the Labour left constituted a threat. This is so because, although their calls were for nothing more radical than the retention of the policy principles of wartime agreements on social politics, post-war politics had shifted. The left's position, therefore, looked like a challenge to 'sensible' [capitalist] economic management. It also came to be seen as a challenge to new bipartisan orthodoxies in the foreign policy field. One of the most important of those orthodoxies was that one of the major allies in the war against Hitler's fascism was now to be regarded as an enemy. The Soviet Union was therefore subjected to 'cold war' policies, primarily from the United States and the United Kingdom. The Cold War brought with it demands for defence spending at a higher rate than could have been anticipated at the end of the 'hot war' and a contributory factor in Labour's consideration of welfare cuts was the need to pay an increased defence bill. As a result of this, the challenge from the left, that the Labour Party should retain its immediate post-war priorities, came to look not only conflictual but also unpatriotic. As it turned out, this battle was postponed by Attlee's decision to call a general election in 1950.

At that election, Labour was returned with an absolute majority of only 17. It struggled on for a year and was then replaced, as a result of the 1951 election, by a Conservative government led by Churchill. Labour's final year did see one last spasm in the battle over the welfare state. This was the dispute between three dissident government ministers and the rest of the Cabinet. The issue was, or at least appeared to be, about the NHS. In fact it was a much wider dispute. As part of a political accord that the Attlee government had with the United States government, Britain was required to re-arm when the United States became embroiled in the Korean War. Gaitskell, by now Chancellor, proposed and successfully negotiated in Cabinet that part of the finance necessary for rearmament (the defence estimates for 1951–4 had risen to £4,700 million) should come from projected NHS expenditure and that the consequent shortfall in NHS income should be made up by charges for service. This now famous decision led to the resignations of two senior ministers, Bevan and Harold Wilson, and one junior minister, John Freeman. The resignations were specifically about the direction of foreign and defence policies and how they affected domestic expenditure. That is, they were about the politics of priorities. They came to be seen simply as resignations over prescription charges.

Labour's creation of a welfare state provides us with a number of interesting issues. In the first place, although comprehensive state welfarism provided a radical departure from what had gone before, it was also shot through with conservative social values. In health, as in social security, the ideas of the past played almost as prominent a part in policy development as did the ideas of the present. Those values influenced the Labour government, for instance, to place the views and interests of the professional expert above those of the consumer of welfare. As we shall see, this essentially Fabian approach was to leave doctors with a near monopoly of power in the NHS until the early 1980s. It was to place the views of teachers above those of parents, at least until the great debate on education three decades later. It was, in other words, to make clientism one of the most prominent features of the welfare state.

On the other hand, elements of welfare state policy were clearly concerned with issues of quality and equality. Bevan's wish, though it remained that of council housing for all, had at its core the idea of social mixing and the breakdown of social class. It was about the provision of high-quality housing distributed equally. Similarly, the same minister's insistence on high standards in council house builds was an attempt to spread access to good-quality housing more widely.

One final issue, which was to return throughout post-war social policy, relates to the relative roles played by central and local government in social policy. Bevan's decision to nationalise the hospitals tipped the Government into the centralist camp, despite Morrison's opposition, as did his close direction of the house building programme. These issues were to prove difficult throughout the post-war period as we will see later in the book.

The Labour Party on the welfare state, 1952

Labour . . . looks upon social security and social services as the birthright of every citizen, normally speaking without test of means. There will, of course, always be special circumstances when an assessment of need is inevitable, but this must be the exception and not the rule.

Labour, then, reasserts its belief in the development of social services democratically organised to meet the essential needs of the whole community and in which the whole community participates as a matter of course. It does so because it accepts the moral obligation of making provision for the needs of the old and the weak. It does so because it believes in the economic gain to the whole community as well as to the individual concerned of public spending on the social services. And it does so because it believes that as we develop our social services we can encourage a growing understanding of our common needs and reduce the pressure of the narrow personal acquisitive instincts of a capitalist society.

We recognise, however, that this aim can only be achieved over a period of time and with the positive encouragement of a much closer association of the social services with effective local democracy. It should be made much easier for all who want to do so to help in the work. Much more has to be done to explain the work of the services and how they affect each one of us as individuals. A responsible attitude towards the services can be developed only if we can feel a much closer contact with and pride in them, not merely as users but as providers, too.

We are proud of the great structure of social welfare legislation which has been implemented by the Labour Government, but at the same time we must guard against complacency, as there is still much to be done. The five giants have been subdued. But the battle freedom from want is not yet over. There is still much avoidable distress, for which social action and social effort are needed. The social services will need extending in the years ahead if we are succeed in building a fairer and juster society, and that means that they will cost more. However, social services are not the only claim on the British economy at the moment. There are others no less important and less urgent. We have to carry out our commitments within the United Nations Organisation and contribute our share towards the efforts of the Atlantic Treaty countries. We must play our part in the struggle 'towards world plenty' by building up the standard of life in the under-developed countries. We must export more of our resources in the fight to attain economic independence. We can only achieve all these ends by greater production through the sustained effort of the whole community. If we do not secure this greater output we shall not be able to extend our social services, unless it is at the expense of commitments no less vital and no less urgent. The balance of payments battle is not something remote that only concerns financial experts. It is of day to day concern to all of us. Meanwhile we have to think not only of expanding our social services where it is necessary, but we must also review our existing services so as to eliminate avoidable waste, and get the greatest value for money. When appropriate the services must be simplified, and overlapping between various departments must be cut out. At the same time, we must not allow our welfare services to become cold, impersonal or hidebound. These are the evils that standardisation and centralisation can bring with them. Provision must always be made, in some way or another, for the exceptional case, while opportunities for local action and voluntary initiative must be extended.

We must also consider priorities within the main groups of the social services. For instance, given the limited resources available, would it be better to raise the school-leaving age to sixteen or to make provision for children to start in nursery classes at the age of three? This, and many other problems of a similar character, have to be decided, and it is the purpose of this pamphlet to consider some of the issues of policy that must be faced in the future.

Many critics do not openly attack the great work of Social Welfare legislation of the Labour Government. Instead they concentrate their criticism on two points. First they argue that the Social Services cost too much and are an important influence on our balance of payments difficulties. Second they suggest that comprehensive Social Services cannot be provided without high taxation. Such taxation is undesirable, they say, it reduces incentives and it removes from the citizen the responsibility of spending his own money, which instead the State spends for him. In fact both these criticisms are grossly exaggerated.

. . . The figures for Social Service expenditure of £1,896.6 million for 1949/50 and £1,921,2 million for 1950/51 are not completely up to date. Social Service expenditure accounted for about 16 per cent of the national income in those years and a fair estimate for the present day would be about 17–18 per cent. A recent survey of Social Service expenditure carried out by the International Labour Office covering over twenty nations indicates that some other countries are spending a larger percentage than this on Social Services. These estimates effectively dispose of the argument that social services are swallowing up an unduly large part of the national income, and that Britain is the heaviest Social Service spender. In particular it should be noted that Social Service outlay, both by central and local government, on the widest possible definition, . . . accounts for less than half the budget of national and local authorities. Moreover the amounts shown as transfer incomes are, of course, incomes which were spent by the public in the way they thought fit and not by the Government at all. As transfer incomes amounted to as much as 54 per cent of the national income in 1950–51 only 11 per cent of the national income was in fact spent by the Government directly on the other Social Services including food subsidies. Some may still consider that this proportion is too high. We do not think so. Humane and extensive Social Services are a safeguard for the democratic way of life. They further the principle of human equality and they relieve distress and suffering. As such they bring with them a positive economic gain to the community. Social Service expenditure is an investment in human capital, the most valuable capital that a people have.

What of the future? We want to safeguard our existing services and extend them when need is great. It is here that our difficulties arise and we must face up to them. In the long run the call of the Social Services on the national income will increase despite the ceilings that have been imposed on the health and education services, and despite the cuts in food subsidies. These measures will for the time being more than compensate for the increased allowances that are being paid, but it is unlikely that they will cover the amounts needed as the proportion of old people in the population begins to rise appreciably. Also it is extremely doubtful if these ceilings can be held if existing services are to be adequately maintained.

Many people regard the Social Services as a first charge on the community. But they are not the only charge and consequently the money which can be spent on them is limited. We must also face our commitments in the field of defence; the colonies and the undeveloped countries need our aid badly; our own industry needs plant and machinery; houses, power stations and factories must be built besides schools, clinics and hospitals; our export trade must be expanded.

Future problems of Social Service policy are all concerned with priorities. We have to start with an acceptance of the need for planning the use of our resources, and as we have seen, Social Service expenditure cannot be satisfactorily planned in isolation from all the other relevant facts in the economy. If priorities are to be properly considered, Social Service expenditure must be related to national income as a whole. There is therefore a strong case for ear-marking a proportion of the national income for Social Service purposes. This proportion would of course be subject to review from time to time in the light of economic circumstances, social developments, size of the national income and the demands of competing resources. It would be a great advantage if Social Service expenditure could be looked at from this point of view . . .

However hard we try we can only get a pint out of a pint pot. Therefore a large expansion of expenditure on Social Services is only possible if we increase our national income. But we must never forget that increased effort can only go hand in hand with social justice. That was the secret behind the effort of the British people in wartime and under a Labour Government. Our Social Services must be based on principles of fairness that are plain for all to see. Where the Tories abandon the principle of fairness we must be prepared to put things right. But we need to be ready to do more than that. We have to look at our own handiwork in a critical spirit and strive when necessary to improve it. By our Social Services we can secure freedom from want and at the same time enshrine the principle of equality on which a democratic Socialist Society must be based.

From *The Welfare State* (The Labour Party, 1952)

Conservatism and social policy 1951–64

The 1951 election marked not only the replacement of a government but the installation of Conservatives at the political helm for 13 years and three administrations. During the election campaign, the Conservatives had presented themselves as the party of the welfare state (see Sullivan, 1987, pp. 5–6). They were, they impressed upon the electorate, to be regarded as reliable guardians of the welfare state. So much so that one of Churchill's close advisers and friends teased him that he had 'stolen the socialists' clothes while they were bathing' (Bracken, cited in Sullivan, 1987). On the surface, this claim has clear validity: during the 1951–5 government, the value of pensions was increased in real terms when compared to the 1951 rate; houses were built at a faster rate than under Labour (though at the cost of diverting labour from industrial building and of lowering its quality), and in the last period of government the Conservatives guaranteed the expansion of higher education following the Robbins Report (HMSO, 1963). In general, however, social policy development in this period was fairly low-key. The three Conservative governments that served from 1951–64 continued to support the major post-war social policy innovations. Additionally, they established in the later years of this period corporatist structures to develop tripartite agreement on issues of economic development and its concomitant social policy implications (see Sullivan, 1987).

Yet the apparent continuation of policies, while representing a genuine political continuity with the earlier period, masks interesting real and potential political shifts during the years of Conservative government. It is to these political disputes about social policy that we now turn.

Conservatives and anti-welfarism

From the beginning of this period, pressure to change the parameters of the welfare state became obvious. Indications of this were nowhere more clearly glimpsed than in discussions about the NHS. Following the lead given by a Labour government, the Churchill government imposed charges for dentures and spectacles in 1952. In practice they did what Labour had threatened: to breach the principle of health services free at the point of use. In fact, even this move from the principle of collective provision for individual need was insufficient to satisfy a growing constituency in (and on the fringes of) the Conservative Party committed to moving the boundaries of collectivism.

Early in 1952, *The Times* ran two articles about a hypothesised 'crisis in the welfare state'. The authors of these articles, both Conservative MPs, saw the crisis as a fiscal one. The United Kingdom could not afford the extensive and universalistic services put in place in the immediate post-war years. Arguments about the legitimacy of the welfare state were left to others but, or so *The Times* writers believed, the economic burden of a welfare state – created by Labour with the tacit and sometimes overt support of the Conservatives – was too much to bear (*The Times*, 17 January 1952).

The legitimacy argument was first taken up later by the same authors in an official party pamphlet. Here, Ian Macleod and Enoch Powell, later to be government ministers, argued that health and welfare services should be provided to citizens only on the basis of demonstrable need (Conservative Political Centre, 1952). This was an argument based on ideology as much as on economics. Not only could Britain not afford to finance a universalist welfare state but, and of more significance, a residual welfare state was to be preferred on the grounds of freedom and independence for the many. This contribution to the debate represented a break with the *de facto* cross-party consensus at least as significant as the challenge of the left to the Labour government in the late 1940s and early 1950s. It represented, in the political vocabulary of the left, and indeed of ordinary people, a proposal to return to the 'means test' and to the Poor Law principle of 'less eligibility' in which the means test had been rooted.

The area that caused most controversy then, as now, was the NHS. Writing towards the end of this period, a neo-liberal Oxford professor of economics argued for a reorientation of health service principles which might include the imposition of charges for particular services or the restriction of free service to particular social groups (Jewkes and Jewkes, 1961). The justification for such changes were both economic, despite the relatively clean bill of health given in 1956 to the administration of the NHS by the Guillebaud Committee which looked at NHS expenditure, and ideological. The economic arguments were based on the perceived difficulty of meeting demand for health services out of the public purse and on the assumption, shared with other neo-liberals that the re-introduction of market principles into the health service would improve both efficiency and quality levels, an assumption hardly supported by the pre-war evidence. The ideological arguments revolved around the assertions – for they have never been more – that individual choices about medical cover and treatment, on the one hand, and about disposition of personal income, on the other, are superior to and more 'natural' than the restricted choices or coercion of a state system.

These arguments were fortified by discussions emerging from the Institute for Economic Affairs (a right-wing, free-market think tank). In a persuasive paper, Lees complained that the introduction of a service free at the point of use ignored the most basic economic principles of capitalist organisation: that at zero cost demand becomes infinite; that this situation was exacerbated by the fact that the NHS was a monopoly provider with no incentive to efficient operation, and that free services often implied a restriction of choice (Lees, 1961). More than this, Lees complained that the intervention of the state as a third party into the association between doctor and patient perverted that relationship. And, most important of all, consumer sovereignty was denied by any system that flouted the laws of supply and demand. If the consumer was to be sovereign then the only way to ensure this was through the direct payment for service (Lees, 1961).

These sallies from within the governing party, and from groups on its fringes, represent attempts to influence the welfare agenda. Though they were successful in raising the profile of right wing approaches to health and welfare, there is relatively little evidence that they affected fundamentally the course of government policy-making.

Conservative responses

Reactions to the right-wing's nostrums on the welfare state came from a number of directions, some more unexpected than others. Some of the dissidents of the early 1950s had even become incorporated, by the late 1950s, into a within-party consensus on welfare state issues. A Conservative Political Centre (CPC) monograph on *The Future of the Welfare State* was published in 1958. One of its main arguments was that there was a need for an 'opportunity state' to 'match and sustain the welfare state' (Conservative Political Centre, 1958, p. 7) or, to put it another way, the workings of the welfare state should complement rather than inhibit the private wealth creation needed to nourish economic growth. However, despite this unsurprising defence of the market, the monograph is on the whole a justification of the welfare state. This is nowhere more obvious than in the essays contributed by Macleod and Powell who, as we have seen above, had, at the beginning of the decade, argued for a selectivist and residual welfare state. Macleod, it is true, tries to hide this state of affairs behind an ideological smokescreen. In refuting 'some Conservatives recent discontent . . . that there was no difference between the two major parties; that Butskellism, so-called, was not dead but sleeping' (Conservative Political Centre, 1958, p. 11), he clearly marks his conversion to a universalist welfare state. The difference between the Labour and Conservative conception of welfare statism becomes less one of eligibility for receipt of service and more one of the ideology believed to underlie the administration of a universalist welfare state. Whereas the Labour concept of welfare emphasised the rights of citizens to receive benefits, the Conservative view was that philanthropists or legislators had a duty to provide welfare as part of the obligation to creating 'one nation'. Quoting from an earlier CPC document, Macleod reminded his readers:

> The existence of a nation depends on the steady and indeed instinctive acceptance by those who compose it of a scheme of duties. It may also imply a scheme of rights; but the health and life of the nation are endangered as soon as the rights come to be regarded as more important than the duties, or even as their prior condition. (Conservative Political Centre, 1950, cited in Conservative Political Centre, 1958: p. 14, emphasis in the original)

Even here of course Macleod is not ruling as inadmissible a justification of welfare based, in part, on rights. Rather, he appears to be covering the embarrassment of an apparently naked conversion with the cloak of Disraeli's 'one nation Conservatism'.

Again according to Macleod, Conservatism differed from Labour's quest for social equality but justified welfare statism as a buttress against impermissible and unacceptable levels of inequality. Apparently following Hayek (1944), and echoing Braine (Eccleshall, 1977), he suggests that the 'natural' form of social organisation is one based on inequality and that the ends of welfare include, for Conservatives, the creation of opportunity. Here, at least on the surface of the argument, is a fundamental gulf at the level of ideology: whereas the Labour Party hoped to achieve egalitarian outcomes from social policy, modern Conservatives were in favour of social policies which facilitated equality of opportunity (Conservative Political Centre, 1958, p. 14).

The distinction Macleod draws here is, to some extent at least, a straw man. For, as we have already seen, the post-war welfare system put into place by Labour was ameliorative, rather than egalitarian, in intent as well as in outcome. Social security policies were developed which were designed to ensure that no citizen fell below a certain basic standard of living rather than to create equality of income. Education policies were shaped to make it more likely that attainment correlated with ability than had previously been the case rather than to assist the equality of outcome, and so on.

In effect, Macleod's contribution is a masterly rebuttal of the Conservative right-wing distaste for Butskellism. While appearing to highlight areas of fundamental conflict over welfare statism between the two major parties, he in fact draws attention to a continuing and shared consensual framework for the development of social policies. Political differences undoubtedly existed between the leaderships of the two parties over social and economic politics. Continuity and consensus over the development of the welfare state are, however, equally clear, as is obvious in Macleod's Jesuitical disquisition.

Of even greater surprise, perhaps, is the essay in the same monograph by Powell. Despite Powell's past and future adherence to neo-liberal economics and radical right politics, his essay is, in part at least, a justification for extending universalism in the welfare state (Conservative Political Centre, 1958, pp. 38–46).

Enoch Powell on the welfare state, 1961

The Plowden Report on *Control of Public Expenditure* contained, amongst other nuggets of wisdom, the following sentence which I should like to take as my starting point: 'The social changes of the last fifteen years have altered the incidence of hardship, so that there now may well be excessive social services for some purposes and inadequate ones for others.'

I should have thought that, in the abstract, no one was likely to quarrel with that statement. Indeed, the reference to 'the social changes of the last *fifteen* years' makes it an understatement. . . . The conception of all of them, in more or less recent form, dates from the social revolution of 1942 to 1944. The General Election of 1945 was in some ways only a consequential recognition revolution which took place under, and inside, the Coalition government at the height of World War II, and was announced to the outside world by a cloud of White Papers – on planning, social service, employment, a national health service – much as the election of a new Pope is first evinced by the smoke from the burning papers . . . The conditions in the light of which those policies were then framed were the conditions of the inter-war years . . . If the Plowden Committee had referred more to 'the social changes of the last *thirty* years' instead of, they would have been guilty of no inaccuracy. Those thirty years span some of the sharpest changes of trend in modern history, persistent deflation, for instance, to persistent inflation, or unemployment averaging 10 per cent to unemployment averaging 2 per cent.

Politically . . . the inducements to continue what the Plowden Committee call 'excessive social services' are much stronger than the inducements to discontinue them or to supplement any which may happen to be 'inadequate'. But it would be a cynical mistake to limit the forces of inertia to these narrowly political ones.

It is the characteristic of social services that they become rapidly and strongly institutionalised. True, all acts of government policy create a presumption that they will remain in force and are an invitation to the citizen to adapt his private behaviour accordingly; but the tendency of decisions in the social service field to create vested interests is of a quite peculiar order . . . We see a range of existing social services, entrenched to varying degrees in institutional form, reflecting to varying degrees needs and economic conditions which have passed or are passing away. We see new needs, born of newer economic social conditions, which call to be met. We recognise that logically this demands a transfer of resources and effort from the former to the latter, that in the words I have so often quoted, some social services are 'excessive' and others 'inadequate' – that it was bound to be so and that it is so.

The question for us, for the Conservative Party, is whether, having seen this, we put the file into the 'Too Difficult' tray and 'pass by on the other side'. I can see the expediency of that course; I can see the expediency of Ministers not making addresses which explore this kind of territory and arrive at this kind of conclusion . . . however, I confess that I do not believe a Party, any more than the society which it serves, can fail to suffer if it knowingly allows institutions to fall more and more out of correspondence with contemporary needs. In Britain of the 1960s this challenge of the welfare state is not isolated: it is but one aspect of the challenge which confronts us throughout the whole political field . . . The question falls to be posed in different terms in the different fields of policy. Here in the social services, which, in volume . . . represent between one-third and one-half of the State, the question, it seems to me, cannot be posed by spasmodic *pluses and minuses* but by presenting a conception of the manner in which resources ought to be redeployed to meet modern realities, and this will not be done without soberly assessing but boldly facing the in-built obstacles to that redeployment.

Enoch Powell, *The Welfare State* (Conservative Political Centre, 1961)

Reactions to the right: the challenge of social democracy

In the latter part of the period that this chapter is concerned with, right-wing views of welfare were challenged not only by government ministers but also by left-leaning politicians and academics. Their response was mounted on both political and theoretical levels. These challenges form the basis of a social democratic refutation of neo-liberalism. The first by Professor Richard Titmuss, one of the earliest social administration academics and someone close to the Labour Party policy elite, was a specific rebuttal of the right-wing stance on the NHS. The other two, one from an academic turned Labour politician, Crosland, and the other from Professor T. H. Marshall, were more general theoretical rebuttals of right-wing Conservative views.

Titmuss: in defence of the welfare state

As we have seen above, the political right had mounted a clear argument for profound changes in the NHS. The changes suggested included imposing charges for services and/or the restriction of services to special groups and the establishment of an NHS catering only for a social residue. Titmuss's response to these sorts of plans was clear and unequivocal. In the first place, he argued that simple laws of supply and demand could not be applied in the health service. One of the arguments from the right wing was that the patient should be free to choose the form of treatment for their condition. Titmuss's riposte was that real freedom of choice for the patient was impossible as medicine had become highly technical. There was therefore no alternative for the patient but to trust the doctor. The question raised by Titmuss was whether, in a doctor–patient relationship dominated by financial considerations, such trust could remain. His estimation was that it could not and that the most likely outcomes of supposed freedom of choice, made effective through financial transactions, were 'fee-splitting, commission-taking, canvassing, the dispensation of "secret remedies", and the employment of unqualified assistants' (Titmuss, 1968, p. 249). The outcome of putting health back in the market place would not, he was convinced, lead to an improvement in health care but to its opposite.

It would do so, in part, because it would turn doctors into entrepreneurs. Criticising the emphasis on consumer sovereignty found in the work of Jewkes and Jewkes (1961) and Lees (1961), he disputes the assertion made explicit in the former that '. . . it is reasonable to suppose that even without a National Health Service, Britain would have enjoyed after 1948 medical services more ample and better distributed than those which existed before the war' (Jewkes and Jewkes, 1961, p. 36). Far from the market solving problems of distribution of services it would, he believed, be more likely to make those problems less tractable:

> They will . . . give preferential treatment to consumers who will pay most for what they [doctors] have to sell; consumers who are presumed, as a result of the free play of the market, to be more worthwhile in genetic or productive terms. (Titmuss, 1968, p. 250)

In Titmuss's view, the radical-right approach to the NHS would turn doctors into business people ' . . . the doctor is essentially a small businessman [sic]. He is selling his services so is as much in business as anyone else who sells a commodity' (Dickinson, cited in Carter, 1958, p. 88). Consequently, it would lead to the lowering of standards and the maldistribution of services (Titmuss, 1968, p. 249).

More than this, Titmuss argued that the evidence of periods when British medicine was part of a free market, as during the early years of the twentieth century when many contract practices had existed, hardly pointed to freedom of choice for the consumer (Titmuss, 1968, p. 248).

In any event, as Titmuss was to argue elsewhere, the NHS and the welfare state in general worked because the transactions between individuals were part of a 'gift relationship' (Titmuss, 1970). Extrapolating from his study of blood donation, he argued that the basis of support for collective services was that they were collective. Whereas citizens might freely give, of blood or of income through tax, to support services of which they were themselves consumers or potential consumers, it seemed less likely that such public support for welfare would be forthcoming if it were to be necessary in order to support a residual service for a class of clients who were unable to pay for their own services.

Considering the right-wing critique of the NHS, Titmuss finds its claims unproven and its prescriptions unpalatable. The settlement on health, carved out of conflict with the doctors and fashioned by both Labour and Conservative governments, was to be protected from the wild assertions of politically motivated actors from the pre-Thatcherite right. In this, as we have seen, he had the tacit support not only of Conservative health ministers, including Powell, but also of Macleod who, until his untimely death, was regarded as one of that rarest breed of Conservatives: a political thinker.

Redefining socialism: Crosland and the welfare state

The late Anthony Crosland, initially an Oxford politics don and later a Labour politician, is often credited as being Labour's chief theoretician of social democracy. He is, in the demonology of the political left, both inside and outside that party, also credited with being Labour's chief revisionist thinker. That is to say, he is honoured or blamed for a perceived movement in the Labour Party away from a political analysis owing something to Marxism and towards an accommodation with capitalist values and methods of organisation.

During the period that we are concerned with in this chapter, he was rethinking the means of achieving the Labour Party's goal of more equality. That is to say, he believed that the aims of a party like the Labour Party should include the mitigation of inequality without accepting that its role was the creation of an egalitarian society. This distinction is, as we shall see, crucial in understanding both the development of social democracy, on the one hand, and the justification of the welfare state from the assaults of the right, on the other.

As early as 1952, Crosland was arguing that the capitalism to which Marx and Marxists had referred was dead or, at the very least, had been transformed out of all recognition. The welfare state and the mixed economy were themselves evidence of the transformation of capitalism away from a form of social and political organisation sustained through the exploitation of a labouring class. Capitalism, in the words of another Labour intellectual and politician, 'had been civilised' (Crossman, 1952). For Crosland:

> *while capitalism has not collapsed as a result of internal contradictions, it is possible to see a transformation of capitalism occurring. Since 1945, capitalism has been undergoing a metamorphosis into a different system. (Crosland, 1952, p. 34)*

It had changed, and was changing, for a number of reasons. First, the development of powerful anti-capitalist power blocs, like the trade union movement and the Labour Party, in the early twentieth century had placed policy changes on the political agenda that could not be ignored by conservative or radical governments. Second, or so Crosland believed, the political aspirations of the labour movement were, coincidentally, shared by the British business class. In effect, that class came to support the idea of interventionist economic and social policy because it benefited from so doing.

Full employment, one of the bases of consensus politics, meant guaranteed high levels of production and consumption which in turn meant the generation of high profit levels. The transformation of capitalism and the development of an interventionist state therefore occurred with the support, or the acquiescence of, the capitalist class. Fourth, a dispersion of ownership of the means of production and an increasing separation between ownership and management had occurred in twentieth century Britain and, partly as a result, entrepreneurial capitalism had evolved into a system in which the dispersal of ownership had led to the diminution of exploitation. Finally, according to this thesis, the level of central planning that had developed during the Second World War had made a return to free market capitalism impossible. For Crosland and other revisionist thinkers, capitalism had given birth to a new economic and social system. The metamorphosis amounted to no less than the adoption by the state of the regulation of social and economic relationships, a role previously occupied by the market (Crosland, 1952). The revisionist thesis, then, assumed welfare statism to have been part and parcel of the transformation of an economic and social system and the revision of ideas about the appropriate relationship between the state and civil society in the United Kingdom.

It is clear that for Crosland, as for other revisionist thinkers, the political project for the Labour Party no longer included the overthrow of capitalism. Capitalism had already tamed itself and the Labour Party's main concern should be to work within the framework of post-capitalist politics to ensure the maximum benefits of transformed capitalism for all citizens. This view had clear implications for Labour's economic and social politics as well as for the wider politics of welfare. He drew out these implications in a series of books and political tracts, the most influential of which, *The Future of Socialism*, was published in 1956 in the middle of the period which presently concerns us.

The positive aspects of his arguments were that, in place of a concern with the overthrow of capitalism, Labour should be concerned with the advantages that post-capitalist politics, properly executed, could bring to ordinary people. In this, he saw a crucial role for government in intervening in the economy at a macro-economic level to ensure economic growth. That growth was a necessary condition for achieving what Crosland believed to be Labour's most important objective, *greater* equality. Here the line of argument is quite straightforward. First, government should use Keynesian methods to stimulate consistent growth in the economy. If growth is sustainable, then it is, in itself, redistributive; increases in the general level of real income having an equalising effect (such increases, for example gave access to goods such as motor cars which had previously been the privilege of the few). Crosland, then, believed that, if incomes were to rise steadily for the mass of people, the consumption cleavages between rich and poor would become much less visible (Lipsey and Leonard, 1981, p. 27).

Second, he argued, growth would play a critical role in 'achieving equality without intolerable social stress and a probable curtailment of liberty . . . it requires the better off to accept with reasonable equanimity a decline in their *relative* standard of living because growth has enabled them [almost] to maintain their *absolute* standard of living despite redistribution' (Crosland, 1974, p. 6).

Third, growth, and government action to ensure growth, was necessary in order to fund public services without overburdening the tax-payer. Crosland was, and remained, a firm advocate of developing public services. He was so because he took the view that part of the process aimed at getting more equality, or as he was to describe it later (Crosland, 1974), equality of opportunity, was aided through the public services. Education services provided by the state gave, and would give, access to opportunities in education hitherto not experienced by the mass of ordinary people, and so on and so forth. Without economic growth more social equality was a vain hope (Crosland, 1956; Lipsey and Leonard, 1981, pp. 26–8).

Two further questions are posed and answered in Crosland's work: how was growth to be assured and what would be the nature of the welfare state funded out of growth? His answer to the first question was straightforward, even if, viewed from the 1990s, it appears controversial. In essence he argued that growth could be guaranteed by the following:

1. A substantial market sector where price governed what was produced.
2. A privately-owned and managerially-run productive sector working alongside a state sector and responding to existing levels of profits and incentives in its production and investment plans.
3. A Keynesian state prepared to use its regulatory, fiscal and monetary powers to support growth and sustain full employment.
4. A free trade union movement which pursued its objectives of protecting and improving its members' standard of living in a way compatible with such a mixed economy (see Crosland, 1956).

Fundamentally, the argument being rehearsed here is for what Furniss and Tilton term a 'social security state' (Furniss and Tilton, 1979). In abstract terms, the elements of acceptable activity that make up Crosland's conception of such a state are these.

First, governments should act to correct, supplement and, only if absolutely necessary, displace the market system of exchange. Governments' intention in acting in this way would be the promotion and development of greater equality, democracy and welfare; goals which Crosland believed were the shared property of those allies of welfare statism. Crosland's prescription for this sort of activity takes into account that welfarism, while the shared property of the policy elites of the two major parties, had not necessarily permeated the social and political structure of the system as a whole. The proposition lying behind this prescribed role for government can be expressed thus.

In a liberal-democratic, mixed-economy society, there will exist, notwithstanding broad party political consensus, a plurality of power bases and different sites of economic control. Sometimes, when consensus at the top fails to trickle down, governments would need to be prepared to lay down groundrules, especially in the industrial field, to ensure conformity with the Government's own view of the national interest (Crosland, 1974); or, as Crosland had put it during the period we are now considering:

> to guide the private (and public) sector to forms of collective action to achieve collective goals which individuals cannot achieve with the same measure of success, by their isolated efforts. (Crosland, 1956, p. 61, emphasis added)

Second, governments should use social expenditure and other means at their disposal to *modify* inequalities and injustices associated with a market system of distribution (Crosland, 1956). This prescription acknowledged the potential lack of fit between welfarism and a market system of economic distribution and proposed the solution that governments, when faced with aspirations in the private sector of the economy to maximise profit rather than to meet social and economic needs of citizens, should provide a countervailing system of need satisfaction. Working through systems of social expenditure, governments should redistribute resources through taxation, income maintenance or services in kind (George and Wilding, 1985; Sullivan, 1987).

In more concrete terms, Crosland's views on the role and nature of a welfare state, and its position in a mixed economy, provide interesting reading. They do so because they represented a social democratic manifesto and rationale for welfarism: a justification for maintaining a centrally-funded universalist welfare state; a rationale for the extension of that welfare state to provide more equality through consumption-oriented social policies rather than production-oriented economic policies; a refutation of the right-wing prescription for less welfare, and a rebuttal of the aspirations of the Labour left for a marriage of economic and social policies intended to bring about equality of outcome rather than equality of opportunity.

As has been made clear above, Crosland, like the left of the Labour Party, was unwilling to separate issues of social policy development from issues of economic development. In detail, this meant that full employment and economic growth were indispensable if Crosland's social democracy was to work. The lower the level of unemployment, the more economic power was shared with workers. If labour was in short supply, which would be the consequence of full employment plus economic growth, then a sort of equalisation would occur between unions and management in wage bargaining and negotiations over workers' terms and conditions of employment. Additionally, high levels of employment at reasonable rates of return meant that there would be less call on those areas of the welfare state most used during times of unemployment-related poverty: social assistance, social work and primary health care. Crosland's argument was that the welfare state had eradicated absolute poverty and that economic growth provided the resources to ameliorate relative poverty.

The welfare state *per se* was not to be about creating equality, nor even in many cases to be the major weapon in the attack against relative poverty. Nor was it, as we have seen above, to be regarded as a battering ram to destroy remaining inequalities. In his own words, 'social equality cannot be held to be the ultimate purpose of the social services' (Crosland, 1956, p. 148); rather:

> The object of social services is to provide a cushion of security . . . Once that security has been provided further advances in the national income should normally go to citizens in the form of free income to be spent as they wish and not to be taxed away and then returned in the form of some free service determined by the fiat of the state. (Crosland, 1952, p. 63)

The welfare state in a post-capitalist society was to function to ameliorate the diswelfares created when the interaction between state regulation of the economy and the private industrial sector of the economy failed, without further help, to aid equality of opportunity.

In the political context in which it was made, Crosland's reformulation of the ends and means of social democracy not only clarified, and to some extent changed, the direction of the Labour Party's social politics. It also acted as a firm and important rebuttal of the ideas being floated by the Conservative right. It certainly had an effect on both strategy and policy in the Labour Party. From the mid-1950s until the untimely death of the Labour leader Gaitskell in 1962, the leadership of the party adopted a policy position which, while resisting the direction prescribed by the Labour left, appeared progressive and pro-active. It appeared progressive because it was concerned, albeit using a somewhat different definitional yardstick, with issues of equality, as were the policy positions of the left. It was pro-active because apparently egalitarian policies were developed from the centre rather than the centre reacting to developments from the left of the party, as had often been the case.

More than this, however, it was a direct rebuttal of the policy prescriptions of the Conservative right and the political principles which lay behind those prescriptions. The attack against the views and precepts of the right took the following form.

First, Crosland constructed, as we have seen, an argument for a universal welfare state which, while less extensive in its scope than some would have wished, was a counter-balance to the residualism of the right. Crosland's welfare state was to be universal in coverage, was to be sufficiently resourced to facilitate equality of opportunity for all citizens but was to stop well short of attempting to create equality of outcome. In other words, all were to be catered for but the level of support was to be consistent with seeing the role of a welfare state as providing security rather than equality. This, of course, was entirely consistent with the aspirations of Beveridge and Keynes and with the political centre of gravity in the post-war Labour Party – Crosland had redefined rather than recreated Labour's social policy. However, and this is the crucial point, this approach to social politics attempted to neutralise the Conservative right's major attacks on the legitimacy and cost of state welfare. For Crosland was arguing loudly and clearly that the proper role of a state welfare system was not to bring about equality. The siren call of the political right was that its goal was to do precisely that. Crosland, in accepting that full equality was unattainable, and perhaps undesirable, appears to have taken the political rug from under his adversaries' feet. Welfare statism was legitimate because it was consistent with the values of a reformed capitalism, not inimical to them.

His argument also took on board the apparently genuine view from the right that continued welfare state development was too costly for the British economy to bear or imposed costs, both monetary and to freedom, on the individual which ought to be avoided. The response to this sort of argument is quintessentially Fabian. Welfare is to be financed out of economic growth. If growth falters then so should further welfare development. The welfare state should neither be financed excessively from direct taxation nor should it substantially affect the absolute material health of the rich. A 'growth premium' should be used to finance developments in welfare and those developments should be used to improve the social and economic position of the poorest while only marginally diminishing the wealth of the rich.

Crosland's reaction to the right, then, complements Titmuss's specific rebuttals with a general and theoretical rejoinder which served the purpose of clarifying and justifying Labour's commitment to the welfare state and confronting the principles and prescriptions of conviction politicians on the right.

Citizenship and social policy

The third reaction to the right considered in this chapter is that found in the writings of the late Professor T. H. Marshall (1963, 1975). Unlike either Titmuss or Crosland, Marshall had no close political links with the Labour Party. His analysis and defence of a certain sort of welfare state is in this author's opinion, however, clearly in the Croslandite social democratic mainstream. I therefore part company to some extent with Pinker (1971, 1979) in the categorisation of Marshall as a theorist of the middle way. In essence, Marshall makes explicit Crosland's implicit assumption that social democratic politics and the social politics of consensus are inextricably linked with developments in conceptions of, and actions around, citizen rights. In other words, while I accept the Crosland/Marshall perspective as based on a revisionist analysis of capitalism, the evidence suggests an unmistakeable social democratic orientation in Marshall's work (see Sullivan, 1992).

To understand Marshall's defence of welfare statism, it is necessary to understand that he analysed the role and function of state welfare in the context of the changing nature of capitalism. One clear view that emerges from the analysis is that he, like other theoreticians in the so-called 'citizenship school', believed that unsupplemented markets caused severe insecurity and wide economic inequalities. In effect, one section of the population, the lower paid, bear the costs of progress as capitalism develops while another section, the owners of capital, reap the benefits. Welfare states according to Marshall, in his inaugural lecture as Professor of Sociology at Cambridge, mitigate these tendencies. Or, to put it another way, the welfare state in the United Kingdom is seen as redressing the economic balance of power by giving equal social rights to all (Marshall, 1963).

According to Marshall, the chief goal of post-war social policy was not, nor should it have been, the pursuit of equality. Rather, it was the maximisation of welfare. His critique of the Conservative right would have been that, were their principles accepted and their prescriptions adopted, welfare – the social repayment given in return for economic inequality – would have been minimised rather than maximised.

Marshall claimed that, in some part, the Marxist critique of welfare held true: state welfare was a ransom paid by the ruling class in return for social stability and the maintenance of capitalism. Like the granting of political and legal rights, the concession of social rights, in the form of welfare state policies, were part of a trade-off: social security for social stability. The part of the trade-off threatened by the prescriptions of the right might, if allowed to take place, threaten the other element. Welfarism was therefore an integral part of modern capitalism and the price paid by capitalism, through the welfare state, was the satisfaction of citizens' needs. Need satisfaction, however needs were defined, was seen by Marshall as a process to which the market was particularly ill-adapted (Marshall, 1963).

Put another way, Marshall might have been arguing with Conservative critics that state welfare provision was necessary to honour the social rights of citizens (Marshall, 1963, 1981). In this, he places himself squarely in the social democratic tradition. Titmuss had written of 'services provided as social rights, on criteria of the needs of specific categories' (1968, p. 122). What Marshall does is to stress that such service provision to citizens is not only the mark of a civilised society but also honours a social and political debt.

His emphasis on welfare policies as justified on the basis of meeting need also stresses the requirement that policy makers adopt some sort of objective definition of what constitute reasonable needs. In countering the claims of the Conservative right, then as now, that state welfare is morally corrosive and economically wasteful because it provides either for people's preferences or wants rather than their needs, or that it generates needs that recipients were previously unaware that they experienced, Marshall is protecting the idea of state welfare from the political ravages of the right. If needs are consensually and objectively agreed, then there is no reason, or so he seems to say, for either of the outcomes feared by the Conservative right (Marshall, 1963, pp. 77–82, 1981).

If this needs-based justification of welfare were to be accepted, then clear arguments for the retention and entrenchment of state welfare would also emerge. The arguments as mobilised by Professor Marshall were as follows:

1. The possession of social rights is contingent on the identification of needs and the satisfaction of needs identified.
2. The right to welfare (one of Marshall's social rights) are connected with full membership of the community for the individual. Here Marshall was reinforcing one of Crosland's arguments about the role of welfare. The objective and outcome of state welfare is not the creation of economic equality but the sort of equality that comes, in Marshall's words, 'from full membership of the societal community' (1963, p. 80). The right to welfare, in other words, confers on the citizen rights to be treated like all other citizens in relation to welfare and therefore bestows a sort of equality of regard. This formulation is, of course, not much distanced from Crosland's view that one of the objectives of a welfare state is to secure equality of opportunity rather than equality of outcome.
3. Marshall's third argument leads on from the previous two and it is this. If all citizens are to be treated alike as far as their right to welfare is concerned, then the welfare state must continue to be based on a framework of *universal social policies*. This argument clearly signalled opposition to the Conserva- tive right's preference for a residual welfare state based on *selective entitlement* to the benefits of welfare.

The United Kingdom welfare state was to be protected from political attack because it represented an increase in people's rights:

> from the right to a modicum of economic welfare and security to the right to share to the full in the social heritage and to live the life of a civilised being according to the standards prevailing in the society. (Marshall, 1963, p. 74)

In this, as elsewhere, Marshall is, in fact, defending the social and political settlement chiselled out by the post-war Labour government. It constitutes an aggressive reaction to the right as well as a sophisticated justification of the welfare state. But in dismantling, or seeking to dismantle, the argument from the right, did not this sort of approach fall foul of the left's aspirations for equality through social policy? It may have done so, of course. But on one level at least, it may also have been consistent with those aspirations as Robson and Donnison, following the Marshall tradition, were each to argue later.

One of the sought-for objectives of the Labour left was that of social justice. For Robson, at least, the *right to welfare* approach is not at variance with that aspiration:

> There is . . . a vast difference between a society based on the assumption that free competition and individual enterprise are the highest goods and that the right to possess whatever can be acquired by these means is morally, legally and politically justified, and

a society based on the principle that social justice is essential to the concept of legitimacy. *(Robson, 1976, p. 63, emphasis added)*

Similarly, Donnison in his discussion of poverty argues:

People are poor because they are deprived of opportunities, comforts and self-respect regarded as normal in the community to which they belong. It is therefore the continually moving average standards of the community that are a starting point for an assessment of its poverty, and the poor are those who fall sufficiently far below these average standards. (Donnison, cited in Marshall, 1981, p. 43, emphasis added)

This reaction to the right, like Crosland's, draws attention to the nature of welfare. Universal welfare services, intended to ameliorate diswelfares, facilitate more equality and confer the status of citizenship, while meeting some of the interests expressed by socialists, are entirely consistent with the development of a reformed capitalism. The attack from the right is therefore an attack not only on the political left but on the socially-conscious Conservatism of the 1951–64 governments.

The rediscovery of poverty

The final reaction to the right to be considered in this chapter is that provided in the early work of Peter Townsend. The importance of this work is that it provides an empirical rebuttal of the view from the Conservative right that extensive state welfare was unnecessary. Explicit in the view of this political constituency was the assertion that the post-war welfare state had provided services in cash and kind which had gone beyond the relief of poverty and had contributed to the development of a class of non-poor work-shy. The welfare state had abolished poverty and some more. Perhaps we should also note here that even Labour's political intellectuals, Crosland and Crossman, signed up for the first assertion in this statement also. What became clear right at the end of the period with which this chapter is concerned is that reports of the death of poverty were premature. Townsend and his colleagues found, as a result of rigorous social enquiry, that extensive primary poverty existed in mixed-economy, welfare state Britain. Far from gilding the lily, as it were, the welfare state had been found to have failed in the objectives attributed to it by the Conservative right. If reasons were to be found for the rolling back of the welfare state, they would have to be new ones (Townsend and Abel-Smith, 1965).

Emerging issues

The period we are considering is an interesting one for students of social policy. It is so less because of changes in policy direction than because of development and clarification of issues germane to the function of a welfare state.

The first issue is one of clarification. For in this period, questions raised in the late 1940s about the legitimacy of the welfare state were raised again and clarified in the 1950s. The legitimacy argument that was to rage again in the 1970s was put on the political agenda by some on the right wing of the Conservative Party. The major concerns expressed were that state-provided welfare sapped the ability of citizens to care for themselves and in so doing also sapped the nation of resources that would be better directed to maintaining Britain's international position strategically and industrially. This prompted the centre and left of the party and the Government itself to make explicit its aspirations for the welfare state. They were that welfare statism was a way to facilitate the 'opportunity state'. That is to say, that Conservative governments in the period saw state provision of welfare as a way of ensuring that those with ability prospered and that the class system was structured around meritocratic rather than aristocratic notions.

Emerging as a rebuttal to this idea of the opportunity state was a new Labour emphasis on equality of opportunity. Crosland, the major theorist of modern social democracy, had throughout the late 1940s and early 1950s drawn attention to what the social democrats in the party saw as the taming of capitalism. Capitalism had changed, he believed, out of all recognition and a new sort of welfare capitalist society had emerged as a result of the development of the welfare state. In such a post-capitalist society, Labour's previous emphasis on public ownership was irrelevant. Instead, the party's socialism should be judged by its ability, via the welfare state, to mitigate inequality and increase equality (Crosland, 1952, 1956). So, whereas the official Conservative defence of the welfare state was that it could and should be used to create a meritocracy, Crosland and Labour's view became that its function was to increase equality of access and opportunity. Welfare should be a citizen right that improved citizens' access to other rights. It was this sort of approach, shorn of its explicit social democracy, which informed Marshall's theoretical justification of the welfare state.

Labour and social policy: 1964–9

Labour, as we will see in Chapter 6, attempted to put flesh on the policy bones of the Crosland approach, particularly in relation to comprehensive education; a reform he was to introduce. It also looked carefully once more at the income maintenance system and at NHS structures (see Chapters 5–8). It was, however, the 1970s which saw the beginning of big changes in attitudes to the welfare state. Nonetheless, Labour, which had been elected on a mandate of modernising the British economy set about attempts to usher in a technological revolution. That revolution, it was hoped, would make British industry more likely to compete successfully with its industrial rivals and would help to pay for a welfare state that appeared to grow like Topsy.

CHAPTER FOUR

The welfare state in crisis

Chronology   The 1970s onwards

1970–4   Heath leads Conservative government
           Flirtation with monetarist economic policy before
           interventionist spurt

1973–5   Global oil crisis

1974   Reorganisation of the NHS

1974–9   Labour governments

1976   IMF crisis
           Welfare cuts
           Social Contract
           Lib–Lab parliamentary pact

1979–83   First Thatcher government
           Unemployment rises
           Cuts in social security rates and changes to eligibility
           Review of the NHS
           Right to buy council houses introduced

1983–7   Second Thatcher government
           Griffiths Report on General Management in the NHS
           Fowler Review of Social Security

1987–90   Education Act (1988)
           Housing Act (1988)
           Community Care Report (Griffiths)
           NHS and Community Care Act (1990)

1990–5   Major Conservative governments
           Encouragement of NHS Trusts
           Encouragement of grant maintained status in schools
           Review of the welfare state

Farewell to welfare statism?

Storm clouds were gathering over the welfare state before the Labour government left office in 1970 though they were little bigger 'than a man's hand'. The late 1960s saw the emergence of evidence and phenomena which were to question the efficacy of the welfare state for perhaps the first time.

Poverty and labour

In 1969, the Child Poverty Action Group (CPAG) made public evidence it had which it thought pointed to the fact that poverty had increased under the 1964–70 Labour administrations. In fact the director, Frank Field, had drawn on a memorandum produced by CPAG's former director, Tony Lynes, and had misinterpreted the figures. What was obvious however was that, as Townsend and Abel-Smith had suggested, poverty was stubbornly inamenable to treatment by the welfare state. And if the party most committed to the welfare state could not make it work, perhaps it was unworkable.

The challenge to Keynes and Beveridge

Throughout the 20 or so years following the end of the war, governments had retained faith in Keynesian demand management techniques and the social ideals of Beveridge. Unfortunately, in the late 1960s these consensually-adopted economic and related policies appeared to fail. An economic commentator, writing about the period argued:

> After two decades at least of government attempts to improve the non-price competitiveness of UK exports none of the policy instruments tried so far seems to have had any measurable effect. (Cripps, 1978, p. 170)

With the failure of the economic strategy came the beginnings of the end for the consensus politics that has sustained it and for the bipartisan support of the welfare state, or so it seemed to some. The governments of the 1960s had failed to save the economy from the familiar stop-go cycles of the 1950s but the modernisation programme designed to do just that had meant a rapid rise in public expenditure against the background of a stagnant economy and collapsing profits. Paying for policies like Labour's earnings-related unemployment premium, introduced to ameliorate the effects on families of frictional unemployment, therefore became a burden on the economy without the economic benefits it was expected to accompany. For some, the United Kingdom faced, as early as the late 1960s, a fiscal crisis of the state. The United Kingdom, it was argued by the right, could simply not afford the commitment to welfare that had emerged in the post-war period and particularly during the

1960s. The solution of the Conservative right was, as we shall see in the next chapter, part pragmatic, part ideological: welfare was eating up an increasing proportion of GNP so there needed to be welfare cuts; welfare statism also sapped the moral fibre of the population so there should be a reorientation of the way in which welfare was provided.

This critique of the interventionist Keynesian welfare state appeared to resonate with growing popular discontent with the policies and institutions of social democracy but it posed some problems for the leadership of the Conservative Party, many of whom remained committed to the social democratic compromise. As in the Labour Party in the same period, this tension between the populist right-wing analysis of the pre-Thatcherites and the political predilections of the leadership, many who had been what Deakin (1994) calls the *Rabians* of the 1950s, led to some Conservatives leaving the party and joining or establishing ultra-right political groupings. Unlike the case of the Labour Party, the conflict between the apparent reality of the failure of consensus and the social democratic tilt of the party leadership did not lead to a haemorrhage of members out of the party. This was the result, at least in part, of two factors: the presence of a small number of rightists in the Shadow Cabinet, chief among them Enoch Powell, and a seemingly pragmatic accommodation by the, to use one of Mrs Thatcher's epithets, 'wet' majority to the re-emerging radical right analysis (see Deakin, 1987, on this period).

Powell became, at this point, an articulate promoter of neo-liberal political ideas and a fierce critic of what he saw as a socialist welfare state. His economic liberalism and social conservatism were welded together with a political nationalism, leading him to support not only the maintenance of the union between Britain and Northern Ireland but also the repatriation of immigrants from the New and Old Commonwealths and the imposition of strict immigration control. Though expelled by the leader, Edward Heath, from the Shadow Cabinet for his infamous *rivers of blood* speech (see below), Powell came to be the spokesperson for a growing number of Conservative MPs whom the leadership ignored at their peril. In effect he became the focus of radical right opinion in the party and, with the election of a Conservative government in 1970, one of the most vociferous internal critics of what he saw, despite the Government's early flirtation with post-Keynesian, neo-monetarist economics, as the Heath government's last-ditch attempt to achieve economic growth within the constraints of Beveridge/Keynes social democracy (Loney, 1983).

Economic failure provided a fertile political soil into which Powell and others planted radical right ideas. It was left to Mrs Thatcher to bring in the harvest.

Rivers of blood

In 1968, Enoch Powell – now a member of Heath's Shadow Cabinet but previously a Conservative Minister of Health – made a speech that was to rock even the British political establishment and was to get him sacked by Heath. His infamous 'rivers of blood' speech drew attention to the increasing influx into Britain of immigrants from the Old and New Commonwealths. His arguments were compellingly simple. Large-scale immigration, for that is what he thought the situation to be, would lead inexorably to social unrest as both the indigenous and the immigrant population chased the scarce resources of housing and jobs. Tiber-like rivers of blood would flow in the streets of Britain. Though undoubtedly racist in effect, Powell was tapping into fears of mass unemployment caused by the removal of heavy industry from urban centres and the blight which followed their removal. Government response was swift, with Wilson announcing the establishment of Community Development Projects (CDPs) (Loney, 1983; Sullivan, 1987). The CDPs were the brain-child of a Home Office civil servant, Morrell, who had studied a similar innovation in the United States. The intention was to form teams of researchers and action workers in areas most affected by inner-city blight. They would recommend ways of developing new employment and other activities in the areas in which they were situated and would work with local authorities, the trade unions and local business to action their recommendations. The projects were partnership schemes with local government providing some of the funding.

The 1970s

At the start of the 1970s, the post-war settlement looked insecure. Some months prior to the Conservative election victory in 1970, Heath took his future Cabinet for a weekend social policy discussion to the Selsdon Park Hotel in Croydon. At that meeting, or so it was reported, decisions were made to cut taxes and public spending, to seek trade union reform and to take a tougher line on law and order. It was Prime Minister Wilson who dubbed the outcome of the discussion 'Selsdon Man'. He was to say 'Selsdon man is not just a lurch to the right, it is an atavistic desire to reverse the course of 25 years of social revolution. What they are planning is a wanton, calculated and deliberate return to greater inequality' (Campbell, 1993, p. 254). And Selsdon man appeared to have electoral appeal with evidence showing that the public preferred tax cuts to more spending on the welfare state.

As a result, the Conservative government (1970–4) flirted with post-Keynesian economics and a reduction in state activity in the economy. So-called lame-duck industries were refused further government subsidy and allowed to go to the wall in the eponymous Selsdon Man period before a reversion late in the Heath government to the consensus management of earlier periods.

The Heath administration also saw the emergence of a debate that was to run, in one form or another, for the next 20 or so years. Speaking to the Association of Pre-school Playgroups in 1972, Sir Keith Joseph (the Secretary of State for Health and Social Security) wondered aloud why it was that even in periods of general affluence poverty persisted. His hypothesis was that it was because of a 'cycle of disadvantage' which functioned to pass poverty on from one generation to another (Joseph, 1972). He suspected that a minority of parents transmitted deprivation to their children by equipping them with the behaviours of poverty.

Some poor parents had inadequate child-rearing methods and as a result their children failed at school, became unemployable, were incapable of strong lasting relationships, had children early and became depriving parents themselves. In other words, Joseph wondered whether the poor were poor because they did not have the behaviours and attitudes necessary to climb out of poverty.

Though this suggestion of the inter-generational transmission of poverty can be seen as consistent with a right-wing Seldonesque approach, and indeed was seen as such, it emerged in a period when Joseph's credentials as a one-nation Tory were still impeccable. Famous later for his fascination with ideas and his agonies about their implications, Joseph seems genuinely to have speculated on the causes of a problem which others had started addressing in the late 1960s (Townsend and Abel-Smith, 1965; Loney, 1983). In the furore that followed, Joseph made money available to the Social Science Research Council (SSRC) to undertake a programme of research to test his hypothesis. This episode is more interesting for its reverberations down the years than for its effect on contemporary policy. For, despite the almost universal failure of the sponsored research to find evidence of inter-generational transmission (Rutter and Madge, 1977; Brown, 1978), the idea was to be recycled and emerge as underclass theory, popularised by an American writer (Murray, 1984) and then applied by the same author to the British situation (Murray, 1990). But, as we see later, Sir Keith, along with Mrs Thatcher, was instrumental in the development of a *new Conservatism*. Disappointed with their involvement in the ultimate interventionism of the Heath administration (1970–4), and through the creation of the Centre for Policy Studies, Joseph and Thatcher developed a new, or at least recycled, approach to Conservative politics which came to inform the Thatcherism of the 1980s. It rejected state interventionism in the economy and in social policy as semi-socialism and developed a critique of welfare statism which argued for the removal of large tracts of welfare intervention on the following grounds:

- That welfare statism was responsible for the development of a culture of dependency.
- That it removed incentive by featherbedding claimants and necessitating high levels of taxation on the resourceful.
- That it involved the coercion of the many by the imposition of taxation for purposes about which they had not been consulted.
- Because it was economically imprudent to operate a large social budget in the context of economic crisis (see, for instance, Joseph, 1976).

Explicit in their approach to the welfare state was the argument that the responsibility for welfare should be moved nearer to the individual or family.

These social prescriptions were underwritten by a monetarist approach to economics which saw Keynesian approaches to social spending as part of the problem and Beveridgian social ideas as anachronistic or dangerous. As becomes obvious later, Margaret Thatcher remained a consistent promoter of these ideas throughout her administrations, although successful formulation of radical right policies was inhibited in the early years by a Cabinet weighted towards interventionist Conservatism.

Labour and the welfare crisis

The Wilson governments (1974–6) appeared to abandon the commitment to full employment on which the post-war settlement had been built (Riddell, 1983). It was in the years following 1975, however, that the interventionist state appeared to be 'undergoing an abrupt and fundamental reversal of its whole direction' (Taylor-Gooby, 1985, p.12).

The welfare state in crisis

During the tenure of Labour governments in the last half of the 1970s, the welfare state slid into crisis. Those Labour governments presided over an economy skidding into reverse. Unemployment rates rose alarmingly, if not as spectacularly as in the early 1980s. Inflation at times seemed uncontrollable (Sked and Cook, 1979, ch. 12; Morgan, 1990; Williamson, 1990). Economic crisis followed economic crisis and industrial conflict reached new heights culminating in the 'winter of discontent' of 1978–9. During the winter months of 1978–9 the trade union movement rejected government policies, particularly those on wage restraint, aimed at dealing with Britain's economic crisis and mounted a campaign of industrial action which played a large part in the defeat of the then Labour government in the 1979 general election. If there has been a fundamental shift in the nature and scope of welfare statism, then this period may be regarded by later commentators as a period of transition from a consensus on state involvement and growing state expenditure to one in which fundamental conflict characterised the debate on the role of the state in civil society and the degree of economic intervention and expenditure acceptable in a modern society. Riddell, commenting on this period, argues 'if there has been a Thatcher experiment it was launched by Dennis Healey' (1983, p. 59).

During this period government policies on state expenditure and on state involvement in industry and the public sector of the economy seem to have reflected, on the one hand, a commitment to the interventionist state which had been the political commonsense of the post-1945 period. On the other hand, economic policies also appeared to include elements which portended a future reduction in state activities.

Throughout this brief period, the Labour government attempted to implement Keynesian or neo-Keynesian economic policies to hold down unemployment. It also sanctioned and encouraged increased intervention into other areas of economic management. In particular, the development of a 'social contract' between government and trade unions amounted to state intervention to control pay and prices and was, arguably, the high-tide mark of corporatism in Britain. In effect, at least for a short period, government and state offered, and the trade union movement (or at least its leaders) accepted, the role of a quasi-state agency, monitoring and, where possible, controlling increases in pay. On the other hand, it was this Labour government which introduced an economic strategy part of which was governed by monetarist principles. This development is amply described and analysed in a number of excellent texts (especially McLennan et al., 1984) but appears to have consisted of the following features:

- Attempts to control the money supply (first introduced in 1975).
- Attempts to reduce public expenditure, or at least to halt its rise.
- Application of cash limits to public spending and to curb the Public Sector Borrowing Requirement.

These monetarist policies undoubtedly led to a reduction in state provision in welfare services as in other services and have been seen as paving the way for private provision and privatisation, even if that were not the political intention.

Some have argued that the monetarism of the Labour government in the mid to late 1970s should be seen as a politically expedient response to external pressures rather than as a principled abandonment of Keynesian economic precepts. Prime among these external pressures were the requirements of the International Monetary Fund (IMF) in granting Britain a loan during the sterling crisis of 1976 (Riddell, 1983, p. 59). They point to the 'uncertain mix of policies' (Riddell, 1983, p.60), to monetarist methods of financial management juggled alongside incomes policies and measures to hold down unemployment. They contrast such an eclectic mix with the straightforward monetarism of the later Thatcher governments. Be that as it may, the winds of change in attitudes to state intervention had started to blow in the Labour government in the late 1970s.

Conservatives and social policy

Ideas about social policy radically changed between the mid 1970s and the present. The election of a radical-right leader of the Conservative Party in 1975 marked the beginning of a shift in the emphasis of Conservative economic and social policy. Three Conservative governments headed by Mrs Thatcher introduced new (or reintroduced old) ideas about the role of government and state and their relationship with civil society. As we will also see, those governments not only introduced new ideas but also attempted to shift the direction of social policy and the welfare state. With Thatcher's fall from political grace in 1990 came the elevation of her protégé, John Major. Major's premiership has, according to some, seen the maturity of some Thatcherite social policies and the development of some new ones. This process is documented and analysed below.

In 1979 the first of the Thatcher governments was elected. Its election manifesto had drawn on the work of economists, philosophers and social scientists of the radical right (Hayek, 1944; Friedman, 1962; Powell, 1969; Joseph, 1972, 1976), as well as retaining some elements of the earlier Heathite consensus. Gradually, those consensus trails appear to have been removed as a form of 'new Conservatism' developed as the guiding light of government economic and social policy.

The principles on which Thatcher's Conservatism were based seem to be threefold:

1. A need to reduce drastically government expenditure as the public sector is seen as a burden on wealth-creating sectors of the economy.
2. A firm control of the money supply in order to restrain inflation.
3. A reduction or confinement of the role of government simply to the maintenance of conditions in which free markets may function properly.

It was the articulation of these principles and their translation into government policy which led to promotion of the idea that the British state, after three decades of interventionism, had been 'rolled back' or withdrawn from interference in the affairs of civil society. As we will see, changes occurred in the relationship between state and civil society during this period. An apparent consensus, however limited or extensive, was seemingly shattered. Government aims in this period differed from those of governments in the earlier post-war period, as witnessed by the following claim:

> the aim must be to challenge one of the central prejudices of modern British politics, the belief that it is the proper function of the state to influence the redistribution of wealth for its own sake. (Joseph and Sumption, 1979, p. 232)

Welfarism and the new Conservatism

In May 1979 a Conservative government, pledged to political philosophies quite different from those of the governments of the post-war period, was elected. The new Prime Minister and her senior colleagues presented a programme of change for Britain which had been developed over some years and which owed something to the philosophers, economists and social scientists of the neo-liberal right. The aim of the 'new Conservatism' was to shatter the post-war consensus on interventionism, mixed economy and welfare or, in the words of one Thatcherite, to reject the 'false trails of Butskellism' (Lawson, 1981) and to create a new consensus based on quite different principles. Deliberate attempts were to be made by governments headed by Mrs Thatcher to shift the frontiers between the public and private sectors of the British economy, to introduce policies which would stimulate private enterprise and to encourage the creation of a strong private sector in welfare. The proposed principles which would guide policy making were regarded by the new Government – and by many contemporary writers (Leonard, 1979; Hall, 1979; Gamble, 1979, 1980) – as the antithesis of previously dominant consensus principles. Specifically these new guiding principles included:

- A commitment to large-scale state intervention in social and economic life being replaced by a commitment to a market economy (Howe, 1983).
- A commitment to the authority of the state being replaced by a commitment to the rule of law (Howe, 1983).
- A commitment to large-scale state intervention in welfare being replaced by a commitment only to a *residual* welfare state (Boyson, 1971; Joseph, 1976; Seldon, 1977, 1981; Harris and Seldon, 1987).

Political orthodoxies were cast aside. The new Conservatives saw state interventionism as sapping the initiative of entrepreneurial capitalists. Industry and economy needed to be freed of the fetters of state controls and subject only to the regulation of the market. The economic system, if it were to generate wealth and freedom, needed to be developed around the principle of voluntary exchange.

The growth of the state, and particularly the growth of welfare bureaucracies, had elevated the authority of the state over people's lives to unacceptable proportions (Powell, 1969). The new Conservative proposals included ones concerned with severely limiting the state's paternalistic role and reinstating the rule of law as the primary institution regulating social and economic life (Howe, 1983).

The earlier political orthodoxy – of large scale state provision and control of welfare – was also to be challenged. The 'nanny-state' was to be rolled back. Responsibility for the provision of welfare was to be put back in its rightful place – with the individual, the family and the community – and large areas of welfare provision were to be privatised (Conservative Party, 1979).

In short, the new Conservatives at the beginning of the 1980s promised a transformation of the relationships between state and society – a transformation that was to be based on the economic principle of sound money and the moral principles of individual freedom and individual responsibility. In their analysis, the welfare consensus had created a coercive state in an attempt to redistribute income, wealth and life chances. That coercive state had, at one and the same time, destroyed freedom and the economic growth which was the pre-condition of redistribution. The new disposition, based on a sense of personal responsibility, on a notion of community self-help and on a concept of individual rather than collective justice (Griffiths, 1983, p. 7), presumed, in contrast,

> *a certain kind and degree of inequality . . . If society wants to preserve economic freedom it cannot predetermine equality which can only be achieved by coercion and therefore against freedom. (Griffiths, 1983a, p. 9)*

So, if this was the rhetoric of change, what have been the empirical realities of state intervention in Britain since 1979?

1979–90: the new Conservative experiment

Some have seen the 1980s as the decade of the *Thatcher Experiment* (Riddell, 1983; Hall and Jacques, 1985). During that time, or so it is argued, Conservative governments changed the face of Britain in a social and economic revolution that sounded the death-knell of welfarism.

The 1979 Conservative government came to power at a time when unemployment was rising, industrial relations were sour, public expenditure had been cut and the British economy was in free-fall. Its reaction was to attempt to redefine the appropriate role of government in a modern society. Social policy was one of the central targets of that redefinition.

Dealing with unemployment

Although unemployment had risen alarmingly under the Wilson–Callaghan governments, it had been regarded as an acceptable price to pay for low inflation. The first Thatcher government, on the other hand, appears to have seen high unemployment as a policy in its own right. As has already been observed, the outgoing Labour government had, in 1976, accepted the conditions laid down by the IMF in return for substantial loans. These conditions had included the explicit abandonment of Keynesian budget management and this had, along with pursuant cuts in public expenditure, created higher unemployment.

Mrs Thatcher's first government adopted policies which have been interpreted as signifying the end of the formal commitment to full employment. First, and as early as 1979, the Chancellor reduced rates of income tax. But, unlike President Reagan in the United States, the Government was unwilling to rely on the *Laffer Doctrine* (Stockman, 1985) and wait for the improvements in government revenue that increased individual incomes might yield. Instead, the Government financed its cuts in direct taxation by increasing indirect taxation, including a near doubling of value added tax (VAT) and an increase in social security tax. The result of this strategy was to make spending more difficult and thus to produce higher unemployment. That this was a conscious strategy is in little doubt. The Prime Minister, herself already a monetarist of the Friedman school, had earlier signalled her agreement with the economist's view that unemployment was a necessary part of a low inflation strategy (Sullivan, 1989; Glennerster and Midgley, 1991). It is less clear whether the government recognised at this point that the situation would be exacerbated by other economic and social policies which it would embrace as part of the struggle to keep inflation low. It should be acknowledged that all post-war governments had pursued the holy grail of low inflation. Those governments had, however, sought to keep inflation low by keeping growth high (Cole, 1995). For the Thatcher government, however, the strategy included instead a high interest rate policy and further reduction in public expenditure (especially on capital projects). The result of this combination of policies was to push Britain into recession and further to increase unemployment.

This had two effects. First, it raised unemployment to the status of policy instrument. Second, it led to the accumulation of a budget deficit. These policy developments in the first Thatcher term mark the unequivocal ascendancy of radical-right thinking as a guide for government policy. This *modus operandi* made, of course, a serious impact on the provision of social policy. Cuts in public expenditure ate into the fabric of the welfare state. Consistently high unemployment would make the financing of welfare more difficult. The three-fold increase in social security payments between 1979–82, a direct result of the increase in unemployment, reinforced this view and led to cuts in real terms in expenditure on health, education and housing.

The first major change was, then, the abandonment of full employment. Tacit in this was a rejection of the Beveridge principles that was to be made explicit later. Beveridge had correctly assumed that the successful administration of a social security system and the maintenance of a welfare state were dependent on full employment (HMSO, 1942; Hill, 1990; Sullivan, 1992). Without full employment, paying for welfare became an onerous burden on government and people. The use of unemployment as a policy instrument would therefore create a fiscal crisis which was, as we shall see later, followed and complemented by questions about the welfare state's legitimacy.

A further consequence of the use of unemployment by government was, at least according to some (see for example Walker, 1983; Sullivan, 1989), the suppression of the low pay lobby. The argument here is that the threat of unemployment would tend to extinguish efforts to improve the conditions of those workers on low pay, therefore satisfying the wish for a 'high technology, low pay economy' (Lawson, 1981).

The beginnings of a new social policy were, then, emerging during Thatcher's first term of government and the clearest feature of this embryonic social policy was the acceptance or use of high unemployment.

Public expenditure restrained

The constraint of public expenditure was another policy ambition of the first Thatcher administration. As a strategy, restricting public expenditure was seen as both fiscally necessary and socially desirable. Its fiscal attraction was that it would arrest and reverse the upward trend in expenditure on the welfare state. Its social desirability lay in the fact that less expenditure on welfare meant, or would ultimately mean, less welfare. Given the Thatcher government's views, borrowed from Hayek, Powell and Joseph (see Sullivan, 1989), that the welfare state had created a dependency culture and a work-shy population, public expenditure cuts offered one of the routes to a revitalised, individualistic society with only residual state welfare functions.

In the event, the strategy met with only limited success. Local government spending on education, housing and personal social services was severely curbed but savings on welfare state spending thus made were more than accounted for by the 300 per cent increase in social security expenditure between 1979–82. That expenditure was caused, of course, by the adoption of monetarist macroeconomic objectives. Attempts were made, at least in the social security system, to square the circle. These attempts included: the abolition of some social security benefits; changes in the basis for entitlement to others, and reduction in the real value of selected benefits. The abolition of the Earnings Related Unemployment Supplement, which introduced the principle of graduated unemployment benefits, is an example of attempts to make savings by the removal of a benefit. This benefit, introduced in 1966 by a Labour government, was intended to cushion those made temporarily unemployed during a period of rapid industrial change. It was abolished in 1982. The strategy of reducing the value of some social security benefits was adopted in the decision in 1980 to de-index long-term benefits. In 1974, the then Labour government had linked annual increases in long-term benefits – such as pensions – to whichever was the higher of price inflation or earnings. This was replaced by a decision to relate the benefit to price inflation only and was fully enacted in 1983 (see below) along with further changes in the way that price inflation was calculated. This ensured that further disadvantages accrued to claimants and further savings were made by government (Sullivan, 1989, p. 44). These savings amounted, in the first year of operation, to a sum in the region of £500 million (Riddell, 1983; Sullivan, 1989).

Some have also argued that the policy choice of de-indexing *long-term* benefits had ideological as well as fiscal appeal (Sullivan, 1989, 1992; Mishra, 1990). This attraction, if it existed, lay in the division of benefit recipients into the potentially productive groups, whose benefits were not de-indexed, on the one hand, and the unproductive, including the elderly, on the other.

Another dual-appeal strategy was reducing the level of benefit without making open cuts. One of the most obvious examples of this strategy was the decision in 1982 to tax unemployment benefit. The strategy here was, at one and the same time, to recoup revenue for the Exchequer and to ensure that the level of unemployment benefit was pegged below the wages of low-paid workers. Thus, not only would fiscal imperatives be satisfied but a distinction between the working poor and the non-working poor would be constructed and the operation of a principle of 'less eligibility' reintroduced (Johnson, 1990; Sullivan, 1992).

Despite these strategies, the first administration succeeded only in devoting a higher proportion of gross domestic profit (GDP) to welfare spending. This was, as has already been noted, almost entirely the result of the trebling of unemployment benefit costs during this period. Indeed, the effect of high unemployment throughout the first two Thatcher administrations was to have the effect – further cuts in public spending notwithstanding – of qualifying the goals of government. Instead of reducing the proportion of GDP expended on welfare, the aim became to arrest its upward trend (Johnson, 1990; Hills, 1991; Glennerster, 1992).

Safe in our hands? The National Health Service

Between 1979–82, government considered alternative forms of health cover to the National Health Service (see Chapter 7). It is well known that Mrs Thatcher and her senior ministers and advisers considered the option of replacing the NHS, with its guarantee of treatment free at the point of use, with a system of health insurance (Sullivan, 1989, 1992). In the event, this option was abandoned in 1982 after a fact-finding mission to the United States by the then Secretary of State for Health, Patrick Jenkin. Structural changes in the NHS were to be delayed for a further eight years.

Also during this first term, the Housing Act (1980) introduced the 'right to buy' scheme. Under this scheme, council house tenants were allowed to purchase the homes they lived in as long as they satisfied a length of tenure condition (see Chapter 8). This was presented as a move to 'people's capitalism' and was rightly seen by the Prime Minister, herself, as popular and an electoral asset.

What seems clear is that a new Conservative social policy was beginning to emerge during the first Thatcher administration. That embryonic social policy suggested the replacement of collectivist consensus policies by an emphasis on small government and individual responsibility. That the fiscal effects of the strategy differed from policy intention was in part due to increased unemployment and the failure of this early government substantially to alter the principles governing the receipt of social security benefits. Radical changes would await the election of the second and third administrations.

1983–90: a radical approach to social policy?

During the two administrations which followed 1983, the tentative steps to retrench the welfare state that had occurred in the first Thatcher government gave way to a more sure-footed attempt to tackle what was seen as an overweening welfare state.

Attempts at radical change

The first social policy area targeted for change was the social security system. From the Government's vantage point there were good reasons for this. In the first place, spending on social security amounted to approximately half of all social spending and, in 1983, was the fastest growing element of the UK welfare state (Minford, 1983; Hill, 1990; Hills, 1991; Glennerster, 1992), particularly as a result of still increasing unemployment. This circumstance was exacerbated by relatively generous levels of pensions for a growing elderly population that had been introduced by the last Labour government. Government therefore decided to act firmly in an attempt to slash spending on social security and thus to move some way towards its welfare state spending targets.

There might, of course, have been another reason for seeking to overhaul the social security system. This was the problem of the 'poverty trap'. Radical-right economists who had the ear of government (see for instance Minford, 1983) were concerned about the alleged propensity of the system to act as a work disincentive.

The argument went something like this. Previous Labour and Conservative governments had pitched benefit levels too close to the wage levels of lower paid workers. Consequently, benefit claimants had little or no incentive to find low-paid work. Indeed, Minford (1983) comes close to presenting this alleged system-induced work-shy behaviour as the major contributory factor in rising unemployment. This situation was compounded by the fact that receipt of mandatory benefit acted as a 'passport' to certain discretionary benefits, that either disappeared or were taxed pound-for-pound once the beneficiary found work, and to free services in other areas of welfare (optical, dental and school meals services, for example). Government, its neo-liberal supporters and, indeed, the political left found the existence of a poverty trap an undesirable state of affairs, though right and left differed on the nature of policy solutions to the problem (Minford, 1983; Walker and Walker, 1987).

The solution adopted by the Government to the problem of social security had two parts: one procedural and the other structural. Its first action was to alter the basis on which all benefits would be calculated. Since the 1950s, even those benefits which were not index linked had been uprated annually in line with rises in the general standard of living. In 1983 this changed and was replaced by a previously agreed principle of uprating in line with annual increases in prices only. The outcome of this move was to increase the relative income gap between claimants and those in work. As wages in the real economy increased the relative value of benefits fell. The group hit hardest were the unemployed. Indeed this was part of the policy strategy. Unemployment benefit fell in value when compared with wages. Not only this, but as we have seen above, it became tax-liable. As a result of these changes, benefits were worth only one eighth of average earnings by the end of the decade.

The second part of government strategy was intended to be considerably more significant, though it simply extended the logic of the earlier decisions on benefit levels. In 1984, the then Secretary of State for Health and Social Security announced the Government's intention to mount a detailed review of the social security system. Though the review took two years and was intended to replace the Beveridge principles with something closer to the views of radical-right economists, its outcome was somewhat more modest. In the first place, the intentions of government had included the phased replacement of the State Earnings Related Pension Scheme (SERPS) by private provision. In the end, the reviewers concluded that SERPS should be abolished but stiff opposition from the insurance companies (see below) convinced the Government to modify its stance (see Chapter 9). The privatisation proposal assumed that instead of contributing to a state scheme, individuals would make compulsory contributions to a private scheme and would thus ultimately rid government of responsibility for older people. This policy proposal was opposed not only by the poverty lobby, to which the Government had stopped listening anyway, but also by the private insurance industry. The insurance business took the view that coverage of the whole of pensioners' insurance needs was a risky proposition and preferred to remain as providers of top-up pension schemes to state pensioners (Hill, 1990; Johnson, 1990). Facing up to this, changes in this aspect of social security have merely meant that the state scheme has been made less fiscally attractive and that tax incentives have been introduced to encourage the taking up of private pension schemes.

Other outcomes of the review included the replacement of Supplementary Benefit by Income Support, of Family Income Support by Family Credit and of one-off discretionary payments by a Social Fund dealing largely in loan making. The effect of these changes has been a meaner and leaner social security system. They do not, however, amount to the replacement of Beveridge that the Government appeared to promise and that many feared.

The relative failure of the social security reviews in changing the underlying principles of social security led one radical-right commentator to argue that radical change is best managed in two phases. The first phase involves changes in the administration of public services to bring them closer to the ethos of the private corporation. The second phase, that of privatisation of public services, is thus made easier (Seldon, 1986). This appears to be a strategy that, purposively or accidentally, Thatcher governments adopted in some other social policy areas (see below).

Radical change effected?

More significant success was managed by government in other areas of social policy. This was particularly the case in the third Thatcher administration. Though even here there were instances of spectacular failure.

The Conservative manifesto for the 1987 general election (Conservative Party, 1987) seemed to suggest that the Party was willing to go for broke in introducing radical social policy changes. Here we will consider four policy innovations, three of which were prefigured in the manifesto. They are the introduction of the community charge, the Housing Act (1988), the creation of grant maintained status ('opting-out') for state schools and the NHS reforms.

The community charge, or the poll tax as it is better known, was introduced by government as a replacement for local rates. It required all but a small minority of adults to make a flat-rate contribution to local authorities and thus differed from the previous rating system in that it took the individual rather than the household as the unit for taxpaying purposes. One of the effects of this was that the tax liability of many households was increased and, given that the scheme was flat rate, it failed to take into account the tax payer's ability to pay. The introduction of the poll tax was seen by government as serving several functions: the abolition of a rating system universally regarded as inequitable; the introduction of a notion of fairness in the payment of local tax (a household with one member had previously paid the same rates as a household with many members), and the introduction of a notion of local accountability (it was expected that poll tax payers would punish any council which overspent and therefore made its local taxpayers liable for a greater poll tax burden). In fact the experiment turned out to be an almost total political disaster. The tax was unpopular. Citizens faced with high tax bills in the first year of its operation blamed not allegedly spendthrift local authorities but the government which introduced the tax. Neither was this hostility diminished by the decision of government to increase its grants to local councils in the second year of the poll tax and thus to make poll tax bills smaller. As a result, following the resignation of Prime Minister Thatcher in 1990, the Government gave notice of its intention to ditch the system and replace it with a council tax.

Further failure, or at least relative failure, attended the implementation of the Housing Act 1988 and the Education Reform Act of the same year. Or so it seemed at the time.

The Housing Act permitted council housing to be transferred from the control of local councils to private sector management bodies if the tenants of a street, block or estate so wished. Though government loaded the policy dice in favour of such opt out schemes – a failure to vote in a tenants ballot on transfer of control was originally counted as an assenting voice – few landlords and relatively few housing associations indicated their wish to take over erstwhile council housing.

Initially, at least, the picture was the same in education. One of the key elements of the Education Reform Act (1988) empowered parents to vote to transfer the status of Local Education Authority (LEA) schools to that of grant maintained schools funded directly by the Secretary of State for Education (for more detailed descriptions of the process of transfer see Simon, 1988; Sullivan, 1989). In the first two years of this scheme only 60 UK schools opted to transfer status and moves to grant maintenance were resisted equally strongly in some places by Conservative councillors as they were by Labour councillors (Sullivan, 1991; Glennerster, 1992).

However, there was a clear and resounding policy success during this third term. It was one which was not even hinted at in the Conservative manifesto for the 1987 general election. This is all the more startling because the changes wrought were little short of revolutionary. I am referring, of course, to the results of the NHS review in the late 1980s. The popular affection for the NHS remained unvanquished during the Thatcher years. It seemed to be as much part of the furniture of British life as fish and chips and the monarchy. Certainly, this popularity remained undimmed at the end of the decade (Jowell *et al.*, 1989). Nonetheless, political circumstances of the Government's own making conspired to push reform of the NHS to the top of the policy agenda.

The NHS had been subject to cash constraints for much of the Thatcher period. These constraints contributed, in 1988, to an embarrassing series of exposés of seriously ill children being turned away from intensive therapy units because of staff shortages. Mrs Thatcher's characteristic political luck deserted her over this issue and she was harried successfully over a number of weeks by the Labour Opposition, who reminded her that she had once promised that 'the National Health Service is safe with us'. Though her predicament was uncharacteristic, her eventual policy response bore the hallmarks of a premier used to making policy on the hoof. She announced the establishment of a comprehensive review of the NHS and proudly declared that all policy options, including the abolition of the NHS, would be on the table. If the NHS was not working then maybe it needed to be replaced by a different system of health care.

The review, which was charged to report to the Prime Minister within the year, received submissions from all political directions. Some advice from the political right focused on ways of running down the NHS gradually and replacing it with a system of private health insurance (see Pirie and Butler, 1988). Another suggestion was that the NHS should be replaced by health maintenance organisations (HMOs) on the American model (Goldsmith and Willetts, 1988). The radical right seemed intent on taking Reagan's America as the pattern for a future British health system but most of the other evidence submitted to the reviewers was supportive of the NHS. This evidence drew attention to underfunding of the service and suggested that this state of affairs lay at the heart of the problem. Some commentators suggested judicious experimentation within the existing structures of the welfare state (Barr, Glennerster and LeGrand, 1988) but few outside the right-wing think tanks suggested that the NHS was a suitable case for surgery.

The strategy of abolition and replacement was dropped by the review team almost immediately. There appear to be two reasons for this. The first was timescale. The reviewers had been instructed by the Prime Minister, handbag in hand, to report in no more than one year and this all but precluded in their minds – if not in hers – a thorough review of the evidence on the viability of alternative systems to the NHS. The second reason, and one familiar to students of social policy-making, was the Treasury. Quite simply, the Department was convinced that to follow the American pattern of third-party private health insurance would be to court the disaster that had befallen the American health care system, namely the explosion of health care costs, which had been witnessed by Jenkin earlier in the decade (Barr et al., 1988; Leathard, 1991). The structural changes suggested by the right wing were therefore rejected with the aid of the conservative impulses of the Treasury mandarins. Be that as it may, radical structural changes were proposed by the reviewers and, after refinement, implemented.

The review recommended the introduction of an internal or quasi-market in the NHS. The basic right of the patient to treatment free at the point of use was to remain as was the method of funding the service through taxation. But the reviewers suggested a fundamental internal reorganisation. The idea was that District Health Authorities (DHAs) should commission services from which-ever hospital was regarded as providing the best quality services. In other words, hospitals were to compete with each other for business. A market was to be created in the NHS in which efficient, good-quality hospitals would be rewarded with DHA contracts. The bracing winds of competition would also act as a spur to less efficient under-performing hospitals in that the loss of contracts would impel them to improve performance in order to win contracts in the future. These recommendations were, of course, music to the Prime Minister's ears. They were consistent with the new Conservatism of which she was the prominent public promoter and were consonant with the radical-right belief that competition improved efficiency and performance. The idea itself was not new and had been floated by a leading American advocate of managed competition on a visit to the United Kingdom in 1985 (Enthoven, 1985).

The concept of competition was at the heart of the White Paper, Working for

Patients (Department of Health, 1989). Though the precise form of competition remained ambiguous in the White Paper, the National Health and Community Care Act (1990) appears to have opted for a 'managed competition' approach (see Chapter 7). This became particularly clear at the implementation stage (Paton, 1992). DHAs, instead of providing, managing and funding all services in a given geographical area became simply the purchasers of those services. What emerged from 1 April 1991 was a system which bore close resemblance to the 'preferred provider model' adopted in the American Medicare system and in private health insurance schemes in the United States.

District Health Authorities were expected to purchase services not only from NHS hospitals in their own area but from NHS hospitals, emerging NHS trusts and private hospitals (see Levitt and Wall, 1992; Sullivan, 1992). The NHS, which had always had elements of a mixed economy of welfare about it, moved towards a market model – even if that model was to be managed rather than entirely free (Sullivan, 1987).

Further Americanisation was proposed in relation to the organisation of GP services. The reforms introduced the possibility, opposed by the general public and initially by the BMA and the doctors, for GPs to be part of fund-holding practices. As a result of this change, doctors in larger practices could opt to receive a budget from the Department of Health to purchase services for their patients (Leathard, 1991; Glennerster, 1992; Sullivan, 1992). In this they were to behave similarly to Health Maintenance Organisations (HMOs) in the United States.

The introduction of the internal market constitutes a major change in policy direction. In implementation, however, this revolutionary policy change may have proved less startling than might have been expected by government.

The problem about inserting quasi-American structures into the NHS was, of course, the differences between health markers in the United Kingdom and the United States. The excess supply of beds in American hospitals makes genuine competition possible. In the United Kingdom, by contrast, there is a shortage of supply-side provision, most of which is in any case concentrated in district general hospitals. Consequently, following the enactment of the National Health and Community Care Act, patterns of contract between DHAs and local hospitals remained largely unchanged. DHAs behaved as they had always done when commissioning services, but did so in a way more closely defined by the Department of Health.

The intervention of fund-holding GP practices in the market had a potentially more profound effect. Giving local doctors the power and the resources to purchase care theoretically brings service accountability closer to the patient. It also gives local doctors the potential to be more careful about their choice of patients, the fear being that iller and more expensive patients might come to be seen as unwelcome burdens on the practice budget.

We might conclude, then, that the NHS reforms failed fully to introduce a radical-right approach to welfarism. Markets were introduced but, in the short term at least, refused to behave like markets. To come to this judgement only would, however, be to miss a fundamental point not lost on radical-right lobbyists outside government. The point is this: the introduction of the internal market moved the NHS closer to a private model. The further introduction of NHS Trusts and of GP fund-holding has reinforced this trend and, taken together, the reforms made it easier to privatise the service in the future. Is this the two stage process to which Seldon (1986) refers? (For further discussion on this see Chapter 5.)

Though it is by now clear that by the end of the third administration radical changes in social policy had taken place, the project of 'rolling back the welfare state' had been left undone. Resistance within government played some part in this but there were other factors at play as well.

Public resistance to welfare state dismantling

Despite the chronic political weakness of Labour, the major opposition party for most of this period, the welfare state was neither destroyed nor replaced. This is not to say that fundamental changes were not introduced. Shifts in the direction of welfare occurred during the 1980s in each of the areas we have reviewed above. The NHS became less of a monopoly provider of services than it had been hitherto. In education, the private, or quasi-private, sector has been strengthened. Consumers, or more accurately, surrogate consumers (parents) have been empowered to make choices about the status of their local schools and about where they wish their children to attend school. These choices had previously been the province of professional educators or administrators. Additionally, the higher education sector was visited by policies intended to make it more efficient, more accountable and more responsive to the needs of society, or at least to commerce and industry.

It is quite clear that in both intent and outcome welfare was transformed during the Thatcher years. Policies were sometimes imposed as a result of conviction rather than consensual agreement (look, for example, at the decision by government in 1990 to proceed with NHS Trusts despite opposition from the Labour Party, the Social and Liberal Democrats, the BMA, the health trade unions, the nurse organisations and, as far as can be made out, the populace). But the structure of the welfare state remained relatively intact by the end of Mrs Thatcher's premiership. How then do we set about explaining the gap between intention and outcome in relation to Conservative social policy in the 1980s?

The most plausible explanation is that we should recognise that by the 1980s citizen rights had become firmly embedded in the political consciousness of the United Kingdom population and had been seen as something worthy of protection. To put it another way, the electorate had far from complete faith in the political morality of Conservative social policy (Loney, 1986).

The psephological evidence, such as it is, suggests that 1980s voters were attracted to the promises contained in Conservative economic policy that individual financial gain was more effectively guaranteed by Conservative governments. Tax cuts and counter-inflationary policies appear to have been powerful electoral inducements in all three elections in the decade. Nonetheless, there is powerful and persuasive evidence that, while the electorate were attracted to post-Keynesian policies on economic management, they remained wedded to most areas of the welfare state (for reviews of the evidence, see Taylor-Gooby, 1985; Papadakis and Taylor-Gooby, 1987). According to Taylor-Gooby, the public view appeared to be:

> *support for the mass welfare state services of pensions, the NHS and education [although this is] tempered by concern at unemployment and low pay benefits, council housing and lone parents' benefits . . . strong support for the principle of state welfare with some concern at the cost. (Taylor-Gooby, 1985a)*

In other words, the lack of fit between intention and outcome was influenced by the public's acceptance of the viability of welfarism, despite its rejection by the Conservatives.

Since 1983, the series *British Social Attitudes* has gathered data about, *inter alia*, public attitudes to state welfare. Throughout the period, the data have shown rising levels of public support for core services of the welfare state and an apparent readiness to pay tax at higher levels to pay for the services. The 1989 survey – the last survey before Mrs Thatcher's fall – demonstrates this trend.

Survey respondents were asked to choose between three options about welfare expenditure and Table 4.1 compares the responses with those furnished in 1983 and 1986.

The same series also suggests that support for the welfare state rose most sharply among *social classes I and II* (the managerial and professional classes). Between 1983–9, the increase in social class I/II respondents choosing option 3 above was 29 per cent compared with a jump of 18 per cent among social class III (non manual), 26 per cent among social class III (manual) and 24 per cent among social classes IV/V (Taylor-Gooby, 1990, p. 3).

Table 4.1   Public expenditure and welfare (%)

	1983	1986	1989
Reduce taxes, spend less on health, education and social benefits	9	5	3
Keep taxes and spending on these services the same as now	54	44	37
Increase taxes and spend more on these services	56	32	46

Source: British Social Attitudes: the Seventh Report, 1990

More than this, by 1989 almost half of all respondents who saw themselves as Conservative voters opted for increased taxes and increased services – a jump, in fact, of 100 per cent over the six years (Taylor-Gooby, 1990, p. 3).

The data exposes interesting detail about these overall attitudes. In the first place, while it is clear that respondents believe the NHS to be in desperate need of additional expenditure and the education service to be similarly needy, it is equally clear that income maintenance remained a relatively unpopular service. It also seems to be the case that the Thatcher administrations won the argument on council housing because the option of additional expenditure on council housing is only marginally more popular than increased expenditure on income maintenance (see Taylor-Gooby, 1990, p. 4, Table, on priorities for extra government spending).

Within the relatively unpopular social security field, retirement pension is seen as a candidate for extra government expenditure by over 40 per cent of respondents, as was the case in 1983. Benefits for the disabled are also seen, by a fifth of the sample, as worthy of extra spending. However, benefits for the unemployed, child benefit and benefits for single parents are rarely seen as deserving extra expenditure, and, in the case of the first and last of these categories, they were less popular in 1989 than they were in 1983 (Taylor-Gooby, 1990, p. 5).

Further interesting evidence emerges. In the first place, there is strong suggestive evidence that the public remained unconvinced in the late 1980s of the virtue of privatisation strategies in welfare. In 1989, as in previous years, respondents were asked a number of questions seeking to get to the heart of views about privatisation. In the first place, they were asked to comment on the view that the NHS should be available only as a residual service for people who were unable to afford their own private health insurance. Their responses are reproduced below (Table 4.2).

Indeed, by 1989, the tide of public opinion appeared to be running against private provision unless it was truly private. Tables 4.3 and 4.4 give data resulting from questions about attitudes to private health care.

As we can see, the idea of private practice in the NHS had become much less popular by the end of the decade than it had been in 1983.

The British Social Attitudes surveys make depressing reading for Thatcherites in relation to other welfare issues. This is certainly the case if we look at

Table 4.2 Two-tier services

	1983	1986	1989
Support	29	27	22
Oppose	64	67	74

Source: British Social Attitudes: the Seventh Report, 1990

Table 4.3 Private treatment in NHS hospitals (%)

	1983	1986	1989
Is good for the NHS	23	27	24
Is bad for the NHS	42	40	47
Makes no difference	30	28	24

Source: British Social Attitudes: the Seventh Report, 1990

Table 4.4 Private medicine in general (%)

	1983	1986	1989
Private medicine should be			
Abolished in all hospitals	9	11	12
Allowed in private hospitals only	48	46	50
Allowed in all hospitals	39	41	35

Source: British Social Attitudes: the Seventh Report, 1990

responses to the view that the welfare state should embrace a measure of distribution. In response to questions associated with this proposition: 65 per cent of respondents thought that ordinary people did not get their fair share of the nations wealth; 61 per cent thought that government should spend more money on welfare benefits for the poor, even if it led to higher taxes, and 50 per cent thought that the Government should redistribute income from the better off to the less well off.

Neither does the survey suggest that the population accepted Thatcherite invective about the nanny state and its supposed effect in creating an irresponsible society. Respondents, reacting to a series of images of the welfare state, came up with the information given in Table 4.5.

Table 4.5 The welfare state and responsibility (%)

	1983	1989
The welfare state makes people less willing to look after themselves	52	39
The welfare state encourages people to stop looking after each other	37	32
People receiving social security are made to feel like second class citizens	48	53

Source: British Social Attitudes: the Seventh Report, 1990

Here, the important findings are that right-wing Conservative ideas about a supposedly indulgent welfare state had lost ground dramatically from 1983–9. Indeed respondents were less willing by 1989 to believe that a welfare state has any significant effect on people's altruistic impulses.

All in all, then, there appears to be persuasive evidence that, while Keynesian economics had become less attractive to UK citizens in the 1980s, less significant dents had been made in welfarist approaches to social policy. Keynes appears to have been dead by the end of the 1980s but Beveridge lived on.

The analysis sketched out above might be taken to suggest that the welfare state in the United Kingdom proved relatively durable during the 1980s and did so, in large part at least, because of public support for welfare. This is not to minimise fundamental changes that occurred in the 1980s in welfare. We have already seen that the durability of welfare state structures and public support slowed the process of reversing the welfare state rather than promoting a return it to its pre-1970 form.

A number of writers have taken the failure of the 1980s Conservatives to roll back the state from welfare as evidence of the irreversibility of the welfare state (Offe, 1984; Therborn, 1984; Piven and Cloward, 1985; Le Grand and Winter, 1987; Ruggles and O'Higgins, 1987). But the evidence is capable of another interpretation.

If we take a narrow definition of welfare, then it is easy to see how these writers come to their conclusions. For example, public expenditure in the United Kingdom increased during the first Thatcher administration rather than contracting as planned and anticipated. It did so, however, almost entirely as a result of a dramatic rise in unemployment and the consequential rise in social expenditure on unemployment benefit. This could be seen as an expansion of state welfare activities and thus support some sort of irreversibility thesis of the welfare state (Mishra, 1990, pp. 32–6). It is much more plausible, however, to see this phenomenon as pointing to the opposite conclusion. Why?

First, rising unemployment was accompanied in the medium term by policies retrenching unemployment benefits. This can be seen as part of a strategy to restructure welfare so that the principle of less eligibility was reintroduced. That is, it can be seen as an ideological strategy to separate out those categories of people believed to be undeserving of welfare (the unemployed, who the New Right thought remained unemployed by choice) from deserving categories of people. Whatever the intention, the political processes unfolding over the decade cut across the principles of welfare provision developed after the war. They did so because they included a rejection of Keynesianism and its emphasis on the maintenance of full or high employment and of the notion of earlier Conservative governments of 'one nation' and noblesse oblige. In other words, the principles that had sustained welfare provision at the times of its growth were eroded during the 1980s.

Second, it appears that throughout this decade, and despite public support for welfare, the nature of that support was restructured. In essence, as Papadakis and Taylor-Gooby (1987) suggest, growing support for state welfare was accompanied by growing support or tolerance for other forms of welfare provision. The data analysed by them suggests support not only for a welfare state but also for welfare pluralism (Taylor-Gooby, 1987, pp. 21–7; see also Johnson, 1987, 1990).

In light of this, it might be argued that while support for the heartland services of the welfare state remained, it did so alongside support for private services which would ultimately serve to weaken it. Support for private pension schemes and for the sale of council houses are apt illustrations of how the support for universalism also contained within it support for selective privatisation. According to Taylor-Gooby it is also conceivable that, if standards in health and education were dramatically to fall and if tax concessions were made available to ease exit into the private sector, both support for, and participation in, state welfare might alter:

> *Exit for most people is an impossibly expensive option. However . . . if standards do not improve and if government widens opportunities for exit from direct state provision, loyalty to the mass services may be speedily undermined. This is the effect of the subsidies of the 1986 Act, the discount for home ownership under the 'right to buy' scheme and the provision for transferring from state to quasi-private schooling in the 1987 Education Bill (Taylor-Gooby, 1987, p. 27).*

These considerations led during the decade to a reconsideration of the reversibility of welfare. Therborn came to argue that 'consciously or unconsciously, a dualistic economy and society – a well-off sector and a stagnating, declining sector of low-wage or unemployed misery – is the medium term goal of the New Right' (Therborn and Roebroek, 1986, p. 337).

By the end of the 1980s, then, significant changes had been wrought within the welfare state. Particularly during the third term of office, welfare services were restructured. The creation of 'opt out' positions in health and education (see Chapters 5 and 6) represented the insertion of market mechanisms into public services. But, by the time Mrs Thatcher was removed from leadership of the Conservative Party, welfare state services remained publicly funded and part of the state apparatus. That they did so, and that Conservative policy outcomes did not match intentions, seems, in large part, the result of public resistance. Public opinion, while failing to halt the strategic march to a different welfare principle, slowed down the progress of Thatcherism.

The Major governments and social policy

In late 1990 Mrs Thatcher was toppled as leader of the Conservative Party and as Prime Minister following a 'palace coup'. During her tenure as premier, her governments had, as we have just seen, attempted radical and structural changes to the welfare state. While succeeding in reversing the upward trend in welfare spending and in getting the NHS reforms on to the statute book, those governments were certainly less than immediately successful in rolling the state back from welfare. While it is beyond doubt that those governments intended to smash the welfare consensus, the indications are that it was less than completely successful in that intention. But it is still possible, while acknowledging that the Thatcher years represent an incomplete revolution in social policy, to see the fruits of that failure as becoming, in policy terms, pragmatic first and second steps towards a radical-right utopia of stateless welfare.

1990–5: development of the Thatcher project or its demise?

Mrs Thatcher was replaced in November 1990 by John Major. Though the new Prime Minister had been her Chancellor of the Exchequer, political pundits opined on whether his accession would mean a break with the policy principles with which she (and, incidentally, he) had been associated or whether continuity would characterise the policy agenda in social policy and elsewhere. This was not, of course, merely journalistic puff. Major, early in his first term as Prime Minister, declared his political aspirations to include the creation of a classless society. He did not mean the same by this, of course, as had Karl Marx! Rather, he was talking about the creation of a society in which personal effort and equality of opportunity became political bedfellows in the project of making Britain a society 'at peace with itself'. Surely, then, the policy agenda and policy intentions were to change. Would not the creation of a harmonious Britain depend, in part, on government following a different social policy trajectory? Perhaps the Major premiership would mark a break with the policies and policy aspirations of Conservative governments since 1979.

Words are, of course, sometimes deceptive and the words of career politicians often open to a multiplicity of interpretations. There is, on one reading at least, evidence to suggest that a social policy audit of the two Major administrations implies continuity and development of Thatcherite policies rather than a disjuncture with them.

Health policy and the Major governments

The Major governments have introduced no major new policies in the health field. Neither, however, do they seem to have deviated from the course charted for them by the now Lady Thatcher. Indeed, secretaries of state in these administrations have energetically implemented policies emerging at the butt end of the Thatcher years. The idea and practice of an internal market has remained at the heart of policy on the NHS (Levitt and Wall, 1992) and the movement of NHS hospitals to Trust status has accelerated and been robustly encouraged by both of Major's Secretaries of State for Health. In the run up to the 1992 general election, William Waldegrave, Major's urbane then health minister, indicated that there was little alternative for district hospitals and other health units but to become NHS Trusts. If the Conservatives were elected, he suavely reassured, there would be no attempt to compel units to opt out of DHA control. Rather, NHS Trusts would simply be the Government's 'preferred policy option, our preferred model' (*The Guardian*, 6 March 1992). The political message was clear, however, and health service managers needed no help in decoding it. For Waldegrave had made clear a point reinforced by his successor, Virginia Bottomley. Trusts would, at least in the short run, be the beneficiaries of greater resources than non-Trust hospitals. The effect, of course, has been to translate the trickle of hospitals applying for Trust status before the election into a flood. The same is the case with the GP fund-holding scheme, the entry criteria of which have been made easier by government.

It might therefore be reasonable to conclude that, in health at least, Conservative governments in the early 1990s have remained faithful to the policy principles of the Thatcher years. More than this, they seem to have experienced no discomfort in propelling those policy principles into life. At the time of writing (1995), in excess of half of the United Kingdom's hospitals have become Trusts or have declared an interest in doing so next year (Department of Health, 1993). A similar picture is emerging in relation to GP fund-holding. Structural changes to the NHS, started by the Thatcher governments, seem to have been developed and intensified under Major. But how radical are these changes politically and ideologically?

Measured against the original thoughts of the first Thatcher administration or the advice of early radical right privatisers (Harris and Seldon, 1979), the changes are much less than right-wing Conservatives hoped for and many non-Conservatives feared. A National Health Service, funded out of taxation remains in place. Despite the growth of private health care provision (Higgins, 1988, 1990; Leathard, 1991; Johnson, 1990; Sullivan, 1992), encouraged by government and further fostered by the assumption that DHAs will now buy some services from the private sector, NHS hospitals, Trusts or otherwise, remain the preponderant providers of health care.

Privatisation of the Service has not, then, occurred. Perhaps Conservative governments in the 1990s, like their counterparts in the 1980s, have judged such a dramatic change in policy politically dangerous. Certainly, as we shall see later, abolition of the NHS would prove less than popular with the electorate. Nonetheless, the change in policy direction has been significant. First, the service monopoly previously held by the NHS has been broken: private health care still remains a small part of total health care provision but the principle of a mixed economy of provision has been conceded. Second the introduction of a quasi-market in health has moved the NHS nearer to the private model and has made the privatisation of the service in the future a much shorter step.

Education policy in the early 1990s

There is an essentially similar story to tell in relation to education policy. Policy changes in education came thick and fast in the Thatcher years: parental preference; the reintroduction of formal testing; the introduction of a national curriculum; the encouragement of efficiency measures, and greater competition in higher education, and so on (Sullivan, 1989; Johnson, 1990; Jones, 1991). The Major governments have introduced no new policy trajectories but have implemented these earlier policy changes with vigour. The grant maintained status option opened to schools as a result of the Education Reform Act (1988) yielded less than impressive results up to 1992. Indeed, in its first two years of operation the response from schools was derisory. However, during the general election campaign in 1992, the then Secretary of State for Education made it clear, in terms which strikingly resembled Waldegrave's words about NHS Trusts, that, if returned, the Government would prefer schools to become grant maintained rather than continuing in LEA control. Following that election, the dam has burst and large numbers of schools have declared their wish to transfer status. It was estimated at the time that by 1996 over 80 per cent of schools will have severed their links with LEAs (Aitken, 1992). These predictions now seem wildly optimistic as opt outs have remained a trickle rather than a flood. So much so that the Government appears to be considering the virtue of legislating to make all schools adopt grant-maintained status (*The Guardian*, 21 November, 1995).

Thatcher governments' concern with competition in the higher education sector has been acknowledged and acted upon. This is most sharply seen in the second Major administration's implementation of an earlier policy proposal to dissolve the binary line in this sector. Accordingly, since 1992, erstwhile polytechnics which meet certain eligibility criteria have been allowed to transfer into the university sector. One of the reasons behind this move was that the new universities had developed as successful polytechnics by adopting market values. As a result they had often been more effective than the established universities in attracting non-government funds for applied research and consultancy. The insertion of these institutions into an enlarged university sector would, it was hoped, further encourage the old universities to compete for contracts in the real world of the market.

There were, of course, other equally important policy intentions behind this particular initiative. Two such, which are of prime importance, were a concern with educational opportunity and an interest in efficiency. The nature of both these concerns owed much to the political philosophy which had nurtured Thatcherism and appears to have been a significant influence on the Major governments.

First, then, let us take educational opportunity. In words reminiscent of the intellectual architect of post-war social democracy (see Crosland, 1974), the Major government, like the Thatcher governments before it, has declared an interest in increasing access to higher education. The political motives behind increased access have, however, been quite different from those embraced by social democrats. While the impetus for social democracy's emphasis on equality of educational opportunity was a belief that a modification of the inequalities in educational opportunity would have a carry-through effect into the managed labour market, contemporary Conservatism appears to dance to a different political drum. Here, the attraction of increasing access to higher education appears to be a belief that government should act through education to increase the number of people equipped to compete in an unmanaged market economy. That is to say that, whereas the principle of equality of educational opportunity had previously been associated with social democracy's sister concerns with a labour market policy (Furniss and Tilton, 1979; Sullivan, 1992), the Conservative emphasis on increased access appears to be connected with a desire to increase the numbers of citizens equipped to face the rigours of unmanaged capitalism. There are, in any event, concerns at the time of writing that increasing access to higher education, whether through the enlargement of the university sector or by other means, is likely to be unsuccessful in expanding the pool of students benefiting from high-quality education. Rather, say some, the outcome is likely to be the lowering of academic standards as higher education institutions seek to reach the targets for increased recruitment set for them by government (Association of University Teachers, 1991, 1992). Arguably, then, the outcome of this policy emphasis, whatever its intention, has been to decrease access to quality education.

The concern with efficiency which has been associated with the dissolving of the binary line can be expressed simply. The erstwhile polytechnics, though administered for most of their existence by LEAs, were seen as having secured their continuation, in part, by the adoption of efficiency strategies familiar in the world beyond the ivory tower (performance-related pay, performance reviews and the like). One of the hoped for outcomes from a merger of the new universities and the old was a permeation of the system as a whole by the attitudes lying behind these strategies.

The changes in education occurring in the period we are now considering appear to some to have been momentous. And indeed they may turn out so to be. It may be that grant maintained status in the school sector is a Trojan Horse bearing the threat of later complete privatisation. It may be that changes in the higher education sector will transform the nature of degree and post-degree education. At the time of writing, it is too soon to say. What can be said is that, inasmuch as government education policy represents a radical break with post-war consensus politics, the impetus for change came from a policy environment created by its predecessors. Conservative governments since 1990 have merely, though importantly, acted to encourage the widespread adoption of policy strategies in education set in place before the downfall of the Prime Minister's predecessor.

In health and education, then, there looks to be no sign of the demise of the Thatcherite social policy project. Indeed, in areas like 'school opt-outs' and the creation of NHS Trusts, the Major administrations appear to have breathed life into Thatcher policy reforms. As we have already seen, the Thatcher governments of the 1980s had mixed fortunes in implementing post-consensus social policies. As we shall see below, in some policy areas at least this led to rethinking the policy agenda. But, in the two areas of policy that have been reviewed above, political principles established by the Thatcher regimes have been fostered and nurtured.

Rethinking the policy agenda

There is some evidence, however, that the Major governments have rethought aspects of the Thatcher social policy agenda.

Shortly after the replacement of Mrs Thatcher as Prime Minister the new Major Cabinet made plans to replace the community charge (poll tax) with a council tax which, it is believed, takes more account of citizens' ability to pay and partly reverts to the principle of taxing according to property value. This new scheme, implemented in 1993, and the policy process which created it, were, in no small measure, a response to public outcry, sometimes bordering on civil disobedience against the poll tax. Sufficient tax payers refused to pay and thereby created a crisis in local authority finances. This and the general displeasure with the policy led the Government to conclude that there was no political alternative but to remove it.

There are also indications that new thinking is taking place in relation to the social security system. Once more, this review of previous policy seems to have been forced on government. The Fowler Review, as we have already seen, was nowhere near as radical in its outcome has had been intended. Moreover, since the implementation of the Fowler system, additional problems have become apparent: administrative costs have remained high (and higher than in any other area of state welfare); there have been runaway costs in certain benefit areas, and particularly in invalidity benefit where GPs appear to be sanctioning its receipt as an alternative to unemployment benefit, which is paid at a lower rate; the Social Fund, by which local offices administer loans for one-off expenditure to claimants, is budget limited and appears to work on a first come first served basis rather than on any objective need measuring footing, and so on. The result of these problems has been to raise the question about the need for a 'new Beveridge' at the highest reaches of government, leading Mr Michael Portillo, then Chief Secretary to the Treasury, to announce in 1993 a fundamental review of public spending which would 'question the principles of the welfare state'. Time will, of course, tell whether any changes in the social security system amount to more than tinkering.

The Major administrations and social policy

In summary, we might make the following observations about social policy developments since 1990. First, there has been a large degree of continuity between the welfare ideology and social policy innovations of the Thatcher and Major governments. Indeed, where policy revision has occurred – or is occurring – it appears to be as a result of public political pressure or of fiscal and administrative crisis. Second, where there have been changes, there appears to be no consistency in policy direction. That is to say, that, while the replacement of the council tax may come to be seen as a liberalisation of Thatcher policy, any future changes to the social security system may well turn out to have the effect of making it less generous than the system administered in the Thatcher years.

Social policy and new Conservatism: an appraisal

What then are we to make of the changes in social policy since the breakdown of the post-war consensus? On one reading, the changes are less fundamental than new Conservatism promised: the structure of the welfare state remains largely, if not completely, intact; privatisation, though it has occurred, has been less extensive in outcome than in policy intention, and the provision of welfare still appears to be a citizen right. Read another way, the changes have been gradual but profound.

Long-term strategy and incremental change

A not implausible reading of the contemporary politics of social policy is to see continuity rather than conflict between the rhetoric of policy change and the reality. While it is true that the most radical policy intentions of recent Conservative governments have not been translated into policy outcomes at the first attempt, it is possible to discern the process as one where long-term strategy is the guiding principle behind incremental change.

Viewed from the 1990s, this might seem to be the case in the principal welfare state areas. In housing and in personal social services, as in health, education and social security, the accumulated changes in policy direction have been significant.

Though the early rhetoric of rolling the state back from welfare has not been fully realised, the welfare state now more fully resembles market organisations than would have seemed possible 20 years ago. That this transformation has, in large part, seen recent Conservative administrations as the midwives of change is not in question. This seems to hold as true when we look at the governments headed by Mr Major as it does when we consider the earlier Conservative administrations. There have been five Conservative governments between 1979 and the time of writing. Each of those administrations has engaged in incremental changes to the fabric of welfare. From 1993, those increments have come to look more and more like pieces in a strategic jig-saw puzzle.

Further reading for Part One

Addison, P. (1982). Considers the factors associated with the post-war settlement on a welfare state, mixed economy and full employment.

Addison, P. (1992). Analyses the influence of Churchill on the development of domestic policy.

Ashford, D. (1986). Looks at the emergence of the welfare state in comparative context.

Barnett, A. (1984). A thoughtful contribution to the debate on the welfare consensus.

Barnett, C. (1987). A development of the author's thesis that the new Jerusalem of welfare statism put comfort before economic security.

Barnett, C (1995). Argues that the creation of the welfare state bankrupted the UK.

Calder, A. (1965). Considers the effect of the Second World War on peace-time policy making.

Deakin, N. (1994). A history of the political process of policy making in the welfare state.

Foot, M. (1975).

Fraser, D. (1982).

Glennerster, H. (1995).

Harris, J. (1981).

Hennessy, P. (1992). A social history of the immediate post-war years.

Hill, M. (1993).

Jones, K. (1991).

Lowe, R. (1993).

Mishra, R. (1984).

Mishra, R. (1990).

Morgan, K. O. (1985). Looks at policy in periods of Labour government.

Morgan, K. O. (1990). Considers whether the 'people's war' led to peace-time developments in welfare.

Pimlott, B. (1988). Argues that the post-war welfare consensus was a limited one.
Sainsbury, E. (1977).
Sullivan, M. (1987).
Sullivan, M. (1989).
Sullivan, M. (1992).
Taylor-Gooby, P. (1991).
Taylor-Gooby, P. and Dale, J. (1981).
Timmins, N. (1995). An impressive general history of the welfare state.
Williamson, B. (1990). A social history of post-war developments.

PART TWO

Welfare state services

CHAPTER FIVE

Post-war education policy: continuity and change

Chronology	Education policy in the post-war years
1945–1951	The development of the comprehensive school principle
	Government support for the bipartite system
1951	Labour adopts the comprehensive school idea
1950s	Official support for bipartite system but growth in the number of comprehensive schools
	Parents oppose the bipartite system
	Industry argues for a new education system
	Sociological and psychological research suggest system is failing
1959	Crowther Report
1963	Newsom Report
1963	Robbins Report on Higher Education

We have seen in Chapter 2 that the war-time years saw a major development in education policy with the enactment of the Butler Act. When Labour formed the immediate post-war government, it set about implementing that act, straying little from the policy parameters laid down by Butler and his Labour deputy, James Chuter Ede. The Act had made secondary schooling between the years of 11 and 15 compulsory and free. It had abolished fees in all maintained schools, save for the direct grant grammars – a sort of halfway house between the state and private sectors – and elementary schools appear to have been consigned to the dustbin. The Act also legislated for the provision of school milk and, where necessary, of free school meals. In the higher education sector, it placed powers and obligations on local authorities to provide some scholarships to cover the cost of university education.

The Education Act (1944), though rightly regarded as a landmark in education policy, was, however, a monument to Britain's late acceptance of the legitimate role of the state in the provision of education. In the century before its passage, public education provision was guided by a relatively light central state hand on the tiller (see Chapter 1) and had become almost solely the property of local government. This had posed problems for Butler, who was constrained by this and other factors into crafting an Act whose main central powers were reserve powers. Central government found itself permitting local authorities to act in one way or another but often without the statutory power to compel it so to act. So, for instance, the Ministry of Education might advise on curriculum and syllabus in the nation's schools but had no legitimate right to lay down what should be taught (a problem with which a Conservative Secretary of State for Education was to tussle in the late 1980s).

Local authority resistance to central control was, and remained throughout the post-war period, firm as ministers introducing and progressing the comprehensive school reform were to find out to their cost. And, though the shared responsibility for educational provision was to create diversity, it made the system almost impossible to modify from the centre.

The Labour government and the Butler Act

However, what the Act is chiefly remembered for is the establishment of a tripartite system of secondary education. That is to say, that it is seen as establishing a secondary sector divided into grammar, secondary modern and, in theory at least, technical grammar schools (see Chapter 2). In fact, as we have already seen, the Act did not prescribe this division but it had been the clear anticipation of Butler that in general it would become the dominant pattern. Labour's post-war education ministers were to remain faithful to this tripartite organisation of secondary schooling despite a strong commitment in the party to the idea of multilateral or comprehensive schooling. The major policy discussions during the rest of that government's tenure were to be in the form of disputes about the organisation of schooling.

On the eve of the Government taking office the 'caretaker' Conservative government had published a policy statement on education which had argued that there already existed, in embryonic form, a *de facto* tripartite secondary education system following the Hadow reorganisation. It further argued that this system should be developed rather than a new unified system evolved (Ministry of Education, 1945).

In addition, the authors of *The Nation's Schools*, as this document was called, did not foresee any need to increase the number of grammar schools available from then existing numbers. This latter suggestion certainly appears to contravene the principle, which was said to be behind the 1944 Act, that working class children should have the same opportunity to attend grammar schools as middle class children. Such a principle would have implied the provision of a greater number of grammar school places. The Conservative document claimed, on the other hand, that since, in 1938, 40 per cent of secondary school leavers had not taken the School Certificate and 25 per cent had left before the age of 16 years, many children had obviously been receiving an education beyond their capabilities. In fact, the statement argued, the numbers of places available in grammar schools might actually be reduced. Moreover, should a larger number of working class children than hitherto gain access to a grammar school, it might lead to a corresponding decrease in the number of 'talented' working class children entering industrial occupations, a situation which the Conservatives believed would damage the economy by creating a much diminished pool of skilled labour.

Despite the fact that this policy statement had been opposed by the Labour Party at Conference, it was to be accepted as the basis of government policy by the first Labour Minister of Education, Ellen Wilkinson. Within the Labour Party there was to be a constant battle between the two Labour Education Ministers of this period and members of Conference organised and led by the National Association of Labour Teachers (NALT). Throughout the period 1945 to 1951 the Labour ministers were to argue that there were sound educational justifications for the tripartite system and to allow diversions from this organisational pattern only in exceptional circumstances.

The comprehensive issue

This period was, however, a very fertile period for thinking about secondary education. It saw the beginnings of the comprehensive movement emerge from the ashes of Labour's refusal to reorganise secondary education along multilateral lines. It saw the lead in this movement being taken by a small, radical section of the Labour Party and other left-wingers. It also saw the establishment and growth of the tripartite system ensured by the two Labour administrations. A review of the major events in this period will serve to illustrate the issues of importance and controversy in this period.

The debate within the Labour Party

At the 1946 Labour Party Conference NALT called on the Minister to repudiate *The Nation's Schools* and to reshape the education system 'in accordance with socialist principles'; in other words, to initiate a multilateral reorganisation. NALT introduced this call in an amendment to the composite motion on secondary education because it was unhappy that many Labour-controlled

LEAs were responding to the Ministry's encouragement to develop a tripartite system of secondary education. The Minister, Wilkinson, was not to be convinced by NALT's arguments for reorganisation. She firmly defended tripartism claiming that parity in material resources between different types of schools would lead to parity of esteem. In addition, she argued that distinctions between the schools were made on the basis of objective educational criteria and not, as had previously been the case, on the basis of unjustifiable social criteria. The NALT amendment was carried – despite the attempt by a National Executive Committee (NEC) spokesperson to prevent an open rupture in the party on this issue – but the Minister continued to defend tripartism during the rest of her time in office. When Wilkinson died in 1947 she was succeeded by George Tomlinson, till then Minister of Works. He published a policy statement almost immediately (Ministry of Education, 1947). Though this document, *The New Secondary Education*, had been prepared during the tenure of the previous Minister, he defined the position it outlined as his own. In essence, this document was a further defence of tripartism. Like the 1944 Act, it did not completely close the door on the establishment of multilateral schools, and consequently the rebuke he received at the 1947 Labour Party Conference was not one for discouraging the establishment of multilateral schools but for being insufficiently positive in encouraging them.

In the late 1940s, the spearhead for reform initially provided by NALT was sharpened by a growing number of delegates to the Annual Conference who made public statements in favour of comprehensive reorganisation. In 1948 resolutions which called for a more positive approach to reorganisation were put to Labour Party Conference, were carried, and Tomlinson censured. Following this defeat at Conference, a delegation from NALT met with Tomlinson. They did so to persuade the Minister of the error of his ways only to find, at least according to one of the delegation, that the Minister regarded the difference between them as one of strategy rather than principle.

Responding to a question about Labour thinking on the comprehensive school policy in the late 1940s, one of the delegation appears to downplay the idea of ideological fissure between the rank-and-file left and the party leadership. As seconder of the pro-comprehensive school motion moved by NALT at the conference, he had been invited, along with them, to see the Minister:

> I went with a NALT delegation to see George Tomlinson who was then Education Minister and he was sympathetic but cautious. I think he was saying that the system wasn't ready for it yet and there weren't the resources and he was sympathetic to the idea but it was in a vague sort of way and I think his attitude then was probably typical of a lot of Labour controlled education authorities . . . very proud of their grammar schools and very proud of the opportunities they gave working class kids . . . George Tomlinson's attitude seemed to be of that kind. Not against comprehensives but not willing to push it on LEAs. (Prentice, 1991, emphasis added)

This judgement appears to be entirely consistent with Tomlinson's own statement to the House of Commons in 1947:

In the field of secondary education, I do not envisage any uniform system over the country as a whole. I want to encourage variety and I shall welcome carefully conducted experiments in suitable cases with multilateral schools and the like, provided that they are designed to cater for the needs of all the children. (Hansard, 3 March 1947)

That the NALT and segments of the constituency section of the party regarded this sort of response as unsatisfactory; that it regarded it as a demonstration of the Government's intransigence in the face of an opportunity to implement a progressive social policy is not in doubt. They continued to press the party, in and out of Annual Conference, to relent. In 1949 they submitted a memorandum on comprehensive education direct to the NEC. That memorandum expressed the concern of the Labour Teachers with 'the failure during the life of the present parliament to give encouragement to the comprehensive school as "*a general policy*"' (National Association of Labour Teachers, 1949). It reminded the National Executive of the resolution passed at the 1942 Labour Conference in favour of the common or multilateral school and that the Executive had, as a result, impressed on Mr Butler, as Secretary at the Board of Education, the view that 'schools for all children over the age of 11 years should be brought under a common code of regulations for secondary schools and that a new type of multilateral school should be developed' (Labour Party Conference, 1942). The document went on to remind the NEC that since that time Annual Conferences had consistently voted in favour of the principle of the comprehensive school being aware of the dangers of educational and social segregation. Notwithstanding this, the memorandum complained, the Labour government had failed to implement Conference policy, preferring to administer a scheme developed under a Conservative minister.

The 1949 memorandum made the basis of the NALT's opposition to the Minister clear. Essentially its case was that he had sabotaged the development of the comprehensive school by defending tripartism despite the Labour Party's policy in favour of the former and against the latter.

In the face of this and other criticisms, Tomlinson decided that he must defend himself. In a memorandum to the Home Policy Committee of the Labour Party in July 1950 he defended the policy he had put forward in Ministry Circulars but insisted that he had rejected those LEA development plans which envisaged a comprehensive reorganisation only when he considered that they were not consistent with sound educational principles. He did not accept, he said, that the tripartite system was necessarily pernicious. It would only be so, he said, if the system permanently segregated one social class from another. He expressed fears for the future of bright children in any reorganisation, believing that it was 'foolish to ignore the consequences of neglecting those needs'. As a final justification, he argued that the controversy surrounding

comprehensive schools in educational circles would mean that a reorganisation 'would alienate a large, vocal and influential section of opinion'.

War had raged in the Labour Party over this issue for four post-war years but
outside of parliament the footsoldiers of the comprehensive school movement
had started marching in the opposite direction.

But outside, a movement away from the comprehensive idea

In the year following the conclusion of the war there was a discernible
movement by teacher organisations away from the concept of multilateralism.
Those organisations which had helped pioneer the multilateral idea in the
1920s and 1930s cooled in their enthusiasm following the passage of the 1944
Act. Indeed the idea of common schooling no longer appeared to be anywhere
on the teacher unions' agenda. This movement was particularly obvious among
grammar school teachers who perhaps thought that the promised equality of
status for other types of secondary schools would lower their own status. The
view of many grammar school teachers was given expression in an article by
Eric James, High Master of Manchester Grammar School, who argued that the
common school would inevitably produce 'grave social, educational and
cultural evils' and 'may well be a national disaster' (*Times Educational
Supplement*, 1 February 1947). The same author claimed, in a book published
two years later, that such schools would lead to 'a narrowing and impoverish-
ment of the whole content of education' (James, 1949).

Of perhaps greater significance is the fact that the National Union of Teachers
(NUT) Conference in 1948 heavily defeated a motion opposing tripartism. The
20 years since the publication of *The Hadow Report and After* had seen a
complete turnaround in the NUT position.

The first comprehensive schools

It is paradoxical that the first comprehensive schools should have been
established in this politically fluid period and ironic that some of the pioneer
authorities should have been Conservative controlled. Immediately LEAs had
been asked to produce development plans for a secondary education system
in their areas, some set about producing plans for comprehensive education.
The London School Plan, adopted by the London County Council in 1947,
envisaged the establishment of 103 comprehensive schools. Coventry, which
had been extensively bomb-damaged during the war, planned for comprehensive schools to cater for 80 per cent of its pupils. The rural areas of
Westmorland, Anglesey and the Isle of Man planned similar reorganisation, as
did the county boroughs of Southend, Oldham, Bradford and Bolton and the
counties of West Riding and Middlesex.

The plans for reorganisation in Middlesex were rejected by the Ministry, which allowed only a limited experiment with the establishment of two 'comprehensive' schools. The London Plan was similarly rejected as was the plan by the West Riding. The development of new types of secondary school did occur, however, in Anglesey and the Isle of Man (which was not, in any case, subject to control by the United Kingdom Parliament). Indeed, in areas of scattered population, comprehensive schooling was accepted by both major political parties as a desirable solution. The London County Council was allowed to establish five experimental 'interim' comprehensive schools by merging selective central schools with modern schools but was prevented from absorbing any grammar schools into comprehensive schools.

The development, then, was severely limited by the Ministry during this period but the seeds of comprehensive education were sewn.

Education and society: 1951–64

If the policy discussion during the tenure of two post-war Labour governments was about the acceptability of tripartite schooling, the preoccupations of the 1951 Conservative administration were to prove strikingly different.

The squeeze on education spending

One of the proud boasts of the incoming government was that it would build more houses than its Labour predecessors. The previous Conservative Party Conference had, much to the consternation of the platform, committed this government to a target of 300 000 houses per annum and the new Minister of Housing, Harold Macmillan, was – with the support of Churchill – determined to give the party what it wanted. To pay for this promise, education, like health, was to be squeezed.

On appointment, Butler, now Chancellor of the Exchequer, was to declare a moratorium on school building which, given that precious little building had occurred during the late 1940s, was to have serious implications. More than this, Florence Horsburgh at the Ministry of Education was to spend the next three years fighting against Treasury proposals to raise the age of school entry from five years to six years and to pull the school leaving age back to fourteen. Other Treasury ideas included the reintroduction of fees for state schooling and the levying of a charge for those pupils who stayed on beyond the statutory leaving age. Despite having been the author of expansionary education legislation, Butler argued: 'We must think in terms of major changes in policy as well as constant pruning' (Simon, 1991, p.164). The stranglehold on education was to be relaxed only on the succession of Sir David Eccles to Horsburgh's post in 1954.

Expansion replaces squeeze

Eccles took over the Ministry of Education a year before a general election. In that context, he made clear to the Cabinet that it could no longer thrive politically if it failed to invest in education. More than any other education minister since the war, he understood that educational expenditure was investment in the economy. Accordingly he told Eden, who became Prime Minister shortly after his own appointment, that he intended to breathe life into the Butler Act. This was to be the beginning of what Simon analyses as the 'educational break-out' (Simon, 1991) which was to reach its zenith with the Robbins expansion of higher education. As a result, expenditure rose significantly and school building, delayed for so long, proceeded apace. This allowed new schools to be opened to deal with the post-war baby boomers and to get rid of the all-through schools that had been the legacy of the inter-war system. Between 1954–63 over two thousand new schools were built.

Throughout the 1950s and into the 1960s, a variety of factors were to play a part in moulding governments' education policy. Changed attitudes, together with information yielded by research, Britain's economic position and public pressure, worked to create a consensus for changes in education of significant scale. This is nowhere more obvious than in relation to secondary education where the campaign for comprehensive schools gathered momentum between the mid 1950s and mid 1960s.

Comprehensive schooling: the continuing debate in the Labour Party

As seems usually to be the case, the Labour Party was a more unified force early in opposition than it had been in government. The trend set by the growing number of pro-comprehensive delegates at the annual conference was confirmed in 1951 by the publication of the document, *A Policy for Secondary Education* (Labour Party, 1951), which sought to commit the Labour Party to a policy of comprehensive reorganisation. This pledge was reinforced by a statement in favour of comprehensivisation at the 1952 Conference by the NEC spokesperson, Alice Bacon, who, nevertheless, warned Conference that the chances of such a reorganisation were diminishing as the tripartite system became further established. She urged Labour-controlled LEAs to take note of Conference decisions, remarking that many had accepted the tripartite system because they saw it as having been encouraged by a Labour government. The NEC, anxious to generate momentum on the issue, set up a social services sub-committee to review the structure of education which reported in 1953.

The conclusions of the sub-committee, substantially accepted by the NEC, were published in a document entitled *Challenge to Britain* (Labour Party, 1953). The section on comprehensive secondary education attacked the 11-plus selection procedure on the grounds that it labelled children at an early age as belonging to different intellectual 'types' and segregated them accordingly. This separation had a tendency to be permanent as transfers from modern schools to grammar schools were usually hindered by curriculum differences. In contrast, the comprehensive school was portrayed in the report as delaying rather than eliminating selection, as offering *all* children education in *one* school in the studies to which they were most fitted. Any early judgements concerning the child's ability and aptitude would, the argument ran, be subject to regular review in the comprehensive school, arrangements being sufficiently flexible that they could easily be altered.

Hard on the heels of commitments to comprehensive education made by the Labour Party Conferences in 1952 and 1953 followed a concern in certain sections of the party about how to present the policy to the electorate and how to implement it when the Labour Party was returned to government. Margaret Cole, in a memorandum from the party's Advisory Committee on Education, highlighted the need to ensure party unity on the issue before presenting Labour's plans to the electorate. Such internal unity was necessary, she argued, to persuade reluctant LEAs to implement a comprehensive policy when the Labour Party returned to power because 'it is no part of Labour's intention to force LEAs to embark on new experiments' (cited in Parkinson, 1970). In expressing this view, she opened a debate within the party about the use of legislation in introducing the comprehensive policy which was to continue over the next two decades. The NALT and the publicity and policy sub-committee of the Labour Party disagreed with Cole's arguments, claiming that if the policy was to be implemented successfully at a national level, then Labour would have, sooner or later, to introduce legislation obliging LEAs to carry out a comprehensive reorganisation.

This debate continued. In 1955 a study group on education was established and the discussion was enlivened in May 1957 by a memorandum to the group from Michael Stewart MP, a future, if short-lived, Education Secretary. The memorandum argued that the Labour Party would have to mount a campaign of explanation and propaganda on the issue of comprehensive education if a future Labour government were to have enough support to implement such a policy. This process should start, he argued, by collecting information from local Labour groups and Labour-controlled LEAs on how to implement their plans for comprehensive schools locally. The substantive claim of the memorandum was supported by an opinion poll in 1957 which showed widespread ignorance of the issue of comprehensive education among the public and little opposition to segregation (Parkinson, 1970; Bellaby, 1977; Reynolds and Sullivan, 1987).

These findings appeared to affect the views of the Labour Party concerning the type of propaganda which might be used in a political campaign to promote comprehensive education. The study group working on this question argued that the appeal of the comprehensive school lay in emphasising the educational benefit which would be derived from it by children who failed to

134   *The development of the British welfare state*

gain grammar school places. That is to say, it came to the conclusion that the comprehensive school should be presented as a 'grammar school for all' if the policy were to be electorally attractive, a conclusion not lost on the future leader of the party, Harold Wilson, as we shall see below.

At the end of 1957 the study group reported and pinpointed a number of ambiguities in Labour's previous statements on secondary education. The two main areas highlighted were, first, the reluctance of the party to pose comprehensive education as entailing the disappearance of the grammar school and, second, the party's ambiguous stance on the use of legislation to introduce the policy when it returned to government. The study group report argued that Labour could not continue to avoid the issue of the dissolution of the grammar school in its presentation of the comprehensive idea but it was unable to come to any recommendations concerning the question of whether the comprehensive policy should be implemented by legislation or by co-operation with LEAs.

A further memorandum that year outlined the advantages and disadvantages of legislation. Legislation, it argued, would be an advantage in that it would enable a Labour government to make firm the basis of the comprehensive system during one term of office. On the other hand, the memorandum suggested, a major disadvantage would be that a future Labour government could be accused of interfering with the autonomy of the LEAs – an autonomy which was very closely guarded by local authorities.

During the mid and late 1950s the Parliamentary leadership appeared to lead a retreat from the support for comprehensive education offered earlier by the party. It was reported that not all of the leadership were convinced that the orthodox, 'all through' school was the answer to the problem of secondary education reorganisation. In fact, Hugh Gaitskell, the Labour leader, seemed to be among the doubters. In a public speech in 1958, he argued that the term 'comprehensive' did not mean that all children should attend the same kind of huge, impersonal school; instead, it meant 'something simpler than that, that we abandon the idea of permanent segregation' (cited in Williams, 1979, p. 466).

The core of Gaitskell's argument was that the abolition of permanent selection alone would lead to the creation of an educationally-sound and socially-just system of secondary education. Beyond this many arrangements seemed permissible. Strangely, the 1958 Conference did not object to the sentiments expressed in the speech (Craig, 1982).

In 1959 Roy Jenkins argued for the retention of the 'good, established grammar school' to act as a bridge between the state sector and the private sector (Jenkins, 1959). In his scheme, comprehensive schools would play only a limited role, being created where new schools were to be built or where reorganisation was necessary for any other reason. Such a view was supported by Emmanuel Shinwell who criticised the Labour Party for sacrificing the grammar school, which gave many working class children an opportunity for advancement, while it feared to intervene more widely in secondary education by opposing the continued existence of the public school sector (Parkinson, 1970; Reynolds and Sullivan, 1987).

This seeming revision of the policy by leading members of the party once more caused disarray. However, the document *Learning to Live* published in 1958 appears to suggest that the leadership's view had gained ascendancy in the party discussions over the form of comprehensive education (Labour Party, 1958). While the document repeated Labour's commitment to comprehensive education, it included an explicit commitment not to use legislation to reorganise secondary education and, although it remained ambivalent on the question of the future of the grammar school, it seemed to be presenting the comprehensive school as an institution that would replicate the important features and traditions of the grammar school and would be, in Gaitskell's phrase, a grammar school for all. It was on this sort of conception of comprehensive education, related to an emphasis on the wastage of talent in the tripartite system, that Harold Wilson, the new leader of the Labour Party, was to advocate comprehensive reform in his famous 'Science and Socialism' speech to the 1963 Party Conference (Craig, 1982).

The Labour left resurgent or . . . ?

How then do we explain Labour's approach to the comprehensive school policy throughout the 1950s and into the 1960s. After all, the acceptance of one kind of comprehensive school policy or another marked the period, whereas the Labour governments following the war set their face against such a partisan stance. And the policy appears to have moved from being the political property of the left to become, by the early 1960s, the common-sense of all sections of the party. One of the explanations available suggests that the apparent policy turn around can be understood in terms of a resurgence of the left in the party during the 1950s. Such an argument runs thus. Labour, in the early 1950s, as in the early 1980s, became not a party hedged in by the realities of government but a party which returned to its radical roots. The consolidationists within the party were weary people unprepared for, or at least incapable of, success in a political fight with the left. Moreover, Labour was clearly more prone to the adoption of left-wing policy stances when it was out of government given the Annual Conference's higher profile as a policy-making forum when Labour is in opposition (Minkin, 1980). In such circumstances the dead hand of the party leadership is lifted and the locus of power shifts, if not to rank-and-file members, closer to the Annual Conference. More than this, or so the argument goes, left-wingers of some political substance engaged for the first time in the battle over education policy.

On the surface, this is not entirely implausible. It is certainly the case that internal Labour Party documents promoting the comprehensive school policy became more convincing, less reliant on rhetoric and better constructed than had previously been the case. Following the rather unspecific policy statement in favour of the comprehensive school at the 1951 Annual Conference and an ambiguous and contentious presentation of the policy in *Challenge to Britain* (1953) (see above), three middle-range Labour parliamentarians reported to the social services subcommittee of the NEC. The report, written by Alice Bacon, Richard Crossman and Peggy Herbison was, among other things, a reasoned left-wing case for comprehensivisation.

In the first place, Labour's handling of the issue of secondary education since the war was attacked as socially conservative in its orientation:

> Neither in Let Us Face the Future nor in the 1950 or 1951 programmes did the Party put forward any challenging policy for education. Indeed, it seemed to be assumed that the application of the 1944 Act would be a sufficient task for the Labour Government. (Labour Party Social Services Subcommittee, 1953)

It went on to argue that deficiencies in that strategy had become clear and that the tripartite organisation of secondary education had not worked. The argument contained in the document proceeded as follows:

> By now deficiencies, not only for a socialist but for a democrat, have become clear. The Act, as administered, has not achieved the expected progress towards the ideal of ensuring that every child, irrespective of class or family income, should have an equal chance to develop his or her talents.

> . . . the examination to which every child is subjected at eleven plus creams off an elite for the grammar schools and leaves those who go to the modern schools with a false, but nonetheless deadening, sense of failure.

> The next Labour Government must come to grips with these problems. Not only does socialist principle demand it, a policy which showed how to do away with the gross inequality of the present system could win a great deal of popularity. (Labour Party Social Services Subcommittee, 1953)

Though written in a style reminiscent of declamations to the Soviet Politburo, the memorandum contained, perhaps for the first time, an attempt to link socialist principle with empirical concerns about whether selective schooling was efficacious. For the authors went on to say ' . . . such a policy is also essential if we are to *increase our productivity* and carry out the five year plan to make Britain pay her way' (emphasis added).

Here, then, were *parliamentary* representatives of the left widening the appeal of earlier left-wing calls for comprehensive education. Those earlier petitions were almost exclusively couched in the language of the equality. This one linked concerns with social and educational equality with apparently hard-headed concerns about the effect of talent wastage on the national economy. If the left was resurgent, then its approach on this particular issue was aimed to chime in with the political sentiments of a wider constituency in the party and in the polity. Its success was that it not only satisfied left wingers in the party but also developed arguments consistent with a redefinition of Labour Party socialism (or social democracy) occurring during these years.

. . . A redefinition of social democracy?

The elevation of the comprehensive school policy from the status of a rather embarrassing item on the policy agenda of the Annual Conference, to that of more or less common property of the party from Westminster to Blackpool also seems to have coincided with, and to have been in no small part influenced by, the wider redefinition of social democracy occurring within the party. This ideological revision was an attempt by centrist supporters of the Chancellor, later to become leader, Gaitskell, to redefine Labour's principles in a way attractive to the electorate. It was also, as was made abundantly clear, an attempt to modernise the party, to ditch allegedly redundant ideological baggage and to wrench the party out of the reach of the Bevanite left. The ideologue of this movement in the mid to late 1950s was, of course, Crosland (Crosland, 1956). The principles on which this redefined social democracy were based have been discussed in Chapter 3. We underline here those elements of the Crosland thesis that have a direct bearing on the comprehensive school issue.

Labour's concerns, according to Crosland and the group around Gaitskell, should, as we have seen, move from concern with nationalisation to concern with the creation of equality through the operation of the welfare state, should be less with production and more with consumption (Lipsey and Leonard, 1981, pp. 10, 24). It is in this respect that Crosland's views and his later activities as a government minister had the most direct impact on the comprehensive policy issue. His clear belief was that governments should use social expenditure and other means at their disposal to *modify* inequalities and injustices associated with a market system of distribution (Crosland, 1956). In education the aim must be, or so Crosland thought, to create as much equality as possible through the creation of a non-selective secondary school system.

In the political context in which it was made, Crosland's reformulation of the ends and means of social democracy clarified, and to some extent changed, the direction of the Labour Party's social politics. It certainly had an effect on both strategy and policy in the Labour Party. From the mid-1950s until the untimely death of the Labour leader Gaitskell in 1962, the leadership of the party adopted a policy position which, while resisting the direction prescribed by the Labour left, appeared progressive and pro-active. It appeared progressive because it was concerned, albeit using a somewhat different definitional yardstick, with issues of equality, as were the policy positions of the left. It was proactive because apparently egalitarian policies were developed from the centre rather than the centre reacting to developments from the left of the party, as had often been the case.

In this progressive and proactive social democracy, the idea of comprehensive schools had a significant part to play. For Crosland himself, the attraction of ridding the country of the selective secondary education system was clear. The establishment of a comprehensive system of education would remove once and for all educational selection, which tended to confirm social class and social status positions. Comprehensive schools, in his view, would postpone rather than remove academic selection but the postponement would allow for children to be rigorously assessed over a considerable period of time rather than once and for all at age 11 (Crosland, 1956).

Giles Radice, one of Labour's shadow education ministers in the 1980s but, during the mid to late 1950s, a researcher for a trade union, an active Fabian and seeking a Labour parliamentary seat, remembers further significance being endowed to the comprehensive school principle during these years. That significance was, he believes, that it played a central role in 'the redefinition of socialism that occurs in each decade in the Labour Party' (Radice, 1991) rather than simply being a reflection of it:

> There were a number of influences . . . that seemed to point towards comprehensive education, particularly at the time when you were trying to redefine socialism as not about ownership but as about changing or getting rid of the inequalities . . . what was Crosland's phrase . . . getting rid of the factor which divided people. I mean The Future of Socialism, if you remember, was about comprehensive education. And he'd gone to the United States and Sweden for his research and so those of us who were revisionists in the party also looked to comprehensive education as a sort of alternative to public ownership. So it had some ideological importance. (Radice, 1991)

The Future of Socialism was not simply about comprehensive education, of course. The point that this former Crosland supporter is struggling towards is, however, a substantial one. The social democrats, along with sections of the party left, had, in the 1940s, looked to a mixture of nationalisation, municipalism and welfare as the way forward to a New Jerusalem. However, or so it seems, the reformation of social democracy, particularly under Gaitskell's political leadership and Crosland's intellectual influence, was so immense that the route maps to the New Jerusalem would need to be thrown away and replaced by new maps to a different destination. That destination was, of course, a political philosophy and a set of political actions which focused on the consumer rather than the producer. Labour's consumer socialism was to supplant the producer socialism of the earlier years. It was to focus on the achievement of a modicum of equality rather than on replacing private with public property. It was to be as concerned with the effect of policies on the consumers of services as it was with the conditions in which goods and services were produced. Consequently, the replacement of private ownership of the means of production in post-capitalist society was seen as irrelevant unless it was responsive to consumer need. For the new social democrats, the idea of further nationalisation, that might simply replace inefficient private management with a similarly inefficient public management structure, should be consigned to the dustbin of political history where they believed it belonged.

Much more important were those welfare policies, made possible by economic growth, that would transform the nature of relationships between social classes and individuals. Here the hope was that a system of comprehensive education, in which the children of the coal miner and the cabinet minister attended the same school, might facilitate the greater social equality sought by Gaitskellites and Croslandites (a consideration which appears lost on the present leader of Her Majesty's Opposition). That it might do so in the context of equalising educational opportunity as well as social mixing was an equally important consideration (Crosland, 1956, 1974).

This is what I think Prentice, a Labour Secretary of State for Education in the 1970s, was aiming at in an interview given to the author in 1991:

> *There was always an argument around 1950 as to whether the Labour Party should be going for another big advance to socialism or a consolidation period. Gaitskell argued, as I myself and other people on his wing of the party did, that we were in favour of socialism. By socialism I mean a society with more equality and more co-operation between people, but I don't necessarily mean wholesale nationalisation and all that. But translating actual policies . . . one of the tools for creating the egalitarian society is to change the education system. There are sound educational reasons for doing it. There are also social reasons. But dividing children up the way we did at the 11 plus was both unfair and socially divisive. It was wrong and I think that he felt a need . . . and there was a clear political need for his supporters to show that they had socialist ideas and socialist policies that were as good as, though different from, the traditional left.*

This short excerpt is, I think, fascinating. Prentice was, by the early 1950s, already a 'back room boy' for the Gaitskell campaign to replace Attlee as leader of the Labour Party when the latter decided to retire.

His recollections are that, at the beginning of the period we are concerned with here, the major internal political divide in the party was between those on the left, like Bevan, who wished to construct a radical programme for the short-lived 1950 Labour government and a group of consolidationist senior ministers. In essence, both of these aspirations were in part pragmatic responses to the small majority gained by Labour in the 1950 election as well as revealing the political orientations of the different factions. As many political commentaries and biographies of the period show, the left were convinced that a 'socialist programme' – by which they meant something akin in its impact to the 1945 programme – would attract the electorate to Labour and ensure a comfortable majority when Attlee decided to call a further general election. The consolidationists, on the other hand, were equally firm in their belief that the electoral popularity of the party would be enhanced if Labour simply got on with administering the raft of legislation it had enacted between 1945 and 1950.

As we know, the consolidationists won the day in Cabinet and in the NEC and 18 months after the 1950 election Attlee called for a mandate from the people which they disobligingly refused to give him.

What Prentice appears to be suggesting is, of course, entirely consistent with Radice's view but it rounds it out. In the years following Labour's defeat in 1951, the political constellation of the party appears to have changed. While the left in the party, and particularly the Bevanites, stressed the importance of producer socialism, the social democrats around Gaitskell moved away from an emphasis on consolidation. As a consequence, that battle for the soul of the Labour Party (and, of course, for its leadership) developed into a contest between the traditional left, represented in Parliament by the likes of Bevan, Crossman, Driberg and Castle, and a reformed social democracy. This social democratic approach appears to have taken as its own the political language of the left, while massively differentiating its policy stances from both the left and the old consolidationist wing of the party. Its adoption of the comprehensive school principle had both philosophical advantages. As suggested earlier, it offered a new way, in Britain at least, of looking at the nature of the socialist enterprise. Its practical attractions included the one acutely observed by Prentice; namely, that it provided the Gaitskellites with a distinctive policy slant which allowed them to display their supposed socialist credentials while distancing them from the left.

To understand the role which the comprehensive school policy played for the Gaitskell group it is necessary to understand the theoretical underpinning of Labour social democrats' approach to social policy issues. Part of that underpinning paradigm has been outlined above. Crosland's manifesto for social democracy was, however, a reworking and adaptation of Marshall's understanding of the role of social policy in capitalist society. In his inaugural lecture at Cambridge in 1950, Professor T. H. Marshall had attempted to analyse the nature of citizenship in Britain (Marshall, 1963). He had concluded that citizenship rights had been extended in Britain, first by the addition of civil rights to the population, then by the granting of political rights and then, during the twentieth century, by the enhancement of social rights. These latter rights included the right to a modicum of financial security and access to a number of services in cash or kind which improved citizens' social security (for a detailed discussion of the significance of Marshall's analysis to the understanding of social policy development, see Sullivan, 1987, 1992).

Marshall had also drawn his audience's attention to the relationship between these extensions of citizen rights and the development of capitalism. He had concluded that social rights, like civil and political rights before them, were complementary to the development and maintenance of capitalist organisation. They were so because they made their recipients stake-holders in the form of social and political organisation from which these rights had emerged.

Though social rights, when added to the other rights, were intended to lead to a sort of equality, it was an equality of regard between citizens rather than an equality of condition.

Crosland's reworking of Marshall led him, as we have already seen, and the Gaitskellites to an appreciation of social policy as a means of stabilising a sort of humane capitalism – though Crosland, of course, preferred to see it as post-capitalism. And it is in this respect that we can fully recognise the phenomenon that Radice sees as a redefinition of socialism and Prentice regards as 'socialist ideas and socialist policies that were as good as, though different from the traditional left'. In truth, this was the zenith of the Labour establishment's embrace of post-war British capitalism.

This redefinition of socialism, and the theoretical rationale underpinning it, clearly had effects on the way in which the party saw the issue of comprehensive education. Radice and Prentice have implied as much but have glossed over the transformation of the policy occasioned by its adoption by the social democrats. The left, it will be remembered, were concerned that it act as a sort of equality machine, facilitating equality of educational and social outcome, inasmuch as that was possible. The new social democracy appeared to have regarded it as a vehicle which would enhance the chances of equality of opportunity. That much we already know. It became clear, however, that in its journey from the left to the centre of the party even more ideological baggage had been sloughed off.

As we have seen, by 1956, an NEC committee could argue:

> *To abolish selective education immediately would cause confusion in many areas where no provision has been made for such a measure. Labour Ministers should be prepared to use compulsion to secure the abolition of the 11-plus. But at this stage it might not be necessary to insist that any consequential reorganisation must be on comprehensive lines. We should merely reaffirm that Labour will make available to LEAs the best advice concerning the possibilities of each method of organisation. (Labour Party Policy and Publicity Subcommittee, 1956)*

Equality of educational opportunity, then, is seen as achievable through the abolition of the 11-plus examination. Implicit here is an acceptance that the schools emerging from the implementation of such a policy would be multilateral rather than comprehensive in the sense understood by the policy's early advocates. That is to say, in this advice at least, there appears to be a preparedness to see the continuation of selective schooling under one roof, with schools having grammar school, modern school and technical school sides. The advantages over the system extant at the time would simply be that allocation to one side or another would be dependent on long-term assessment rather than the sudden-death method of the 11-plus and that, in theory at least, transfer from one 'side' to another would prove easier than transfer between different schools. Of course, the advice also reinforced a view held by the Labour policy establishment since the mid 1940s: that progress to educational reform could be by consent only. Local authorities would set the pace and the agenda in any future implementation of policy.

In itself, however, neither this redefinition of the goals of Labour politics, nor the policy proposals that stemmed from it (ranging from the policy under consideration, through the support for public control rather than ownership of key industries, to the attempt to remove Clause 4 from the Labour Party Constitution), are likely to have been enough to get the comprehensive school policy from the policy agenda to the point of implementation. Internecine warfare, particularly, though not exclusively, at the Annual Conference, appears to have led electors to question the reality of political reorientation in the party (Morgan, 1990). In 1959, at least, electors seemed to regard as more credible Macmillan's claim that they had never had it so good. Other factors appear to have helped the process along.

Evidence from sociological and psychological research studies

Throughout the 1950s, evidence was emerging which suggested that tripartite secondary education was flawed. The work of Halsey and Gardner (1953) and Floud (1957) demonstrated that children of manual workers who possessed 'grammar school ability', according to the criteria currently used, were under-represented in grammar schools and that the children of middle class parents were over-represented. The National Foundation for Educational Research (NFER) claimed in 1958 that even the best available tests which sought to measure academic ability at the age of 11 could not eliminate a 10 per cent margin of error in the selection of children to one or other type of secondary school. The Crowther Report (HMSO, 1959) published results of a survey carried out among recruits to the Armed Services. These results showed that a substantial number of the sons of manual workers in their sample had been wrongly placed at the secondary school stage. These findings suggested, then, that 'intelligence tests' used to sort out the academic sheep from the non-academic goats were massively unequal to the task.

Moreover, further evidence was becoming available at this time which questioned the theory on which the intelligence test rested. Vernon (1957) questioned the extent to which intelligence, as measured in the intelligence test, was an inherited characteristic and Bernstein (1959, 1960, 1961) suggested that poor academic performance of working class children might reflect a lack of knowledge of the formal language used in conceptual frameworks but not used in the public language of the home. Douglas (1964) presented a framework to explain how an 'interlocking network of inequalities operated to the detriment of working class children' in terms of educational achievement.

The rationale and operation of the tripartite system was thrown into question by these and other findings. In effect, according to Halsey, a rapidly expanding technical economy was being ill-served by a system of secondary education which functioned to confirm social status (already privileged middle class children were associated with the grammar school) rather than to generate much-needed talent and to even out differences in social status (Floud *et al.*, 1956).

Changes in the schools and changing attitudes among parents

The ground upon which the tripartite system stood was further shaken during the late 1950s both by internal developments and by the changing attitudes of a vocal section of the population to the organisation and operation of secondary education.

One of the fundamental arguments used by the earlier architects of the tripartite system was that some children were capable of the abstract conceptualisation necessary if they were to benefit from an academic education while others did not possess such capabilities. However, in the late 1950s, changes occurred in the curriculum and examination policy of grammar and secondary modern schools which made a nonsense of this already discredited distinction. Firstly, as the children of the first post-war 'baby boom' achieved secondary school age a smaller proportion of the 11-year-old population gained grammar school places (as no extra provision had been made). This resulted in modern schools receiving children from a wider section of the ability range – as defined by performance on intelligence tests – than had hitherto been the case. Many modern schools responded to this change by developing a more academic curriculum for some of their pupils and entering growing numbers of pupils for GCE 'O' level examinations. Thus the conceptual framework of the tripartite system was challenged, as it was by a broadening of the curriculum to allow more vocational subjects to be taught in grammar schools (Reynolds and Sullivan, 1987).

Running parallel to these changes, and apparently resulting from the broader social class composition of the modern schools, there evolved pressure, largely from middle class parents, against the selective system. This pressure reflected the hitherto unknown failure of access of considerable numbers of middle class children to the grammar school. That pressure was felt not only by the government of the time but by Labour MPs. And it seems to have made a lasting impression. James Callaghan, who was to become Prime Minister in the late 1970s, recounts the views of his Cardiff constituents at the time:

> The parents began to get quite agitated about the 11-plus and there was a feeling that the 11-plus was really a handicap and I can't go further than that. But it was a strong feeling that came together with the views of what you call the equality of opportunity strand in the party to fuse into a view that something could and must be done. This wasn't helped by the local authorities. You mustn't neglect the strength of the local authorities. We had a large number of Labour authorities, very proud of their schools,

very proud of their grammar schools. You can sum up the argument by saying that on the one side [the parents] there was talk, and it was very controversial talk, of class distinction in the grammar school and the other side [including some Labour LEAs] it was of mass production in large educational factories of two thousand children and all this . . .

In further conversation, Callaghan clarified the issues raised here. His argument was that, in the period to which he was referring (roughly 1957–9), a number of issues coalesced to convince even the sceptics in the party of the need for educational reorganisation. First, there was the research evidence about the injustice and inefficiency of the selective system. Second, there was the ideological shift in the party itself. Then there were the concerns expressed by industrialists about the inappropriate nature of British education. Of prime importance in shifting the issue up the policy agenda at this time was – at least in Callaghan's view – the expressed perceptions of parents.

Prentice, who was to become a minister of state at the Department of Education and Science (DES) in 1964, and was, by the end of the 1950s, a firm Gaitskell supporter, though more cautious, makes the same points:

Yes, you see, we were keen to catch an issue with popular support. We believed in the comprehensive school, of course, but here was an issue that could become an electoral asset. The Tories had refused to increase grammar school places even though the post war baby boom was 11 in the late fifties. There were some very angry parents. And the more articulate ones got in with CASE and other pressure groups and I remember the party being deluged by delegations from here and delegations from there. If there was any doubt about the policy, that would have settled it. And the beauty of it was of course that it fitted in with our new ideas about socialism. (Personal communication)

Another dimension to our understanding of parent pressure is provided by Lord Glenamara who, as Ted Short, was Wilson's first Secretary of State at the DES. Throughout the mid to late 1950s, he had carried out a watching brief for the NEC on the comprehensive school issue. Glenamara's firm memory is that the social composition of the movement pressing for change was of crucial importance in moving comprehensive schooling to near the top of the policy agenda:

Historians and the like make the mistake of seeing the pressure from parents as a middle class thing. It wasn't only that, you know. In some parts of the country, you didn't stand a chance of getting to grammar school if you were from an ordinary family. That was the turning point for the comprehensive school policy. An opinion poll I had done for the party in 1957 showed that the grammar school was very unpopular with many of our traditional supporters as well as with the articulate middle class parent. That, I think, really settled it. (Personal communication)

So Glenamara is clear that the coalition in support of educational change was one constituted of parents from all social classes.

The opinion poll to which he refers, however, suggested discontent with the relatively small proportion of children gaining grammar school places rather than support for common schooling.

Education and economy

As we have seen above, concerns emerged during the late 1950s and the early 1960s about the capacity of the selective system to produce the sort of technologically-flexible work force that would be necessary if Britain was to close the gap between herself and her industrial competitors. It will be remembered that industrialists were of the opinion that the grammar school tended to produce people with too abstract a turn of mind for this project; that the secondary modern schools were producing, on the whole, a labouring class rather than a cadre of technologically proficient workers, and that the small number of technical schools was unable to produce sufficient workers for the nation's industrial needs. Though there is relatively little evidence that this issue exercised the minds of the NEC, there is evidence from one of my respondents, and in the speeches of one who professed himself too forgetful to take part in the research, that this issue was of some concern to Labour's Cabinet in waiting in the late 1950s and early 1960s.

Prentice had entered Parliament in 1957 and had quickly been made Shadow Minister of Labour. He recalls his concerns thus:

> I became very interested in training policy, manpower policy. I didn't think the Government was solving those problems. I don't think that any government has solved those problems. It seemed to me that two things were clear. One was that the traditional education system – the 11-plus divide – often failed people of middle ability and the sort of people who would be good craftsmen, foremen, technicians. And our failure then, as now, was not having enough training for middle level manpower. And a comprehensive system ought to provide, if well organised, more scope for such people. Allied to that is another question and that is that the traditional grammar school was not necessarily the right place for the bright boy or girl who was a potential engineer. They would be channelled far too much into other subjects. (Personal communication)

Though there is little evidence that these concerns percolated as far as the Shadow Education Secretaries of the time, they were certainly at the top of the mind of the man who became leader of the Labour Party in 1963. The basis of Wilson's attack on the Conservatives was that they had mismanaged the economy and that as a consequence Britain's competitive position was parlous (Wilson, 1964). In order to kick-start economic growth there was, according to Wilson, an imperative need to modernise the economy. That modernisation process demanded, as did considerations of social and educational justice, that Britain's educational system be reorganised in order to produce personnel capable of 'stoking the white heat of the technological revolution'. Though persisting in describing comprehensive schools, as had Gaitskell, as 'grammar schools for all', the reorganisation of secondary education along comprehensive lines was among his priorities for government action (Crossman, 1975). So much so, that along with the creation of a technological higher education sector, it became the highest profile issue, save for economic mismanagement, in the 1964 election.

This much seems clear, however. Wilson's ideas, and those of his Shadow Education Secretary, were more closely akin to the principle of comprehensive education proposed in the Gaitskell years. His attachment to the grammar school, which had been his own route to Oxford, Labour politics and the premiership, made him instinctively reach out towards the Shinwell position. His political skill over this issue was to present grammar school education as something which would be available to all in comprehensive schools. Additionally, there appears to have been a genuine anticipation that a comprehensive system would contribute to the solution of Britain's modernisation problem. Alongside all this, Wilson's left-wing credentials, bogus though they may have been, and the obfuscation of political decisions in his marriage of socialism with science may well have given the appearance that Wilson, too, was concerned with the issues which preoccupied the left.

The period of Conservative Party government between 1951–64 saw, then, movement in the Labour Opposition towards full acceptance of the need for comprehensive reorganisation, though the concept of the comprehensive school appears to have undergone substantial redefinition by the Parliamentary leadership. At the same time the Conservative Party had sanctioned the establishment of comprehensive schools only in extraordinary circumstances and appears to have moved by the early 1960s to a position of hostility to the comprehensive school idea, seeing it as the product of socialist egalitarian ideology. Dissatisfaction with selection in secondary education had been aided in the late 1950s, however, by the publication of research findings which questioned the predictive accuracy of the intelligence test and also the notion of inherited general intelligence.

The attitude of the Conservative Party

If Labour had moved, sometimes painfully, to redefine socialism in a way that placed comprehensive education at the top of the agenda by the early 1960s, what about the Conservatives? During their 13 years in government between 1951–64 the Conservative Party seemed to move to a position of almost complete hostility to the idea of the comprehensive school. In the early years, Florence Horsburgh, the Minister of Education, was prepared to allow limited experiments with comprehensive schools but only if the LEA was to initiate the reorganisation. Such experiments were only allowed, however, if they took place within the context of a set of selective schools. Any proposals to merge a grammar school with other schools to form a comprehensive school were rejected. This policy continued when the first Conservative Minister, Florence Horsburgh, was succeeded by Sir David Eccles. His view was that it was impossible to enlarge the nation's 'grammar school stream' without changing the character of higher education and the grammar school. The solution to the increased demand and need for higher standards of secondary education was to be found, he believed, in the improvement of the modern schools and not in the reorganisation of the secondary school system.

The Conservatives repeatedly attacked the Labour Party's advocacy of the comprehensive school, claiming that it arose out of an ideological commitment to equalise life chances rather than from a consideration of educational arguments.

Though Eccles was succeeded in 1962 by Edward Boyle, who became an advocate of the comprehensive school, attitudes within the Conservative Party had hardened to such an extent that he seemed powerless to act against his colleagues.

Paradoxically, while the two major parties' positions on comprehensive education became increasingly polarised in Parliament, developments were taking place in some LEAs which ran contrary to the positions held by the parties nationally. Many Labour-controlled LEAs were reluctant even to seek permission to establish comprehensive schools and some Conservative authorities were in the vanguard of the development of the small number of such schools opened in this period. (The Leicestershire reorganisation – a pioneer reorganisation – was presided over by a Conservative County Council.)

Though the political battle continued to rage, the decade and a half before the publication of Circular 10/65 saw the generation of a great deal of evidence from government reports and independent research studies that the process of selection, which lay at the core of the tripartite system, was functioning to produce a wastage of talent and create inequality of educational opportunity.

In 1964, a Labour government was elected which was to develop and implement policy in this area. By this time pressure had mounted to such an extent that change seemed inevitable.

Reports and more reports

The late 1950s and early 1960s saw the publication of three government-sponsored reports on education, all of which were responded to by government with policy enactment and implementation. The first of these reports, the so-called Crowther Report, was published in 1959 (HMSO, 1959). It was concerned with the further education of school-leavers. To place this report in its context it is necessary to remember that the United Kingdom was already lagging behind most other European countries in terms of economic growth. The report's recommendations address themselves, therefore, to the solution of this problem as well as to the widening of access to education for this group of young people. Crowther came up with a 20-year development plan for intermediate technology that would include day-release and block-release schemes so that young people would be able to acquire further, usually vocational, qualifications and educational experience, even after they had started work. Though never fully implemented, Crowther schemes gave, and continue to give, many ordinary young working people access to tertiary level education.

The second of the reports, published in 1963, was the Newsom Report, *Half Our Future* (HMSO, 1963). It was concerned with children of lower-than-average ability between the ages of 13 and 16 years. The Newsom Committee believed that these children who represented 'half the pupils in secondary schools, half the citizens, workers, mothers and fathers of the future' were ill-served by the existing secondary school system. The collective result of the aggregate of individual educational disadvantage was that talent was lost to society and economy. The recommendations of this report included the raising of the school leaving age to 16 years, the adoption of teaching method and content that made these children's educational experience more relevant and accessible and the establishment of a working party to look at social problems in inner-city areas. The last of these was taken up by the establishment of the Plowden Committee while the other two recommendations were acted on – though in the case of ROSLA not for a further nine years. The third of this trilogy of reports was the Robbins Report, to which we now turn.

Expansion in higher education: the Robbins revolution

Pressure for changes at the school level fed into and was accompanied by pressure for change at the tertiary level of education. By 1960, the number of children remaining in school beyond the statutory leaving age had doubled compared with 1950 numbers (Lowe, 1988, p. 75). Those achieving two or more 'A' levels increased from around 25 000 in the mid 1950s to 64 000 by 1964 (*ibid*, p. 151) and the Macmillan government of the early 1960s came under increasing pressure to match the increase in sixth-form students with an increase in places available in higher education. It was in this context that the idea of reviewing the pattern of higher education was born and in February 1962 a review committee under Lionel Robbins was established. Robbins was the same Robbins who had worked for Beveridge at the LSE, had been one of the Keynesian economic advisers to the war-time government and who, since the war, had established friendships with Macmillan and Sir David Eccles, the latter of whom he had taught.

Robbins' job was to look at the current expansion in the higher education sector following the establishment of Colleges of Advanced Technology (CATs) in the late 1950s and the expansion of teacher training to deal with the demand presented by demographic factors. Having reviewed these phenomena, he was charged with making recommendations to government about long-term developments.

The timing of the committee's establishment was propitious and made it easier for Robbins to turn this rather pedestrian brief into a manifesto for expansion. There was strong pressure for expansion as a result of both demography and the additional numbers of children taking 'A' level examinations. More than this, there was a perception that Britain needed modernising emerging from both industry and the opposition parties. Finally, during the time in which the committee sat, the Leader of the Opposition, Harold Wilson, was allying Labour with the modernisation of British industry, a process that would demand the development of technology and which required increased numbers of graduates. As part of this technological drive Labour was planning 40 new universities.

Into this maelstrom of political activity, emerged the Robbins Report in October 1963. Its most important recommendation was that 'courses in higher education should be available to all those who are qualified by ability and attainment to pursue them and who wish to do so' (Robbins, 1963, p. 8). In effect, this was to mean two things. First, that all candidates with good enough 'A' level passes would be eligible (thus satisfying the ability criteria). Second, however, it meant that local authorities would be committed to funding all candidates accepted by higher education institutions. For the recommendations of the Anderson Committee that all students in higher education should be grant-aided had been implemented while the Robbins Committee was sitting.

The implications of the Robbins proposals were momentous. First, the report assumed a 50 per cent increase in the number of higher education students by 1967, turning into a 250 per cent rise by 1980. As the bulk of these were to be in universities, new universities would need to be built. As the need for technological development was recognised by the committee, the Colleges of Advanced Technology (CATs) were to be translated into universities.

On the day of the report's publication, the new Conservative Prime Minister, Sir Alec Douglas-Home, with an eye no doubt to the 1964 general election, took the unprecedented step of appearing on television and accepting it. In doing so, he committed governments to a 10-year programme costing £3.5 billion pounds – or just less than one-third of all public spending.

The 14th Earl, as Wilson sometimes mischievously called the Prime Minister, was in no position to implement Robbins, however. That was left to the Labour government that succeeded the Conservatives in 1964.

CHAPTER SIX

Education, retrenchment, privatisation and consumers

Chronology   **Education policy; the last thirty years**

1965   Circular 10/65 introduces comprehensive education as Labour government policy

1970   Conservative government issues Circular 10/70 rescinding Circular 10/65

1976   Education Act makes comprehensive reorganisation compulsory Prime Minister Callaghan initiates a 'great debate' on education following concerns about curriculum and standards

1980s   Increased emphasis on consumerism, standards and a move towards a national curriculum in schools

1988   Education Reform Act allows schools to opt out of local authority control and to become grant maintained. It also removes polytechnics from local authority control

1988–   Removal of the binary line
Student loans in higher education
Expansion of student numbers and cuts in funding

Throughout the 1960s and 1970s, education policy, like all other aspects of social policy, was to be affected by worsening economic conditions. It was also characterised, paradoxically, by growth as the new universities took root post-Robbins. Education, during these two decades specifically, also saw the consolidation of comprehensive schooling and disputes about its efficacy. The 1980s saw the development of policies of semi-privatisation and consumerism in education.

Education policy and the Labour governments: 1964–70

The Labour government and comprehensive education

In October 1964 a Labour government was elected with a majority of three seats over all other parties. Michael Stewart became Secretary of State for Education. In January 1965 he declared his intention to issue a Circular to initiate comprehensive reorganisation of the secondary education sector and was assisted in this development by one of his ministers of state, Reg (now Sir Reg) Prentice. In fact he was replaced as Secretary of State by Anthony Crosland in April 1965. Tony Crosland, who, as we have already seen, had become the ideologue of social democracy, was the youngest member of Wilson's Cabinet when he arrived at Curzon Street. The appointment of Crosland was inspired. His own work in *The Future of Socialism* and *The Conservative Enemy* marked him out as someone who understood the primacy of education in creating equality of opportunity. He was now charged with seeing through a reform aimed at just that and at modernising the economy and British industry.

In July 1965, after it had been redrafted following consultation with the LEAs and teacher organisations, Crosland issued Circular 10/65. The Circular made clear that it was the Government's intention 'to end selection at 11-plus and to eliminate separatism in secondary education'. Local authorities were requested to submit, within a year, plans for reorganisation along comprehensive lines. The Circular did not, however, lay down a single pattern of organisation. Instead, six different patterns – all of which were in operation in the areas which had comprehensive schools or were under discussion – were offered for consideration. Of these six patterns of organisation all but patterns 5 and 6 below were regarded by the Labour government as suitable permanent patterns for the organisation of comprehensive secondary schooling. The six suggested patterns of organisation were:

1. The single-tier or 'all through' school catering for all children from the ages of 11 to 18.
2. A two-tier system whereby all children were transferred from a lower school to an upper school at age 13 or 14 years.
3. A two-tier system comprising comprehensive schools for the age group 11–16 years with sixth form colleges offering education of the 16–18 age group. (It was envisaged that only a limited number of experiments would be allowed on this pattern.)
4. A two-tier system comprising a 'middle school' for all children aged 8–12 years (or 9–13 years) and an upper school for the age group 12 (or 13) to 18 years. (Again the utilisation of this pattern would be strictly limited.)
5. A two-tier system in which only those children who intended to sit public examinations transferred from junior to senior comprehensive school.

6. A two-tier system in which pupils were transferred at age 14 years from a junior comprehensive school to two types of senior school, one catering for those who did not wish to stay in school beyond the statutory school leaving age and another type for those who did.

Social reform by administrative circular

Two questions are prompted by the decision to introduce comprehensive education by circular. The first, and most obvious, is why did the Government embark on a non-legislative route in introducing comprehensive schooling as government policy? Second, why did the Circular allow for a wide variety of patterns of internal organisation for the new schools, some of which retained elements of academic selection?

The first question is quite important because, at first blush, the use of a Circular to initiate a major policy change was, up to 1965 at least, quite unusual. The establishment of compulsory secondary education had been seen to require the force of legislation. The revamping and extension, by Labour's post-war administration, of the Liberal social security measures – a process influenced to a massive extent by the Beveridge Report – Social Security and Allied Services (1942), had merited two government Acts. The implementation of Bevan's NHS plans had followed the passage of legislation through the House, as had the widening of access to higher education in the early 1960s. What then could account for the introduction of a major social policy change by Circular?

The second question which addresses the matter of the internal organisation of the new schools is no less pressing.

Numerous plausible solutions are provided in the literature to these puzzles. One argument is that the policy emerged via the Circular route because it did *not* represent a major policy change. The logic used here is that the comprehensive school reorganisation was merely an extension of the spirit of the 1944 Act rather than, in some ways, running counter to it. Indeed this is an explanation given some weight by Crosland in conversation with Professor Maurice Kogan (Kogan, 1971). Another suggestion, which appears to adopt the principle of prospective precedent, is that the introduction of major policy changes by Circular is not unusual. Witness, the argument goes, the use of Circular 10/70 by an incoming Conservative Secretary of State to reverse Labour's policy on comprehensive schooling. The most popular answer to our second question suggests that the multiplicity of comprehensive school models acceptable to the Secretary of State simply reflected the Government's commitment to local democracy and the appropriate functions of local government (see Crossman, 1975 as well as Crosland, 1974).

The need not to involve Cabinet

One possible explanation for taking the Circular route relates to constraints on Cabinet time. The preparation of legislation would have required a considerable amount of Cabinet consultation and the establishment of a Cabinet Committee to look at proposed legislation. Lord Callaghan, for instance, believes that Crosland 'was in part influenced by the full agenda for change already before Cabinet'. Similarly, Crosland's Minister of State understands, as a result of a conversation he had with Crosland at the time, that a Cabinet log-jam was part of the reason why legislation was not considered: 'Tony said that the PM had told him to get on with it' (Prentice, 1991).

No need to involve Cabinet

Another explanation might be that there was, indeed, no need to involve Cabinet and that, given this fact, the quickest and easiest way to proceed was by a Departmental Circular. This is clearly the view of one of the actors:

I think that Cabinet agendas are funny things. They will tend to concentrate on matters where Departments are divided or need reconciling one with another. Here was a policy that was really confined to the DES, the Welsh Office of course had to help in it, but the policy had been formed in the DES ... There were no other Departments really concerned except the Treasury over resources. But there was no need for the Cabinet to discuss it really. I mean, quite big policies, and this happens in all governments, go ahead if the policy is clear and accepted by the Minister in charge. No one has any complaints about the way he's carrying it out so it doesn't get on to the agenda. I mean when I was a member of cabinet in the seventies, I seem to recall, now this might not be literally true but its the way it seemed, that in the first few weeks that we were in government in 1974, the most common item on the Cabinet agenda was the future of the alkaline inspectorate. Because Michael Foot, as the new Employment Secretary was introducing the new health and safety legislation and the Department of Environment very much wanted to hold on to that inspectorate. So it kept cropping up. (Prentice, 1991)

So, for the Minister of State at the time, the issue did not become a legislative concern because it was uncontroversial; Cabinet was busy and did not need to spend time on it because they approved of the way it was being handled by the Secretary of State.

No legislative space

Put simply, the argument is that, given the slim majority held by the 1964 Government, it seemed inevitable that another general election would be called sooner rather than later. Though Labour ministers hoped that the timing of the election would be in their hands, there was no way of guaranteeing that this would be the case. On more than one occasion, and particularly when two Labour MPs looked set to oppose the Government's attempt to renationalise the steel industry, Labour looked like falling. The priority, therefore was to enact as much legislation as possible before a further election. This pressure was increased because the party had been out of government for 13 years and was faced with a stock-pile of policy commitments. In the then Chancellor of the Exchequer's words:

> When I think about it, we had a small political majority in 1964. We came back to power after 13 years in the wilderness. There were a lot of things that we wanted to do and the struggle to get a legislative slot in the first programme after you've won an election is as difficult as you can imagine. Every Minister has got his own pet project: its in the party manifesto; he's promised everybody everything, you see. And then when he gets back he's got to fight for time in whatever it is, 76 days of legislative time. The Chief Whip comes along and says 'Look here, do you realise you've got x days for this project and y days for the Opposition and you've only got 76 days. You can't get all of these Bills through'. Now Tony Crosland wanted to do something, and do something quickly. He could push out a Circular but he couldn't get legislative time against the other things we were doing. Big things, if you remember. My memory is that he said to himself 'that's the way I'll go'. (Callaghan, 1991)

This is a view with which Prentice concurs:

> . . . like most governments, we had too much legislation to get through and therefore the Leader of the House, the Chief Whip and so on would have argued strongly against finding room in the programme for a Bill of this kind. Though that's probably not the main reason. I don't think we were pressing for it. (Prentice, 1991)

This is almost certainly the case. One of Wilson's secretaries of state remembers talking to Michael Stewart (who had held the education brief fleetingly when Labour came to power in 1964) about this. He remembers conversations with Stewart about the issues involved if the 1944 Act was to be amended legislatively to allow comprehensivisation:

> I remember talking to Michael about this. He had thought about legislation and got the DES lawyers working on it. Their advice to him was that it would be impossible to amend the Act without a major rewrite. That would then mean that it was more likely to run into trouble at the Committee stage and to take even more time. He took the view that if it [the comprehensive school policy] was to be introduced quickly it meant abandoning the idea of legislation. (Glenamara, 1991)

On the face of it, then, whatever other factors may have been involved, the lack of legislative space argument seems to have some credibility. For most of this time, after all, Cabinet and Parliament were addressing industrial and economic issues seen as vital to the modernisation project and it may well have been seen as strategically more sensible to enact some sort of educational reform quickly, especially as it had figured so prominently at the time of the 1964 general election.

Central–local relations

One of the decisions implicit in implementing policy by Circular is the loss, by central government, of the power to compel. In this case, because a decision had been made to use the non-legislative route, the DES could only request that local authorities reorganise their secondary education and submit their plans to the Department. A key reason in opting for policy implementation by Circular seems to have been to do with the appropriate relationship between central and local government. Prentice puts it this way:

> Now I still personally took the view that we should have legislated, [a view, incidentally that Crosland regarded as 'empty toughness'] should have required them or at least have put require in the Circular. But of course the Permanent Secretary and others said that we couldn't require because we had no legislative clout. So the Circular gave a lead instead. If we gave a lead then we knew that a lot of authorities would follow it. Some sooner, some later. Even old-fashioned Labour authorities who were proud of their grammar schools would follow. They varied but they'd be inclined to respond to a Circular. (A) Because it was enshrined in a Conference decision and I think a lot of them still literally believed that the Conference made policy and that therefore they had to change for that reason. So, in other words we could make a lot of headway without actually compelling authorities who didn't want to move. (B) Because it was a Circular from their Government. (Prentice, 1991)

This sort of view is supported by Lord Callaghan: 'You see, we were very strong in local government and education had been seen as a matter for local government. It might have been very foolish to compel them' (Callaghan, 1991).

Concern about the respective roles of central and local government had been a feature of earlier discussions in the party on welfare state policies and, as a glance at undergraduate social policy texts will reveal, it has been a political problem that has dogged policy interventions in housing, social services as well as in education. It has, of course, been an issue at the centre of political disagreement between the Conservative governments and the Labour Party in recent years, particularly over the establishment of grant-maintained ('opted-out') schools, as well as over central government interference with local taxation (rate capping, charge capping and the like). The argument being promoted here is that it was politically expedient to observe the distinction between central and local government competencies. This was so not simply because such observation left intact a particular view of local democracy. It served other political purposes as well. That, at least, is the view of some of the political actors.

First, it sought to optimise the Government's political influence with Labour local authorities by stressing the necessity of partnership over this issue. Second, it appealed to party loyalty in implementing a policy that was unpalatable to some Labour authorities – it was a circular from their government. Third, it appealed to a, by then, mythical view of the power and role of Annual Conference. In Prentice's estimation, implementation by Circular was bolstered by the belief of many Labour councils that Conference and Conference alone determined policy.

A politically prudent attention to the relations between central and local government seems to have played some part in the decision to take a non-legislative route over this issue.

The Labour Party and the professionals

Though the within-party process over this policy issue may have shown little sign of being substantially influenced by sympathetic academics before 1965, it seems extremely likely that the route to policy implementation was influenced by professional influence. Teachers, particularly through their unions, seem to have played a key role in the decision not to legislate. This seems to key Labour politicians to have been based on an assessment of the readiness of local authorities and teachers in different parts of the country to support reorganisation. This appeared to mean that at one and the same time the unions, and particularly the NUT, wished to support a rapid move to comprehensive schooling in areas where it enjoyed the support of councillors and teachers while, at the same time, sustaining the right of teachers and councils in other areas to retain selective schooling, albeit temporarily. Radice expresses the influence of the teacher unions thus:

> *I think the role of the teachers was absolutely crucial. I mean they were putting together the experiences of the people on the ground. They had experience of comprehensive schools that already existed, the ones that worked and the ones that didn't. (Radice, 1991)*

Prentice illustrates this point by reference to his dealings with the general secretary of the NUT as an education minister:

> *Now of course all the other pressures were against compulsion. The local authorities didn't want it, the civil servants didn't want it. The NUT didn't want it. Ronnie Gould certainly didn't want it. I remember he brought a deputation to see me. They were saying don't go too fast and don't compel. We believe in it where it works . . . but there are other areas where they will make a mess of it until they come to support it. The NUT seemed to be supporting Tony whose instincts were always cautious, step by step instincts. (Prentice, 1991)*

Crosland, in conversation with Kogan, certainly supports this argument. He recalls how, before an irretrievable decision had been made and once the

Circular had been drafted, he consulted widely with the teacher unions (Kogan, 1975, p.113). He did so, he says, for two reasons. First, the teachers would be at the front line of any reorganised system of schooling and, second, because he believed their opposition to any policy form would be fatal. It would be so, he judged, not only because of their political influence outside Parliament but also because of the number of Labour teachers who had become MPs.

Here, then, political realities and Fabian-like deference to the expert played a part in the decision of the Minister.

Avoiding opposition in the House

A final reason for the decision not to legislate is that to have done so would have risked opposition in the House of Commons, delay and possibly defeat: 'We had a majority of six that fell to two. We had a number of sick Members and some who didn't agree with the policy. How could he be sure that he would get a piece of controversial legislation through the House?' (Callaghan, 1991). As a development of this, the former MP for Cardiff South East adds: 'anyway, we were going to have to go through another election. If he didn't act with haste, how did he know he'd be there to do anything?'. As it turned out, of course, Labour romped home in the 1966 general election, but the point is no less powerful for that.

One of the virtues of Circular 10/65, then, seems to be that it was used to implement policy not only without significant Cabinet discussion but also that it ushered in substantial change without reference to the House.

The major educational policy change of the 1960s, then, had involved Labour in a series of tactical and strategic decisions about implementation. In the event, the use of the administrative circular was to prove enough to encourage the majority of LEAs to reorganise by the mid 1970s, despite discouragement from the 1970–4 Conservative government. That it was implemented at all is as much to do with the internal politics of the Labour Party as it is to do with the other factors described above. For comprehensive education became a flagship of the revisionist wing of the Labour Party who were largely successful by the early 1960s in translating Labour's earlier obsession with public ownership into a new emphasis on equality of opportunity.

Conservatives and education: 1970–4

At the 1970 general election, much to the surprise of the pundits and spin doctors, the Conservatives defeated Labour. The new Prime Minister, Edward Heath, installed a relatively unknown politician as Secretary of State for Education. She was Margaret Thatcher, the MP for Finchley and the daughter of a Grantham greengrocer. She was, as *The Times* noted on her appointment, 'less enthusiastic about comprehensive schools than Sir Edward [Boyle]', her predecessor as education spokesperson who had decided to leave politics and become Vice-Chancellor of the University of Leeds.

Mrs Thatcher and the comprehensive schools

Displaying the certainty, and penchant for action, that were later to be her hallmarks as Prime Minister, Thatcher issued Circular 10/70 on education within a fortnight of taking office. The Circular cancelled Crosland's 10/65 and informed local authorities that they could keep their grammar schools if they wanted to. Unlike Crosland who had consulted professional and local authority interests before developing his policy, Mrs Thatcher acted unilaterally and the local authorities and teaching unions were outraged. Some Conservative authorities saw their chance, however, and withdrew their plans for comprehensive education (Timmins, 1995, pp. 288–9). Labour launched a vote of censure and the Conservative Bow Group's journal described the decision as bad not only for education but also for the Conservative Party.

In fact, 10/70 proved to be a storm in a teacup. Although there followed three years of sometimes robust argument about comprehensives and although some LEAs were able to put off the day when they would reorganise, the comprehensive movement had gathered a momentum of its own. The Secretary of State would, much to her chagrin, preside over a period when the numbers of comprehensive schools rose more rapidly than under any previous or future education secretary (Simon, 1991, p. 415). By the time she left office, the proportion of children attending comprehensive schools had doubled to 62 per cent (Simon, 1991).

'Margaret Thatcher, milk snatcher'

The author's first memory of Mrs Thatcher was of taking part in a trade union demonstration against the abolition of free milk for primary school children in 1970. The favourite chant of the demonstrators included the words of the heading to this section. In one fell swoop, the Minister abolished cheap welfare milk and removed school milk from children. It was hardly a clever political move, even if it did appear to give some substance to the Tories' Selsdon Manism. For one of her unofficial biographers it was 'an absurd issue on which to enter the national demonology' (Young, 1990, p. 73). The move saved little more than £8 million pounds per year and the Minister faced charges of damaging the health of the nation's children; a charge that was presented as all the more heinous because the policy was implemented by a woman. It was rumoured that Thatcher was so upset by the reaction that she confided in her husband Denis that she might resign. In the end, she did not and has said that this was the point at which 'iron entered my soul' (Young, 1990, p. 74).

An expansionary minister

If nascent neo-liberalism and controversy were to mark her first two actions as Secretary of State for Education, Mrs Thatcher was, in fact, to settle down as a conventional expansionary education minister. She successfully spiked the Treasury's guns in 1972 when she insisted that the school leaving age should be raised to 16 years (one of the moves canvassed in the 1944 Education Act), despite the cost. In the same year, she saved the Open University from closure just as the first students were to enrol. This is all the more surprising because the university was the brain-child of Harold Wilson as Prime Minister and was conceived as part of the attempt to harness the 'white heat of the technological revolution'. Whatever its virtues, many Conservatives regarded it as the spawn of socialism and Iain Macleod had, before his untimely death, determined to kill it off. This latter intervention is reckoned by an early Thatcher biographer to have been about her 'strong belief in giving educational opportunity to those prepared to work for it' (Gardiner, 1975) or it might have been influenced by her permanent secretary's information that an Open University degree cost only half of an Oxbridge one.

Mrs Thatcher was at her most expansionary, however, in the White Paper, *Education: A Framework for Expansion* (1972). This was a plan for tremendous expansion over the next decade in all sectors of education. It picked up the Plowden Report's call for more nursery places and called for half of three-year-olds and 90 per cent of four-year-olds to be in nursery education by 1982. The teaching force was to be increased by 40 per cent over a decade to improve teacher/pupil ratios and to allow for nursery expansion. Higher education was anticipated to grow by over 60 per cent to 750 000 students by 1981. This anticipated expansion was more than even Robbins had suggested.

Mrs Thatcher's tenure at Curzon Street was a masterpiece in contradiction. There were indications of the radical rightist who was to emerge later in her approach to the comprehensive school issue and in her abolition of free school milk. However, for the most part, Thatcher was no more a Selsdon person than other cabinet ministers in the Heath government. Indeed, on most major issues, she proved surprisingly willing to argue for increased spending and, indeed, for equality of opportunity. An example of this was her support of Plowden-type improvements of school buildings. She had authorised a blitz on unsuitable buildings and school repairs which was not before time given that many of the schools had been built in Victorian times. Her reason?

> *You found by the time children came to school at five, a lot of them were already behind because they came from homes where no interest was taken in the children, where the parents didn't talk to them . . . Of course, the state can never take the place of good parents . . . But it can help redress the balance for those born unlucky. (Gardiner, 1975, p. 111)*

Political life, it seems, is full of contradictions!

Education policy during the Labour governments: 1974–9

The tenure of two Labour governments between 1974–9 saw legislation to abolish direct grant schools, the development of the comprehensive school policy and a major debate on the nature of education in Britain. The period was covered by three secretaries of state for education: Reg Prentice (who was later to cross the House and become a member of the Conservative Party) from March 1974 to June 1975; Fred Mulley from June 1975 to September 1976, and Shirley Williams, who was to be one of the founders of the Social Democratic Party in the 1980s, for the rest of the government's tenure.

Labour was as good as its word on direct grant schools. In October 1975, the House of Commons passed the legislation necessary to abolish them. Of the existing 150 schools in this sector 51 became comprehensive schools. The rest severed their link with the state system and decided to become independent. If Mrs Thatcher had been responsible for overseeing the biggest growth in comprehensive education, Labour now found itself creating more independent schools than any government in living memory.

The comprehensive issue

The battle over comprehensive education was, however, to be longer running. Labour's hand was forced by the election of a Conservative council in Tameside in early 1976. The new council decided to overturn the previous Labour council's decision to go comprehensive. They were supported by a petition of close on half a million signatures in support of the grammar school arranged by the usually liberal Conservative education spokesman, Norman St John Stevas, and his right-wing political adviser, Stuart Sexton. Mulley, the then Secretary of State for Education, required the council to reverse the decision on the grounds that it was unreasonable but the council, using free legal representation provided by Leon Brittan, who was later to become a Conservative minister, took on Mulley in the courts. The issue ultimately went to the Law Lords who decided in Tameside's favour. It was this, more than any other issue, that convinced the Government that it would have to legislate to coerce the minority of recalcitrant LEAs to reorganise.

The 'great debate' on education

A small junior school in Islington was the spark that ignited the so-called great debate on education. At this school, teachers had created a highly permissive, apparently child-centred approach to learning. The result, as far as many parents were concerned, was chaos and a complete breakdown of authority. Parents complained and removed their children from the school in large numbers. Their protests to the LEA yielded an inspection by Her Majesty's Inspectors of Schools. In response, the staff, claiming that it was their right alone to decide on what was taught and how it was taught, went on strike. The Inner London Education Authority, anxious to defuse the row, set up an inquiry. The inquiry criticised the local authority for not intervening earlier and the Taylor Committee on the role of school governors, which had been set up while Tyndale was raging, made suggestions about the local management of schools. The William Tyndale affair, however, went close to the knuckle of concerns throughout the previous decade about standards of education, the curriculum and the accountability of schools.

These concerns had been fanned by the editors of, and contributors to, the *Black Papers on Education*. Mistakenly attributing responsibility to the new schools, the Black Papers drew attention to an alleged slippage in academic standards, to the radicalisation of the curriculum and to the supposed loss of freedom involved in the abolition of the grammar school (Maude, 1969; Cox and Dyson, 1969, 1970, 1971; Cox and Boyson, 1975).

But the Labour Party had also been exercised by these issues and none more than James Callaghan who became Prime Minister in 1976. Callaghan became aware of the seriousness of these issues and, in a break with previous Labour practice, opened up the policy debate not only, or even primarily, to the educational administrators and the teachers but to the public itself (see Rose, 1989). His policy unit chief, Bernard Donoughue, remembers it thus:

> *Basically the situation was this. Mr Callaghan became Prime Minister and every new Prime Minister wants to put his foot-prints on one or two issues . . . I indicated that my impressions were that, given his history, he might be into education. He wrote back immediately and said that he would like to follow it up and asked us to prepare an initial draft, which we did. The Prime Minister and the Unit both had an impact on this process. Mr Callaghan then called for other inputs . . . The Department of Education provided one of their customary drafts with which you can't do anything. His own private office wrote some very good paragraphs. The relationship was good because we had empathy on this subject. We talked about bits of educational experience that nobody around him had. He had sort of assumed that, like the others, that I was one of these Oxbridge, typical highly educated persons. I mean most people have come up through the velvet drain-pipe: the elite and the privileged go in at the bottom and quite naturally rise to the top. It's very comfortable and they have no idea what it's like to be outside it but I was a below decks person. I went to a secondary modern school in Northampton. So we had empathy. Our concern was about education and that it wasn't delivering to the people most in need. At the end of this he said, 'Look Bernard, I don't know all the answers but I'd like to open up the debate and I'd like everyone to take part. And I'd like the parents to think that they can give their own views. I don't just want it to be the Department of Education and the Teacher Unions because they have been in charge and they are the ones who are not producing'. (Donoughue, 1991, emphasis added)*

In essence, Callaghan appears not only to have side-stepped the DES, the teacher unions and the like who, with considerable sympathy from ministers, had influenced the policy process thus far. He also appears to have elevated consumerism to the most prominent position in the policy-making process.

Before the Ruskin Speech, Callaghan had involved himself in some consultation exercises:

> There were complaints from the parents which were very strong at the time about the failure of their children with the three Rs. They really were complaining very bitterly and very deeply. And there were also complaints from industry about the incapacity of people they were receiving. I got hold of Len Murray [then General secretary of the TUC] and we talked about it and we started up a little thing. I don't remember how far it went, but one night he, the President of the CBI and myself went to a school in north London. You won't know this. But we sat on the platform and we talked about education to a lot of people and we listened. Now this went on with other people and other places. (Callaghan, 1991)

The concern of parents, of industrialists, of the head of his policy unit, and the flaccidity of the DES all contributed to the Prime Minister believing that a high-profile intervention was necessary. This he made at Ruskin College, Oxford.

Callaghan's intervention marked a life-long interest in education. In conversation with the author, and in his own memoirs (1987), he recalls how, after Wilson's decision to move him from the Treasury in 1967, he had requested to go to Education. Donoughue was a useful lieutenant because of his strong suspicion of the vested interests of teacher unions. They had, Callaghan thought, 'become a major part of the problem. In all my dealings with the NUT at the time I never once heard mention of education or children, only money'.

Callaghan's Ruskin Speech hinted at his preference for a core curriculum, for higher and universal standards, for the closer involvement of parents and industry in the running of schools and for a greater emphasis on technology. He argued that a method of monitoring individual school performance against national standards was necessary. He made it clear that he did not see his words as supporting the views of the Black Paper writers but the issues raised in the speech were, he made clear, 'proper subjects for rational debate based on facts' (Baker, 1993, p. 30).

From such a propitious beginning, however, the key components of this important debate were chipped away over the next three years. A Green Paper emerged in July 1977. This apparently had to be redrafted because the then Secretary of State, Shirley Williams, had omitted reference to a core curriculum (Callaghan, 1987, 1991). Callaghan clearly suspects that, within a short period of time, she had 'gone native': 'I asked Shirley to do a Green Paper. She was reluctant but she did it. It was all right but I had to send it back and then get the policy unit to do it. She was strangely reluctant' (Callaghan, 1991). And Donoughue (1991) remembers that 'Shirley took a curious position, appointed by Jim to see to this problem but she supported the DES line [against a core curriculum]'.

In fact, the legislation that finally ensued – The Education Bill (1978) – made no mention of a core curriculum, although it did recommend greater centralisation of education, particularly in order to protect academic standards in the schools. By this time, however, Labour was a minority government, kept in office only by a political pact with the Liberals. The latter were unwilling to support legislation which reversed the devolved power that had character- ised education policy since 1944 and the Bill fell with the Labour government in 1979.

Thatcher governments and education

'Cuts, Cuts, Cuts' thundered the banner headline of the *Times Educational Supplement* in November 1979. Mrs Thatcher's first education secretary, Mark Carlisle, had been charged with saving £280 million off the education budget. His proposals were included in an Education Bill in 1980 which reduced local authorities' responsibilities to provide school meals and transport. He also repealed the Education Act (1976) which required LEAs to go comprehensive. The Act, when it became so, also introduced parental choice of school and parent governors in a way consistent with the previous government's ideas. Perhaps the most controversial Carlisle policy was the introduction of the Assisted Places Scheme, whereby the DES would pay the independent school fees of state school pupils who wished to move to the private sector and who were selected. Neil Kinnock, Labour's education spokesman, pledged himself to abolish what he saw as an elitist scheme when Labour next formed a government.

In 1981, the government turned its eyes to higher education and told the universities that they were to be subject to an 8.5 per cent cut in funding. This was to lead to job cuts for 10 000 academic and non-academic staff at a time when the relevant student age group was still rising. However, the Government overlooked the fact that, although it could control the university sector, it could not control the polytechnics which were local authority institutions. As a result, disappointed would-be university students found their way onto courses offered in the polytechnic sector and spending overall was not reduced.

In 1981, Mrs Thatcher acceded to Sir Keith Joseph's request and moved him from the Department of Trade and Industry to Education. As is evidenced by his time at the Department of Health and Social Security, Joseph was fascinated by ideas and he was to fall for a number of them while he was at Curzon Street. The first idea to emerge from the Prime Minister's policy unit was the notion of vouchers, first floated in the 1970s by Rhodes Boyson and peddled since then by the Institute of Economic Affairs (IEA). The idea was that parents would be given a voucher equivalent to the cost of state education. They could use this voucher to choose a state school of their choice or could supplement it if they wished their child to receive private education. In fact, the idea never got off the ground, largely because the Deputy Secretary at the DES, Walter Ulrich, spent two years presenting Joseph and his advisers with every conceivable objection to vouchers. What is more, at this point, schools did not manage their own budget so it was difficult to see how vouchers could be dropped into a system where their recipients would not know how to use them.

Though this idea fell, Joseph was not idle. He revamped teacher education, arranged for the publication of Her Majesty's Inspectorate (HMI) reports on individual schools and ushered in the GCSE examination to replace GCE 'O' level. The core curriculum idea was, however, never floated. In the university sector, he made some money available to counter the effects of the Carlisle cuts and thus made possible modest recruitment of staff in the three years following 1983.

The substantial underfunding in the first two Thatcher governments (DES, 1983; Flather, 1988) were accompanied during the third term by changes at the level of organisation and curriculum. In the case of primary and secondary education, the most significant restructuring came during this later period. Legislation was introduced to allow primary and secondary schools to 'opt out' of control and funding by their local education committees (LEAs) and to take on grant maintained status with financing coming directly from the DES (or in Wales from the Welsh Office). Opted-out schools can, under the provisions of the Education Reform Act (1988), hire and fire their own staff and determine terms and conditions of employment. In common with their LEA counterparts, they are self-managing with school governors occupying a pivotal management role. Unlike schools in LEA control they are unaffected by LEA policy decisions (Simon, 1988; Dale, 1989; Sullivan, 1991). Significant changes have also occurred at the level of curriculum. During the third term of government, Mrs Thatcher's administration introduced a national curriculum with the overt intention of standardising and rationalising the learning process of UK pupils. This proved contentious, not because of the stated aims but because of a set of alleged covert aims which included the intention to 'rid the school curriculum of subjects regarded as potentially politically or morally subversive: peace studies, political or civic education, sex education and sociology' (Sullivan, 1989, p. 67).

A further change introduced under the Education Reform Act has been the right of parents to opt, through the parental preference scheme, for the school of their choice for their children. Here, as in health, a form of consumerism lies at the heart of the changes.

Further and higher education policy has also introduced some major changes. Expenditure on higher education has been substantially cut in the last 10 years or so: government expenditure on universities being cut by 15 per cent between 1980–90 (DES, 1990). As a result of these economies, 19 per cent of university posts were lost between 1979–88 (Association of University Teachers, 1989) and up to 12 universities have faced bankruptcy during the period. As early as 1984 the University Grants Committee, a quasi-governmental, though formally independent, body which administered government funding to universities before its replacement in the late 1980s by the Universities Funding Council, was claiming:

> *these cuts are so severe that great harm has been done. Academic planning has been disrupted, morale has been impaired, thousands of young people have been denied university education, confidence in government has been shaken and will be difficult to restore. (University Grants Committee, 1984)*

The intention behind this apparent underfunding of the university sector of higher education was clear: universities should establish closer links with commercial and industrial enterprises, should bid for research and consultancy contracts and should seek to make good the short-fall in government funding through access to this sort of private funding. This policy direction was also followed in the polytechnic sector where increases in the number of students attending these institutions had not been matched by increases in government funding. This had led to reductions in the level of spending per student of around 20 per cent between 1980–4 and had prompted the National Advisory Board on Higher Education (a sort of University Grants Committee for the polytechnics) to warn as early as 1984 that '[it is] not possible to achieve the triple objective of access, maintenance of standards and a continued downward move of the unit of resource' (National Advisory Board for Higher Education, 1984).

By the third term of Thatcher government, these financial strictures had been supplemented by wider policy considerations. So that, the Education Reform Act (1988) removed polythechnics from local authority control (a sort of compulsory opting out) and made them private institutions in the way that universities are private, and removed from university teachers' contracts the clauses which had hitherto granted them permanent job security. This has been seen by some as an instrument to effect not only the ability of universities to keep within restricted budgets by making academics unemployed but also as a means of controlling, through the fear of termination of contract, the freedom of expression of politically dissident academics. The issue here is not whether such a development was to be applauded or regretted. Rather the issue is that, as with the most recent NHS reforms, the Thatcher government was prepared to arbitrarily change the terms and conditions of professional workers in order to increase accountability.

In the education sector, as in the NHS, Conservative social policy has sought to elevate the position of the consumer; to restrict, where necessary, the power of the professionals; to marginalise areas of learning seen as inappropriate or subversive, and to introduce through the opting out mechanism a market-place in school provision. This last intervention is ideologically very interesting because it appears, on one analysis at least, to epitomise radical right thinking about social policy.

In the first place, the reform introduces the notion of consumer choice. Parents as consumers, both as represented on school governing bodies and as the final arbiters through ballot, are the key actors, at least in theory, in choosing whether their school applies for grant maintained status. Second, the reform can be seen as being at the cutting edge of a radical-right-inspired campaign against large welfare bureaucracies – in this case LEAs. It is so because opted-out schools free themselves from the policy direction of the local council, and in so doing break down the power of those welfare bureaucracies. Third, opting out can be seen as consistent with a long-held desire of the radical right to privatise welfare because many regard the opting out provisions as a halfway house not only to the recreation of selective education but also to private education. This is so because it is believed that grant-maintained schools will, in the short to medium term, be allowed to become independent schools.

As we have seen earlier in the book, the Major governments have added little in the way of education policy. Though working energetically to make grant-maintained status the preferred option for schools and managing finally to resolve the dispute with teacher unions about diagnostic tests of children's ability, it has not introduced many new ideas in education. Certainly, following Mr Major's election victory in 1992, the higher education sector was subject to change as polytechnics were given the status of new universities and the binary line dissolved. But little else of note has emerged until recently. This may be changing as a recent Cabinet reshuffle has led to the merging of the Department for Education with the Department of Employment to form the Department for Education and Employment. It is certainly the case that the Queen's Speech at the opening of a new parliamentary session in November 1995 has promised the expansion of the nursery sector by the use of education vouchers and that ideas about legislating to enforce grant-maintained status on all schools are in the wind. How significant these policy innovations are remains, of course, to be seen.

CHAPTER SEVEN

Health policy and the National Health Service

Chronology	Health policy highlights
1948	Establishment of the NHS
Early 1950s	Concern at expenditure on the NHS
1955	Guillebaud Committee on health service expenditure reports that NHS expenditure has not kept pace with inflation or demographic trends
1962	Powell's Hospital Plan and plans for community care New district general hospitals built but fewer than planned and insufficient resources devoted to community care
1974	NHS reorganisation
1983	Griffiths Report on General Management in the NHS
1988	NHS Review Griffiths reports on community care
1989	White Papers *Caring for People* and *Working for Patients*
1990	National Health Service and Community Care Act
1993	Community care provisions enacted

This chapter looks in some detail at the development of health policy since the end of the Second World War. It is concerned not only to chart the policy directions and stages in the making of health policy but also to elucidate factors associated with policy development and policy shifts.

The creation of the National Health Service

As we have seen in an earlier chapter, the establishment of the NHS was fraught with conflict and difficulty. The post-war Labour government faced opposition on at least two fronts. In the first place, doctors, or at least some doctors, were hostile to the idea of a state health service. This led to pitched battles with the BMA which were finally resolved only by making concessions to doctors' professional self-interest. A lesser struggle also took place within the House of Commons. The Conservative Opposition, which generally acquiesced in the development of welfare state services, saw the opportunity to embarrass the government and took up arms on the doctors' part to protest about the creation of a state monopoly of health care in which professionals were at danger of becoming mere salaried employees.

Aneurin Bevan: speech to the House on the National Health Service, 1946

Mr Bevan The first reason why a health scheme of this sort is necessary at all is because it has been the firm conclusion of all parties that money ought not to be permitted to stand in the way of obtaining an efficient health service. Although it is true that the national health insurance system provides a general practitioner service and caters for something like 21 million of the population, the rest of the population have to pay whenever they desire the services of a doctor. It is cardinal to a proper health organisation that a person ought not to be financially deterred from seeking medical assistance at the earliest possible stage. It is one of the evils of having to buy medical advice that, in addition to the natural anxiety that may arise because people do not like to hear unpleasant things about themselves, and therefore tend to postpone consultation as long as possible, there is the financial anxiety caused by having to pay doctors' bills. Therefore, the first evil that we must deal with is that which exists as a consequence of the fact that the whole thing is the wrong way round. A person ought to be able to receive medical and hospital help without being involved in financial anxiety.

In the second place, the national health insurance scheme does not provide for the self-employed, nor, of course, for the families of dependants. It depends on insurance qualification, and no matter how ill you are, if you cease to be insured you cease to have free doctoring. Furthermore, it gives no backing to the doctor in the form of specialist services. The doctor has to provide himself, he has to use his own discretion and his own personal connections, in order to obtain hospital treatment for his patients and in order to get them specialists, and in very many cases, of course – in an overwhelming number of cases – the services of a specialist are not available to our people.

Not only is this the case, but our hospital organisation has grown up with no plan, with no system; it is unevenly distributed over the country and indeed it is one of the tragedies of the situation that very often the best hospital facilities are available where they are least needed. In the older industrial districts of Great Britain hospital facilities are inadequate. Many of the hospitals are too small – very much too small. About 70 per cent have less than 100 beds, and over 30 per cent have less than 30. No one can possibly pretend that hospitals so small can provide general hospital treatment. There is a tendency in some quarters to defend the very small hospital on the ground of its localism and intimacy, and for other rather imponderable reasons of that sort, but everybody knows today that if a hospital is to be efficient it must provide a number of specialised services. Although I am not myself a devotee of bigness for bigness sake, I would rather be kept alive in the efficient if cold altruism of a large hospital than expire in a gush of warm sympathy in a small one.

From *Hansard, Parliamentary Debates*, House of Commons, 5th Series, vol. 422, Cols 43–5 (April 1946)

The Labour Health Minister, Aneurin Bevan, ushered the service into existence against this opposition by appealing to doctors' pecuniary interests as well as their anxiety to be at the centre of policy-making in the NHS. Not only did he 'choke their throats with gold', he also allowed general practitioners to retain their status as private contractors and hospital doctors to retain private practice.

Notwithstanding this, the NHS has often been seen as the main, perhaps the only, socialist achievement of the Attlee government. This is so not only in the perceptions of Labour supporters but also in the minds of some doctors and academics. In the late 1970s, for instance, Julian Tudor Hart – a socialist GP in a south Wales valley community and the author of the 'inverse care law' hypothesis (Hart, 1975) – could still describe the NHS as 'an island of socialism in a sea of capitalism' (Hart, 1979). Given this dogged belief in the socialist pedigree of Bevan's health service, despite the apparent capitulation to medical interests at its establishment, we are forced to address a central problem. Whose victory was the establishment of the NHS?

Viewed from one perspective, Hart's (and indeed Bevan's) view appears sustainable. Introducing the NHS Bill in the Commons in 1946, Bevan presented the service as divorcing the right to receive best service from the ability to pay and from geographical location. In other words, the NHS would redistribute service and life-chances by making the same standard of health care available to all, irrespective of income, class or region. On this reading, the establishment of the NHS can, indeed, be seen as a victory for ordinary people and as rooted in socialist ideas.

However, this is far from the whole story. For, the establishment of the NHS can also be seen as reflecting not the socialist ideas of Bevan but a sort of rational managerialism. Looked at from this angle the war-time departmental civil service and the medical profession collaborated to rationalise the complexities and inequalities of the pre-war health service. Thus, the principles which guided the emergence of the NHS are seen as having been consensually established during the tenure of the war-time coalition government.

Klein's attempt to square this circle is persuasive (Klein, 1989). He points to the need to appreciate that different policy actors and different political priorities were influential at different stages of the policy debate. During war-time, the civil service worked to create and nurture a consensus on the need for a national health service. They operated within a politics of health care in which the views of the medical profession were acknowledged as key constraints. Bevan, on the other hand, chose to move outside these internal politics. And so, the post-war policy debate on health became a public domain discussion.

This is not to say, of course, that the views of the medical profession were unimportant during this new phase of policy making as is witnessed by the concessions which Bevan made to their interests. He, and the government of which he was a part, were, however, prepared to tolerate conflict in the development of policy.

We should not, however, over emphasise the importance of conflict in the emergence of the NHS. Shared assumptions and common ground were as prominent in the emergence of the NHS as were disagreements and discord. For example, the creation of a universal, free health service represented the mutual political property of both Conservative and Labour parties, as did the belief in the capacity of medical science to conquer ill-health. Though surprising at face value, issues of distributional equality failed to separate the political parties. In other words, the goal of establishing a national health system was a consensual goal. Conflict emerged less over ends than it did over means.

It was the Labour government's choice of political means that brought policy makers into head on conflict with professional interests. That battle was over the devices used by the Government to translate goals into policy. As we have seen in an earlier chapter, the jury is still out on who won the battle over political means. On the one hand, concessions were made to the doctors: GPs were allowed to retain their contractual position and hospital doctors were bought off with money, prestige and influence. However, these concessions did not confer positive rights but rather the power to block changes.

This conflict of interests was accompanied by a conflict of values. The values that the emergent NHS represented were rationality, efficiency and equity. The NHS was intended to provide health services in a rational, efficient and fair way. It is at this level that Hart's 'island of socialism' analysis is more convincing. These values reflected a victory over other values, of course. Chief among these contending arguments about political means was local government's preference for the local administration of the health service and Morrison's promotion of their interests. This view about means was rooted in a value of localism which prized local accountability above efficiency, difference above uniformity and self-government above national and equitable standards of service.

What emerged from these conflicts were contradictions which were built into the structure of the NHS on establishment. These contradictions have been the focus of policy discussion, and sometimes change, in the 50 years since the establishment of the NHS.

From conflict to consolidation

As we have seen above, the NHS was the child of both consensus and conflict. Consensus on aims was accompanied, at least in the early post-war years, by conflict over means. The dispute over means was one that was carried out in the public political sphere and is nowhere better highlighted than in Foot's biography of Bevan (Foot, 1975). Once the NHS had been established, however, conflict appeared to abate. Writing in 1958, the Conservative minister, Ian Macleod, was to claim that 'the National Health Service, with the exception of recurring spasms about charges, is outside of party politics'. This claim pithily describes the transformation of the debate about the NHS in the preceding decade. Once the NHS was safely set up, political priorities turned to consolidating that achievement. Or, to put it another way, the NHS became depoliticised, at least in the arena of public politics. With the exception of the bitter struggle within the Labour government over health charges between 1949–51, the politics of the NHS were, during the 1950s, essentially internal politics. Nonetheless, the 10 years following establishment threw up difficult policy questions which have characterised debates over health policy in particular and social policy in general ever since.

Demand and supply

One of the major problems to loom during this period materialised within the first year of operation. By December 1948, it became clear that the estimated annual costs of the service had underestimated demand. Original estimates for 1948/9 had been £176 million. However, barely four months after the establishment of the NHS, it appeared that actual costs for the year might be £50 million in excess of this figure. In a memorandum to his Cabinet colleagues, Bevan explained that:

> The rush for spectacles, as for dental treatment, has exceeded all expectations . . . Part of what has happened has been a natural first flush of the scheme, with the feeling that everything is free now and it does not matter what is charged up to the Exchequer. But there is also . . . a sheer increase due to people getting things they need but could not afford before. (Public Records Office, 1948)

These were not, however, the only factors involved in the situation. The salary and wages bill for NHS employees had turned out to be much greater than the Minister had anticipated because of the award of rises above the level of inflation by a couple of the NHS pay boards.

Cost continued to be a problem. Supplementary budgets (of £59 million in 1948/9 and of £98 million in 1949/50) failed to stem the tide and it came to seem as if NHS expenditure was out of control. As we will see, the problem was by no means as serious as it appeared. However, the Ministry of Health appeared unable to calculate even short-term demand and were thus invariably incapable of providing accurate estimates. A number of solutions were prescribed to alleviate the ostensible problem of overspending. In the first place there was an attempt to tackle the issue at source. The establishment of the NHS had effectively devolved decisions about resources to doctors, the prescription of drugs in GP surgeries or the referral to hospital, or to regional hospital boards (RHBs). This meant that those responsible for levying taxation to pay for the NHS were, in effect, excluded from expenditure decisions. As a consequence, it was suggested that RHBs be abolished and their planning functions absorbed by the Ministry of Health. It was also suggested that a generic list of prescription drugs be drawn up and GPs required to prescribe cheaper listed drugs rather than more expensive branded drugs. In 1949, and despite Bevan's reluctance, the Government introduced legislation to impose a shilling charge on prescriptions. The aim was to raise revenue but also to suppress demand. In 1950 Bevan, who had resisted the imposition of these charges in Cabinet, agreed instead to the imposition of a cap on NHS expenditure. In the same year Attlee set up a Cabinet Committee, with himself in the chair, to monitor health expenditure. In 1951, Gaitskell, as we have already seen, introduced charges on dental and optical services in order to keep expenditure below the ceiling agreed by Cabinet (at £400 million, more than twice the original annual estimate).

This was a major factor in Bevan's resignation, along with Harold Wilson, from Cabinet. In fact, tensions had been rising in Cabinet for a considerable time. Although Bevan had gone along with some reluctance with the *idea* of imposing health charges, he remained an implacable opponent of their actual introduction. He was also unhappy with the Government's timid and, as he saw it, un-socialist approach to policy in general (Foot, 1975). The specific issue over which Bevan resigned brought him into head-on conflict with the Chancellor of the Exchequer, Hugh Gaitskell. Gaitskell argued for charges for dental and ophthalmic services, claiming that this would suppress demand only in non-essential areas of health care and would raise revenue for the NHS. Moreover, unlike the imposition of prescription charges, this strategy could not lay the Government open to the charge that it was moving away from the idea of a free health service. Bevan had evident difficulty in following this Jesuitical justification and claimed, in any event, that the reason that the Chancellor wanted cuts in health spending was to help finance re-armament. He was convinced that it would be impossible to spend the defence estimates of £1250 million in the financial year and therefore saw the saving of £13 million on health as unnecessary. More than this, he argued that re-armament was hardly the issue on which the principle of a free health service should founder. In the event, Gaitskell's view prevailed, Bevan left the Government, health charges were introduced and the defence estimates were undershot by a considerable margin.

The episodes described above appear to illustrate the problem of finite resources and infinite demand (Sleeman, 1978) that is sometimes said to characterise social policy. And, indeed, they may do so. They also illustrate the battle that was raging within the Labour Party over political priorities. Most of all, they represent the Government's inexperience of running a major state welfare service.

For, in fact, things were much less serious than they appeared at the time. Reporting in 1956, the Guillebaud Committee – which had been set up in 1952 to investigate NHS expenditure – gave the NHS a relatively clean bill of health (HMSO, 1956). According to the committee, NHS overspending had been much exaggerated and had been, in large part, a function of both general inflation and of health service inflation which was already running ahead of general inflation. In fact, as the committee was able to establish, health expenditure had risen only modestly between 1948–54. In the financial year of Bevan's resignation it had actually fallen as a proportion of GNP!

Consolidation

The Guillebaud Report dispelled the myth that health spending had been extravagant. Though dismissed as a 'blue book full of whitewash' by some, it was seen by others as an 'impressive document' (Abel-Smith, 1964, p. 36). In retrospect, it cleared the air and presented information that could sensibly be used as a basis from which to plan future health policy.

The major achievement of the report was that it related health expenditure to inflation and economic growth. This sort of approach had not been used before and allowed the report writers to authoritatively dispel the idea that health costs had spiralled since 1948. The research officers responsible for calculating these data were Titmuss and Abel-Smith; strange though perhaps inspired appointments to what was intended to be a Conservative cost cutting exercise.

The report concluded that *per capita* health expenditure had remained virtually static since 1948; that in relative terms it had actually fallen from 3.75 per cent to 3.5 per cent of GNP, and that expenditure on hospitals, far from being profligate, was dangerously low at only a third of pre-war levels. The report also presented evidence that the increase in health costs associated with the growth in the elderly population could easily be accommodated as a result of economic growth. The report therefore recommended that radical reorganisation of the NHS be resisted and that attention be given, instead, to consolidating its achievements. Though it recognised the relative inefficiency of the tripartite structure developed in 1948, it believed that a further administrative upheaval would increase rather than decrease inefficiency levels. Time was needed, it counselled, for attitudes to change within the service and more, rather than less, capital expenditure was indicated by its investigations. This latter recommendation astonished the Treasury which had expected the committee to recommend cuts in expenditure.

As a consequence, the report came under attack. The specific criticisms were as follows. First, while disagreeing that there was some objective measure of demand, the report gave little advice to government about how demand in a free service could be regulated or what proportion of the national product should be invested annually in the NHS. Second, although the Committee had come down firmly in favour of expenditure on old people's homes rather than on extra elderly beds in hospital and had favoured conservation in dentistry, it largely accepted, as Bevan had, the medical professions penchant for heroic, curative medicine. It argued, for instance, that 'those who have criticised the health service for spending far too much on disease and far too little on prevention have tended to overstate their case' (HMSO, 1956). Third, it rejected many of the contemporary ideas for raising revenue: the raising of existing charges, the imposition of further charges, the introduction of a hotel fee for hospital treatment, the extension of the pay-bed scheme and the exclusion of services, like ophthalmic and dental services, from core NHS concerns. Indeed, it recommended the abolition of charges for dental and ophthalmic medicine introduced by the post-war Labour government, believing that these charges had a significant effect in deterring citizens from seeking treatment. The committee's critics saw these weaknesses as indicating that the committee's major concerns were with maintaining the status quo.

In a sense, the Guillebaud Committee ensured the consolidation rather than the reform of the NHS in the 1950s. The Conservative government felt inhibited while the committee was sitting and discouraged from change by the committee's recommendations when it reported. Nonetheless, two issues were given very careful consideration by government following the publication of the committee's report: the redirection of resources from curative to preventive medicine and the financing of the NHS entirely out of contributory insurance.

The first of these policy ideas was dashed, somewhat surprisingly, by the Treasury. Although it understood that preventive care provided best value for money, it was reluctant to support such an idea because of worries about the control of public expenditure. This meant that any new health expenditure had to be offset by cuts in another part of the health budget. Because of Bevan's concessions to the hospital specialists, consultants were in a position to block any cuts. The Treasury view was therefore that it would be prudent to shelve this particular policy idea.

The second policy idea of financing the NHS entirely out of contributory insurance was at the centre of the Conservative government's drive to create an 'opportunity state' rather than a welfare state. In an opportunity state, individuals would be aware of their own responsibility as well as the state's obligations, while in a welfare state, or so this Conservative claim went, the citizen is aware only of the state's obligations and becomes dependent on the state as nanny and dole-giver. This notion had support at the highest reaches of government, indeed the Prime Minister (Macmillan) was counted among its supporters. As we know, it was Beveridge's intention that around a third of the cost of the NHS should be met from contributory insurance, though there remain popular misconceptions that he intended the full cost to be met by insurance and that, at the start at least, this was the way the service was funded. By 1954, insurance contributions accounted for only 6.4 per cent of NHS funding and the Government was interested in transferring the whole cost to this method. The advantages of such a scheme were that it would allow direct taxation to be reduced and that it would, it was believed, instil into doctors and patients a sense of responsibility. If, as in social security (see

Chapter 10), a direct link was perceived between contributions and benefits, then doctors would be more responsible in their prescribing practices and patients would moderate their demands.

There were, however, extensive flaws in this idea. Beveridge had realised that it would be impossible to finance a comprehensive health system on the basis of a flat-rate contributory scheme based on what the poorest contributor could afford. Other practical issues also came into play, particularly the fact that by the late 1950s the Government was already raising national insurance contributions to offset the cost of old age pensions. With some reluctance, this latter idea was therefore also shelved. But not before it could be roundly condemned by the creator of the NHS. In a parliamentary debate in 1958 to celebrate the tenth anniversary of the formation of the NHS, Bevan expounded the reasons for rejecting an insurance-based method of financing. The first reason was one of equity: that the nature of the treatment should not be related to the contribution made: 'We cannot perform a second class operation on a patient if he is not quite paid up!' The second objection was that the Labour idea of the NHS was that it should be redistributive. Financing the service out of general taxation ensured that those who had the most paid the most: 'What more pleasure can a millionaire have than to know that his taxes will help the sick? . . . The redistributive aspect of the scheme was one that attracted me almost as much as the therapeutical'.

In the end, then, and with the help of the Guillebaud Committee, consolidation ruled the day in policy development and the NHS remained substantially untouched during the 1950s. This meant, of course, that the weaknesses as well as the strengths of the service became entrenched.

The hardening of inequalities?

Bevan had justified the creation of a centralised NHS on the basis of universalising the best. That is to say, he believed that central control would avoid the problem of richer areas getting better services. However, during the 1950s this seems to have been exactly what happened, at least in relation to bed numbers. This hardening of inequalities stemmed from the Ministry of Health's decision to accept health authority budgets inherited from Labour rather than starting from first principles and assessing need. This had the effect of rewarding most those authorities which had been most profligate following the establishment of the service, a point that the Guillebaud Committee was quick to see:

> *The criticism is still made, however, that the system favours most the authorities who showed the least degree of financial responsibility in the early years of the service. . . . We agree that the main weakness of the present system of allocating revenue funds is the lack of a consistent long-term objective. (HMSO, 1956)*

The motivation to change this was, however, missing from the report. This is perhaps because any attempt to help the least well off authorities would, during a period of zero growth, have meant redistributing resources. The more favoured authorities were well able to resist this suggestion by pointing to the fact that, despite their relatively favoured position, they were unable to meet need adequately. In this context, the principle of giving priority to maintaining unequal provision rather than changing it won through.

On some other indices, the NHS appears to have mitigated health inequalities, however. In general practitioner services, the NHS developed a system of negative controls which were designed to prevent new practitioners moving into already over-doctored (usually financially well off) areas. The effect of this strategy was to reduce the proportion of patients in under-doctored areas (those where the size of lists was exceptionally large) from 51.5 per cent in 1952 to 18.6 per cent in 1958.

The distribution of specialist hospital services also has to be seen as a qualified success, though the scope of those services has to be seen as a failure. In other words, although the evidence suggests that a softening of inequalities occurred in this area, significant general shortages pertained throughout the 1950s.

As early as 1948, the Ministry of Health produced a plan for specialist services. This set out what were regarded as reasonable consultant norms by specialty and by population. However, financing crises in the NHS ensured that the growth of consultant posts slowed down to a trickle. Attempting to tackle this problem and the problem of geographical distribution, the health ministry established an Advisory Committee on Consultant Establishments in 1953. Its function was to advise the Minister of Health on all applications for additional consultant posts received from health authorities. Within that brief was a negative or vetting function: support would be warmer for applications from under-doctored areas. As a consequence, although numbers of consultants remained lower than anticipated (5316 in 1949, rising to 7013 in 1959) and remained below the 1948 target until 1962, inequalities were mitigated. For within the increased total there was a higher proportion of appointments to precisely those specialties which had been undersubscribed in pre-NHS days: anaesthetics, psychiatry, gynaecology, etc.

The power of the medical profession

The 1950s was also marked by disputes between the medical profession and the Ministry of Health. These disputes, usually about money, permeated discussions between the two parties throughout the decade and beyond. In part, these disputes stemmed from the fact that the NHS was a near monopoly provider of services, thus making it impossible to ascertain the market price for doctors' salaries. Consequently, the decade was scarred by pay disputes and attempts to devise arbitration machinery to deal with the problem. In 1957, the Conservative government established a Royal Commission on Doctors' and Dentists' remuneration to look at ways of reviewing pay.

The Royal Commission found, substantially, for the doctors: 'At the time of our appointment the current earnings of doctors and dentists were too low'. Doctors' salaries had fallen behind those of comparable professions and GPs were seen by the Commission as having done particularly badly (during the 1950s average earnings had increased by about 20 per cent while GP remuneration had fallen by about the same proportion). The Commission recommended all round increases and the establishment of a review body to ensure that doctors' salaries were kept roughly in line with their comparators in other professions.

In crude pay terms then the profession had proved to be ineffectual rather than powerful during the 1950s. It fared no better than other NHS groups whose salaries also fell in real terms. The medical profession's power lay in its ability to win through on narrower NHS issues. This, of course, flowed from Bevan's acceptance that doctors should be able to be members of Hospital Management Committees (HMCs) and RHBs. Its outcome was that throughout the 1950s the medical profession pervaded the decision-making machinery of the NHS. If an issue became defined as an NHS issue rather than a political issue, it was the medical profession that represented itself as the voice of expertise.

The Guillebaud Committee had found that doctors were heavily represented on both HMCs and RHBs (between a fifth and a third of members of the former and between a third and two fifths of the latter). The committee was unperturbed about medical membership and thought that the presence of doctors provided 'invaluable advice to the lay members on medical aspects of hospital management' (HMSO, 1956). And, as we have grown to expect, doctors interpreted 'medical aspects' pretty widely.

Though the medical profession did not run the NHS of the 1950s it developed considerable influence and power in shaping the policy agenda. It was influential in determining which issues were put on the policy agenda for action and it was powerful in defining those issues which should be regarded as medical and therefore the sole province of doctors. Its chief power lay in the fact that it became clear to government that if it attempted to change the structure of the NHS in a way that diluted the institutional power of doctors it would have a battle on its hands.

From ad-hocerey to rational planning

If the 1950s were characterised by a sort of solidification of the strengths and weaknesses of Bevan's NHS, then the next two decades appear to have been an interlude during which rational planning was applied to the NHS. Perhaps the first example of this was the 1962 Hospital Plan.

The Hospital Plan (1962)

The 1960s saw the increasing scrutiny by government of the delivery of health care and the structure of the health service. At the beginning of the decade, Enoch Powell – who had resigned from the Government in 1958 over the Government's failure to cut welfare spending – was appointed Minister of Health. He along with a new permanent secretary (Sir Bruce Fraser) and a new chief medical officer (Sir George Godber) were to be important in this early review of the way in which health care was delivered. The objective of the plan was to guarantee access for patients and doctors to the most modern and comprehensive treatment facilities. It called for the closure of over 1000 hospitals, the extension of about 350 others and the building of a further 90. The idea was to create a national structure of general hospitals which would cater for catchment populations of between 100 000 and 150 000 and have between 600 and 800 beds. Powell took upon himself the role of ensuring that RHBs produced and submitted plans for their local area. He also took the lead in integrating these plans into a national blueprint. He delegated Fraser to persuade the Treasury that through a more concentrated and capital-intensive approach better healthcare could be provided at a relatively low cost.

Unfortunately the plan, though accepted by Treasury and Cabinet, failed spectacularly. By the time that the plan was formally abandoned in the early 1970s, neither the projected savings nor the full complement of district general hospitals had been achieved. Why was this so?

First, the plan was dependent on consistent long-term funding but was, in fact, derailed by short-term expenditure cuts caused by balance of payments and sterling crises during the 1960s and by rising inflation. Nor was there the commitment to public values that would have been necessary to carry the plan through to a successful conclusion: politicians favoured short-term rather than long-term measures so that they could ensure that the benefit fell to them rather than their successors; doctors favoured the distribution of scarce resources on salaries rather than facilities.

The failure of the plan must also be counted as a failure for central rational planning. There were public protests at the closure of hospitals that the plan regarded as obsolete. The public, it seemed, would not, as Bevan believed, prefer to be 'kept alive in the efficient if cold altruism of a large hospital than expire in a gush of warm sympathy in a small one' (cited in Watkin, 1978, p. 71). There was also the failure of central plans to take into account local situations. But the most spectacular failure of the plan was the building process itself. Experiments with a standard, national, architectural plan had disastrous outcomes, leading to the bankruptcy of contractors, poor quality and delayed completion on a scale hitherto unheard of in public building projects.

Crucially, the success of the plan had been contingent on the successful implementation of a parallel community care programme. This programme, described in two White Papers (HMSO, 1963, 1966), was designed to suppress demand for general hospital places by providing alternative treatment in the community for older people, the mentally handicapped and the mentally ill. Powell intended that by 1972 these community alternatives would have yielded 1000 more residential homes, a similar number of training centres for the physically and mentally handicapped and an increase of 45 per cent in local authority staff to care for people in their own homes. However, reality fell far short of objectives and many patients remained in inappropriate, more expensive and ineffective general hospital beds.

It might not be unreasonable to see the failure of community care as a failure of the central planning mechanism. Government, however, drew the opposite conclusion and believed the failure to be, in large part, the result of too little national co-ordination. Uncontrollable local government was painted as the villain. One of the results of this perception was that in the reorganisation of the NHS in 1974 local authority services were clawed into central control.

Financing the National Health Service

Neither had the problem of supply and demand disappeared by the 1960s. Indeed a debate about how to address this problem raged throughout the decade. Supporters of private, market-led health services argued that the problem lay in consumers' natural predilection to demand more services than they were prepared to pay for through taxation. The argument here is a familiar one. If the constraint of cost is absent there is no incentive to restrain demand. The solution to the problem was a simple one: remove health care from the state and make it a private service or set of services. Even for those (the majority) who found this claim unproven or unprovable, the problem of equalising supply and demand remained a real one. The problem, however, led to significant conflict between the medical profession and the policy makers in the Ministry of Health and the Treasury. The battle was between those (the doctors) who saw the aim of the health service as being to provide doctors with resources that would ensure the maximisation of treatment for the individual patient and the Ministry which saw its role as distributing scarce resources in a way consistent with the competing demands of different groups of service users (Owen, 1976).

One way of squaring this circle was to look for new ways of generating more income for the NHS. This was certainly the view of the medical profession. Miller, writing in 1967, argued:

It is the clear duty of the medical profession to present to Government and public the grim and sober truth, that without a vast increase in national expenditure on the hospitals, here and now – and far beyond anything so far envisaged even on paper and for an indefinitely receding future – they will progressively run down, and the present inadequate service will shortly give way to one that is frankly third rate. (Miller, 1967, p. 21)

In the same year, the BMA established a panel to look into the finances of the NHS. It came out, in due course, in favour of an insurance-based system.

If the problem of supply and demand was exercising doctors, it was also proving to be a headache for politicians. In 1968 Douglas Houghton, the Chairman of the Parliamentary Labour Party, opined:

> It can be contended that, judged from the standpoint of the quality and efficiency and adequacy of the services, we are now getting the worst of both worlds. The government cannot find the money out of taxation and the citizen is not allowed to pay it out of his own pocket. (Houghton, 1967, p. 7)

His solution was to raise more money by charging patients for some services. A year later, Richard Crossman, who had succeeded Houghton as Secretary of State for Social Services, addressed the problem straight on:

> The pressure of demography, the pressure of technology, the pressure of democratic equalisation will always together be sufficient to make the standard of social services regarded as essential to a civilised community far more expensive than that community can afford. It is a complete delusion to believe that if we had no further balance of payments difficulties social service ministers would be able to relax and assume that a kindly Chancellor will let each one of them have all the money he wants to expand his service. The trouble is that there is no foreseeable limit on the social services which the nation can reasonably require except the limit that the government imposes. (Crossman, 1969)

The debate over problems of demand unfortunately remained just that. Crossman rejected the idea of additional charges. The Labour government had already had the unfortunate political experience of abolishing prescription charges when it came to power in 1964 only to reintroduce them in the midst of economic crisis four years later and feelings about charges ran high. Instead, Crossman, like Bevan before him, and like his Conservative successor Sir Keith Joseph, asked the civil service to consider the possibility of charging 'hotel' charges during patients' stay in hospital. Even here, the Secretary of State decided that the political furore would far outweigh any financial advantage and so the issue was left as unresolved at the end of the decade as it had been at the beginning of it.

There were, however, interesting aspects to the debate. First, it did not proceed along party lines: Joseph was as aware of the political sensitivity of charges as his Labour predecessors. Second, the Conservative government that took office in 1970 kept charges, as a proportion of NHS income, at roughly the same level as during the 1964–70 Labour governments. Finally, constraints of one sort or another prevented both parties from introducing manifesto pledges. Labour was constrained from abolishing charges by economic crisis and the Conservative government which followed was unable to increase charges by administrative inertia. In any event, both parties maintained a commitment to the NHS which appeared to have dissuaded them from attempting root and branch reform.

... And back to ad-hocerey

The 1974 reorganisation of the National Health Service

This reorganisation was intended to tackle dissatisfaction with the post-war structure of the NHS. That dissatisfaction came from two major sources, doctors and the Ministry of Health. The Ministry was concerned that lines of management and accountability were less than clear. The doctors were also unhappy with the post-war tripartite organisation of health services. They believed that this fragmentation made effective co-ordination of services impossible and led to high-cost hospital beds being filled with patients who would best be served by after care or convalescent places. The system also militated against the development of preventive medicine because of the fragmentation of primary and secondary care services.

As a consequence, the 1966–70 Labour government collaborated with the doctors in what Klein has called 'an organisational fix' (Klein, 1989, p. 90). This led to the publication of a Green Paper in 1968 (Ministry of Health, 1968). It proposed a simple structure for the organisation of health care in England and Wales and anticipated the creation of between 40 and 45 area health authorities (AHAs), accountable to the Ministry of Health and responsible for the *full* range of health services within a given district. Under this plan, AHAs would have responsibility for GP and hospital services, as well as those services currently administered by local authorities. It also suggested that AHAs should have boundaries which were co-terminous with those of the major local authorities which the Royal Commission on Local Government was thought likely to recommend. This was to be so because it was seen as vital that there was closer liaison with social services departments so that issues relating to illness and convalescence could be dealt with as part of the same package of care. A Green Paper in 1970 (DHSS, 1970) rejected the transfer of health to local government on the basis that 'the independent financial resources available to local government are not sufficient to enable them to take over responsibility for the whole health service' (HMSO 1970, p. 7). This was almost entirely specious. The more likely reason for rejection was that the medical profession feared the dilution of their power if services were localised (Hill, 1993).

By 1974, this simple plan had become more complex. First, it was thought that the proposed number of AHAs would create organisations too small for strategic planning of health services and too large for detailed implementation of health policy. Second, the Royal Commission on Local Government had reported and had recommended smaller local government units than had been anticipated. It also created another political problem in that it revived the battle fought by Morrison in the 1940s by suggesting that local authorities should run the health service rather than central government. Final plans for reorganisation suggested the creation of 90 AHAs with boundaries co-terminous with the new local authorities responsible for social services functions (normally counties or metropolitan areas). AHAs were to be responsible to regional health authorities (RHAs) and below them was to be a proliferation of district management committees. The desire for unification was a casualty of the new plan as the executive committees for optician services, GP services and dental services were omitted from the AHA remit and became newly formed family practitioner committees. The Ministry of Health's desire for clearer management lines also went by the board. Membership of AHAs was to be determined not on functional lines but on representative ones. Equal representation on the new organisations was to be granted to the medical profession, local authority representatives and NHS managers. Though the intention of the reform was to create the maximum feasible delegation alongside clear upward accountability, the structure, at least according to Klein (1989), 'satisfied no one'. Once more, administrative tiers proliferated and confusion reigned.

New philosophies: changed service?

Throughout the mid to late 1970s little happened in the way of health policy development. Though the NHS suffered, like other welfare state services as a result of the economic recession and IMF-induced economic retrenchment, little of substance emerged from the policy machinery. All that was to change with the election of Conservative governments in 1979, 1983 and 1987, respectively. Those governments, headed by Mrs Thatcher, were (see Chapter 4) apparently committed to the marketisation of health services and to rolling back the state from welfare. Though, as we shall see, fundamental shifts in health policy were slow in coming. This is no doubt in part because of the affection in which the NHS was, and remains to be, held by the public at large. For, as Papadakis and Taylor-Gooby remind us, the NHS 'remains the most popular component of the welfare stare' (1987, p. 70). Or, in the words of the journalist, Melanie Phillips:

> The NHS . . . rides high in people's affections. Unlike teachers or housing officials, the producers of the service can do little wrong in the eyes of its consumers. The perception is that its faults are caused not by the doctors, nurses or even the hospital administrators but the government. People believe that the health service is not being given enough money. When asked they even say they would happily pay more in taxes to provide more for the NHS. (The Guardian, 23 October, 1987)

Mrs Thatcher's governments were, however, determined to change the nature of the debate about the NHS and to change the institution itself. This was in line with her views that the responsibility for welfare in general should be returned to individuals and families, or at least shared between them and the state:

> The sense of being self-reliant; of playing a role within the family, owning one's own property, of paying one's way, are all part of the spiritual ballast which maintains

responsible citizenship, and provides a solid foundation from which people look around
and see what more they might do for others and for themselves. (Thatcher, 1977, p. 97)

However, the politics of health policy were acknowledged by Patrick Jenkin, one of Thatcher's early Secretaries of State for Health, as a minefield. On returning from the United States in 1982 after a fact-finding mission about private health insurance, he became convinced that the British public would not tolerate such a change in the means of provision. Recognising, or anticipating, the political reality that the NHS remained so popular an institution, the Conservatives, on one reading at least, took:

a succession of Granny's footsteps tiptoeing away from the universal, publicly-funded
comprehensive health service hoping that no one [would] be sufficiently alarmed by the
noise to ask the questions of principle raised by each step. (Cook, 1988, p. 6)

Granny footsteps or not, change was abroad.

More reorganisation

Before the 1974 reorganisation had been given time to settle, a cacophony of criticism created the political circumstances in which further structural reorganisation was inevitable. Opprobrium surrounded the service's apparent inability to make decisions quickly and its structural complexity. It was widely argued that there were too many tiers of administration, too much bureaucracy and too many administrators. The 1974 structure was said to be inefficient and ineffective. In 1979, the Royal Committee on the National Health Service had suggested that one tier of administration could be removed and had recommended that there should be only one tier of authorities below region (DHSS, 1979, p. 376). Events moved quickly. In December 1979, the Government introduced a consultative paper, *Patients First*, which announced its agreement with the Royal Commission. It suggested that AHAs should be replaced by smaller district health authorities (DHAs) which would combine the functions of AHAs and district committees. The Government anticipated that such restructuring would save around 10 per cent of management costs (DHSS, 1979).

The Health Services Act (1980) gave the Secretary of State for Health the authority to restructure. As a result, in 1982 AHAs were replaced by 201 district health authorities which were made responsible for assessment of local health needs, planning, the day-to-day operation of hospital and community services and the employment of staff. DHAs reported to RHAs, whose role remained unchanged.

The central feature of this reorganisation was simplification. But in many parts of the country the abolition of the AHAs meant loss of co-terminosity with those local authorities responsible for the social services function.

Another key feature was that family practitioner committees (FPCs) which administered GP services became increasingly separate from the DHAs, a separation formalised in the Health and Social Security Act (1984) when FPCs became employing authorities in their own right. The attempt, in the 1974 reorganisation, to unify health services lasted less than 10 years.

Marketisation and the National Health Service: the Griffiths Report and general management

As the dust was settling after the 1982 restructuring, even more changes were in hand. As we have already seen, the first Thatcher government subscribed to the idea of minimal government intervention in welfare, to the reduction of public expenditure and the return of a free market economy. This led to notions of dismantling the welfare state. The NHS, however, proved a difficult site on which to start this demolition activity. However, the first administration sought to control the significant increase in health care expenditure by the encouragement of welfare pluralism in health. That is, it encouraged the growth of private medicine as we will see below. Following its re-election in 1983, the Conservative government turned its attention to improving planning and resource management in the NHS.

The new Secretary of State for Social Services, Norman Fowler, emphasised the need for devolution of decision making to the district level wherever possible. To vouchsafe the accountability of a locally-managed NHS to Parliament required ensuring that management structures were equal to the task. Accordingly, an independent inquiry headed by Sir Roy Griffiths (the managing director of Sainsbury's) was established in 1983. Its brief was to scrutinise NHS management practices and to make recommendations, if necessary, for improvement.

The Griffiths team focused on issues relating to the management of hospitals and came up with recommendations which fell short of the need for new legislation (DHSS, 1983). Its major finding was that the NHS suffered from a confusion about the role of management in health care. Its recommendations were therefore based on a belief that the NHS needed to introduce general management at levels below and above the health authority. Its proposals were, therefore, as follows:

- A Health Services Supervisory Board (HSSB) should be established within the DHSS. It would be responsible for setting overall objectives, budgets and strategies for the NHS. It would be chaired by the Secretary of State and its membership would include the Minister of Health, the Permanent Secretary, the Chief Medical Officer and the Chairman of the NHS Management Board (see below), along with two or three non-executive members with management experience outside of the NHS.

- An NHS Management Board, whose chair would be an independent granted civil servant status. It would be responsible for the running of the NHS.
- The appointment of general managers at the regional, district and hospital levels to manage services at the various levels.
- The involvement of clinicians in management through the introduction of resource budgeting.

The Government elected to move speedily and within two years Griffiths's key recommendations were implemented. The main thrust of the Griffiths Report was about changing the NHS from an administered to a managed service. The outcome was a shift away from the consensus management (shared responsibility between doctors, nurses and administrators) that had previously characterised the NHS. Griffiths saw this form of management as management by lowest common denominator. General management, in contrast, vested all responsibility for performance in the hands of one accountable manager.

This was a considerable upheaval and, as one might expect, its introduction was not universally welcomed. The Labour Party criticised the plan only to later accept that general management should be left in place by a future Labour government (Meacher, 1984). The Association of Community Health Councils was to argue that the introduction of general management had led to less democracy as it had led to a decline in the influence of health authority members and a sidelining of the Community Health Councils (CHCs) (Association of Community Health Councils in England and Wales, 1988). In addition, a former Health Minister, Ray Whitney, argued that general management had done nothing to address the problem of centre–periphery relations (1988, p.79).

Be that as it may, the Griffiths model played a part in the marketisation of the NHS. It introduced the methods and assumptions of private commerce into the NHS and cleared the way for the introduction of other strategies intended to dilute the public sector ethos of the NHS (see the discussion below of internal markets). It was also the first health policy document to emphasise the role of consumers.

Marketisation and the National Health Service: competitive tendering

Early in Mrs Thatcher's first administration competitive tendering was encouraged in relation to the provision of non-medical services. By this method, health authorities and hospitals were exhorted to put out to tender for a range of services such as portering, catering, laundry services and the like, which had hitherto been provided by NHS employees. The contracting-out strategy was intended, at least in part, as weakening the grip of public sector unions on the NHS. The Government saw this as a way of ensuring that the NHS was protected from industrial action from ancillary staff like that experienced during the 'winter of discontent'. The first administration relied on persuasion as a policy tool. However, the service proved to be impervious to the urging of government and between 1980–3 contracting out of NHS services actually fell (Ascher, 1987, p. 38). Bearing this in mind, the second Thatcher government decided to move from persuasion to coercion. In autumn 1983 the newly-returned government issued a directive that required health authorities to put cleaning, laundry and catering services out for tender. DHAs were to submit plans in respect of this to RHAs within five months and the latter were given a further two months to submit proposals for the whole period to the Department of Health. Health authorities were also encouraged to consider other areas for contracting out.

Health authorities, while remaining hostile to contracting out, had to appear to comply at the very least. However, by the end of 1985, of the 519 contracts completed less than one quarter had been awarded to outside contractors, the rest having been successfully bid for by in-house groups (Ascher, 1987, pp. 190–1). Government figures suggest that between 1983–8 85 per cent of contracts were awarded to in-house bidders.

Notwithstanding the mixed success, from the Government's viewpoint, of this first round of contracting out, pressure was maintained throughout the 1980s and 1990s as fresh candidates for competitive tendering have been presented. Up to the present, services selected for competitive tendering have included hotel services, including portering, non-emergency transport, sterile supplies, pathology services and building and engineering. Despite early hostility from health authorities, contract culture has gripped the NHS.

Marketisation and health: private practice

Readers will recall that the Callaghan Labour government had introduced a policy of phasing out private practice from the NHS. After an acrimonious dispute between Barbara Castle (Secretary of State for Health in the Wilson government) and the doctors the government established a Health Services Board to oversee a phased run-down of private beds. The first Thatcher government set about reversing this move. The Health Services Act (1980) abolished the Board and made the Secretary of State responsible for ensuring the presence of private beds in NHS hospitals. Though battle was joined with relish, the victory was pyrrhic: the passage of the Act, in fact, coincided with the growth of private hospitals which took increasing numbers from the private patient 'pool'.

The insinuation of private practice into the NHS system was also achieved in other ways. In 1980, the Government introduced changes to hospital consultants' contracts. These allowed consultants to increase their private practice without jeopardising their NHS practice. The contracts allowed a greater proportion of a consultant's salary to be earned in private practice before forfeiting any of his/her NHS salary. They also reduced the proportion of NHS salary forfeited once the cut-off point had been reached (Higgins, 1988; Johnson, 1990, pp. 70–2). According to Higgins, the result of this change was that there was a significant increase in the number of consultants who, while working on full-time or maximum part-time contracts for the NHS, engaged in significant private practice. As Higgins notes:

> In a situation where there were so few wholly private practitioners and where the service was so firmly consultant-led the potential for the expansion of private practice was dramatically changed. Although the increase in private health insurance and the availability of new private sector facilities were important factors, their contribution to the changing scene would have been marginal were it not for the radical restructuring of consultants' contracts and consultants willingness to take on new work. (Higgins, 1988, p. 87)

Consultants also benefited from tax breaks for employees and employers participating in employer-funded private health insurance schemes – a development which led, *inter alia*, to the introduction of private health insurance schemes run by some major trade unions!

Private insurance and private facilities

Along with the growth in private practice came the growth in private insurance schemes and private provision. By 1988 over 10 per cent of the population were covered by private health insurance, double the proportion covered in 1979. This apparently small proportion is, in fact, deceptive because health insurance schemes have tended to exclude older people and those with chronic illnesses and disabilities.

With government encouragement, three provident associations dominated the health scheme: British United Provident Association (BUPA); Western Provident Association (WPA), and Private Patients' Plan (PPP) took the lion's share of the private market. Towards the end of the 1980s, however, a number of for-profit companies have entered the private health market, competition has become fierce and a market in health looks, to some, a near reality. It is, however, a very limited market. Despite the Government's target of 25 per cent of the population to be covered by private insurance by 1990, the most recent figures are well below that.

This steady growth in private health insurance has been accompanied by a growth in the provision of private facilities. Notwithstanding the changes introduced by Conservative governments in the 1980s, the number of private patients treated in NHS hospitals has declined continually over the last 20 years. This has less to do with the number of pay beds available in the NHS, which have remained relatively constant during the 1980s, and more to do with declining rates of occupancy of those beds. Instead private treatment has increasingly occurred outside the NHS. Some commentators see the stimulus for this growth of private facilities as stemming from the attempt by the Callaghan government to phase pay beds out (see above). Whatever the reason, the acceleration of provision of private facilities in the 1980s was substantial: '. . . while in the 1970s around three out of every four private patients were treated in the NHS, the reverse is now the case'. (Griffith *et al.*, 1987, p. 79)

This growth in facilities has been accomplished through the intervention of two kinds of hospital facilities: commercial hospitals and those run by not-for-profit organisations. By the late 1980s they were catering for roughly equal numbers of patients with the two major UK providers, Nuffield (a charitable trust) and BUPA growing more quickly than the others but with American for-profit corporations attempting to break into the market (Higgins, 1988).

Notwithstanding the appearance of an incipient free market in health during the 1980s, the private health sector has grown as a result of its dependence on the NHS as well as its competition with it. In the first place, the NHS increased the potential profitability of private medicine. This was so because it had to treat all patients in need of hospital care. This included the bulk of patients who were not, in any event, able to pay for their treatment and left the private sector to concentrate on the more exotic or more profitable acute cases. Second, private hospitals profited during the late 1980s from work diverted to them by DHAs. This was largely, though not exclusively, the result of central government waiting list initiatives in 1987 and 1989. In both of these years the Department of Health made extra funds available to district and regional health authorities for the purpose of reducing patient waiting lists (£25 million in 1987 and £33 million in 1989). In many, though not all, cases waiting list initiative monies were used to contract out work to the private sector. This was particularly the case with relatively uncomplicated minor operations. Third, the NHS has increasingly subsidised the private medicine business through its use of 'agency' doctors and nurses in locum capacities. The cost of locum consultants has been, on some occasions, equivalent to twice the salary of an NHS consultant (*The Guardian*, 17 June 1987). Last, the NHS heavily subsidises the private sector through its training of medical personnel. Doctors and nurses transferring from NHS to private hospitals bear no responsibility to repay the NHS for their training nor is there any expectation that their new employers will be involved in reimbursement.

The National Health Service reforms

Throughout the 1980s, the purchasing power of the NHS had barely increased, although government had kept pace with inflation in NHS funding. But despite this relative stand-still, demands on the service were increasing. One source of demand was the ageing population which was growing at about 1 per cent per year in the late 1980s. If we take into account the disproportionate use of the NHS by older people, then the amount of resource available for each member of the population had fallen during the 1980s (King's Fund Institute, 1988). As a result of the consequent control on spending, waiting lists grew, beds were closed and operations cancelled. DHAs were running out of money well before the end of the financial year and doctors resorted to 'shroud-waving'. As we have seen, these events put Mrs Thatcher on the defensive and she announced, under pressure at Prime Minister's Questions, that a review would take place. She thought that 'the NHS had become a bottomless financial pit' (Thatcher, 1993, p. 608) and was keen that something should be done.

Early discussions in the review had centred on two different approaches to funding the service. One was to move the NHS out of general taxation and to move its funding to a health insurance contribution that would be paid alongside national insurance contributions. One of the advantages of this was that the NHS would then be theoretically self-financing and outside the Annual Consideration of Public Expenditure (PESC) round. The other approach was to expand the contribution that private finance could make and the review committee looked at ways to boost private health insurance. According to Nigel Lawson, Thatcher's Chancellor at the time, he had argued over dinner with the Prime Minister that private market solutions to the NHS problem would not work. In fact he believed that the NHS was performing well compared to health systems in other countries. Lawson and the Treasury seemed to support the NHS as a public utility because it worked, was popular and made financial as well as political sense (Lawson, 1992; Thatcher, 1993).

The National Health Service and internal markets

In the end, the review recommended a compromise solution. Methods analogous to those of a private corporation were to be introduced into the NHS but it was to remain publicly funded.

Of most significance perhaps was the creation of what has come to be known as an *internal market*. The internal market idea was a brain-child of the right wing of the Conservative Party and found favour with the Premier. It was promoted in the late 1980s by an ultra-right-wing group of MPs known as the *No Turning Back Group* (which had been established to protect the radical right ideas that had informed the policy making of government during most of the 1980s) in the following way:

Particular hospitals and particular areas should be able to specialise, with patients being referred to whichever can provide the cheapest or best service. Excess capacity should be traded across district boundaries instead of having empty places in one location accompanied by shortage in another. (No Turning Back Group, 1988, p. 20)

This move exposed clear political and ideological preferences. First, it increased *competition* in the service with hospitals competing with each other to secure contracts for work from DHAs. Second, it was seen as improving *efficiency* in the service. Efficient hospitals with lower unit costs would reap the reward of more contractual work from DHAs. This would have consequences not only for them but would also act as an incentive to less efficient hospitals to improve efficiency levels and avoid the financial penalties that such a market place in health creates. Here then we see the ideological assumptions of the Conservative government: competition and efficiency are inseparable bedfellows. The post-war NHS had been inefficient *because* it did not operate in a health market place. Monopoly provision had bred waste and the introduction of both external competitors and internal competition was intended to create a service more responsive to consumers and more efficient in its activities.

This development was, of course, accompanied by a further spurt of policy making associated with the White Paper, *Working for Patients* (1989), and the National Health Service and Community Care Act (1990).

Papering over the White Paper cracks

It is well documented that the Prime Minister, anxious that her Chancellor as well as the Labour Party were supporting the principle of a publicly-funded NHS, insisted on a White Paper which would underline the review committee's preferences. This was policy making on the hoof par excellence for the document, suggesting bold departures, left the detail to be worked out as the process unfolded. It created the most tremendous furore. Health service managers were fearful that they would be left with the task of implementing policy without adequate guidance. The Labour Party thundered that the proposals meant the privatisation of the health service. The BMA, which had opposed Bevan's publicly-funded NHS, now argued against the reforms and supported the NHS as it was. Though Kenneth Clarke, the Secretary of State for Health, stuck out against the opposition and saw the legislation through virtually unchanged, the Government was rattled. It slowed down the pace of reform and told health managers to do as little as possible about the reforms before the next election. And, it increased spending on the NHS substantially! More than this the language of commerce gave way once more to the language of the public service:

> In retrospect . . . it is clear that as Mrs Thatcher's grip on office began to weaken, so ministers and their officials began to distance themselves from the stance they had been taking . . . 'Buyers' became 'purchasers' and then 'commissioners'. 'Sellers' became 'providers'. GP budgets became 'funds' and 'marketing' became 'needs assessment'. (Butler, 1992)

The National Health Service and Community Care Act (1990)

Under the provisions of the Act, a number of other measures were introduced with the apparent intention of facilitating greater efficiency, accountability and consumer responsiveness. These include:

1. The separation of the purchasing and service provision roles of DHAs. From 1 April 1991 this separation has been operative with DHAs acting as investigators of health needs, planners of service and procurers, and with hospitals acting as providers of services procured by the DHA.
2. The possibility for hospitals and other service providers to 'opt out' of DHA funding and become self-governing NHS Trusts. Five phases of opting out have now occurred. Trusts are able to control their own funds and appoint their own staff on pay and conditions negotiated between the parties. They are also permitted to enter into contracts with any DHA rather than solely the one in whose area they are situated. The Trusts are funded from earned revenue:

    An NHS Hospital Trust will earn its revenue from the services it provides. The main source of revenue will be from contracts with health authorities for the provision of services to their residents. Other contracts and revenue will come from GP practices with their own NHS budgets, private patients or their insurance companies, private hospitals, employers and, perhaps, other NHS Hospital Trusts. (Department of Health, 1990)

3. The establishment of GP fund-holding practices. As a result of this development, GP practices have been able to apply for self-governing status and receive practice budgets direct from the Department of Health. The link with the local Family Health Services Agency (FHSA) – formerly the Family Practitioner Committee (FPC) – has thus been broken and such general practitioners have become government-sanctioned medical entrepreneurs. The budget they receive is broken down under three heads covering, hospital costs, practice costs and prescribing costs. GP fund-holders may buy services from hospitals and other health providers and may negotiate fixed-price contracts for particular specialisms with individual hospitals. They are allowed to buy services from the private sector as well as the NHS.
4. Additional provisions of the Act included the streamlining of regional health authorities (RHAs), in England at least, and the transformation of the membership of DHAs. Before the Act, DHA membership included a significant representation of local elected councillors. Under the Act, they have been re-formed to ensure that the majority of the DHA membership is made up from the business community.

The changes outlined above constituted, then, an attempt by the Conservatives to restructure the National Health Service in a way consistent with wider free-market ideas, while bowing to pressure not to change the basis of funding. They amount to the practice of managed competition, first promoted by Enthoven (1985) and eagerly supported by the right within the Conservative Party.

Though there have been few new policy ideas in relation to health during the early 1990s, the Major administrations appear to have consolidated changes started during the Thatcher years. The transformation of hospitals into NHS Trusts is all but complete. At the time of writing only a few hospitals remain as units managed directly by health authorities. The effect of this transformation is significant if only because it has created a market or quasi-market within the NHS. From *quasi*-market to real market is a much smaller policy step than from public service to private service. Perhaps, after all, this is where the granny footsteps were leading.

Whither the National Health Service?

What, taken together, do all of these changes signify? On one reading they might be seen as fitting in with the destruction of the welfare state thesis. After all, substantial changes have occurred in the service which made it sometimes difficult to recognise as Bevan's NHS. And, of course, it is not. The changes that have been considered above are profound. But we need not only to understand those changes in the context of some sort of Thatcherite political project but also to appreciate that the changes fell far short of the plan developing in the early 1980s to annihilate the NHS and replace it with a private health insurance scheme. Conservative governments in the 1980s backed away from that strategy. They did so partly because of evident public opposition to the idea and, in part perhaps, because of some internal opposition within the parliamentary party. Instead, a programme of *restructuring* appears to have replaced the proposed devastation of the NHS. That restructuring was intended to move towards achievement of the same goals as abolition but it meant that by 1991, 12 years after the election of the first Thatcher government, the *framework* of the NHS remained relatively intact. The skeletal structure of the service had been bowed to some extent by the reforms of the 1980s and it is undoubtedly the case, despite government protests, that it was seriously underfunded throughout the whole of the period. However, it remained in place and in a recognisable form. As we have seen earlier, the period covered by the Major administrations has intensified the pace of the reforms but has not seen the development of new policy directions in health.

Making sense of it all

What conclusions are we to draw from the evolution in health policy and the NHS during the post-war years? Such a stock-taking exercise has to take account not only of the shifts in policy that have occurred but also of the possible meanings of those shifts.

The first point to be made is the obvious one. From almost its conception, Bevan's NHS ceased to be a service free at the point of use. Despite Bevan's efforts in Cabinet and elsewhere, the introduction of charges for optical and dental services in 1951 compromised one of the basic principles of the NHS on establishment. More than this it had the effect of separating so-called peripheral services from core NHS services. As we have seen, this has led to seemingly endless disputes since about the limits of free healthcare.

Supply and demand

The second theme to run throughout the whole post-war period is that of supply and demand. As we have seen, Bevan was simply wrong in his judgement that, once a post-war backlog of ill-health was dealt with, expenditure on the health service would fall in real terms. It did not and it has not. While resources are necessarily and always limited, demand remains infinite. This is not only because our expectations constantly rise, though this has been a factor, but also because medical science continually advances and is able to provide treatment for a growing number of ailments. This, of course, has placed growing demands for resources.

Demography has also played a part. Declining birth-rates and the fact that people are living longer (itself, partly the result of the success of the NHS) have placed increasing strains on the NHS. And, it should not be forgotten, the last 30 years have seen, if not a decline in the nation's health, a growing disparity between prosperous and less prosperous regions of the country. This was documented in *The Black Report*; the report of a study commissioned by Mrs Thatcher's first government and then buried when its message became clear (Townsend and Davidson, 1982).

In order to deal with supply and demand problems, and to tackle inequalities, rationing or prioritisation procedures have been developed. Ranging from charges on service to the development of blueprints like *The Health of the Nation* in England and *Strategic Intent and Direction* in Wales, these strategies have attempted to develop ways of containing what the NHS should treat. Similarly, the attempt, following Griffiths, to develop a managed service and the introduction of an internal market have been attempts either to manage demand or to drive the costs of treatment down.

The role attributed to DHAs in the 1990s is also concerned with defining or limiting supply and demand. Required to be 'champions of the people' (Department of Health, 1993), their main functions have been to assess health need in their localities and to arrive, via consultation with the community, at commissioning plans which encompass not only which treatments should be purchased from NHS Trusts but also which should be excluded from purchase.

Equality

The NHS has failed to generate equality of access to health services and states of health. It is widely acknowledged that relative inequalities in health have increased during the post-war period whether measured in relation to region, social class or ethnic group (Hart, 1975; LeGrand, 1982; Townsend and Davidson, 1982). If the intention of the founding parents of the NHS was to increase equality it has failed.

Postscript

At the time of writing, the Labour Party, which clearly regards itself as a government in waiting, has released a health policy document, the ideas contained in which will form the party's health manifesto (Labour Party, 1995). It anticipates making only relatively minor changes to the Government's health service reforms. Though it will formally remove the internal market from the NHS by removing purchasing contracts, it in fact recommends a market without money. NHS Trusts will remain although their boards will be democratised. They will provide healthcare commissioned by DHAs and doctors on the basis of a service level agreement. This author has some difficulty in distinguishing between a contract and a service level agreement and takes this policy to be acceptance of the internal market idea along with recognition that the money has not always followed the patient as had been anticipated in the present Government's establishment of the contract mechanism. The only significant divergence from the present NHS structure appears to be a commitment to abolish GP fund-holding and to replace it with GP consortia who will co-operate with DHAs in making decisions about commissioning healthcare.

CHAPTER EIGHT

Personal social services

The post-war personal social services: a summary

Following the Second World War, three state personal social services (PSS) agencies were created. They were administered by local government and replaced in large part the multiplicity of independent and government agencies which had previously carried out personal social service functions. These agencies, which existed until the early 1970s and were primarily concerned with services to children, the physically and mentally sick and disabled and the elderly, carried out a range of mostly statutory responsibilities. These were

195

especially concerned with the provision of residential or substitute care for clients in situations where home-based care was regarded as inappropriate, inadequate or damaging (see Sainsbury, 1977, for a fuller description of the services).

The reorganisation of state social work

In the early 1970s, following the report of the Seebohm Committee (Seebohm, 1968) in 1968 and the passing of the Local Authority Social Services Act in 1970, PSS was re-organised into unified local authority departments charged with the provision of statutory and non-statutory services to those in need. Further developments in PSS have occurred through the 1980s and early 1990s. In the early 1980s, the Barclay Report (1982), recommended the introduction of *community social work* strategies. Local authority social services departments and other PSS agencies were encouraged to develop alternative practices to meet social need. Community social work presumed a movement away from the one-to-one focus of traditional social work towards the encouragement and facilitation of self-help by individuals, social networks and communities. Barclay also recommended that the social work role, for many post-war years that of therapist, should be transformed. An important element of that transformation would be a move to the role of enabler. Social workers would support and enable informal carers rather than provide all care themselves.

The most recent organisational change in PSS has followed the enactment of the National Health Service and Community Care Act (1990). From 1993, local authority social services departments have become the co-ordinating agency for community care. This has significant ramifications. First, these departments will be key players in the assessment of social need, as long-stay hospitals and institutions are closed, to be replaced by care in the community. This immense change has come at a time when form has been given to the social services departments as strategic enablers. In this new world, local authority departments have become the assessors of need and the purchasers of services rather than near-monopoly providers of PSS.

This chapter describes and attempts to understand the development of post-war policy in this area of provision.

Personal social services in the post-war period

The late 1940s and the 1950s were a rather barren period for the development of the personal social services. At central government level, responsibility for the services was divided between the Home Office, which oversaw probation and children's services, and the Ministry of Health, which was concerned with services to the elderly, the sick and the disabled. At the local government level there was a separate committee for children's services, while responsibility for other services was divided between health and welfare committees and between education and housing. Working to these separate committees were separate departments, each with their own staff with their own assumptions, traditions and training. The outcome of this was that it was almost impossible to co-ordinate policy at national or local level and that duplication of services often occurred.

The development of policy was also influenced by pre-war, poor law attitudes among social services workers. In some areas of the country, workers appeared to believe that help for the disadvantaged should be provided by families and charities and not by them (Younghusband, 1978, p. 39). In others service appeared to be guided by moral, or moralistic, stances. One social services manager in the mid 1950s described the role of social services as being to 'ensure that people do as they are told and to make them realise that they will be punished if they don't' (Dixon and Rogers, 1960, p. 111).

Indeed, for some writers of the period, the problems with which the new social services had to deal were likely to be individual rather than structural in nature:

> *The most urgent problems . . . today are such symptoms of a sick society as the increasing number of marriage breakdowns, the spread of juvenile delinquency and the sense of frustration of the worker in spite of improved pay and conditions . . . that is, problems of maladjustment rather than material need. (Hall, 1952, p. 8)*

There were, however, problems other than those created by the social services themselves. Chief among these was resources. So, for instance, although one of the major intentions of the Children Act (1948) was that all children taken into care should be individually assessed in a reception centre before placement in a small family-style home or with foster parents, the resources did not exist. Given the scarcity of funds, labour and material few reception centres and small children's homes were built. The result was that children, and incidentally the elderly, often found themselves in large impersonal residential institutions. Though professionals in the services took the view that it was more effective to prevent difficulties than to react after they had occurred, preventive work was neither sanctioned nor encouraged by central government.

The 1960s: a decade of change

It was only with the coming of the 1960s that things began to change. Early in the decade, the Conservative government became increasingly concerned by the rising rates of juvenile delinquency and by the increased number of older people who, in the absence of alternative forms of institutional care, were occupying hospital beds. In the latter case, Powell, as Minister of Health, was anxious to meet the targets set in his Hospital Plan and introduced a policy of community care. Powell's plans for community care were based in large part on the discovery of drugs which could control the behaviour of mentally-ill people in the community. As a result of this and the dawning realisation that many people with mental handicaps could also be catered for outside institutions, resources were made available and spending on the social services doubled between 1960–8, having remained fairly static throughout the 1950s.

Fundamental changes were also afoot in the attitudes of professionals, or so it seemed. The moralistic assumptions of the 1950s appeared to be giving way, with the employment of a new generation of welfare professionals, to the idea that many of the problems experienced by individuals and families were related to wider structural problems. This understanding was part of the reason why social workers, and particularly the probation service, called for changes in the organisation and practice of social welfare. The probation service suggested in 1964 that there was a need for each local authority to develop a family service which would be preventive in nature. It would be concerned, in part, with the growing problem of juvenile delinquency and would be able to identify abnormal behaviour at an early point in the hope of preventing these behaviours developing into criminality.

The Seebohm Report

This recommendation played no small part in convincing the Labour government to establish a committee to review local authority social services. Headed by Sir Frederick Seebohm, it was established in 1965. Its brief was to 'review the organisation and responsibilities of the local authority personal social services in England and Wales . . . and to consider what changes are desirable to secure an effective family service' (Seebohm, 1968, para. 1). Like Beveridge, the Seebohm Committee decided early on to exceed its authority:

> *We decided very early in our discussions that it would be impossible to restrict our work solely to the needs of two or even three generation families. We could only make sense of our task by considering also childless couples and individuals without any close relatives: in other words, everybody. (Seebohm, 1968, para. 32)*

The committee took verbal and written evidence from interested parties and commissioned some small scale research.

Its eventual recommendations were threefold. First, each local authority should have a unified social services department which would bring together the professional workers previously employed by the children's department and the health and welfare departments. This was not the family service that had originally been envisaged but, as we have already seen, the committee took the view that membership of a family was not a sufficiently inclusive eligibility criterion for use of the service. Second, these departments should be headed by a director approved by the Secretary of State for Health of Social Security, whose responsibility was to ensure that the new social service departments were not 'self contained units . . . but part of a network of services in the community' (Seebohm, 1968, para. 376). The final recommendation was that generic training and further research should be encouraged. The Committee's recommendations were included in the Local Authority Social Services Act (1970), passed in the dying days of the Labour government with the co-operation of the Conservatives. The departments prescribed in the report were established in 1972 and their boundaries changed, following local government reorganisation, in 1974.

The Seebohm principles became, however, the source of controversy. The report, while commenting on the organisation of personal social services, provided no explicit justification of social work. It was silent on the criteria by which service priorities should be established. And, while the report listed a series of objectives and defined client rights, it neither costed nor quantified these proposals. The result was to be that aspirations for this universalist service were often dashed because no one had thought to calculate the cost of a trip to New Jerusalem; or, in Pinker's words, 'expectations raced ahead of available resources and the Babel of universalist aspirations overwhelmed the language of priorities' (Pinker, 1979).

Community development

In the late 1960s, the Labour government also introduced, as part of its anti-poverty strategy, the Community Development Project (CDP) initiative (Loney, 1983). Drawing on American War on Poverty initiatives, precipitated by Powell's Rivers of Blood speech and steered by the Home Office civil service, CDPs were seen as intervening in inner-city communities, often blighted by high levels of unemployment. The intervention of the CDPs was intended to help communities formulate or reformulate their own plans for social and economic regeneration. They are also notable for the joint financing basis of the initiative by central and local government. Though ultimately they failed, indeed how could they succeed in the context of seemingly perpetual economic crisis, they are striking for their emphasis on intervention at the community, rather than at the individual, level and their similarity in this respect with the principles behind the Seebohm Report.

The 1970s: filling the gap between aims and resources?

Almost immediately, then, the new social services departments, and the new social work that was implied, presented the two problems. What sort of

approach was consistent with the fresh challenges set by Seebohm departments? And, how could the gap between aims and resources be filled?

The clear implication of Seebohm's analysis that personal problems were
often reflections of wider structural problems was that the old emphasis on
psychodynamic approaches was inappropriate in this new world.

The response to this insight was two fold. The first, and conscious, reaction
was to change the nature of social work education so that the accent moved
from a concern with personal and family dynamics to training social workers
to carry out generic tasks. This transformation of training appears, in
retrospect, to indicate a misunderstanding of Seebohm by the social work
profession. He had stressed that the new social services departments should
be generic. The profession, in contrast, set about trying to create generic social
workers rather than sufficient numbers of specialist social workers who, when
brought together, might satisfy the new generic function.

The second response was more serendipitous. Searching for an intellectual
basis for the new genericism, the profession appeared to swallow whole an
approach to social work popularised by American social work theorists.
Nineteen-seventy-three saw the publication of Pincus and Minahan's *Social
Work Practice: Model and Method* and Goldstein's *Social Work Practice: A
Unitary Approach* (Pincus and Minahan, 1973; Goldstein, 1973). This was
followed in 1977 by the first British contribution in this genre (Specht and
Vickery, 1978). The nub of all these books was that individual and family
problems should be seen through the lenses provided by systems theory.
Problems, when they occur, are seen as arising from the dissonance between
elements of the individual's or family's social system, including the
community in which the individual lives, the society of which she is a part
and the policies prescribed by that society. The role of the social worker in this
literature is to act as a change agent, engineering change in whichever sub-
system is responsible for problem causation. In order to perform this role,
social workers would need skills in social casework, groupwork, and
community development. This sort of approach became popular in part
because it filled the intellectual gap, left by Seebohm, about the methods by
which generic activity was carried out. Though the contradiction of state
employees (for that was what social workers are) sometimes acting to change
the state was never resolved, systems theory seemed, for a while at least, to be
the panacea to social work's post-Seebohm ills.

The most significant gap, between aims and resources, was however not
bridged. Sir Keith Joseph, as Secretary of State for Health and Social Security
in the early 1970s, had found the money to implement the Seebohm
programme and had also released resources that were to start a decade of
apparently uncontrolled spending on the personal social services. Between
1970–4, spending on PSS increased by an average of 12 per cent per annum.
From 1975 on, the increase in expenditure slowed, as the British economy
ground almost to a halt, but the rate of increase was still respectable. However,

aims always outstripped resources, which was one reason why Mrs Thatcher's first government tried again and appointed Sir Peter Barclay to carry out yet another review of social workers' tasks and roles.

The 1980s: community social work arrives

We might expect that such a committee, at such a time, established by such a government would have produced recommendations calculated to strike fear into the social worker's heart. For Mrs Thatcher's own views were clear. Often citing the work of the radical right, ministers, or the Premier herself, signalled a restructuring of PSS that would involve voluntarism and residual-ising the state.

Such a pre-eminent role for voluntary, family, or community services, and a consequential residual role for state social work, is clear in the advice of Patrick Jenkin, then Secretary of State for Social Services, that 'The Social Services departments should seek to meet directly only those needs which others cannot or will not meet . . . Their task is to act as a safety net . . . for people for whom there is no other, not a first port of call' (*The Guardian*, 21 January, 1981).

Thatcher herself told the 1981 annual conference of the Women's Voluntary Service that the main burden of social welfare provision should fall on the voluntary sector of welfare, with statutory social services functioning simply as residual gap fillers, underpinning the work of the voluntary sector.

Barclay, picking up on these themes, did emphasise the role of voluntarism and community action. He emphasised the need for social work to be transformed from the role of change agent, if that role had ever successfully been adopted. Instead social workers should practice community social work. Social services departments should enable the provision of services rather than provide all of them themselves. They should co-ordinate the efforts of volunteers and community groups and advise on access to resources. But, neither the abolition of local authority departments nor the eclipse of social work was recommended:

> In spite of all the complexities and uncertainties surrounding the functions of social workers, we are united in our belief that the work they do is of vital importance in our society, as it is in other modern industrial societies. It is here to stay, and social workers are needed as never before. But it is important that we use a scarce and costly resource – the trained social worker – in a creative and effective manner. (Barclay, 1980, p. xi)

The vote of confidence in social work is as resounding as Seebohm's though the realignment suggested was much less significant. Similarities between Barclay and Seebohm are eerily close. Both were plucked from the chairmanship of the National Institute for Social Work, both were bankers and both had been involved throughout their life in charitable activity. Though the attraction of Seebohm to a Labour government is obvious, it is less easy to understand why Barclay's *curriculum vitæ* should have commended itself to Thatcher or her neo-liberal Secretary of State, Patrick Jenkin.

. . . and disappears

Barclay, *per se*, disappeared from the scene as quickly as it had emerged. Though there are traces of Barclayism in Conservative government policy throughout the 1980s and 1990s, the report's direct impact was decidedly underwhelming.

Community care, again!

Hard on the heels of the death of Barclay came a number of care in the community initiatives. Between 1985–9 four major reports on community care emerged. All four pointed to the principled agreement of all interested parties that community care should be supported. And all four drew attention to the unwillingness of government to implement such proposals:

> At the centre, community care has been talked of for 30 years and in few areas can the gap between political rhetoric and policy on the one hand, or between policy and reality in the field on the other hand, have been so great. To talk of policy in matters of care except in the context of available resources and timescales for action owes more to theology than to the purposeful delivery of a caring service. (Griffiths, 1988, p. iv)

The intensification of interest in the provision of services by means of community care was signalled by an Audit Commission report which found 'progress towards community care to be slow and uneven' (Audit Commission, 1986) and was emphasised in a report from the King's Fund Institute that 'there is clearly no articulated national policy on community care'. Following the criticisms contained in the Audit Commission report, Sir Roy Griffiths was commissioned once more to sort out the problem.

Inasmuch as community care policies and practices were evident they were spread between the Department of Health, the new Department of Social Security and the Department of the Environment. In Griffiths's words, community care was 'the poor relation; everybody's distant relative but nobody's baby' (Griffiths, 1988). How, the Government wanted to know, could this situation be changed and community care co-ordinated. From the start, Griffiths was determined that one route that should be avoided was the establishment of an entirely new body to oversee community care. He also came to rule out the NHS as the appropriate agency to take the lead in community care. For one thing the service was in upheaval and about to be subject to its own review. For another, Griffiths was fearful that if the NHS led on community care it would become medicalised. Instead, and to the surprise and disapproval of government, he plumped for local authorities as the most appropriate body to co-ordinate community care policy and practice: 'any government has got to differentiate between the free health service and the means-tested social services. If you start putting them both under the health service, you are blurring a very crucial line' (Timmins, 1995, p. 473).

Griffiths's decision to recommend local authorities as the co-ordinators of community care caught the Government on the hop. It was certainly not what it had been expecting and, given the record of Mrs Thatcher's administrations in relation to local authorities, it was unwelcome. Unsurprisingly, they followed the well trodden road and played for time. They published the report on the day after the 1988 Budget, thus ensuring that it received little publicity and then set up an inter-departmental committee of civil servants to scrutinise the report. In fact, the committee concluded that Griffiths had got it about right.

The Government's allergy to local (especially local Labour) government had, in any case, partially blinded it to the fact that 'Griffiths Two', as it came to be known, was in fact orthodox, straight-down-the-line welfare pluralism of the sort that the Government approved and usually promoted. It anticipated that local government's role in the provision of services would diminish and that there would be a significant increase in the involvement of the informal, voluntary and private welfare sectors:

> The primary function of public services is to design and arrange the provision of care and support . . . There is value in a multiplicity of provision, not least from the consumer's view, because of the widening choice, flexibility, innovation and competition it should stimulate. It is vital that social services authorities should see themselves as the arrangers and purchasers of care services – not as monopolistic providers. (Griffiths, 1988)

Local authorities should then enable, design, purchase and organise non-health-related community care. Griffiths believed that they should be charged with:

- Assessing community care needs in their localities, objective-setting and formulation of community care plans.
- The financial management of community care funds to be transferred from social security and health authorities.
- Monitoring and regulating performance.
- The provision of information to consumers and providers of care.
- The assessment of individual need and the design of packages of care to meet need.

Under these arrangements, social workers were to become case managers, designing packages of care aimed at achieving effective services in the community.

Though Kenneth Clarke, as Secretary of State for Health, and Mrs Thatcher were, from different wings of the party and for different reasons, unhappy about the Griffiths proposals, they appear to have been saved as a result of an equally unlikely ministerial paring. David Mellor, the 'wet' Minister of State for Health, and Nicholas Ridley, the paper-dry Secretary of State for the Environment, both pressed for the adoption of Griffiths: Mellor because it struck a balance between private and public services rather than attempting to abolish the latter and Ridley for quite other reasons. He was well known as an enemy of local authorities, believing them to be expensive to run and expansionist in their aspirations. In the late 1980s they also tended to be Labour. However Ridley, at the time of the publication of the report, had just finished writing a pamphlet for the Centre for Policy Studies. Its title was *The Local Right* and it argued, as had others, for local authorities to be enablers not providers, to be stimulators and monitors of service provision rather than monopoly providers.

In other words, and probably for different reasons, Griffiths Two chimed with the views of the radical right on the role of local government. The report also pointed the way, wittingly or otherwise, to a coherent Thatcherite social policy by means of which services remained publicly funded but market forces were introduced into them. The creation of quasi-markets, at least in the view of the right-winger, Arthur Seldon, would make the final move to privatisation of services easier in the future.

However, Griffiths could count on a far wider constituency of support than the radical right. Labour local government backed him. Here the motive was almost always that, having been stripped of much of their role in housing and education, community care gave them an important policy function. And, despite the continuing scepticism of Clarke, the Government finally accepted the Griffiths proposals in July 1989. The proposals, or at least many of them, were to emerge as the community care bit of the National Health and Community Care Act (1990) and since 1993 it has been fully implemented.

Understanding personal social services policy

How then do we explain the development and objectives of PSS throughout the whole of the post-war period?

It appears clear that, for two post-war decades at least, PSS policy was driven by the same social democratic engine that drove education. That drive was based on essentially Fabian notions of human nature, professional action and the appropriate role of the state. In other words, thinking about policy and its enactment was coloured by a belief in the perfectibility of humankind. Sometimes such views are made explicit. Slack, commenting on the introduction of state social work with children, says of the Curtis Report, '[it] was based on a *new and more sympathetic* approach to human need. Emphasis was laid on the differences of each child and his value as an individual' (Slack, 1966, p.111, my emphasis).

It reflected, in large part, a commitment to meet need through the activities of government and state: 'whenever or wherever a social service is introduced it is to meet a need that has, whether soon or late, been recognised as real or unmet' (Slack, 1966, p. 93); or, as Titmuss suggests: 'As the accepted area of social obligation widened, as injustice became less tolerable, new services were separately organised around individual need' (Titmuss, 1963, p.21). However, this sort of view was one that was to be assailed by both the political left and right.

The left critique

Much of the left critique emerging in the 1950s and 1960s was that the social services had less to do with helping individuals and families deal with their problems than with achieving social and attitudinal conformity.

The state, according to this perspective, always safeguards the interests of capitalism. The post-war British welfare state therefore functioned to promote capital accumulation (O'Connor, 1973), economic efficiency and social stability (Saville, 1957) and ideological conformity (Barratt-Brown, 1972).

The place of PSS in this scheme was that of a state institution operating primarily, though not exclusively, to promote social stability and the conformity of working class people to ruling class ideology. During the period under consideration, this function had been carried out in a number of ways including the use of social case work techniques '. . . a pseudo-science – that blames individual inadequacies for poverty and so mystifies and diverts attention from the real causes' (Case Con Collective, 1970). Capitalism was also protected by other, and seemingly more progressive, forms of social work activity such as group work and community work. Such activities served simply to pathologise the group or the community rather than the individual. Social work, then, whether practised in the form of case work, group work or community work, acted socially to integrate or socially to control, working class people. In Corrigan's words, 'throughout the western world, states are characterised by one of the two major symbols of control in capitalist society; the tank or the community worker' (Corrigan, 1975, p. 25). Social case work, one of the major tools in the armoury of the post-war PSS, was a coercive activity which defined socially caused problems as family or individual crises (see Wilson, in Cowley et al., 1977). Community work and group work are seen as '. . . means by which society induces individuals and groups to modify their behaviour in the direction of certain cultural norms' (Gulbenkian Foundation, 1968, p. 84).

However, some left writing, though it was critical of social work as theory and practice, suggested that the picture was less black and white than had been presented by the radicals. For these writers, the state exhibited, during the post-war period, a limited autonomy from the British ruling class.

For many writers from this perspective (Corrigan and Leonard, 1978; Bolger *et al.*, 1981; Jones, 1983), PSS in post-war Britain reflected a dialectic of welfare (Leonard, in Bean and MacPherson, 1983).

To some of these writers, social democratic theory is at least half right: post-war capitalism was qualitatively different from its inter-war forebear. Co-ordinated services were established and operated for most of the period in a changed political atmosphere and structure. The spirit of 1945 was sustained throughout much of the period (Jones, 1983). PSS legislation and social work practice during that period reflected the clear influence of the social democratisation of state structures and social values. State policies and social work practices, while stopping far short of the provision of total welfare, demonstrated a tendency for state social provision progressively to meet some of the social needs of ordinary people as well as being concerned with containment and control (Gough, 1979; Leonard, in Bean and MacPherson, 1983). From this perspective, then, co-ordinated state services managed at one and the same time to effect the contradictory aims of meeting some of the social needs of its clients while meeting the economic and political 'needs' of a dominant class in capitalist society. Welfare state social work moved from punishment to rehabilitation. Post-war social democratic politics had pro-vided 'the ideological climate for [the] more liberal and humane welfare theories and practices to be extended to the unorganised and impoverished dependent poor' (Jones, 1983, p. 39). However, for these Marxists at least, such changes in practice and aims represented little more, at times, than a replacement of biological determinist theories of social problem causation by a set of family pathology explanations. Nonetheless such a shift, though limited and still ideologically useful to powerful social interests, is seen as having effected a move towards understanding social problems within a wider social context than hitherto.

Policies and practices related to youthful delinquency and family problems were seen, from this perspective, as reflecting the social democratisation of welfare. The Children and Young Persons' Act (1969) was therefore concep-tualised as part of a process which tended both to liberate and control.

Here, the argument is that the 1969 Act and the reorganisation of personal social services, with which it was associated temporally and philosophically, point up both the progressive and conservative nature of PSS under social democracy. The Act and the reorganisation are seen as products of the contradictions inherent in the capitalist system. For both sought to establish the primacy of a welfare model in the theory and practice of social welfare: the Act by elevating the welfare needs of young offenders above abstract considerations of justice in sentencing; reorganisation by promoting the idea that the new social service departments would provide for the welfare needs of all in a non-stigmatising way. At the same time, however, both social policy developments were rooted in an ideology of family pathology which saw residual problems in social democratic Britain as the result of malfunctioning family units. Such an ideology reinforced a new form of social control in social work. Individuals, previously held responsible for their own difficulties were, in late twentieth century British social democracy, to be subject to social control through treatment rather than punishment. They were to be controlled through the identification and policing of families – often seen as the root of problems of deviance and poverty (see Donzelot, 1980).

For all left critics the crucial weakness in social democratic welfare theory and practice was this: in one form or another, citizens were regarded as responsible for socially-induced problems. For social democracy theorised, and social democratic welfare practice operated, an ideology of pathology. If the individual was liberated from responsibility for social problems, then the family or the community took the individual's place (Clarke, 1980). If social democratic PSS policy had virtue then it was, for the left, in the practical implications of the move from an ideology of punishment to an ideology of treatment.

This was, as we have seen above, to change during the 1980s and 1990s as responsibility for problems and their solutions were, to a greater extent, placed back with the individuals, families and communities who experienced them. More than this, ideas of the market and market practices were imported for the first time into the provision of social welfare. In this context the left critics became supporters of the social democratic welfare project.

The attack from the right

As we have seen in Chapter 3, radical-right formulations see social welfare as having developed as the result of the creation of a bogus consensus on the need for state provision. Many, if not all, of the arguments adduced by proponents of anti-collectivism in relation to welfare in general were adduced in the specific cases of social work provision and PSS policy.

For the ultra-right, state provision of PSS, like other state social services, led post-war Britain towards state coercion (Hayek, 1944, p. 52; Friedman, 1962, p. 13). PSS, by according citizen rights to all sections of the population, contributed to social discord (Friedman, 1962, ch. 10) and, because of its increasing call on the public purse, to reducing economic growth and prosperity. State social work was seen as having diminished individual responsibility because it, 'reduces the breadwinner's individual responsibility for his family's well being, and for the pursuit of independence it substitutes permanent mutual dependence as the much more fragile basis of mutual respect' (Bremner, 1968, pp. 52–3).

Personal social services provision, by superseding 'the voluntary co-operation of individuals' (Friedman, 1962, p. 13), also reduced freedom: it reduced democracy, choice, respect, the role of the family and contributed to social disorganisation.

The new right apologists of the post-war years not only attacked PSS social democratic style. In its place, they prescribed a much reduced role for state social work in contemporary British society. Instead of offering a more or less universal service, social welfare services were best undertaken in the main by the family and the community. Thatcher, echoing Friedman, argued that 'if we are to sustain, let alone extend, the level and standard of care in the community, we must first try to put responsibility back where it belongs, with the family and with the people themselves' (Thatcher, 1977, p. 83). Pre-Thatcherite apologists, then, assigned both reduction in PSS functions and changes in the pattern of PSS provision.

Personal social services and the new Conservatism

As we have seen above, the election of Conservative governments throughout the 1980s and into the 1990s has effected changes to PSS policy.

The scene was set, then, for the transformation of statutory PSS agencies into enabling organisations. Those organisations would enable informal carers or the neighbourhood (*pace* the Barclay Report) or act as commissioners of service, in a situation where much provision was offered by voluntary or private welfare bodies.

At one level at least, the new Conservatism of the 1980s and 1990s has encouraged a return to pre-welfare state approaches in PSS. While carers get on with caring and the independent and private sectors carry out state-financed philanthropy, the state is being slowly removed from centre stage in the provision of PSS. In so doing, of course, an attempt to bury the trails of social democratic welfare, perhaps ultimately doomed to success, is being made. For this marginalisation of state PSS activity also marginalises the totems of social democracy itself.

First, the idea that the state has a responsibility to meet all welfare needs has been superseded by the idea that the state's responsibility is to enable informal carers, or kin, or the community to care. Second, the professional-isation of welfare, seen by Thatcher's new Conservatives and the radical right as largely responsible for the growth of welfare monopolies, is being swept aside by the elevation of informal and untrained care. Last, the social democratic idea that individual needs are best met by collective state provision is severely dented.

At the time of writing, we appear to stand on the cusp of removal of the state from large-scale *provision* of PSS. Whether services will be further rationalised must remain, for now, a matter of conjecture. But a quasi-market has been introduced into personal social services and that in itself might point to an intention to privatise at some point in the future. For as Minford argues:

Many of these personal social services are capable of being privatised. Nothing decrees that . . . [they] be paid by the state . . . these services could be provided by private companies. A system of vouchers would enable consumers to exercise choice . . . They would ensure that the services were provided in the combination suitable to the user and, because of the spur to competition between private producers, . . . at the lowest possible cost. (Minford, 1992)

CHAPTER NINE

Post-war housing policy

Chronology	Housing policy since the war
Late 1940s	The birth of council housing
Early 1950s	Macmillan's housing drive
Mid 1950s–late 1960s	Slum clearance The market in housing policy Rachmanism Homelessness High-rise developments
1970s	Homelessness The failure of high rise Social housing re-emphasised Housing associations
1980s	'Right to buy' Housing Act 1988

As we have seen in Chapter 3, Labour's post-war housing drive was detrimentally affected by both resource shortage and the climate! As we have also seen, when the Conservatives returned to power in 1951, housing was made a priority as a result of a 'peasants' revolt' in the usually well-behaved Conservative Annual Conference when the floor demanded a target of 300 000 new builds a year.

Housing policy: the post-war years

By the end of the war it was clear that the population yearned for the provision of decent housing. In Burnett's words:

there was no longer any hesitation by the state in involving itself in a housing policy. The Labour Government elected in 1945 needed no persuading that it would have to play the major part in promoting new homes at a time of urgent national need. (Burnett, 1986)

By 1951, the Labour government had presided over the building of 900 000 houses. Though this was an impressive feat, they had fallen well short of their own target and the housing shortage remained acute.

Macmillan and housing

On any reading the record of the Conservative housing minister in the 1951 administration was impressive. Committed to build 300 000 houses per annum, Macmillan actually managed to oversee the building of 319 000 houses in 1953 and 348 000 in 1954. The increase was in part the result of his decision to relax the standards set by the Labour housing minister, Dalton, in 1951. And these were, in turn, a relaxation of the rigorous standards set by Bevan during his tenure. Macmillan's council houses were often made with inferior materials and their dimensions were less generous. Additionally, increasing numbers of two-bedroomed (as opposed to bigger) dwellings were built (Timmins, 1995). With a flair that was to characterise Macmillan's career, he presented this shift as a response to demographic change, pointing to the increasing number of one generation households with smaller numbers of dependent children. In an attempt to stimulate the growth of private property he also relaxed and then removed licences on private house building. By 1955, he had also approved the sale of 3000 council houses following his instruction to local authorities to offer their stock for sale to sitting tenants. This move was designed to reduce the Treasury subsidy to local authorities for rents and to generate capital to be ploughed back into house building. In doing this, he was bowing to the Conservative desire to create what later came to be called a property-owning democracy: 'We wish to see the widest distribution of property. We think that of all forms of property available for such distribution, house property is one of the best' (Macmillan, 1951 cited in Timmins, 1995).

The return of the market

Though Macmillan's tenure is marked by the significant numbers of houses built by local authorities for rent, the Conservative government was anxious to reinstate the market to a prominent position in housing. This anxiety was reinforced by evidence emerging in 1952 that housing was falling out of use faster than new houses could be built (Macmillan, 1969, p. 444). One of the reasons for this related to the private rented housing sector. In the early 1950s, this sector accounted for about one third of the housing stock and was therefore an important element in meeting housing need. However, rents on many properties in this sector had been frozen at 1939 levels. Rent income was often, therefore, insufficient to encourage landlords to carry out repairs and housing degenerated into slums or became completely unsuitable for use. By 1954 the hell-for-leather race to build new council housing was therefore scaled down and emphasis placed instead, as in post-war Germany, on repairs and slum clearance. Government estimates suggested the existence of around about 500 000 slum households. In 1953, Macmillan proposed that councils should be empowered to buy slum houses for their site value. They would then be able to engage in slum clearance, replace the slums with new housing and charge an economic rent which would cover repairs. In 1954, the Housing Repairs and Rents Act (1954) removed Treasury subsidies for new builds while retaining them for repairs and for slum clearance. Remaining need for new houses would, the Government hoped, be met substantially by the private market. The success of this strategy appears to be in no doubt: while in 1945 only 26 per cent of houses were owner occupied, the 1964 figure was 47 per cent. Though the re-introduction of the market in the housing sector appeared to work initially: 'The general expectation seems to be that the Act will, as promised, make rather more accommodation available' (*Manchester Guardian*, 1 December 1958), it made for no permanent improvement. Demographic factors, such as the establishment of service industries in London, drew those in search of work to the capital. New Commonwealth immigrants, sucked into a buoyant labour market, were also searching for homes in large numbers. Slum clearance was moving apace and numbers were well in advance of new houses being built. The result was that the housing crisis deepened, homelessness was on the increase and rents were, on the renewal of tenancies, rocketing.

Rising higher

Another solution to the housing problem was the decision, in the mid 1950s, to favour the building of high rise flats. In 1956, Duncan Sandys, Macmillan's successor as Minister of Housing, started paying higher government subsidies for high rise blocks:

> Since construction in practice costs more as you go higher, the result has been that flats in low blocks have been more heavily subsidised in relation to costs than flats in high blocks. Apart from being inequitable, this has unintentionally influenced local authorities to concentrate on building blocks of three, four and five storeys, which, I believe, many honourable members will agree are most monotonous. (Hansard, 17 November 1955)

Honourable members did agree and the scene was set for one of the biggest disasters in British housing policy.

The issue of density clearly influenced the Minister. Here was a way of accommodating more people in less space. In fact, high rise was to prove to be more expensive than low rise building but that was far from clear in 1963 when Keith Joseph, as housing minister, was to sanction a blitz of high rise building. Though he was later to regard this as 'the best of intentions, the worst of results' (*The Guardian*, 12 November 1973), it seemed like a good idea at the time. Not only was high rise build more expensive than traditional methods but in execution it proved to be a lower quality method. The concrete slabs that constituted the core of these often prefabricated buildings were soon to crack, sometimes to free themselves from other elements of the building and on occasions to crash to the ground. More than this, the new tower blocks were to prove dangerous. That danger was often in the form of criminality or over-exuberance. One of the most popular designs was to have decks running around the outside of each storey onto which the flats opened. These proved to offer thieves and others easy access to properties and to provide children with their own adventure playgrounds as they swung Tarzan-like from one deck to the next.

There were other clear disadvantages. Chief among them was that they clearly replaced the community spirit of admittedly slum dwellings with individualism and anomie as councils re-housed slum-dwellers in anonymous tower blocks. Amenities were often poor, with little thought being given to the proximity of shops and leisure facilities. Mothers with young children found themselves almost literally imprisoned within the confines of the block as facilities and kin were often at some distance.

Conservatives and the market

By the mid 1950s, the market was being presented as the major mechanism by which to solve the housing problem. It was the problem of rents that was to make it so. As we have suggested earlier, much of the private sector was subject to rent regulation. This had some unforeseen effects. First, council housing often proved to be more expensive to rent than private accommodation and thus tended to attract the labour aristocracy rather than the semi-skilled and the unskilled. Connected to this, although wages had risen considerably faster than inflation during the 1950s, those in privately rented accommodation had become used to low rents. In order to intervene in this situation Sandys introduced the Rent Act (1957). Under this legislation higher rents were deregulated by stages over three years. While this affected the usually middle class tenants of high-rent properties, lower rents were raised but remained regulated. However when tenancies of these relatively low-rent properties ended these also would be deregulated. The Act was seen by Labour as class-biased legislation and the party promised to repeal it when it formed a government.

The New Towns

Another development, starting in the mid 1950s was the construction of whole New Towns like those at Harlow, Cwmbran, Milton Keynes, Telford and the like. Here the idea was to solve the housing crisis by creating new communities. The composition of the New Towns was heavily weighted towards young couples who were seeking to establish new households. Indeed, Harlow New Town became known as 'Pram Town'!

They too posed early problems as housing tended to be in satellite estates at some distance from the shopping centre, reinforcing the privatisation of tenants' lives. Their big advantage, however, was employment opportunities. For example, by 1961 40 per cent of the female population of Harlow was working, a pattern common to all the New Towns.

Three major trends continued into, and beyond, the 1960s. First, there was a combination of increasing population and fragmentation of lifestyle; secondly, there was an increase in prosperity, and thirdly, a drift away from rented accommodation matched by a move towards owner occupation.

Housing policy in the 1960s: the 'affluent society' and why Cathy didn't come home

Demographic change

During the 1960s the pattern of fragmentation of households, already established in the early post-war years continued apace. Households previously comprising two- and three-generation families broke down as each generation sought their own housing space. The housing stock, already inadequate to demand, was further stretched by this phenomenon.

During the 1960s, the United Kingdom population increased by about two and a half million. At the same time, the average number of people within each household declined from 3.1 in 1961 to 2.7 people by 1981. The result of these two trends was that between 1961–81 an extra 15 million families were looking for their own home.

These were, at least in the early 1960s, the 'never had it so good' years. The wages of manual workers continued to increase at levels above inflation, average working hours decreased and the 'affluent worker' was, at least according to Goldthorpe and Lockwood (1969), a reality.

But behind the undoubted *embourgeoisement* of a labour aristocracy lay a darker country altogether. The flip side of the affluent worker was the perpetuation of a class of unemployed and low paid people to whom affluence had not trickled down. These were the slum-dwellers of the 1960s, 'the private squalor midst public affluence' (Galbraith, 1976). Housing policy and the abuses of those seeking to be housed during the 1960s have to be seen in this context.

In 1961, the Conservative government, struggling with evidence that the crisis was deepening not tapering out (Banting, 1979), re-introduced substantial subsidies for new build but, under Joseph, the Ministry of Housing was already turning to new ideas about housing for the poor. Officials seeking non-state solutions to the housing problem visited Scandinavia to investigate their not-for-profit housing associations. Sir Keith, already an innovator, invested £25 million in a pilot project in 1961. In 1963, the fruit of that investment, twelve two-bedroomed flats in Birmingham, took their first housing association tenants. Here then, though from social democratic Scandinavia, was an idea that was to take root 20 or more years later in education and health: the publicly funded but independently managed provider of services. In the dog days of the Conservative government, a jubilant Sir Keith announced a £100 million grant to the newly formed Housing Corporation so that the idea of housing associations could spread.

Rachman, rents and reaction

All housing policy in the early 1960s was, however, overshadowed by the man who gave his name to Rachmanism. Perec Rachman had, since the mid 1950s, capitalised on the housing shortage in London. Buying up swathes of sub-standard property at end of lease, he would terrorise those sitting tenants who were unprepared to vacate Rachman's premises. He would then subdivide the property and let it at high rent to those who failed to find other housing provision. The conditions were often appalling:

> . . . A young girl near to tears . . . the pitifully small room in which she and her husband had to live. There was no water except for a cold tap in the back yard down three flights of dark, rickety stairs. The one lavatory for the eleven people in the building was too filthy to use. Cooking facilities had to be shared. The house was rat-infested and the walls so ridden with bugs and beetles that the girl was afraid to replace the ancient wall-paper which helped to some extent to keep them from crawling into the room.

thus thundered The Times (29 August, 1963). Labour exposed this exploitation in Parliament during a debate on the Profumo Affair. Mandy Rice-Davies had, according to one speaker, been one of the, by now, late Rachman's mistresses. But of less salacious interest and of more importance was the anger with which Labour tore into the Government. Wilson, the new leader, argued that Rachmanism had been encouraged by the Rent Act (1957) and the consequent rent rises. He pledged that Labour would repeal the legislation and with that pledge the housing debate appeared to shift. Landlords were tarred with the brush of Rachman. The Conservatives were tarred with their association with landlordism and Labour was helped, by the issue, to victory in the general election held the following year.

Labour and housing policy: 1964–70

On election, Labour repealed the Rent Act as it had promised and replaced it with one of their own. It restored tenants' security of tenure and established rent tribunals to adjudicate in cases where tenants felt their rent to be too high. Additionally, it allowed rent rises to occur every three years. Despite Labour's earlier commitment to the municipalisation of the rented sector, Crossman's Rent Act (1965) was acceptable across the political spectrum. It was so because he attempted to strike a balance between landlord and tenant rather than driving landlords out of business. Of equal significance was Labour's White Paper, *The Housing Programme 1965–1970*, in which Labour recognised owner occupation as the dominant form of tenure.

Back to the numbers game . . . but a new ideology

Crossman, on his appointment, persuaded Wilson that building targets needed to be set. These finally fell out as 150 000 council houses and 250 000 private homes in 1965. This figure was missed in 1965 as the Chancellor scaled down Crossman's ambitions. It was met in 1966 but stiffer targets lay ahead. In 1965 Crossman had introduced a White Paper which had set a target of 500 000 builds per annum by 1970. Economic crises and devaluation in 1967 ensured that these targets were never met. In 1968, 350 000 houses were built but from then on numbers fell off. But, as has been suggested above, the White Paper also signalled the end of Labour's affection for council housing. In it, Crossman argued that once 'slumdom and obsolescence' had been banished Labour's programme of council house subsidy should be scaled down.

This new commitment to owner occupation was demonstrated in Crossman's decision to exempt owner-occupied houses from capital gains tax and the introduction of 100 per cent mortgages and option mortgages which provided low-interest loans to the lower paid. By the time that Labour left office in 1970, more than half the households in England and Wales were owner occupied for the first time.

The death of high rise

The collapse of Ronan Point, a London County Council (LCC) tower block in east London, spelt the end of the misplaced confidence in high rise provision. On 16 May 1968 a gas explosion blew out the load-bearing walls of the tower and rooms on one corner of the block progressively collapsed into one another leaving five people dead and seventeen injured.

Surveys by councils in the wake of Ronan Point were frightening reading. Many of them were shedding brickwork and some were downright dangerous.

Though high rise towers were to continue to house tenants, the disaster spelt the end of high rise as a policy. In any event the 1968 White Paper, *Old Houses into New Homes*, was promoting the idea of renovation rather than new build. This was the final nail in the high rise coffin.

The result of all these measures, and of dreadful economic circumstances, was that the government managed to facilitate the building of 1.8 million houses between 1965–9, with the peak being reached in 1968. The houses built were split roughly equally between the private and public sectors (Hill, 1990).

Cathy come home

Throughout the 1960s, as we have already seen, the increasing poverty of the few proved a painful counterpoint to the increasing affluence of the many. This fact was given academic respectability by two left-leaning LSE academics, Brian Abel-Smith and Peter Townsend. In research carried out during the late 1950s and early 1960s, they had found that the welfare state had not, in fact, eradicated primary poverty as had been believed. Rather, it was a growing, if minority, problem (Townsend and Abel-Smith, 1965). This report gained publicity as did the work of the Child Poverty Action Group (CPAG). CPAG went one step further and claimed, erroneously as it turned out, that the poor were poorer under Labour than they had been under the Conservatives. The allegation, made in fact by CPAG's director Frank Field, drew the rage of Crossman and the disapproval of Abel-Smith, who fell out with Townsend briefly because the latter had accompanied Field to a tense meeting with Crossman at which the former had been present as the Minister's political adviser! Nonetheless, what was being claimed contained within it a germ of truth. The poor were the casualties in and of an affluent society (Galbraith, 1982). The welfare state allowed some to slip through the safety nets and to end up homeless and hopeless. Cathy, the subject of Ken Loach's play *Cathy come home*, never did. She and her family were the undeserving in the new affluent Britain and slid into homelessness and separation. As if by coincidence, one month after the broadcast, *Shelter* was born in December 1966 to campaign for the rescue of homeless families in housing blackspots in the major cities.

Heath and housing: the record of the Conservative government, 1970–4

When Edward Heath somewhat surprisingly won the 1970 general election, he appointed Peter Walker as Secretary of State for Environment, in which department housing was now based. A one nation Tory, his major intervention in housing policy was the Housing Finance Act (1972). This legislation re-directed housing subsidies away from buildings and towards people. He made rent rebates mandatory and dependent on individual eligibility. At the same time he made tenants in privately rented accommodation eligible for the benefit. This was at the expense of council house tenants, whose homes were to be subjected to gradual increases to economic rent level. Walker was able, nonetheless, to sell this move as a redistributive one: the better-off working class in the council house sector subsidising the less well-off working class in the private rented sector (Timmins, 1995).

Walker also declared war on slums and approved further slum clearance. But, mindful that the provision of new housing in the previous 20 years had torn communities apart, the Secretary of State made improvement grants available so that new homes could be made out of old houses. Walker's record was, in fact, a reasonable one but it was overshadowed by the passions aroused over the rise in council rents. Crosland, shadowing Walker, attacked the Act as 'the most reactionary and socially divisive measure likely to be introduced in the life time of this Parliament' and promised that it would be repealed. Perhaps Crosland was trying to hang the Selsdon Man label around Walker's neck. If that was the intention, it was peculiarly ill-adept. For new houses were still being built and the slum clearance programme continued. Though, as the economy worsened, the slum clearance programme slowed down, and the completion of new housing fell from 307 000 properties in 1970 to 241 000 homes in 1974.

Labour and housing: 1974–9

The Conservative government fell in February 1974, following an election fought on its handling of the miners' strike (1973/4). The incoming Labour administration inherited a financial crisis that, as we have seen, became a tornado by 1976. The sterling crisis of that year led to the government cutting £1 billion from public expenditure. Of this, £150 million was cut from the housing budgets of local authorities.

The 1975 Housing, Rents and Subsidies Act gave back to local authorities the power to set rent levels and also increased subsidies under a block grant scheme designed to give local authorities greater flexibility in the use of resources. As a result, public sector housing compilations increased, even against the general backdrop of economic recession, from 111 500 in 1974 to 147 300 in 1977. But work fell back sharply to 95 400 homes built in 1979 as the downturn steepened and began to take its toll in the form of deep cuts in public expenditure (Hill, 1990).

Thatcherism and housing policy: a tale of three administrations

On 4 May 1979, tired of the inability of the Labour government to avert economic crises and battered by a 'winter of discontent' by the trade unions, Britain once more elected a Conservative government. This time it was headed by Margaret Thatcher who had drawn the political centre of gravity of the party rightwards. Though her first Cabinet was jam-packed with one nation Tories (those she was later to dub 'wets'), it was clear that in social as well as in economic policy she regarded small government as good government.

In social policy terms, little positive was to happen, or at least be completed, during Mrs Thatcher's first government term. But during that time unemployment rose inexorably and appeared to be used as a policy instrument. Ultimately unemployment was to reach nearly 4 million at its peak in 1985. The effect on the social security budget was horrific, particularly as, by this time, the government had had little success in changing benefit levels.

The development of housing policy in the 1980s has to be seen in this context. But it was also developed in accordance with two fundamental precepts which marked these governments out from earlier Conservative administrations. The first was a belief in the efficaciousness of the market. The second was a prejudice in favour of deregulation, an inclination to lift controls and reduce subsidies in order to encourage the private housing market and promote owner occupation.

The 'right to buy'

These ideological preferences were clear in the Housing Act (1980). Its most important feature was that it granted most council tenants the 'right to buy' their homes at heavily discounted prices and required local authorities to provide mortgages to allow them to do so. Relatively few were excluded from the scheme, which required that eligible purchasers had been tenants for at least three years. Nor were there extensive claw-back mechanisms: if a new owner sold the house on within five years then merely 20 per cent of the discount was required to be returned to the council (Willmott and Murie, 1988).

The 'right to buy' was a piece of sheer political brilliance. It was people's capitalism of the most populist kind as tenants were offered the opportunity to become part of a mortgage-owing democracy for the first time. It was also an incredibly good financial deal with discounts up to 50 per cent of market value being given originally. In further moves in 1984 and 1986 the discount was increased to a maximum of 70 per cent.

Over six years more than a million council houses were bought by their tenants but this overall figure masked relatively wide geographical variations (more sales in the south than in the north of the United Kingdom, more sales to middle class and skilled working class people than to unskilled working class people). The policy was clearly attractive and tapped into a peculiarly British desire to own the houses in which we live. It was also politically astute because it increased the stake that the new householders felt they had in maintaining the status quo; that is, a Conservative government (Malpass, 1993).

But there were losers as well as winners. The effect of the policy was that the best houses were the ones most likely to be purchased by their tenants and the poorest stock was most likely to be left in council ownership. As a result of the policy the condition of the council stock therefore declined. Council house sales also meant financial loss for councils. Some councils found themselves repaying 60-year Treasury loans on properties they no longer owned. More than this, and as a means of ensuring that the revenue from council house sales did not go back into building council houses, the Government also restricted the use to which receipts could be put. The Government took increasingly tight control over council housing, the fixing of rent levels in the public sector, the determination of levels of subsidy, and the use of capital receipts from council house sales. As we have seen above, council house purchasers tended to be middle-aged skilled workers. Elderly people, the young, single parents and people on low incomes were excluded from the bonanza. First, it was more difficult for them to attract mortgages. Second, many of their dwellings were regarded by them as unsuitable for their long-term needs (Burnett, 1986). They too might be regarded as losers.

Be that as it may, the policy marked a transition: from high quality council housing as the province of the respectable working class to its status as a residual, low-quality service reserved for the marginal poor.

The Housing Act (1988)

If the sale of council houses appears bold and radical, then more radicalism was to come in the third term. Mrs Thatcher wanted the withdrawal of the state from housing 'just as far and as fast as possible' (Thatcher, 1993, p. 600). Her Housing Minister, William Waldegrave, looked forward, in 1987, to the removal of the state as a big landlord. The same principles that drove the opt-out option in relation to schools also held sway in housing. The Government applied similar tools to the job as well. For the Housing Act (1988) allowed tenants to opt out of local authority housing by choosing to transfer their tenancy to any number of new, approved private landlords. Under the Act's provisions landlords would be allowed to bid for property and for the worst, run-down estates, the government introduced Housing Action Trusts (HATs) which would take over the properties and improve them before passing them over to the private sector. Though introduced by the buccaneering free-marketeer, Nicholas Ridley, the policy – so radical in intent – failed to lift off the ground. It proved, said this Secretary of State for the Environment, 'most unpopular and it didn't achieve its objectives' (Ridley, 1991, p. 89). For reasons that seem more to do with distrust of Mrs Thatcher than with self-interest, tenants of even the most ghastly estates failed to vote for the improvement monies tied to transfer of tenancy. For the most part, they opted to stay with the local authority.

Or maybe such tenants were displaying clear, shrewd common-sense. A change of landlord could have serious consequences. First, the change would not protect rent levels because the Act abolished tenants' entitlement to an adjudication of 'fair rent'. Second, this deregulation also involved a loss of secure tenancy. Thus tenants who could not afford to pay an increase in rent could more easily be evicted. Furthermore, the 'right to buy' legislation applied to local authorities and to housing associations, but not to the private sector. The tenants of homes transferred to private landlords would lose the right to become owner occupiers. Added to these factors, housing benefit was not available for rental costs on houses which became parts of privately managed estates (Willmott and Murie, 1988).

In view of the disadvantages I have just enunciated, many tenants felt that they would be ill-advised to leave council tenure for the unknown perils of the private sector landlord. It can come as no surprise to learn that many tenants' groups fought hard to resist the privatisation of their homes. Some groups feared that the legislation would deliver them into the hands of Rachman-like landlords and such fears were not wholly without foundation or precedent. The deregulation of rents in the 1957 Rent Act had led to exploitation in rent increases and other practices which clearly contributed to the defeat of the Tory government in the 1964 general election.

In 1988 the lessons had been learned and many groups of residents formed themselves into tenants co-operatives and sought to use tenants, choice legislation to transfer management to themselves, and thus, to keep the predator landlords at bay. Local tenant groups were also very active in leafleting estates in order to forewarn residents of the actual and potential consequences of change.

Indeed, even before transfers were actually mooted, large numbers of pre-emptive ballots were held by tenants' groups all over the country. High turn outs were achieved, and large majorities opted to stay with their local council. So it is that the 1988 Housing Act, has not, hitherto, been a success in this regard. Very few estates indeed have opted for change.

But for some groups, the legislation did offer a new kind of housing tenure that they wished to adopt. Some tenants' associations opted to take a role in the management of the dwellings in which they lived. Equally, there have been some, but only a few, instances in which a move to a private landlord was the preferred choice.

Though tenants could see little advantage in the Act's provisions, that was not the case with all councils. Some of them saw the Act as allowing them to off-load their housing stock, whatever the views of tenants. The capital earned could be put to other purposes like paying debts or lowering the poll tax or building amenities. By 1994, 30 local authorities (almost all of them Conservative) had disposed of 150 000 houses to housing associations (Timmins, 1995, p. 436).

Post-war housing policy: a critical summary

The major struggles in housing policy appear, throughout the period, to be ones relating to whether provision should be predominantly state provision or largely private provision. Bevan's preference was clear. He wanted local government to be the near-monopoly providers of new housing and, albeit romantically, his vision was of houses of such high standard that all would wish to live in them.

Throughout the years following the defeat of Labour in 1951, that certainty was never to return. Macmillan, while inheriting Bevan's mantle, re-introduced the market as a more significant player during his tenure as Housing Minister and, as Prime Minister, approved measures to attract or retain private rented accommodation. It was left to Rachmanism and the Labour Party to tilt the balance back towards the council as the favoured provider of rented housing. That, however, masks a move in Labour's approach since Bevan. For the 1964–70 Labour governments, as enthusiastically as Mrs Thatcher was to do later, encouraged the growth of owner occupation. It was during the period of these two governments that the proportion of dwellings in owner occupation became a majority, helped no doubt by Crossman's introduction of preferential mortgage schemes for the lower paid. It is one of the peculiarities of the United Kingdom that home ownership is seen as the preferred alternative by both citizens and governments. In other European countries a more diverse housing market is evident and encouraged. Be that as it may, Labour in the 1960s had as much right to be seen as the party of home ownership as the Conservatives in the 1980s.

The major political divergences over housing policy occurred during the 1980s. Though it was to revise its view in later years, Labour initially opposed the 'right to buy' policy on the grounds that it was an attempt both to weaken local councils and to buy votes with the sale of houses on the cheap. In this example of 'people's capitalism' Labour saw also the permanent run-down of councils' housing stock and the first move towards the privatisation of housing.

That fear appeared to have been realised by the appearance of the Housing Act (1988). For here was the means by which councils could be divested of those properties which had not been removed by council house sales. Though theoretically and ideologically that fear was understandable, few tenants took the opportunity to transfer tenancy to other bodies. Some councils have seen the opportunity of off-loading their housing stock as attractive but on the whole, the policy has proved a failure. It appears to have been so in some part because of its association with the twilight of Thatcherism and in part because of the relative affection with which council provision is regarded in many parts of the country. Though attempts were made, Bevan's legacy to people's housing remains. Battered, bruised but unvanquished.

CHAPTER TEN

Social security since the war

We have already seen in Chapter 3 that social security was one of the major policy planks of the post-war Labour government's welfare state. James Griffiths, the Minister for Social Security, had introduced a scheme of national insurance to cover earnings interruptions. It was based on an insurance principle and yielded flat-rate benefits from flat-rate contributions. Also introduced was a scheme of national assistance to provide relief in those cases where claimants were ineligible for national insurance. Old age pensions at full rate were introduced immediately, rather than phased in over 20 years as Beveridge would have preferred. One of Beveridge's five giants was, then, being addressed by post-war social security policy.

Conservatives and social security: 1951–64

Though there were other sites for policy conflict during this period, social security policy seems to have rested in the arms of a quiet consensus. This is not to say that the area was without its problems. By 1954, nearly two million claimants were claiming national assistance benefits, although it had been anticipated that it would be a small, safety-net provision. Despite the fact that Powell and Macleod had understood, as early as 1952, that there was something fundamentally wrong with a system in which the safety net became immense, little was said or done about it in policy terms. In fact, this was the beginning of a continuous, if often silent, debate. For the Conservative government, and indeed the Labour Opposition, exhibited confusion about the purposes of the two schemes. Sometimes it would increase national insurance more significantly than assistance and the Government would claim that it was reducing the role of means-tested national assistance and Labour arguing that resources were not going to the most needy. At other times the Government would increase national assistance more substantially than national insurance and the debate would occur in reverse (Hill, 1990).

Pensions

One area of mild controversy became prominent in the mid 1950s. By this time Griffiths' decision not to phase in old age pensions had led to a dawning realisation of the financial burden that the state had taken on thereby. The national insurance fund was in massive deficit. More than this, as Titmuss and colleagues at the LSE found, there was a growing gulf between those old age pensioners who had an occupational pension and those who simply had a state pension. The latter group often had to receive a national assistance top-up to pay for rent. Titmuss's view was that: 'The outlines of a dangerous social schism are clear and they are enlarging' (Titmuss, 1958, p. 73).

Labour, seeking to argue that under the Conservatives the welfare state had stopped being redistributive, focused on pensions. In 1955, Richard Crossman was asked to head a committee to look into the pensions problem. Its other members included Douglas Jay, formerly Labour's President of the Board of Trade, Richard Titmuss, Brian Abel-Smith and Peter Townsend. According to Jay:

The two central principles that in the course of the argument became increasingly clear to us, and in the end won unanimous agreement, were these; first that since the ordinary man or woman would rather pay £1 a week as an insurance contribution than as income tax, and so feel that he or she had earned their own pension, the contributory principle was right; and secondly since a single fixed contribution and pension for all must mean either too high a contribution for the lowest paid, or too low a pension for the well paid, it was inevitable that the contribution and pension must be earnings-related in the future if pensions were eventually to ensure a decent living standard in old age. (Jay, 1980, p. 70)

One of the problems was that the numbers of occupational pensions had mushroomed since 1948 and employers would no doubt resist paying increased premiums to the state scheme as well as spending on occupational schemes. The solution suggested by Crossman *et al.* was a compromise. In such situations employers would be able to opt out of higher premiums. Though Crossman thought the plan only three quarters baked (Crossman, 1981, p. 584), it was released in May 1957 and enthusiastically accepted by the party. Thus Labour abandoned the flat-rate principle. Earnings-related pensions would mean that the better-off received higher pensions and marked a distinct move away from Beveridge's subsistence principle. Rather, the proposals being made by the Labour Party were more akin to the graduated pensions schemes in the countries of continental Europe.

The Titmuss scheme was supported by the trade union movement (Hill, 1990), who favoured a state scheme because occupational schemes were often not portable, and increasingly by Conservatives. Here was the start of a cross-party consensus on pensions that broke radically with Beveridge. Notwithstanding this, Boyd-Carpenter, the relevant minister, dismissed Titmuss and his colleagues as 'a skiffle group of professors' (Ellis, 1989) and believed that they had got their calculations wrong. And he, and Beveridge from the Lords, cautioned that higher contributions from employers would mean higher prices in the shops as the increase was passed on. His response was to introduce in 1959 a much more modest, graduated scheme for those earning between £9–15 per week. The scheme brought the parties to verbal blows in the 1959 election with Labour condemning the plan as a 'bucket shop swindle' and the Government selling it as a good bargain. Until 1964, however, things were to settle back into quiescence.

Poverty and social security: Labour and

However, things were about to change because of a mixture of demographic and economic factors. Further to this, the so-called rediscovery of poverty brought the issue of the role of social security into the open in the form of a furious political and academic battle between the new right's Institute of Economic Affairs on the one side, and the Labour Party and allies on the other.

Demographic and economic crisis

When Labour came into office in 1964, it faced a balance of trade deficit of £800 million. It inherited aid from the Paris Club of advanced industrial nations and the International Monetary Fund amounting to over £350 million. These international economic pressures were exacerbated by a gradual but distinct shift in the make up of the population at home. The birth rate was falling and the proportion of elderly people was growing rapidly (Jones, 1991). As a result, a smaller working-age population supported through tax and national insurance an increasing population of elderly people. The combination of economic adversity, a growth in unemployment to around 60 000 in the late 1960s and a demographic imbalance towards older people, put pressure on the social security system. In this context discussions about the possibility of abandoning universality raged. In November 1967, the Labour government submitted to the inevitable and devalued sterling.

Throughout this period, evidence was also accruing of the failure of many old age pensioners to take up means-tested national assistance top-ups for which their poverty made them eligible (Deacon and Bradshaw, 1983, p. 103). To overcome old people's perception of stigma about claiming, the Labour Party had promised, in the run up to 1964, to introduce an income guarantee. This was to be a minimum income granted without means-testing. Douglas Houghton, who was to become the social services overlord in the first Wilson government described it as income tax in reverse: government would take from those who had taxable incomes and give to those at the other end of the spectrum (Houghton, 1967, p. 12). The idea would have involved the integration of tax and social security systems and in the end foundered because the housing and social security needs of pensioners proved unmeetable by an affordable income guarantee.

What emerged instead was the Supplementary Benefits Commission (SBC) that took over from the National Assistance Board. It in turn was merged into the Ministry of Pensions to become the Ministry of Social Security. The SBC made more benefits mandatory and worked with increased benefit levels. The idea was to make means-tested benefits rights-based benefits, an idea that was to be common currency of both major parties until the Fowler social security reviews of the mid 1980s. Thus, though some discretion was retained, once the means test had been passed basic benefit became an entitlement. Alongside supplementary benefit, an earnings-related supplement to unemployment benefit and more generous sickness benefits were introduced. The former of these initiatives took Britain further away from Beveridge's flat-rate principle and nearer to other European social security systems.

The rediscovery of poverty

In 1960, Richard Titmuss had delivered a Fabian Society lecture entitled, *The Irresponsible Society*. In it he chastised the Conservative government for allowing the welfare state to atrophy. His most stinging indictments were reserved, however, for government social security policy. He argued that 'in terms of the relationship of national insurance benefits and allowances to average industrial earnings, most beneficiaries are worse off today than they would have been in 1948'. Government policy had the effect, according to this argument, of pauperising the poor by creating dependence on the supposedly safety net national assistance for increasing numbers of claimants.

More than this, poverty was being rediscovered among large sections of the claimant class. As we have already seen (Chapters 3 and 8), in 1965, two Fabian academics from the LSE, Peter Townsend and Brian Abel-Smith, published a study called *The Poor and the Poorest*. The work demonstrated that the growth of affluence throughout the 1950s had not percolated down and that a sub-class had been left in poverty, particularly large families on low incomes. They used the benefit scales used for National Assistance as their measure of the poverty line. Their results underlined the problems, particularly of those on very low wages, and of many retired and unemployed citizens who failed to take up the national assistance benefits to which they were entitled.

The rediscovery of poverty provoked the formation of anti-poverty pressure groups and particularly of CPAG. They lobbied and campaigned for changes in the benefit system and informed poor people of their rights and encouraged them to exercise them. The success of CPAG prompted, according to Jones (1991), two unforeseen effects. These were disjointed incrementalism and ammunition to the Opposition. The poverty lobby's favoured tactic was to turn the spotlight on a particular benefit or benefit rule and thereby to expose injustices and inequalities caused by its form or administration. The effect of this 'long march through the benefits' was *ad hoc* change as each benefit was modified to take account of criticisms. Policy developed therefore by increments but, as changes to one benefit were rarely related to changes in another, the incrementalism was disjointed rather than focused.

The work of the anti-poverty pressure groups also gave succour to the enemy in Jones's estimation. The sometimes frontal approach on government policy and the exposure of the failure of some benefits to meet need, was pounced upon by the political right. It led to a critique which started with the belief that social security was failing and continued by arguing against such provision on philosophical grounds First, a state social security monopoly restricted freedom and choice. Second, the lack of competition suppressed incentives towards greater efficiency and caused waste.

These criticisms found their expression in the Institute of Economic Affairs (IEA), particularly in the *Hobart Papers* on the welfare state.

Reappraisal on the left

Given the economic circumstances, the political left had, by the late 1960s, also reconsidered its commitment to universalism. Abel-Smith (1964), for example, reluctantly conceded that in practice the social security system had been selective. It had not, in fact, provided coverage from the cradle to the grave nor had selectivism via means tests ever been abolished. The way forward appeared to lie in the development of selective benefits to meet particular needs (see, Houghton, 1967), a theme taken up in the first White Paper of the Heath government (Alcock, 1987).

The Heath government and social security

In October 1970, Anthony Barber introduced a White Paper on social expenditure which made selectivism respectable:

> We intend to adopt a more selective approach to the social services. There will be increases in expenditure on basic structure – schools, hospitals, payments to those in need. But we aim to confine the scope of free subsidised provision more closely to what is necessary on social grounds . . . Instead of the present indiscriminate subsidies, help will go where it is most needed. (HMSO, 1970)

In the last years of the previous Labour government, Crossman had introduced a plan for superannuable pensions which had fallen with the government. One of the first casualties of the new selectivism was that Joseph, the new Secretary of State, decided not to proceed with it. Other cost-cutting approaches included the decision not to pay sickness benefit for the first three days. Joseph got into most trouble, though, over an apparent breach of manifesto promises.

During Labour's dispute with CPAG over the latter's claim that poverty was worse under a Labour government, Heath and his future, if short-lived, Chancellor, Ian Macleod, had endorsed CPAG's policy of increasing family allowances and clawing the money back through reducing the tax allowances of the well off. Macleod had died in July 1970 and the new Chancellor was unhappy about the idea of clawing expenditure back in this way. More than this Joseph on his appointment had done his own calculations. He told the House of Commons that he had uncovered the following:

- That about one third of the working families earning less than the supplementary benefits level had only one child and would therefore not be helped by increasing family allowance.
- That any rise in family allowance that did not involve astronomic sums would be of insignificant help to the poorest.
- That tax thresholds had fallen so far back that the claw-back would leave little money in the hands of the poor.

Sir Keith and Family Income Supplement

As a result of his calculations, Joseph decided not to increase family allowances but to introduce a new benefit, Family Income Supplement (FIS). Family Income Support had originally been considered by Labour when Houghton was social services supremo but had been rejected. The benefit was to supplement income once eligibility had been established via a means test.

The political reaction to the plan was deafening. Joseph was accused of reintroducing the Speenhamland relief scheme, of demoralising the workforce and of using a state benefit to allow employers to drive down wages. Notwithstanding this furore – or because of it – take-up of the benefit was low, at about 60 per cent at its peak. So worried was Joseph by this that he wrote a personal letter to each social worker in the land asking them to encourage eligible claimants to claim the benefit (Timmins, 1995).

In fact FIS worsened the poverty trap. For not only did it pay only half the difference between benefit level and a notional wage level, it also clawed back 50 per cent of every pound earned. However, tax thresholds were so low that for those at the higher end it was not unheard of for 85 pence of every pound to be lost.

Expansion

Notwithstanding the FIS fiasco, the rest of Joseph's tenure marked the introduction of new targeted benefits to meet special needs. A new attendance allowance was introduced to help those caring for the sick and disabled at home. A new invalidity allowance was introduced and widow's pension was widened to include women between 40 and 50. Pensions for those aged over 80 years were increased and the Government introduced a Family Fund administered by the Joseph Rowntree Trust (perhaps the first example of privatisation of services). This fund, of about £3 million, was to be made payable, at the Trust's discretion, to families with severely handicapped children to offset the cost of holidays, special equipment and transport. The Government also introduced a rent allowance to help low income families in privately rented accommodation.

Stormy weather

Economic crisis in the form of the Middle East oil crisis hit in 1973 and provoked a re-appraisal of welfare spending. Inflation as a result of the oil shocks soon moved into double figures and led to benefits being uprated annually rather than biennially as had been the previous practice. *Ad hoc* solutions were applied. For example, a £10 Christmas bonus was introduced to offset the decreasing value of old age pensions. But the biggest re-appraisal occurred when Joseph found that the flat-rate principle could not be sustained. As a result of the 1973 spending round, there was simply not enough resources to maintain the principle. As a consequence, the Minister decided to give bigger increases to pensioners and those on invalidity benefit than to the unemployed and the sick. The reasoning behind this decision was that those seeking work and those on sickness benefit were more likely to be able to return to work and solve their own problems than the former groups. Consequently, Joseph operated a rough and ready judgement of need. The result was the introduction of a two-tier system dividing the long-term benefits from the short-term ones.

Consciously or not, Joseph was making the old Poor Law distinction between deserving and undeserving claimants. Forced by economic constraints, he used the lower level of short-term benefits as an incentive to find work while accepting the impossibility of this eventuality in the case of pensioners and those on invalidity benefit. This was to go hand-in-hand with the breaking of another Beveridgian principle for the new invalidity benefit was to be both non-means-tested and non-contributory (Glennerster, 1995).

Integration of tax and social security

Despite the previous Labour government's failed attempt to integrate the two systems, Joseph also set off in search of the holy grail of integrated tax and social security systems. This tax credit scheme was based on the same principles as Labour's income guarantee and was similarly to founder on the rocks of finance.

The Conservative stewardship of social security between 1970–4 was, then, a mixed bag. On the one hand, Joseph proved to be an expansionary minister, and one certainly not afraid of the big idea. Certain benefits were improved and new ones introduced to meet the specific needs of vulnerable groups. Gathering economic storm clouds, however, forced review and retrenchment and the sight of the Minister taking refuge in distinctions between the deserving and undeserving poor.

Labour governments and social security policy

When Labour took office in 1974, the economy was sliding into reverse. Throughout its first two years in office 'stagflation' became the order of the day. Though economists believed that rampant inflation and industrial stagnation were mutually incompatible, in the mid 1970s Britain experienced both.

Despite these difficult circumstances and as part of a social contract with the unions, Labour introduced some early additions to social security policy. For example, in 1974 Child Benefit was introduced. Replacing family allowance it extended cover to the first-born child. Labour also introduced the Social Security Pensions Act (1975) which initiated a state earnings-related pension scheme (SERPS). This was a policy descendant of Crossman's superannuation scheme in which the level of contribution would determine the level of benefit. It was inflation-proofed and brought Britain in line with other major European countries. As we will see later, the pressure that this scheme put on the Exchequer was to lead to attempts during the 1980s to remove it.

Thatcher governments and social security

Prelude: the 1976–8 review

On appointment as Prime Minister in 1976, Callaghan had set up a review of supplementary benefit. The review team made a number of recommendations. First, they argued for a simpler social security structure. Second, the team argued for limiting the amount of discretion available to benefits officers in their decision making. Third, the review advised that there should be equality of treatment between married women and their husbands by establishing the right for couples to nominate a breadwinner. Fourth, the team argued for a simplification of the scheme for short-term claimants. They recommended that fixed amounts should be included in benefits to cover housing rent and fixed sums for each child. Fifth, the review recommended the extension of the long-term supplementary benefit rates to those unemployed citizens who were ineligible for unemployment benefit. In the event, the Government fell before it could respond fully to the review but there was a clear recognition that the system was in need of an overhaul (Johnson, 1990).

The first Thatcher administration

With the election of Mrs Thatcher the locus of social security policy changed almost immediately. Chancellor Howe's first public expenditure White Paper set the boundaries within which subsequent social security policy operated. Howe argued in the White Paper that high public expenditure was at the heart of Britain's economic difficulties and that attempts should be made to reduce it.

Social security was made a prime candidate for expenditure cuts. Howe was at pains to stress, however, that the genuinely poor would be protected: 'our general policy is to make substantial reductions in public expenditure, but that must not be done in a way that bears unfairly on the most vulnerable members of society' (House of Commons Debates, 1979). The Government's aim was to be directed elsewhere, or so it seemed.

'Annus horribilis': 1980

Two key pieces of policy emerged in 1980. The first Social Security Act introduced measures in line with the supplementary benefits review carried out under the Labour government (1974–9). The Act also broke the link between average earnings on the one hand, and pensions and other long-term benefits on the other.

However, that year's Budget was even more significant. According to Donnison:

> *From time to time in the course of its history a nation crosses a watershed in its political journey – a point at which the whole landscape of popular assumptions and aspirations seems to change. The crest of the watershed we have just crossed was so early marked that I almost heard the crunch as we passed over. To be precise, it was at about 3.00 p.m. on 26 March 1980 – Budget Day. (Donnison, 1982, p. 206)*

The Budget is notable for three reasons. First, it cut the real value of child benefit by 9 per cent. Second, it announced plans for a second social security act in which the Government would take the unprecedented step of cutting into the value of the main national insurance benefits for those below pensionable age. This cut was to be achieved through the imposition of a 5 per cent 'abatement in lieu of taxation'. Thirdly, the Bill would, it was announced, abolish the national insurance earnings-related supplement, which had been payable for the first six months of sickness, unemployment, maternity or widowhood.

Additionally, as a sign of the future, the legislation would, it was planned, cut off benefits to those involved in trade disputes.

Scroungerphobia

Even before the Budget, the Government had announced a campaign against fraud and abuse in the benefit system and had allocated about one thousand extra staff teams investigating such abuse. Though this option had been considered by Joseph in 1973, it had been rejected and Joseph had told his party's Annual Conference that it 'ought to face the fact that there are a large number of people who are not employable . . . too inadequate to hold down jobs. And should their children starve? Of course they should not' (Conservative Party Conference Record, 1973, p. 98). This time, however, the Government was adamant about proceeding, whatever the facts of the matter. In the event, more resources were devoted to fraud detection than were recovered through prosecutions and, in any event, social security fraud was of minimal significance compared to tax evasion (Sullivan, 1989). In this latter case, government actually cut the number of investigating officers in the same period. All in all, and despite Howe's reassurance, the message seemed to be 'down with the poor' (Boyson, 1971).

The second administration: the Fowler review

By far the most significant development relating to social security policy was the establishment in 1984 of a review of social security. The then Secretary of State, Norman Fowler, set it up because of evidence emerging from commissioned research that the system was failing to reach the most vulnerable because of its complexity as well as its underfunding.

The central aim of the review was to create a 'social security system consistent with the Government's overall objectives' for the economy. Fowler established four review teams to look at benefits at different stages of the life-cycle. Their recommendations were published in a Green Paper in 1985 which also listed three main objectives. First, the social security system should be capable of meeting genuine need; second, the social security system should be consistent with the Government's overall objectives for the economy; third, the social security system should be made simpler to understand and to administer. The review had been announced in an atmosphere of apparent near-panic. Fowler, perhaps with an eye to SERPS, had already expressed the opinion that social security was a time bomb (Wicks, 1987, p. 96). In the event, the review proved to be something of an ideological damp squib. The Green Paper made the following recommendations which were implemented as a result of the Social Security Act (1986).

Income support

The supplementary benefit system was to be replaced by 'income support'. Income support was made up of two elements: a system of personal allowances and premiums for specific categories of claimant. Income support eliminated the previous distinction between long-term and standard rates of benefit and between householders and non-householders.

Family credit

This was the replacement for Joseph's ill-fated FIS. Like FIS, it was to be means-tested and was paid to families where there was at least one dependent child and where one parent was working at least 24 hours a week.

Housing benefit

Housing benefit rates were reduced significantly and additional savings were recommended and implemented by tightening the eligibility criteria and by insisting that all families paid at least 20 per cent of their rates.

Social Fund

The Social Fund that emerged from the review replaced discretionary payments. It was responsible for the payment of grants and loans for contingencies such as pregnancy and child birth, funeral expenses and community care grants. Its most far-reaching change on previous practices was the replacement of exceptional needs grants by a system of loans.

SERPS

Though introduced with all-party agreement in 1978, SERPS was regarded by the Thatcher governments as a millstone. It was concerned about the costs of the scheme and about its disincentive effect on occupational and private pensions. The 1985 social security White Paper had estimated that there were in the region of 10 million people dependent on SERPS and another 11 million in occupational pensions. However, it was estimated that the SERPS population of pensioners would grow to 13.2 million by 2035 and cause an explosion of costs. The White Paper argued that SERPS removed the flexibility of future governments and stored up impossible public spending commitments for governments in the next century. The Government's preferred option had therefore been to abolish SERPS but outcry from the insurance companies forced it to reconsider. In the event, it was scaled down rather than removed.

The changes involved in scaling down were these:

- The original scheme calculated pension on the basis of the pensioner's 20 highest earning years; the modified scheme changed this to a calculation on lifetime's earnings.
- The amount payable to pensioners was scaled down from 25 per cent of earnings to 20 per cent of earnings.
- In the future widows will inherit only half of their spouse's pension rights rather than all of them.

These modifications obviously acted to make private pensions more attractive and their attractiveness was enhanced by terms of the Social Security Act (1986) which allowed SERPS premiums to be used to pay for a private scheme.

The promise of radical change

John Moore arrived at the DHSS in 1987. His arrival was seen as heralding major changes in social security. Like John Major, one of Mrs Thatcher's favourites, he was seen as a future leader and was well known for his radical-right views. Three months after appointment, he made what was seen as a most significant intervention in the debate about social security. His argument was that the welfare state had created a culture of dependency. Citing the American Charles Murray (1984), he argued that social security benefits, far from helping the poor, had created an underclass, dependent on welfare provision.

Moore's argument, like Murray's, was deceptively simple. The welfare state had led to a situation where, under the appearance of compassion, poor people were defined, and came to define themselves as victims of circumstance. Social security claimants should be moved 'away from dependence and towards independence' (*The Independent*, 1 July 1987). He called for the greater modesty in government spending on social security and heralded the moral superiority of private pensions over state-provided ones. Resources should be targeted where they were most needed and not wasted on those who could help themselves (*The Independent*, 24 November 1987).

As good as his word, Moore froze child benefit and redirected the money thus saved into the means-tested family credit. Though this may have seemed the red meat of Thatcherism, it landed the Government in trouble. In a vote on the issue the Government's three figure majority was halved. Not to be intimidated by the backbenches, however, Moore offered in the 1988 spending round to taper the benefit away to nothing for the better off or to tax it. In doing so he found himself confronted by an unusual adversary. The party's 1987 manifesto had promised that child benefit would continue to be paid to all mothers and none less than Mrs Thatcher reminded Moore of this fact. He did the most he could do and froze the benefit for a second year.

Following a bruising humiliation where he had to re-instate £100 million worth of savings from housing benefit (the 1986 changes had just been implemented) and his oversight of the NHS review under question, he found that his one-time patron, Thatcher, had lost patience with him and split the DHSS, giving the health brief to Kenneth Clarke. He was soon to lose social security as well but not before he had introduced and seen through the Social Security Act (1988).

The Social Security Act (1988)

In the final significant social security developments of Mrs Thatcher's governments, Moore attempted to claw back resources. Fowler's review had promised to deliver a system 'capable of meeting the demands into the next century' (Timmins, 1995), but Moore had already made the case for permanent revolution.

The Act altered the age of qualification for income support from 16 years to 18 years. This change was 'designed to avoid the damaging effects for young people of moving straight from school into the benefit culture'. The idea fitted in with Moore's views and with Mrs Thatcher's own instincts. It also resonated with the views of Beveridge, with which the Government was usually at odds. Beveridge had argued that ideally there should be no automatic benefit for young people but that instead they should be provided with work-related training (HMSO, 1942). Its results seem to have played little part in youngsters remaining at home, or in providing training places, but may well have had some effect on the numbers of homeless beggars in the city streets of the United Kingdom.

The end of the line for Moore came in May 1989 when he spoke out against Townsend's use of the income support level as the poverty line. Moore argued that if such a view were accepted then raising the benefit level simply raised the poverty line also. He protested that it was bizarre to claim, as Townsend and colleagues were, that one third of the population were living in or on the margins of poverty (Townsend, 1979). He argued that what Townsend was measuring was not poverty but an abstract set of statistics:

What the new definition of relative poverty amounts to in the end is simple inequality. It means however rich a society gets it will drag the incubus of relative poverty with it up the income scale. The poverty lobby would, on their definition, find poverty in paradise. (Moore, 1989)

In the technical sense, it is hard to fault the logic. But politically this attack by a graduate of the LSE on one of its favourite sons proved to be political suicide. There were howls of protest. CPAG argued that Moore was trying to define poverty out of existence. And his case was made no stronger by ordinary people's perceptions of growing unemployment and homelessness.

Moore found himself under attack from Labour and from his own side. One back-bench Tory sneered that Moore was trying to 'use an academic proposition to prove physical fact' (*The Observer*, 14 May 1989). Seldom can Professor Townsend and his colleagues have been the recipients of support from such a strange political direction! Moreover an official survey published at the time proved to be more trouble for the embattled minister. *Social Trends 1987* (HMSO, 1989) demonstrated that in the late 1980s inequality was growing, however it was measured. Little more than two months later Moore was sacked and replaced by the emollient Tony Newton.

On one set of accounts, Moore had proved to be a spectacular failure. No great policy innovations had been introduced and the darling of the right found himself consigned, so soon after his elevation, to peremptory decline. Nonetheless, it would be mistaken to underestimate the long-term influence of Moore's tenure. The idea of an underclass emerged as one of the common-senses of the 1990s. Murray, at the invitation of the IEA, turned his attentions to Britain and the political left felt bound to defend welfare all over again.

Emerging issues

How then should we characterise the effect of Thatcher governments on social security? What are the major issues to emerge from a consideration of the policy direction of her three administrations?

A preference for means-testing

Taken as a whole the period of Thatcher government marked a move from universality, more or less observed, to an emphasis on targeting and means-testing. If the Fowler reviews achieved little else, they marked the transition to a period where selectivity became the guiding light for social security policy.

Retaining work incentives

Social security policy under the Thatcher administrations was also aimed at retaining work incentives and discouraging welfare dependency.

Fraud and abuse

Another major element of Conservative policy under Thatcher was the pathologising of poverty. This is clearly seen in the continued emphasis on fraud and abuse. The 1983 party manifesto claimed a clampdown on abuse as one of the main achievements of the first term in office.

Less public was the shift from prosecution as an indicator of success to the recovery of overpaid benefit following 'non-prosecution' interviews. In 1988, the *Training for Employment* White Paper was used to announce the allocation of further resources to fraud investigation as part of a nation-wide 'drive against fraud and abuse'.

Another significant policy instrument was the cutback in provision for those in board and lodgings. 'Costa del dole' headlines and Conservative backbench pressure led to a series of increasingly harsh measures, arrested temporarily by setbacks in the courts. Young people were the main victims, allowed to claim ordinary board and lodging payments in any one area for only between two and eight weeks. Although these time limits were subsequently abolished, the benefit provision proposed for this group was so inadequate that young people simply could not afford to live in lodgings. Though intended to drive young people back to their parental home, it appears to have led to increasing homelessness and begging.

Racist attitudes

Another group subject to increasing control has been the black community. Complaints have grown about the increase in passport checking, partly a product of the introduction in 1980 of the legal power to hold a sponsor liable for the maintenance of an immigrant relative. Although the original proposal in the Fowler review for a 'presence test' was dropped, under the income support scheme claimants who entered the country within the previous five years were subject to a special interview, and the information provided was forwarded to the Home Office.

The small state

As we have seen, John Moore argued for the injection of 'some long overdue modesty into government's attitude towards its own role in welfare'. Perhaps he had not been looking but the Fowler review had attempted to introduce just that. This was clearly one element in the preference for abolishing SERPS and in its eventual down-scaling. It was also the intention in the creation of the Social Fund and in the earlier introduction of the Family Fund, the latter of which arguably started the charitabilisation of welfare.

Self-reliance and independence

The reduction in the role of the state has also had a clear ideological aim. One of the assumptions in the 1985 Green Paper was that a Conservative approach to social security would bolster independence rather than extend the power of the state. This theme was repeated by John Moore, who argued that 'the next step in the long evolutionary march of the welfare state in Britain is away from dependence towards independence' (Moore, 1988).

The Fowler review's most visible contribution towards shifting responsibility from the state to the individual was the promotion of private pensions subsidised by public tax relief. The original proposal to abolish the state earnings-related scheme was abandoned in face of overwhelming opposition, but the modifications made seriously weakened the scheme, and in particular those elements that favoured women and other groups unable to build up a continuous contribution record.

Self-help was seen as important because of an aversion to what has become known as the dependency culture. The Social Fund was justified by Nicholas Scott (Minister of Social Security) in a letter to the Chair of the Social Security Advisory Committee, in these terms: 'it has been a consistent objective of the reforms to give people a sum of money within which they manage for themselves, reducing their dependence on the "benefits culture" for extras' (Scott, 1987).

So even more than targeting, the main thrust of John Moore's period in office as Social Services Secretary lay in his belief in personal independence. 'A welfare state worthy of the name,' he claimed, 'while accepting its obligation to care for the distressed and needy, also works to encourage the resourcefulness and enterprise that are the true foundations of both personal and national success' (Moore, 1988). Some saw his pronouncements as the opening shots in the debate about workfare (Sullivan, 1992). Indeed, the withdrawal of the right to benefit from most 16- and 17-year-olds was seen by one author as a 'youth workfare system without question' (Burton, 1988).

A residual welfare state

Changes to social security policy during the premiership of Mrs Thatcher have been seen by some as steps along the road of residualising of the welfare state. It was a period 'characterised by increasing inequality, deepening poverty, greater reliance on the means test, a growing role for the private market and consequently social division and conflict' (Wicks, 1987, p.9). The model pursued by Mrs Thatcher's secretaries of state for social security arguably owed more to Reagan's United States rather than to continental Europe where models of social security emphasise security and protection for all citizens however imperfectly this is achieved.

The 1990s

The Thatcher effect in social security also seems to have permeated policy debates since her overthrow.

Workfare

A distinctly Moore-like perspective can be discerned in the second Major government's attraction to workfare. The idea that claimants should be compelled to work for their benefits, first mooted by the unfortunate John Moore, received the Prime Minister's personal backing in a speech to the Carlton Club in February 1993. By April of that year, it was announced that the Employment Secretary would be launching the first pilot workfare scheme in Britain. In July the Secretary of State visited workfare schemes in the United States, and by December plans were floated to withhold benefit from those who failed to find work. A limited type of workfare has since been introduced whereby the long-term unemployed are robustly encouraged to carry out community-based work.

The march of the 'bastards'

With or without the Prime Minister's encouragement, three right-wing cabinet ministers attempted in the 1990s to turn public opinion against certain classes of benefit claimants. In August 1992 Peter Lilley, the Secretary of State for

Social Security, had revived the dependency culture debate, expressing concern about teenage pregnancies and the cost of single parents to the state. These remarks were echoed in September 1993 by the then Treasury minister Michael Portillo, who feared that single teenage parents could be led into a life of poverty-stricken dependency by the state's provision of what he called over-generous benefits.

Later, on a visit to a housing estate in south Wales, John Redwood (Secretary of State for Wales until his leadership challenge to John Major in 1995) returned to the lone parent debate, suggesting that young women were becoming pregnant with no intention of living with the father of their child. In such a situation, they knew, Redwood argued, that the state would take care of their social security and housing needs. He therefore called for a change to policy and attitudes.

The extent to which these interventions were made with the Prime Minister's support is unclear. Though he was to refer to these three cabinet ministers, when he thought he was off-air, as 'the bastards' the epithet was earned for their anti-European stance rather than their views on welfare.

Be that as it may, dependency culture ideas have remained part of the currency of the Conservative government in the 1990s, even if their British populariser proved to have been a political failure.

The journey from 1945

Radical changes have occurred, then, since the introduction of national insurance and national assistance in 1948. As we have seen, the Beveridge principles have been diluted or rejected as governments added earnings-related schemes or moved from the contributory principle. The major ideological shift on social security did not occur, however, until the election of Mrs Thatcher's three governments. Those governments moved the debate, and sometimes the policies, away from universalism and towards selectivity, away from state responsibility and towards self-help. Those principles, most clearly enunciated by the ill-starred John Moore at the end of the 1980s, though leading to much more modest changes than he would have liked, have continued to trickle down into the 1990s.

Further reading
for Part Two

Barr, N., Glennerster, H. and LeGrand, J. (1988). A consideration of the 1980s health service reforms.

Bellaby, P. (1977). Looks at the reasons behind the development of comprehensive education.

Banting, K. (1979). Looks at the effect of the poverty lobby on poverty policy.

Burnett, J. (1986).

Dale, R. (1989).

Donnison, D. (1967).

Donnison, D. (1982).

Eckstein, H. (1959).

Fabian Society (1968).

Fenwick, I. G. K. (1976). A history of the comprehensive school movement.

Field, F. (1982).

Godsen, P. (1976).

Higgins, J. (1988). A look at private medicine in the 1980s.

Hill, M. (1990).

Klein, R. (1989),

Leathard, A. (1991).

Malpass, P. and Murie, A. (1987).

Murray, C. (1984). Argues that modern societies have an underclass which become dependent on welfare.

Murray, C. (1990). A specifically British treatment of Murray's earlier argument.

PART THREE

From the cradle to the grave

CHAPTER ELEVEN

From the cradle to the grave: the beginnings, development and demise of the welfare state?

This book has been about the development of social policy in the United Kingdom this century. It has briefly traced some of the pre-war influences which contributed to a political atmosphere in which the welfare state was created and has suggested that, in understanding those influences, it is important to acknowledge the continuities with the embryonic social reforms of the early-century Liberal government and the development of the Labour Party from an anti-statist to a welfare-statist party. So we have seen the beginnings of the welfare state. One of the purposes of this chapter is to consider whether we are also seeing its endings. But before we get to that point, some other stocktaking has to be done.

Was the welfare consensus real?

Implicit in the earlier chapters of this book has been the claim that the post-war welfare state was created, nurtured and sustained by a widespread agreement that the state should be involved in the provision and funding of welfare. That consensus, or so it is believed, held more or less successfully until the economic crises of the 1970s and the election, in the late 1970s, of a Conservative government more obviously committed than previous adminis-trations to free-market economics and conflict politics: 'for me, consensus seems to be the process of abandoning all beliefs, principles, values and policies' (Thatcher, 1979). But if that consensus was real – and it is my contention that it was – what sort of agreement was it?

Clearly, early twentieth century political values which had, with the exception of the Liberal governments, emphasised individualism and the market were on the move by the 1930s. The obvious privation and the mass poverty induced by unbridled capitalist principles acted as a spur for a coalition of forces around the Labour Party to call for radical change. It was this period that saw SMA plans for a national health service and calls from the Labour Party and the teacher unions for a state system of education that would guarantee secondary education for all.

This movement of political opinion was significantly assisted by the development of Keynes's general theory and a growth of professional, economic and administrative opinion that governments could and should intervene to establish economic equilibrium and consistent economic growth (Sked and Cook, 1979).

During the war years, and for reasons we have looked at in Chapter 2, this movement developed into majority political and civil service opinion and a consensus was forged, or so it seems. That agreement is sometimes seen as a political settlement between labour and capital.

Keynes plus Beveridge

One historian of the period has argued that the seeds of the 1945 settlement were, in fact, sown by the inter-war Conservative administration of Stanley Baldwin. Attlee's government, like Baldwin's, managed to epitomise a set of ideas and conventions, to some extent shared by other political parties, about the proper role of the state in modern British society (Addison, 1975). For Addison the policy direction of the post-war Labour government represented a set of assumptions and expectations also held by the policy-making elite in other parties, if not by the general population (Addison, 1975).

Clearly, for Addison the consensus forged, or re-forged, around war-time co-operation and the policies of the post-war Labour administration marked a fundamental political shift. In part, that shift constituted a healing of the political fractures of the 1930s when the rump of the Labour Party, which refused to follow MacDonald into coalition government waged, within parliament and without, a campaign of opposition to the class politics of the Chamberlain government.

For another commentator, the existence of a post-war consensus is also clear but its dimensions are specified more clearly. Kavanagh has argued that the political consensus can be broken down into two constitutive parts: style and policy. His argument is that continuity of style and support for a core of policy principles were the hallmarks of government from the late 1940s through to the mid 1970s, whichever party formed governments.

The style referred to is one of 'institutionalised consultation' (Kavanagh and Morris, 1989, p. 3); that is, the expectation and execution of a process of consultation between government and the major economic interests, most notably the trade unions and the employers' organisations. This is, in other words, Middlemas's 'continuous contract' (Middlemas, 1979). It had the effect of translating economic interest groups into governing institutions.

The range of policies referred to are of course those stemming from the war-time and post-war acceptance of the economic philosophy of John Maynard Keynes and the social philosophy of Sir William Beveridge.

Keynesian economic policies were ones which assumed, or were consistent with, the intervention of government through fiscal and monetary techniques to regulate demand and encourage full employment. Beveridgian social policies were intended to contribute to the development of comprehensive welfare services, access to which would confer a sort of social citizenship. Accordingly, Keynes plus Beveridge were seen to equal Keynesian social democracy, or welfare capitalism, or consensus.

The elements of that consensus settlement can also be conceptualised in the following way. In the first place, the settlement represented a political turnabout. The inter-war years had been dominated by the presence of one political party at the helm of government. Although Labour formed two short-lived administrations, the Conservative Party, on its own or in coalition with the rump of other parties, monopolised the politics of policy-making in government. The formation of a genuine coalition government, seen as politically expedient by Churchill when he took over as war-time Prime Minister, was the first step in this turnaround. The landslide victory of the Labour Party in the 1945 election completed the change. Instead of the *de facto* one-party system of government of the inter-war years, a new, two-party system emerged in which both parties enjoyed relatively stable and relatively equal support.

The 1945 settlement is also said to have been forged around policies that can be sharply distinguished from the politics of the inter-war years. Indeed some commentators see that settlement, which included the social security elements of the Beveridge report, the establishment of the NHS, the introduction of compulsory and free secondary education and the full employment policies of Keynes, as representing the creation of new citizenship rights (Parker, 1972; Gamble, 1987; Sullivan, 1989). Indeed, it has been seen as 'a sustained attempt to reduce inequality through public action' (Gamble, 1987, p. 190).

A third element of the settlement is often seen as foreshadowing what was to happen in later years both in the politics of industrial relations and in the politics of social policy making. That is, in accepting that the trade unions, which had co-operated with government throughout the war years, had a right to be consulted and even incorporated into decision-making processes of government, powerful state and private interests were embarking on a momentous change in direction from inter-war practices and principles. Of special significance to us is that this shift is argued to have legitimated the tripartite structure of decision-making in industry (for example, establishment of National Economic Development Councils by a Conservative administration in the 1960s), and in wider areas of policy, including social policy (for example, the corporatist structure of government consequent on the negotiation of a social contract between the Labour administration and the trade unions in the mid 1970s). This view of the 1945 settlement is, of course, quite consistent with the role played by powerful interest groups in the development of certain social policies in the post-war period.

The role of teachers and articulate middle class lobbies in the development of Labour's comprehensive school policy is but one example (Reynolds and Sullivan, 1987; Weeks, 1986; Sullivan, 1991). The role played by the poverty lobby in resisting or influencing the direction of anti-poverty policy (McCarthy, 1986; Whiteley and Winyard, 1987) is another.

The drift of the argument is of course that post-war, or at least pre-Thatcher, Conservative administrations that followed the 1945–51 Labour government were willing to administer a historic compromise put into place by Attlee and his colleagues.

One variant of the argument finds this entirely unremarkable. After all, many policy planks that supported the settlement were developed in ministerial subcommittees of the war-time coalition government (Harris, 1981; Thane, 1982). This approach emphasises areas of broad agreement between Labour and Conservatives in that administration and places less stress on the sharp differences of emphasis and sometimes of principle which on occasion lurked behind that broad agreement.

Another approach points, at least in part, in another direction. It identifies a relative lack of enthusiasm exhibited by the 1951 Conservative administration for certain elements of the settlement established by Labour (Gamble, 1987).

Nationalisation policy, it is said, is one illustration of this. As part of a strategy intended to meet the twin aims of efficiency and social justice, the post-war Labour government had established a mixed economy in which public and private corporations co-existed alongside each other. A number of major industries including coal and steel were nationalised between 1945–51 as part of this process. Though the subsequent Conservative administration retained most of these industries in public ownership, it denationalised steel, which had, in any case, emerged as one of the most contentious items on the nationalisation shopping list, and exhibited lukewarm enthusiasm for the other still-socialised industries. The 1951 Churchill government placed private businessmen at the head of nationalised industries and encouraged them to operate in similar ways to private enterprises (Greenleaf, 1983; Blake, 1985).

According to this approach, the 1951 Conservative administration had drawn a line through the most partisan feature of the post-war settlement while accepting other elements such as full employment policy and the welfare state as both evolutionary and desirable developments (Sked and Cook, 1979; Marwick, 1982; Morgan, 1990; Williamson, 1990).

Neither of the above approaches attempts to make the claim, however, that the supposed consensus at the top was necessarily reflected in the views of rank and file members of the two political parties. Though it might well have been the case, as Gamble opines, that 'majority opinion in both parties came to see the post-war arrangements and the post-war policy regime as an acceptable compromise' (Gamble, 1987, p. 190) that proved durable but enthused few, it is also possible to argue, as does Pimlott, that ordinary partisans perceived not consensus between the parties over key elements of state policy, but sharp conflict (Pimlott, 1988). We return to this latter perception later.

There are of course differences of emphasis in the arguments reviewed above but all of them attest to the existence, over near on 30 post-war years, of a *de facto* political consensus at the level of political leadership on a mixed economy, full employment and a welfare state. That consensus might primarily have been at the level of ideas leaving sufficient space for partisan political disagreement, sometimes sharp. This might appear to be the case in the process leading to the establishment of the NHS where disputes about structure, organisational framework and professional accountability led to rancorous battles between the Conservatives and the medical profession on the one hand and the Labour government on the other (Lowe, 1983; Campbell, 1987; Sullivan, 1987).

If we follow this view, post-war consensus politics might be more noteworthy for the contrast they offer with the conflict politics of the 1930s than for any consistent political agreement at the level of individual policy; an implicit claim in Gamble's argument. Such policies may or may not have carried with them the enthusiastic support of ordinary members of the major political parties. Be these things as they may, there is clear agreement that consensus politics were, in some senses, the pivot of the discourse and the craft of UK national politics in the pre-Thatcher post-war period. Keynesian economic management and Beveridge's social philosophy had acted as midwives to a relatively durable form of welfare-capitalism.

Consensus as back-door tyranny?

Another group of commentators take a rather different approach. This group, often with overt sympathies for neo-liberal economics and radical right politics, acknowledge and resent the creation and operation of political consensus. For many post-war years, the general approach outlined in the previous section was as dominant as a guide to political action as it was as an analysis of empirical reality.

During these years, those who saw consensus politics as socialism by stealth or as back-door tyranny were voices crying in the political and academic wildernesses. Their analyses have gained the status of orthodoxy latterly and have for some time replaced the erstwhile Keynesian social democracy as a guide to political action. The enduring claims of these writers and thinkers have included the following.

- The development of state interventionism in the advanced nations of the twentieth century represents embryonic state socialism and is one step on 'the road to serfdom' (Hayek, 1944) and the loss of individual freedom.
- The development of welfare states and of protective legislation has removed responsibility for behaviour from individuals (Glazer, 1988), including the responsibility to provide material and other goods as a result of independent action. Welfare states have, as a consequence, created irresponsible societies (Boyson, 1971) in which individuals, families and communities look to the state for the provision of resources in cash and services which they ought to have provided for themselves (Boyson, 1971, p. 5). These themes have been rehearsed in the literature of the new right for almost half a century. They bear brief re-rehearsal here in order to understand this distinctive viewpoint on consensus politics.

Consensus politics, or so it is believed, was the creation of misguided, though possibly genuine, political reformers. They legitimated wide-ranging interventionist activities for the state in intervening in the economy, industry and issues of personal welfare. As a result of this, they distorted the true and historic independent status of the individual.

Instead of engaging in unregulated exchange relationships with employers, sellers of goods and services and other individuals, citizens have been made into servants of the state. Instead of social rights, consensus politics have conferred the status of serfdom where each citizen's actions are circumscribed by the all-pervasive regulatory and interventionist activities of the state. One of the results, intended or otherwise, of interventionist consensus politics has been that the state has replaced the family head in the role of pater familias.

Unlike its familial analogue, it has, because of resources made available through high rates of taxation, been able to satisfy – partially or wholly – ever-increasing demands. In Powell's view, consensus politics translated aspirations into citizen rights (Powell, 1972, p. 12), though at a price.

Additionally, because consensus politics have legitimated state interference in the market through strategies which include state ownership of industries, price and wage regulation and the subsidisation of certain goods and services, they have perverted the workings of a free-market system. Where this has happened, it is has also weakened individual freedom. This is so because, according to the radical right, free markets guarantee liberty by establishing a separation between social groups which hold political power and countervailing forces which hold economic power and use that power to block state coercion (Friedman, 1962). More than this, consensus politics have fostered waste and inefficiency because they have allowed, and sometimes encouraged, monopoly formation in industry and welfare (for example, the NHS, see Harris and Seldon, 1979, 1987).

Radical right commentators seem in little doubt that the development of consensus politics in the United Kingdom in the 1940s led to a transformation in the nature of the relation between state and market. The state, as a result, changed from a minimalist state with residual economic and social functions to a collectivist state with extensive central planning functions in the economy and welfare (Hayek, 1960).

The processes and the outcomes of consensus politics have been analysed in masterly polemics published in the late 1980s and mid 1990s by the military historian, Corelli Barnett. In his *Audit of War* (Barnett, 1987) and *The Lost Victory* (1995), the author presents consensus politics as the legitimate progeny of Labour Party social democracy and the bastard-child of misguided Conservatism.

The outcomes of consensus politics are, for Barnett, both clear and damaging. Concentrating on issues of economic development, he argues that the consequences of war-time consensus politics and their continuation into the peace have been disastrous for Britain. War-time government had failed to establish the base for a thriving post-war industrial sector. Instead, foundations had been laid for an uncompetitive and unprosperous future. These foundations included an acceptance of the full employment ideology of Beveridge (HMSO, 1942; Beveridge, 1944) and the demand-led economic strategies of Keynes. They also included the development of a welfare state which sapped the health of the British economy as a result of two outcomes consequential on its development. In the first place, access to welfare benefits has proved a disincentive to work and thus a threat to profitability. Further, welfare state growth, in placing 'parlour before plant' (1995, p. 69), has eaten up ever-growing proportions of the gross national product thereby leading finally to a fiscal crisis (Barnett, 1987, pp. 276–304).

Barnett's analysis of the process of putting consensus on the political agenda has striking similarities with the accounts of radical right apologists. An intellectual and political elite imposed the 'dream of a new Jerusalem' (Barnett, 1987, p. 11) on a war-time coalition government, state functionaries and the general public alike.

These moral entrepreneurs included in their numbers not only the contemporary representatives of Christian socialism, Soper, Stockwood, Temple (see Barnett, 1987, pp. 12–16), but also government advisers. Keynes is said to have been convinced of 'the importance of ethical considerations in . . . economic thought' (1987, p. 17) and Beveridge quite clearly exhibited a similar concern for the place of morality at the heart of politics (Harris, 1981).

Pride of place among the New Jerusalemers is reserved, however, for Labour politicians in the war-time coalition government. Churchill had, of course, placed many of the home front departments in the hands of Labour ministers. The result, for Barnett at least, was the beginning or acceleration of a crusade whose destination was the New Jerusalem of social and economic equality. The crusaders' vehicle was consensus politics. The earliest model of this vehicle was the Ministry of Information, whose Parliamentary Secretary, Harold Nicolson MP, was entrusted with the task of drafting a memorandum on peace principles to lift public morale after the evacuation of Allied forces from Dunkirk. That memorandum contained the following exhortation:

> We should proclaim that we intend to make a better world at home in which the abuses of the past shall not be allowed to reappear. Unemployment, education, housing and the abolition of privilege should form the main planks of such a programme. (McLaine, 1979, cited in Barnett, 1987, p. 20)

Consensus politics then equals egalitarian politics. Egalitarian politics means welfare statism and welfare statism leads to economic disaster. With vividness of expression, Barnett has taken us to the core of one element of the radical-right critique of consensus politics. Britain has failed to remain a great nation for much of the post-war period because it has been brought to its knees by the operation of consensus politics. Here then is one deleterious effect of statism: its inefficiency.

Scepticism about consensus

One of the relatively rare examples of such scepticism is the attempt by the political historian, Ben Pimlott, to dissect what he regards as 'the myth of consensus'. In a short essay published at the end of the 1980s he questions the assumption that consensus politics were a significant feature of the post-war period (Pimlott, 1988). His scepticism arises from the following concerns.

First, Pimlott suggests that consensus theory is based on what Saville has called a 'myth of a golden past' (Saville, 1966). In this case harmony is assumed in the past to underline the conflict of the present. Another way of putting this is to argue that from the vantage point of the conflict politics of the Thatcher era, earlier periods and earlier politics indeed appeared to be consensual in nature. While he is prepared to allow that major changes had occurred in prevailing political ideas during the 1980s, Pimlott is less happy to regard this as entailing a lost consensus (Pimlott, 1988, pp. 135–6).

Second, he argues that if consensus existed as the lodestone of political thought and action for pre-Thatcherite politics, it was a secret well kept from the political actors themselves. Political conflict raged, or so the author believes, over key elements of the supposed consensus (Pimlott, 1988, p. 136).

This was the case with the Beveridge proposals (HMSO, 1942) which provided the basic rationale for, and recommendations in respect of, a post-war welfare state. The response of government was less than unanimous, or so Pimlott contends, with Churchill and many Conservative ministers seeing the proposals as expensive and potentially divisive. This judgement is consistent with the views recently put forward by Kenneth Morgan (Morgan, 1990) and indeed by Beveridge's biographer (Harris, 1977, 1981). These authors also point out that Labour ministers in the coalition, especially Ernest Bevin – Minister of Labour and trade union leader – were also less than enthusiastic supporters of the proposals, believing them to allow a future Labour government insufficient flexibility in the introduction of social welfare and social security measures. Bevin also quite clearly believed that the proposals, if implemented, would weaken trade unions' ability to secure adequate wage settlements for their members because of the existence of a 'social wage' (Bullock, 1967; Harris, 1981; Thane, 1982).

If there was a consensus over this issue it was, or so this argument goes, between back-bench opinion in the Parliamentary Labour Party and an enthusiastic public that queued to obtain copies of the eventual report.

Support for Pimlott's position can also be found in some commentaries on the introduction of the NHS. Here, the argument is that the opposition to Aneurin Bevan's plans for a service accountable to parliament through the minister and for a salaried medical profession and a nationalised hospital system amounted to political conflict rather than to disagreement over detail. Despite support for a national health system from the war-time government and from elements in the medical profession (Thane, 1982, pp. 230–8), Labour's plans, especially those countenancing a curtailment of professional power, were opposed by the Conservatives and by medical interests (Foot, 1975; Willcocks, 1968; Thane, 1982). Bevan's concessions to the doctors over salaries and accountability – 'I choked the doctors' throats with gold' – can be seen, by this account, as a response to political *conflict* rather than as a manifestation of *consensus*.

Similarly, the acrimony of the ideological debate over the reform of secondary schooling in the 1950s and 1960s might be seen as reflecting sharp differences between the major political parties (Rubinstein and Simon, 1972; Reynolds and Sullivan, 1987; Weeks, 1986), although its implementation in the 1960s and 1970s is often seen as reflecting *de facto* consensus (see Sullivan, 1991).

As a final example, Pimlott cites Conservative hostility to the principle of universality in the administration of welfare services, most often latent but increasingly overt since the mid 1960s, as an illustration of the mythical nature of consensus politics (1988, p. 137).

In conclusion, Pimlott addresses the question of the existence of a popular consensus in the British population in the post-war years. His conclusion is that it was conspicuous by its absence. Countering the claim that '. . . party government had given rise to an agreement on the common good which . . . fell short of unanimity but . . . did accomplish the aggregation of the preferences of the electorate' (Beer, 1982), he retorts that ordinary voters appear to have been more divided during the supposed period of consensus than they have since its assumed demise. He supports this by drawing his reader's attention to the stability of voting patterns, reflecting, he believes, rigid party loyalty, in the two decades following the 1951 general election (1988, pp. 139–40).

For Pimlott, then, a period of consensus politics is much more difficult to find than for a number of other commentators. Nonetheless what remains undisputed even in this account is a theory of consensus, *pace* Kavanagh, which allows for sharp policy differences within a generally agreed framework of support for a mixed-economy, full-employment welfare state.

Even in Pimlott's treatment a welfare consensus is grudgingly acknowledged. It operated at the level of framework and was shared, almost exclusively, by party elites. But it nurtured the establishment and growth of the welfare state. As we have seen, that is a regrettable state of affairs as far as the radical political right is concerned. It might have been expected then that the terms of office, during the 1980s, of a government headed by one of their own number would have seen fundamental changes.

Has the consensus been smashed?

It was clearly Mrs Thatcher's hope and anticipation when she took office in 1979 that the welfare consensus would be smashed. But that hope was to founder on any number of rocks.

First administration blues

Whatever the Prime Minister's expectations, the first administration was to prove, as we have already seen, a graveyard for her preference to roll back the state from welfare. Prepared to use unemployment as a policy tool, her government found it impossible fundamentally to change the value of unemployment benefit. The result was that by 1983, spending on social security had doubled and public spending, as a whole, had increased. Neither were embryonic plans for the NHS to come to fruition. Early in the administration, she had sent Patrick Jenkin, the Health and Social Security Secretary, on a fact-finding mission to the United States. His brief was to develop ideas about the privatisation of healthcare. In the event, the difficulties facing the American healthcare system convinced Jenkin and Thatcher that abolition was simply not an option. Instead, while encouraging the growth of private insurance, the Prime Minister felt forced to reassure that 'the National Health Service is safe with us'. In any event, Thatcher and her supporters were hidebound by a commitment made during the 1979 election. Labour's plans, if it had formed the 1979 government, were to pump more money into the NHS.

Jenkin, the Secretary of State in waiting had panicked when he was billed to appear with his Labour opposite number, David Ennals, on BBC2's *Newsnight* programme. He phoned the Shadow Chancellor to seek permission to announce that the Conservatives would match Labour's spending plans. He got that permission, made the statement and was to hold off the Treasury and the Prime Minister from radical changes to the service and from starving it of resources.

Part of the Prime Minister's difficulties were that she had, in 1975, inherited a Shadow Cabinet with a Heathite majority and she was to take most of them into her first Cabinet. Though she was gradually to dispense of their services and was to regard them from the beginning as 'wets', she had, in fact, inherited a majority of consensus-minded politicians who retained an affection for the institutions of the welfare state, even if they acknowledged the case for restricting its further growth.

The bandwagon gets rolling: 1983–90

With her election in 1983 for a second term, Mrs Thatcher obviously felt confident enough to create Cabinets more in her own image. Even the remaining wets came to take on a dry exterior form. Whether by intent, which is my judgement, or for other reasons, the relative timidity of the first administration gave way to the construction, brick by brick, of a strategic approach to the welfare state.

The National Health Service

Unable to make the abolition option stick, a more gradual commercialisation of the service took place in the second and third administrations. As we have already seen, this started with the introduction of general management into the NHS and was followed, after the NHS review in 1988, by the insinuation of a quasi-market into the service in the 1990s. It is clear that though the NHS remains structurally intact, that structure has changed in such a way that it is now mid-way between a public service and a private corporation. Government may have no intention to move the further step. But that step, to remove public funding and replace it with private finance, is a much smaller one – achievable by a couple of granny footsteps – than it was in 1983. Such a strategic approach, if that is what it was, was in any event, made more sensible than the big bang approach by the hardening of public opinion in favour of retention and public resourcing of the NHS (see Chapter 4).

Education

A similar story can be told here. The introduction of the Education Reform Act (1988) was as significant a landmark as Butler's Education Act of 1944. For the

256 *The development of the British welfare state*

legislation, ably guided by Kenneth Baker, loosened the bond between LEAs and schools. Grant-maintained schools, as a result, receive their funding from the Secretary of State and are to all intents and purposes independent save for this. Even LEA-funded schools are now budget-holders and have a much more semi-detached relationship with LEAs than was previously the case.

To semi-privatisation has been added greater consumer choice and participation. For parental choice of schools has been supplemented by the inclusion by statute of parent governors on school governing bodies.

Social security and personal social services

Changes in the second and third terms have instituted significant if not fundamental changes in social security policy. The re-crafting of the social security system has included not only cuts in expenditure but has, as a result of the Fowler reviews, been reorganised to emphasise individual responsibility and self-help.

Not insignificant changes also occurred in the personal social services. Throughout this period, local authority social services departments have been encouraged and then required to develop internal markets as a result of which they are responsible for purchasing services rather than assuming provision of all of them.

Housing

And finally, though the effects are still to be fully appreciated, substantial changes have occurred in housing policy. The sale of council houses must be counted as one of the Government's greatest political successes in social policy. The initiative chimed with citizen aspirations and this piece of people's capitalism had, finally, to be accepted by the Labour Opposition. The Housing Act (1988) was intended to relieve local authorities of their housing function. Though less than completely successful in execution, the principles behind it are those found in education and health: the semi-privatisation of a welfare state service.

In summary, the welfare consensus was not smashed by the Conservative governments of the 1980s. Nor was it replaced by a new consensus. But the old consensus was bent so that while the appearance of change was relatively minor, the reality of change was significant. This was Thatcherism by stealth.

From a viewpoint at the end of the 1980s, we would have to say in response to one of our opening questions that we had not witnessed the ending of the welfare state. But more was to come.

Majorism and welfare

As we have already seen, the biggest contribution of 'Majorism' has been to intensify the reforms planned by Thatcher's administrations in relation to health and education policy. But to leave the story there is to leave it unfinished.

Social policy spending

When Major succeeded Thatcher in 1990, social policy spending accounted for 22 per cent of GDP. This rose by 1993 to nearly 27 per cent, considerably higher than in 1979. Consequently the new Chancellor, Kenneth Clarke, decided to use the new autumn budget to raise taxes. More than this, his deputy, Michael Portillo, announced a fundamental review of spending on the welfare state. This is, as we have seen, not particularly new. Butler had attempted something similar in the early 1950s, Healey in the mid 1970s and Lawson in the early 1980s. Whether the outcome is as unsuccessful as the earlier attempts remains to be seen.

Emphasis on morality: squaring the circle

The last couple of years have also seen the Government returning to a favourite tune from the Thatcher hymn-sheet. Worried about the rebellion of the Conservative right on Europe, Mr Major appears to have decided to give right-wing ministers their head on social issues. As a result the old concerns about social security fraud and lone parents and public housing have re-surfaced (see Chapter 9). Not prepared to let 'the bastards' have their way over Europe, an issue that led to Major calling a leadership election in 1995, he has let them re-introduce distinctly Thatcherite ideologies of the family and the responsibilities of individuals. Nothing, it seems, changes.

The welfare state: 1945–95

Forced to make an analysis, we would have to say that we have not yet witnessed the entombment of the welfare state. It may be however that it is seriously ill. The 1945 idea of welfare as a citizen right has been transformed in the last decade and a half. Now the evidence is of a residualised welfare state. The receipt of welfare is hedged around with qualifications and stigma. Though the final blow is a long time coming, both Mrs Thatcher's governments and Mr Major's have taken us a considerable way down the road to the commercialisation of welfare. But on the road from 1945 to 1995 there have been continuities as well as changes.

Continuity and change

The equality debate

As we have suggested in an earlier chapter, social inequality has increased over the last 15 years or so and it is tempting to see this state of affairs as an effect of Conservative social policy. Though it has played its part, the hardening of inequalities has been a feature of the welfare state throughout its life. As early as the late 1950s and early 1960s evidence was emerging that the welfare state had proved incapable of eradicating poverty. Similarly, the first 30 years of the NHS saw the widening of the health gap rather than its narrowing. And so on. Though Conservative governments of the 1980s and 1990s have been more comfortable with the creation of inequality, their record might reasonably be seen simply as an exacerbation of the inequalities inherent in welfare capitalism rather than an about-turn. This sort of interpretation is masked by Labour's emphasis since the late 1950s on achieving equality of some sort. But Labour ministers as well as their Thatcher/Major counterparts have consciously wrought changes in the welfare state, the effect of which has been to increase rather than mitigate inequality. A good example of this are the earnings-related schemes, including an earnings-related unemployment benefit and SERPS, which were grafted onto but stood in contradiction to the flat-rate principle in social security. Another would be the benefit accrued by usually middle class home owners by Labour's commitment to mortgage tax relief. And, of course, there have been those factors which are outside political control. As LeGrand (1982), among others, has shown, welfare state professionals have tended to direct more services in the direction of articulate middle class service users than their working class counterparts.

Professionals and welfare

If inequality has been one of the continuity factors then the role of professionals in the welfare state has been an area where the governments of the left and right have broken, since the mid 1970s, with previous practice. It is no exaggeration to claim that the welfare state was established, albeit sometimes reluctantly, in the image of the professionals. Labour's association with the teachers was a key feature of its developing educational policy. Bevan, with some reluctance, conceded power in the NHS to doctors' representatives as the price of getting the service off the ground. The welfare state was, then, created and succoured by an emphasis on the producers of service rather than the consumers.

By the mid 1970s that was changing. Callaghan's great debate on education moved the policy spotlight onto consumers for the first time. The development of parental choice of school and the introduction of parent governors in the

1980s continued this new trend. In health, where Bevan had choked the doctors' throats with gold, Thatcher's governments were determined to loosen the stranglehold they had on the governance of the NHS. First, the idea of management was introduced and then the health reforms of the late 1980s were pushed through despite the doctors' opposition. This led not only to an alliance between the BMA and the Labour Party to try to prevent the reforms but also to the health secretary facing the doctors down. In a neat inversion of Bevan, he told a doctors' dinner meeting that whenever he talked about changes doctors felt for their wallets.

So, where now?

Despite the changes, and the continuities, the welfare state has worked well enough up till now as a 'universal savings bank' (Glennerster, 1995). Citizens pay weekly or monthly to finance welfare state services and call in their credit when it is necessary. Throughout the 1980s and 1990s that sort of approach has been called increasingly into question. In health, encouragement to take out private insurance has been the order of the day. In education, the idea of a school voucher which can be topped up out of private income has once more been floated. In relation to pensions, Portillo suggested in 1994 that citizens should increasingly cater for their own old age. Health authorities are, in the chill financial climate of the 1990s, attenuating their commitment to long-term care of the elderly and moving that responsibility not only to local authorities but also to families. Residential care is increasingly financed out of the savings garnered over a life-time.

Perhaps this is, after all, the way forward and not only if the Conservatives win a record fifth consecutive general election.

Labour and the welfare state in the 1990s

Potentially radical changes are also occurring in the approach to welfare adopted by the Labour Party. Its relatively new leader, Mr Tony Blair, has been responsible for the re-packaging of the party as *New Labour* and, since his elevation, Labour – hungry for government office – has reconsidered its approach to the welfare state as it has other areas of political discourse. Despite the recommendations of the Borrie Commission (1995), the major opposition party seems to have opted for shadowing many erstwhile Conservative social policy approaches. The re-orientation has included – or so it seems to this author – an inversion of the party's previous emphasis on social rights so that social responsibility is now seen as the lodestone of social policy. Specific examples of the new policy approach are outlined below but at heart it has involved a re-orientation of Labour social policy principles.

From class to community

In a Fabian lecture delivered in 1995, the leader of the Labour Party outlined his preferred political trajectory (Blair, 1995). Styling himself as a millenarian revisionist, Mr Blair argued for the replacement of Labour social democracy's pre-occupation with social class with an emphasis on *community*. This communitarian approach, borrowed in part from the United States, emphasised the importance of redefining socialism or, more accurately, social democracy, as about citizens' responsibilities for themselves and for their neighbours. The social policy implications of this perspective were clear. The state should play a less prominent part in the provision of social policy but should enable citizens and welfare providers to negotiate the basis of provision. Collective funding would remain a significant plan of welfare provision but might be made less significant by the re-location of part of the responsibility, via the tax system, to individuals. In this light, the Shadow Chancellor's recent, publicly expressed aspiration to reduce the lowest band of income tax to 10p or 15p in the pound (*The Guardian*, 17 November 1995) takes on significance, for reductions in taxes might pave the way for greater individual financial contribution to welfare expenditure.

The re-making of a party: the death of social democracy?

One of Labour's most successful Prime Ministers, Harold Wilson, is credited with arguing that 'the Labour Party is a crusade or it is nothing'. The nature of that crusade for mid-century Labour social democrats was the nurture and furtherance of Marshallite welfare capitalism. The creation of a 'hyphenated society' (Marshall, 1972), in which welfare is promoted within the context of capitalism, was seen by most Labour politicians of the period as requiring a careful attention to the needs of the most vulnerable in society as well as to the economic requirements of an ailing capitalist economy. Labour's method was to negotiate the tension between welfare and capitalism by a Crosland–Marshall emphasis on collectivity and collective rights. In such an emphasis, social rights, pre-eminently a welfare state, were seen as the *sine qua non* of capitalist organisation, as one side of a balancing act in which full membership of a welfare society counterbalanced the inequalities inherent in capitalism. But that welfare society presumed that individual welfare could only be vouchsafed by collective commitment to and provision of welfare. Blairite Labourism appears to have transcended or betrayed such commitments and sometimes to see the vulnerable as a problem rather than as the legitimate focus of welfare activities. Note, for example, the Shadow Home Secretary's polemic against aggressive begging and the 'squeedgy boy' society (*The Guardian*, 13 November 1995). Here, as elsewhere, the casualties of an apparently polarised society, the homeless and the unemployed, are seen as boils on the body politic to be removed, rather than as unfortunates to be rescued by a welfare net. New Labour appears, at least on the surface, to involve a re-definition of the principles of twentieth century social democracy: to misquote Bevan, '...suffer the children is now only something that is said from pulpits'. His belief that prioritisation of the needs of the vulnerable had been woven into the fabric of political life seems strangely anachronistic in the Labour social politics of the 1990s.

Economic prudence

The modern Labour Party also appears, at least in this author's eyes, to have committed itself to national book balancing in economic policy. The economic heirs of the Thatcherite project seem as likely to be found in the Labour Opposition as in the Conservative government. With a prudence that Baroness Thatcher would, no doubt, be proud of, Labour, in the form of its leader, has committed itself to lower social expenditure (Blair, 1995).

The most recent policy directions discernible in the Labour Party suggest that, while the revolution might not be complete, Blairism has re-defined the welfare mission of the party.

The acceptance of internal markets in the National Health Service

Labour's most recent policy document on the NHS makes clear that, while it wishes to transform fund-holding GP practices into purchasing consortia, it has accepted the rationality of the commissioner/provider split in health (Labour Party, 1995). In a Labour future, GPs would assist health commissioning authorities (revamped DHAs) in the planning and commissioning of services. Given the reality and good sense of prioritisation of services, this appears to be an entirely wise decision. But only if significant resources are made available to the service. The winter of 1995/6 has seen the concept of commissioning thrown into question by huge projected health authority overspends, to be recouped in following financial years. Provider units have been placed in the difficult position of having to close beds to deal with the shortfall in purchasing and, once more, this has had the effect of sporadic cancellations of non-urgent treatments (*The Guardian*, November 1995). For the market to work, sufficient resources are required in the system and Labour's apparent commitment to reducing welfare expenditure sits uneasily with the demands of the situation.

From welfare to workfare

The Labour leadership, with an eye to forming a government in the late 1990s, also seems to have set about re-defining social rights in relation to employment and social security. Announcing controversial plans (*The Guardian*, 17 November 1995), the Chancellor-in-waiting, Gordon Brown, has unveiled plans to make benefits dependent on claimants accepting one of a number of government-created employment opportunities. Though the party had opposed the introduction by the Conservative government of a job seeker's allowance, it seems that the principles of workfare lie at the heart of Labour's intention to get Britain back to work. These are quintessentially New Labour attitudes. Previous Labour governments have accepted and administered pecuniary punishments for claimants refusing to take up work, and contemporary internal opposition in the party accepts this principle. The departure, for good or ill, is the emphasis by the leadership of *social responsibility* rather more heavily than *social rights*.

Opting out of schools

Changes also appear to be afoot in relation to Labour policy on grant-maintained schools. Following the Labour leader's decision to send his son to an opted-out secondary school, the party's opposition to government policy in this area has softened. In an apparent about face, Labour now accepts the durability of the grant-maintained sector and is looking for improvements in LEA-controlled schools to match the allegedly high standards of the opted-out sector.

From universalism to selectivism

Labour's new policy armoury also appears to suggest a movement away from earlier support for universalism in social policy. Though the welfare state was founded on the provision of universal services, and although the development of Labour policy for much of this period kept faith with universal provision, policy intentions certainly appear to be changing. Notwithstanding recent rhetoric (*The Guardian*, 17 November 1995), Labour has accepted – and for obvious reasons – prioritisation and rationing in the NHS and with it an element of selectivity managed by the medical profession and NHS managers. Labour's social security trajectory also appears to mark a wider acceptance of selectivity than had previously been acceptable (see above). And Labour, under the influence of the 'new market left', appears poised to accept targeting as potentially more redistributive in the social security field than universalism (Hewitt, 1989). Gone, though not forgotten by unreconstructed 'old Labourites', is the sanctity of universalism.

Nineteen nineties Labour, then, might reasonably be seen as re-mapping the political territory in which it wishes to operate. In doing so, it appears to have moved towards modern Conservative nostrums about the welfare state. Its aspiration appears to be the creation of an opportunity state, based in part on individual effort and individual responsibility, rather than the rescue of a welfare state now in indifferent health. Notwithstanding the less than complete success of Thatcherism and Majorism in fracturing the welfare consensus, Labour seems to have at least on eye on accomplishing that goal. That at least is, as Bevan might have said, one truth. Other analyses are, of course, strong contenders in explaining the apparent welfare shift within Labour.

Ineffectiveness and inefficiency and consumerism in the old welfare state

One such argument is that the pre-Thatcher welfare state was inefficient and ineffective and concentrated on producer needs rather than the needs of consumers. The argument is a familiar one, popularised by Powell (1969) and re-cycled by the radical right in the 1980s. It is that the welfare state, like other service providers occupying monopoly or near-monopoly positions, was inefficient and ineffective because there was no incentive for efficiency and effectiveness. More than this, such services had become dominated by the concerns of providers because the lack of competition made it unnecessary to elicit consumer views. Consumers had nowhere else, or few other places to go.

What is new is that this public sector model was seen as problematic by the so-called market left as well as by the market right (Glennerster, 1992). The argument here is that a modern social democratic party like the Labour Party should develop ways of identifying and satisfying consumer preferences (LeGrand and Winter, 1987). The apparent Labour aspiration to emphasise individual rights and to promote markets and quasi-markets in welfare is therefore an attempt not to kill the welfare state but to re-focus its activities on the receivers of service. It is also an attempt to make the market work to improve efficiency, effectiveness and, therefore, service.

Labour and consumer choice

Labour may also be seen to be responding to increasing evidence of the electorate's preference for systems of welfare which allow them to have a voice, a choice and an ability to exit to other service providers (Papadakis and Taylor-Gooby, 1987). This argument suggests that not only is efficiency improved by competition but so also is consumer power, from identification of service needs through to choice of service provider and the ability to reconsider that choice at a later date. Labour's new-found faith in competition or managed competition may, then, mark its development into a consumer-responsive party in welfare. To other transformations must, then, be added the transformation from provider 'socialism' to consumer 'socialism'.

The jury remains out on Labour's actual social policy direction if it forms a government, although readers will have discerned my belief that a future Labour government is likely to follow the directions already emerging in policy documents. Some (Hill, 1990, for example) might see this as the only sensible way to proceed if the provision of welfare in the next century is to remain affordable. But, it would be an ironic sort of symmetry if the party that was at least one of the midwives of the classic welfare state also proved to be its funeral director!

Bibliography

Aaronovitch, S. (1981) *The Road from Thatcherism*, London: Lawrence & Wishart.

Abel-Smith, B. (1964) *The Hospitals 1800–1948*, London: Heinemann.

Abel-Smith, B. and Titmuss, R. (1959) *The Cost of the National Health Service*, Cambridge: Cambridge University Press.

Abel-Smith, B. and Townsend, P. (1965) *The Poor and the Poorest*, London: Longman Green.

Addison, P. (1975) *The Road to 1945*, London: Quartet.

Addison, P. (1982) *The Road to 1945*, London: Macmillan.

Addison, P. (1992) *Churchill on the Home Front*, London: Cape.

Aitken, I. (1992) 'Raising a glass amid the gloom', *The Guardian*, 13 April.

Alcock, P. (1987) *Poverty and State Support*, London: Macmillan.

Ascher, K. (1987) *The Politics of Privatisation*, London: Macmillan.

Ashford, D. (1986) *The Emergence of Welfare States*, Oxford: Blackwell.

Association of Community Health Councils (1988) *Financing the NHS: The Consumer View*, London: Association of Community Health Councils in England and Wales.

Association of University Teachers (1989) *Annual Report*, London: Association of University Teachers.

Association of University Teachers (1991) *Annual Report*, London: AUT.

Association of University Teachers (1992) *Annual Report*, London: AUT.

Audit Commission (1986) *Making a Reality of Community Care*, London: HMSO.

Baker, K. (1993) *The Turbulent Years*, London: Faber & Faber.

Banting, K. (1979) *Poverty, Politics and Policy*, London: Macmillan.

Baran, P. A. and Sweezy, P. M. (1968) *Monopoly Capital*, Harmondsworth: Penguin Books.

Barclay, P. (1982) *Social Workers: Their Roles and Tasks*, London: Bedford Square Press.

Barnett, A. (1984) 'Beyond consensus', *New Socialist*, 18, pp. 33–5.

Barnett, C. (1987) *The Audit of War*, London: Macmillan.

Barnett, C. (1995) *The Lost Victory*, London: Macmillan.

Barr, N., Glennerster, H. and LeGrand, J. (1988) *Reform and the National Health Service*, London: LSE.

Barratt-Brown, M. (1972) *From Labourism to Socialism*, Leeds: Spokesman Books.

Bean, P. and MacPherson, S. (eds) (1972) *Approaches to Welfare*, London: Routledge & Kegan Paul.

Beer, S. (1982) *Britain Against Itself*, London: Faber & Faber.

Bellaby, P. (1977) *The Sociology of Comprehensive Schooling*, London: Methuen.

Bevan, A. (1951) *In Place of Fear*, London: Davis & Poynter.

Beveridge, W. H. (1941) *Social Insurance: General Considerations*, inter-departmental memorandum.

Beveridge, W. H. (1941) *Social Insurance: General Considerations*, private note to members of the Committee on Social Security and Allied Services.

Beveridge, W. H. (1943) *The Pillars of Security*, London: Allen & Unwin.

Beveridge, W. H. (1944) *Full Employment in a Free Society*, London: Allen & Unwin.

Beveridge, W. H. (1945) *Why I am a Liberal*, London: Jenkins.

Beveridge, W. H. (1968) *Power and Influence*, London: Hodder & Stoughton.

Blair, A. (1995) Speech to the Fabian Society Annual Conference.

Blake, R. (1985) *The Conservative Party from Peel to Thatcher*, London: Fontana.

Board of Education (1943) *Educational Reconstruction*, London: HMSO.

Bolger, S., Corrigan, P., Docking, J. and Frost, N. (1981) *Towards Socialist Welfare Work*, London: Macmillan.

Bosanquet, N. (1983) *After the New Right*, London: Heinemann.

Boyd-Carpenter, J. (1980) *Way of Life*, London: Sidgwick Jackson.

Boyson, R. (ed.) (1971) *Down with the Poor*, London: Churchill Press.

Bremner, M. (1968) *Dependency and the Family*, London: Institute of Economic Affairs.

Brown, M. (1978) *Introduction to Social Administration*, London: Hutchinson.

Bullock, A. (1967) *The Life and Times of Ernest Bevin*, London: Heinemann.

Burnett, J. (1986) *A History of Housing: 1815–1985*, London: Methuen.

Butler, J. (1992) *Patients, Policies and Politics*, London: Open University Press.

Butler, R. A. (1971) *The Art of the Possible*, London: Hamish Hamilton.

Cairncross, A. (1992) *The British Economy Since 1945*, Oxford: Blackwell.

Calder, A. (1965) *The People's War*, London: Paladin.

Callaghan, J. (1987) *Time and Chance*, London: Collins.

Callaghan, J. (1991) Interview with the author.

Campbell, J. (1987) *Nye Bevan and the Mirage of British Socialism*, London: Weidenfeld & Nicolson.

Campbell, J. (1993) *Edward Heath*, London: Jonathan Cape.

Case Con Collective (1970) 'Case Con manifesto' in *Case-Con, 1*, London: Case Con Collective.

Castle, B. (1993) *Fighting all the Way*, London: Macmillan.

Clarke, J. (1980) 'Social democratic delinquents and Fabian families' in *Permissiveness and Control*, Fitzgerald, M. *et al.* (eds), London: Macmillan.

Cole, J. (1995) *As I Remember It*, London: Cape.

Conservative Party (1977) *The Right Approach to the Economy*, London: Conservative Political Centre.

Conservative Party (1979) *Conservative Manifesto: 1979*, London: Conservative Central Office.

Conservative Party (1979) *Conservative Manifesto 1979*, London: Conservative Political Centre.

Conservative Party (1983) *Conservative Manifesto: 1983*, London: Conservative Central Office.

Conservative Party (1987) *Conservative Party Manifesto, 1987*, London: Conservative Political Centre.

Conservative Political Centre (1952) *Social Services: Needs and Means*, London: Conservative Political Centre.

Conservative Political Centre (1958) *The Future of the Welfare State*, London: Conservative Political Centre.

Conservative Political Centre. (1976) *The Right Approach*, London: Conservative Political Centre.

Conservative Way Forward (1991) *Conservative Philosophy in Action*, London: Conservative Political Centre.

Consultative Committee to the Board of Education (1926) *The Education of the Adolescent*, London: HMSO.

Cook, R. (1988) Speech in the House of Commons.

Corrigan, P. (1975) 'Community work and political struggle', in *The Sociology of Community Action* Leonard, P. (ed.), Keele: University of Keele.

Corrigan, P. (1977) 'The welfare state as an arena for class struggle', *Marxism Today*, March, pp. 87–93.

Corrigan, P. (1979) 'Popular consciousness and social democracy', *Marxism Today*, December, pp. 14–17.

Corrigan, P. and Leonard, P. (1978) *Social Work Practice Under Capitalism*, London: Macmillan.

Cowley, J. (ed.) (1977) *Community or Class Struggle*, London: Stage One Publications.

Cox, A. and Mead, M. (eds) (1975) *A Sociology of Medical Practice*, London: Collier-Macmillan.

Cox, C. and Boyson, R. (eds) (1975) *Black Paper 1975*, London: The Critical Quarterly Society.

Cox, C. and Dyson, A. (eds) (1969) *Black Paper 1*, London: The Critical Quarterly Society.

Cox, C. and Dyson, A. (eds) (1970) *Black Paper 3*, London: The Critical Quarterly Society.

Cox, C. and Dyson, A. (eds) (1971) *Black Paper 1971*, London: The Critical Quarterly Society.

Craig, F. (1982) *Conservative and Labour Party Conference Decisions: 1945– 81*, Chichester: Parliamentary Research Services.

Cripps, F. (1981) 'The British crisis: can the left win?', *New Left Review*, 128.

Cronin, J. (1984) *Labour and Society: 1918–79*, London: Batsford.

Crosland, C. A. R. (1952) 'The transition from capitalism', in *New Fabian Essays*, Crossman, R. H. S. (ed.), London: Turnstile Press.

Crosland, C. A. R. (1956) *The Future of Socialism*, London: Jonathan Cape.

Crosland, C. A. R. (1974) *Socialism Now*, London: Jonathan Cape.

Crosland, S. (1982) *Tony Crosland*, London: Jonathan Cape.

Crossman, R. H. S. (1950) *Socialist Values in a Changing Society*, London: Fabian Society.

Crossman, R. H. S. (ed.) (1952) *New Fabian Essays*, London: Turnstile Press.

Crossman, R. H. S. (1969) *Paying for the Social Services*, London: Fabian Society.

Crossman, R. H. S. (1975) *Diaries of a Cabinet Minister: Volume 1*, London: Jonathan Cape.

Crossman, R. H. S. (1981) *Diaries of a Cabinet Minister: Volume 3*, London: Jonathan Cape.

Curtis, M. (1946) *Report of the Committee on the Care of Children*, Cmnd 6922, London: HMSO.

Dale, R. (1989) *The State and Education Policy*, London: Open University Press.

Deacon, A. and Bradshaw, J. (1983) *Reserved for the Poor*, Oxford: Blackwell.

Deakin, N. (1987) *The Politics of Welfare*, London: Heinemann.

Deakin, N. (1994) *The Politics of Welfare*, Hemel Hempstead: Harvester Wheatsheaf.

Dennis, N. and Halsey, A. H. (1988) *English Ethical Socialism*, Oxford: Clarendon Press.

Department of Education and Science (1983) *Report of Her Majesty's Inspectors of Schools*, London: HMSO.

Department of Education and Science (1990) *Statistics on Education*, London: HMSO.

Department of Health (1962) *A Hospital Plan for England and Wales*, Cmnd. 1604, London: HMSO.

Department of Health (1989) *Working for Patients*, Cmnd. 555, London: HMSO.

Department of Health (1990) *National Health Service and Community Care Act*, London: HMSO.

Department of Health (1993) *NHS Trusts*, London: Department of Health.

Department of Health and Social Security (1970) *Green Paper*, London: Department of Health and Social Security.

Department of Health and Social Security (1979) *Patients First*, London: Department of Health and Social Security.

Department of Health and Social Security (1983) *NHS Management Enquiry*, London: HMSO.

Department of Health and Social Security (1986) *The Reform of Social Security*, London: HMSO.

Digby, A. (1989) *British Welfare Policy*, London: Faber & Faber.

Dixon, J. and Rogers, B. (1960) *Portrait of Social Work*, Oxford: Blackwell.

Donnison, D. (1967) *The Government of Housing*, Harmondsworth, Penguin.

Donnison, D. (1982) *The Politics of Poverty*, Oxford: Martin Robertson.

Donoughue, B. (1987) *The Conduct of Policy Under Harold Wilson and James Callaghan*, London: Jonathan Cape.

Donoughue, B. (1991) Interview with the author.

Donoughue, B. and Jones, G. (1973) *Herbert Morrison: Portrait of a Politician*, London: Weidenfeld and Nicolson.

Donzelot, J. (1980) *The Policing of Families*, London: Hutchinson.

Doyal, L. (1983) *The Political Economy of Health*, London: Pluto Press.

Eccleshall, R. (1977) 'English Conservatism as ideology', *Political Studies*, 25 (1).

Eckstein, H. (1959) *The English Health Service*, London: Oxford University Press.

Edwards, E. and Roberts, I. (1980) 'British higher education: long term trends in student enrolment', *Higher Education Review*, 12.

Ellis, B. (1989) *Pensions in Britain: 1955–75*, London: HMSO.

Enthoven, A. (1985) *Reflections on the Management of the NHS*, London: Nuffield Provincial Hospitals Trust.

Fabian Society (1896) *Annual Conference Proceedings*, London: Fabian Society.

Fabian Society (1968) *Poverty, Socialism and Labour in Power*, London: Fabian Society.

Fenwick, I. G. K. (1976) *The Comprehensive School: 1940–70*, London: Methuen.

Ferguson, T. and Rogers, J. (1986) *Right Turn*, New York, Hill & Wang.

Field, F. (1982) *Poverty and Politics*, London: Heinemann.

Flather, P. (1988) 'Education matters' in *British Social Attitudes: the fifth report*, Jowell, R. et al., Aldershot: Gower.

Floud, J. (1957) *Social Class and Educational Opportunity*, London: Heinemann.

Foot, M. (1975) *Aneurin Bevan: 1945–60*, London: Paladin.

Foot, M. (1982) *Aneurin Bevan: 1945–60*, London: Paladin.

Foot, M. (1983) *Loyalists and Loners*, London: Collins.

Foote, G. (1986) *The Labour Party's Political Thought*, London: Croom Helm.

Ford, J. (1969) *Social Class and the Comprehensive School*, London: Routledge & Kegan Paul.

Fraser, D. (1982) *The Evolution of the British Welfare State*, London: Macmillan.

Friedman, M. (1962) *Capitalism and Freedom*, Chicago: Chicago University Press.

Friedman, M. and Friedman, R. (1980) *Free to Choose*, Harmondsworth: Penguin Books.

Furniss, N. and Tilton, T. (1979) *The Case for the Welfare State*, Bloomington: Indiana University Press.

Galbraith, J. K. (1976) *The Affluent Society*, London: André Deutsch.

Galbraith, J. K. (1982) *Mass Poverty*, London: Penguin Books.

Gamble, A. (1979) 'The decline of the Conservative Party', *Marxism Today*, November, pp. 6–12.

Gamble, A. (1980) 'Thatcher: make or break', *Marxism Today*, November, pp. 14–19.

Gamble, A. (1985) 'Smashing the state: Thatcher's radical crusade', *Marxism Today*, June, pp. 21–6.

Gamble, A. (1987) *The Free Economy and the Strong State: The Politics of Thatcherism*, London: Macmillan.

Gamble, A. (1990) *Britain in Decline* (new edition), London: Macmillan.

Gardiner, G. (1975) *Margaret Thatcher: From Childhood to Leadership*, London: Kimber.

George, V. and Wilding, P. (1985) *Ideology and Social Welfare* (revised edition), London: Routledge & Kegan Paul.

George, W. (1958) *My Brother and I*, London: Allen & Unwin.

Ginsburg, N. (1979) *Class, Capital and Social Policy*, London: Macmillan.

Ginsburg, N. (1992) *Divisions of Welfare*, London: Sage.

Glazer, N. (1988) *The Limits of Social Policy*, Boston: Harvard University Press.

Glenamara, Lord (1991) Interview with the author.

Glennerster, H. (1985) *Paying for Welfare*, Oxford: Basil Blackwell.

Glennerster, H. (1992) *Paying for Welfare in the 1990s*, Hemel Hempstead: Harvester Wheatsheaf.

Glennerster, H. (1995) *British Social Policy Since 1945*, Oxford: Blackwell.

Glennerster, H. and Midgley, J. (1991) *Social Policy and the New Right*, Hemel Hempstead: Harvester Wheatsheaf.

Godsen, P. (1976) *Education in the Second World War*, London: Allen & Unwin.

Goldsmith, M. and Willetts, D. (1988) *Managed Health Care: a New System For a Better Service*, London: Centre for Policy Studies.

Goldstein, H. (1973) *Social Work Practice: a Unitary Approach*, New York: Free Press.

Goldthorpe, J. H. (1962) 'The development of social policy in England', *Transactions of the 5th World Congress of Sociology*.

Goldthorpe, J. H. and Lockwood, D. (1969) *The Affluent Worker*, London: Macmillan.

Gough, I. (1975) 'State expenditure in advanced capitalism', *New Left Review*, 92, pp. 53–92.

Gough, I. (1979) *The Political Economy of the Welfare State*, London: Macmillan.

Green, D. (1982) *The New Right*, London: Macmillan.

Greenleaf, W. H. (1983) *The British Political Tradition: The Rise of Collectivism*, London: Methuen.

Greenleaf, W. H. (1987) *The British Political Tradition: a Much Governed Nation*, London: Methuen.

Griffith, B., Iliffe, S. and Rayner, G. (1987) *Banking on Sickness: Commercial Medicine in Britain and the USA*, London: Lawrence & Wishart.

Griffiths, A. (1971) *The Reorganisation of Secondary Education*, London: Routledge & Kegan Paul.

Griffiths, B. (1983a) *The Moral Basis of the Market Economy*, London: Conservative Political Centre.

Griffiths, R. (1983b) *NHS Management Enquiry*, London: HMSO.

Griffiths, R. (1988) *Community Care: Agenda for Action*, London: HMSO.

Gulbenkian Foundation (1968) *Community Work and Social Change*, London: Longman.

Hailsham, Lord (1975) *The Door Wherein I Went*, London: Collins.

Hailsham, Lord (1990) *A Sparrow's Flight*, London: Collins.

Hall, S. (1979) 'The great moving right show', *Marxism Today*, January, pp. 14–20.

Hall, S. (1988) *The Hard Road to Renewal: Thatcherism and the Crisis of the Left*, London: Verso.

Hall, S. (1992) 'No new vision, no new votes', *New Statesman and Society*, 17 April.

Hall, S. and Jacques, M. (1985) *The Politics of Thatcherism*, London: Lawrence & Wishart.

Halsey, A. H. and Gardner, L. (1953) 'Selection for secondary education and achievement in four grammar schools', *British Journal of Sociology*, March.

Halsey, A. H., Heath, A. F. and Ridge, J. M. (1980) *Origins and Destinations*, Oxford: Oxford University Press.

Handler, J. (1973) *The Coercive Social Worker*, Chicago: Rand McNally.

Harrington, W. and Young, P. (1978) *The 1945 Revolution*, London: Davis-Poynter.

Harris, D. (1987) *Justifying State Welfare*, Oxford: Blackwell.

Harris, J. (1977) *William Beveridge*, Oxford: Oxford University Press.

Harris, J. (1981) 'Social policy making in Britain during the Second World War', in *The Emergence of the Welfare State in Britain and Germany*, Mommsen, W. (ed.), London: Croom Helm.

Harris, J. (1990) 'Enterprise and welfare states: a comparative perspective', *Transactions of the Royal Historical Society*, 40.

Harris, R. (1965) *Welfare Without the State*, London: Institute of Economic Affairs.

Harris, R. (1971) *Choice in Welfare*, London: Institute of Economic Affairs.

Harris, R. and Seldon, A. (1979) *Overruled on Welfare*, London: Institute of Economic Affairs.

Harris, R. and Seldon, A. (1987) *Welfare Without the State*, London: Institute of Economic Affairs.

Hart, J. T. (1975) 'The inverse care law', in *A Sociology of Medical Practice*, A. Cox and M. Mead (eds), London: Collier-Macmillan.

Hart, J. T. (1979) *The National Health Service*, Lecture at University of Wales, Cardiff.

Hart, J. T. (1988) *A New Kind of Doctor*, London: Merlin Press.

Hayek, F. A. (1944) *The Road to Serfdom*, London: Routledge & Kegan Paul.

Hayek, F. A. (1949) *Individualism and the Economic Order*, London: Routledge & Kegan Paul.

Hayek, F. A. (1960) *The Constitution of Liberty*, London: Routledge & Kegan Paul.

Hayek, F. A. (1973) *Law, Legislation and Liberty*, Vol. 1, London: Routledge & Kegan Paul.

Hayek, F. A. (1976) *Law, Legislation and Liberty*, Vol. 2, London: Routledge & Kegan Paul.

Hayek, F. A. (1976) *Law, Legislation and Liberty*, Vol. 3, London: Routledge & Kegan Paul.

Hayek, F. A. (1980) *1980s Unemployment and the Unions*, London: Institute of Economic Affairs.

Hennessy, P. (1992) *Never Again*, London: Jonathan Cape.

Hewitt, P. (1989) 'A way to cope with the world as it is', *Samizdat*, 6, pp. 3–4.

Higgins, J. (1988) *The Business of Medicine*, London: Macmillan.

Higgins, J. (1990) *Caring for People, the Government's Proposal for Community Care: a Commentary*, Southampton: Institute for Health Policy Studies.

Hill, M. (1990) *Social Security Policy in Britain*, Aldershot: Edward Elgar.

Hill, M. (1993) *The Welfare State in Britain: a Political History Since 1945*, Aldershot: Edward Elgar.

Hills, J. (1991) *The State of Welfare*, Oxford: Clarendon Press.

HMSO (1926) *Report of the Royal Commission on National Health Insurance*, Cmnd. 2956, London: HMSO.

HMSO (1942) *Social Insurance and Allied Services*, Cmnd 6404, London: HMSO.

HMSO (1944) *Social Insurance*, Cmnd 6550, London: HMSO.

HMSO (1956) *The Guillebaud Report*, London: HMSO.

HMSO (1959) *Fifteen to Eighteen* (The Crowther Report), London: HMSO.

HMSO (1963) *Half Our Future* (The Newsom Report), London: HMSO.

HMSO (1963) *Report on Higher Education*, Cmnd. 2514, London: HMSO.

HMSO (1970) *Social Expenditure*, London: HMSO.

Home Office (1965) *The Child, the Family and the Young Offender*, Cmnd 2742, London: HMSO.

Home Office (1968) *Children in Trouble*, Cmnd 3601, London: HMSO.

Houghton, D. (1967) *Paying for Social Services*, London: Institute of Economic Affairs.

Howard, A. (1987) *RAB: the Life of R. A. Butler*, London: Macmillan.

Howe, Sir G. (1961) *Reform of the Social Services*, London: Conservative Political Centre.

Howe, Sir G. (1983) 'Agenda for liberal Conservatism', *Journal of Economic Affairs*, January.

Hyndman, H. M. (1881) *England for All*, London: Social Democratic Federation.

Hyndman, H. M. (1883) *The Historical Basis of Socialism in England*, London: Social Democratic Federation.

James, E. (1949) *The Content of Education*, London: Harrap.

Jay, D. (1980) *Change of Fortune*, London: Hutchinson.

Jenkins, R. (1959) *The Labour Case*, Harmondsworth: Penguin Books.

Jessop, B. (1977) 'Recent theories of the capitalist state', *Cambridge Journal of Economics*, 1, pp. 353–73.

Jessop, B. (1980) 'The transformation of the state in post-war Britain', in *The State in Western Europe*, Scase, R. (ed.), London: Croom Helm.

Jessop, B. (1988) *Thatcherism: a Tale of Two Nations*, Cambridge: Polity.

Jewkes, J. and Jewkes, S. (1961) *The Genesis of the National Health Service*, Oxford: Oxford University Press.

Johnson, N. (1987) *The Welfare State in Transition*, Hemel Hempstead: Harvester Wheatsheaf.

Johnson, N. (1990) *Restructuring the Welfare State*, Hemel Hempstead: Harvester Wheatsheaf.

Jones, C. (1983) *State Social Work and the Working Class*, London: Macmillan.

Jones, H. (1971) *Crime in a Changing Society*, Harmondsworth: Penguin Books.

Jones, H. (ed.) (1981) *Society against Crime*, Harmondsworth: Penguin Books.

Jones, K. (1991) *The Making of Social Policy in Britain: 1830–1990*, London: The Athlone Press.

Joseph, Sir K. (1972) 'The cycle of deprivation', Speech delivered to a conference of the Pre-School Play Association.

Joseph, Sir K. (1976) *Stranded on the Middle Ground*, London: Centre for Policy Studies.

Joseph, K. (1977) *Monetarism is Not Enough*, London: Centre for Policy Studies.

Joseph, Sir K. and Sumption, J. (1979) *Equality*, London: John Murray.

Jowell, R., Witherspoon, S. and Brook, L. (1989) *British Social Attitudes: the Fifth Report*, Aldershot: Gower.

Jowell, R., Witherspoon, S. and Brook, L. (1990) *British Social Attitudes: the Seventh Report*, Aldershot: Gower.

Jowell, R., Witherspoon, S. and Brook, L. (1991) *British Social Attitudes: the Eighth Report*, Aldershot: Gower.

Kavanagh, D. (1987) *Thatcherism and British Politics*, Oxford: Clarendon Press.

Kavanagh, D. and Morris, P. (eds) (1989) *Consensus Politics from Attlee to Thatcher*, Oxford: Blackwell.

King's Fund (1988) *Health and Health Services in Britain: 1948–88*, London: King's Fund Institute.

Klein, R. (1974) *Social Policy and Public Expenditure*, London: Centre for Studies in Social Policy.

Klein, R. (1989) *The Politics of the NHS*, London: Longman.

Kogan, M. (1971) *The Politics of Education*, Harmondsworth: Penguin Books.

Labour Party Research Department (1985) *Breaking the Nation*, London: Pluto Press/New Socialist.

Labour Party (1922) *Secondary Education for All*, London: Labour Party.

Labour Party (1929) *A Policy for Education*, London: Labour Party.

Labour Party (1945) *Let us Face the Future*, London: Labour Party.

Labour Party (1958) *Learning to Live*, London: Labour Party.

Labour Party (1964) *Let's Go with Labour for the New Britain*, London: Labour Party.

Labour Party (1983) *Campaigning for Britain*, London: Labour Party.

Labour Party (1987) *Britain Will Win with Labour*, London: Labour Party.

Labour Party (1989) *Policy Review Document on Health*, London: Labour Party.

Labour Party (1990) *Policy Review Document on Local Government*, London: Labour Party.

Labour Party (1991) *A Fresh Start for Health*, London: Labour Party.

Labour Party (1995) *A Policy for Health*, London: Labour Party.

Lawson, N. (1981) *The New Conservatism*, London: Conservative Political Centre.

Lawson, N. (1992) *A View from Number Eleven*, London: Bantam.

Laybourn, K. (1988) *The Rise of the British Labour Party*, London: Edward Arnold.

Laybourn, K. and Reynolds, J. (1984) *Liberalism and the Rise of Labour*, London: Croom Helm.

Leathard, A. (1991) *Health Care Provision: Past, Present and Future*, London: Chapman Hall.

Lees, D. (1961) *Health Through Choice*, London: Institute of Economic Affairs.

LeGrand, J. (1982) *The Strategy of Equality*, London: Allen & Unwin.

LeGrand, J. and Goodin, R. (1987) *Not Only the Poor: the Middle Class and the Welfare State*, London: Allen & Unwin.

LeGrand, J. and Robinson, R. (eds) (1984) *Privatisation and the Welfare State*, London: Allen & Unwin.

LeGrand, J. and Winter, J. (1987) *Not Only the Poor*, London: Allen & Unwin.

Leonard, P. (1979) 'Restructuring the welfare state', *Marxism Today*, December, pp. 7–13.

Leonard, P. (1983) 'Marxism, the individual and the welfare state' in *Approaches to Welfare*, Bean, P. and MacPherson, S. (eds), London: Routledge & Kegan Paul.

Levitt, R. and Wall, A. (1992) *The Reorganised National Health Service*, London: Chapman & Hall.

Lewis, R. and Maude, A. (1949) *The English Middle Classes*, Harmondsworth: Penguin Books.

Lindsey, A. (1962) *The National Health Service: Socialised Medicine in England and Wales*, Chapel Hill: University of North Carolina Press.

Lipsey, D. and Leonard, D. (1981) *The Socialist Agenda: Crosland's Legacy*, London: Jonathan Cape.

Lloyd, T. (1986) *From Empire to Welfare State*, Cambridge: Cambridge University Press.

Loney, M. (1983) *Community Against Government*, London: Heinemann.

Loney, M. (1986) *The Politics of Greed*, London: Pluto Press.

Loney, M., Boswell, D. and Clarke, J. (1984) *Social Policy and Social Welfare*, Milton Keynes: Open University Press.

Lowe, K. (1983) *Dilemma of a Democratic Revolutionary*, University of Salford, unpublished MA thesis.

Lowe, R. (1988) *Education in the Post-War Years*, London: Unwin Hyman.

Lowe, R. (1993) *The Welfare State in Britain Since 1945*, London: Macmillan.

Macleod, I. and Powell, E. (1954) *The Social Services*, London: Conservative Political Centre.

Macmillan, H. (1938) *The Middle Way*, London: Macmillan.

Macmillan, H. (1969) *Tides of Fortune*, London: Macmillan.

Malpass, P. (1993) 'Housing policy and the housing system since 1979', in *Implementing Housing Policy*, Malpass, P. and Means, R. (eds), Milton Keynes: Open University Press.

Malpass, P. and Murie, A. (1987) *Housing Policy and Practice*, London: Macmillan.

Mandel, E. (1968) *Marxist Economic Theory*, London: Merlin.

Marquand, D. (1988) *The Unprincipled Society*, London: Faber & Faber.

Marshall, T. H. (1963) 'Citizenship and social class' in *Sociology at the Cross-roads*, London: Heinemann.

Marshall, T. H. (1965) *Social Policy*, London: Hutchinson.

Marshall, T. H. (1972) 'Value problems of welfare capitalism', *Journal of Social Policy*, 1 (1).

Marshall, T. H. (1975) *Social Policy* (revised edition), London: Hutchinson.

Marshall, T. H. (1981) *The Right to Welfare and Other Essays*, London: Heinemann.

Marwick, A. (1974) *War and Social Change in the Twentieth Century*, London: Macmillan.

Marwick, A. (1980) *Class, Image and Reality in Britain, France and the USA since 1930*, London: Collins.

Marwick, A. (1982) *British Society Since 1945*, Harmondsworth: Penguin Books.

Marwick, A. (1990) *British Society Since 1945*, Harmondsworth: Penguin Books.

Marx, K. (1974) *Capital*, London: Dent.

Marx, K. and Engels, F. (1968) *The Communist Manifesto*, Harmondsworth: Penguin Books.

Maude, A. (1969) 'The egalitarian threat', in *Black Paper 2*, Cox, C. and Dyson, A., London: The Critical Quarterly Society.

Maude, A. (1977) *The Right Approach to the Economy*, London: Conservative Political Centre.

McCarthy, M. (1986) *Campaigning for the Poor: CPAG and the Politics of Welfare*, London: Croom Helm.

McLennan, G., Held, D. and Hall, S. (1984) *The Idea of the Modern State*, Milton Keynes: Open University Press.

Meacher, M. (1984) Speech to Labour Party Annual Conference.

Merrett, S. (1979) *State and Housing in Britain*, London: Croom Helm.

Middlemas, K. (1979) *Politics in Industrial Society*, London: André Deutsch.

Middlemas, K. (1986) *Power, Competition and the State, vol. 1: Britain in Search of Balance*, London: Macmillan.

Miliband, R. (1969) *The State in Capitalist Society*, London: Weidenfeld & Nicolson.

Miliband, R. (1978) *Marxism and Politics*, Oxford: Oxford University Press.

Miliband, R. (1982) *Capitalist Democracy in Britain*, Oxford: Oxford University Press.

Minford, P. (1983) *Unemployment: Cause and Cure*, Oxford: Martin Robertson.

Minford, P. (1984) 'State expenditure: a study in waste', *Economic Affairs*, May/June.

Minkin, L. (1980) *The Labour Party Conference*, London: Heinemann.

Ministry of Education (1945) *The Nation's Schools*, London: Ministry of Education.

Ministry of Health (1944) *A National Health Service*, Cmnd 6502, London: HMSO.

Ministry of Health (1968) *Findings of Enquiry Concerning the Care of the Elderly*, London: HMSO.

Mishra, R. (1984) *The Welfare State in Crisis*, Hemel Hempstead: Harvester Wheatsheaf.

Mishra, R. (1990) *The Welfare State in Capitalist Society*, Hemel Hempstead: Harvester Wheatsheaf.

Moore, J. (1989) Speech to Greater London Areas Conservative Political Centre, 11 May.

Morgan, K. O. (1985) *Labour in Power*, Oxford: Oxford University Press.

Morgan, K. O. (1990) *The People's Peace*, London: Oxford University Press.

Murray, C. (1984) *Losing Ground*, New York: Basic Books.

Murray, C. (1990) *The Emerging British Underclass*, London: Institute of Economic Affairs.

National Advisory Board for Higher Education (1984) *Report of the National Advisory Board*, London: NABHE.

National Association of Labour Teachers (1949) *Memorandum on Comprehensive Education*, London: NALT.

National Institute for Economic and Social Research (1991) *Economic Review* (136), London: National Institute for Economic and Social Research.

No Turning Back Group (1988) *The NHS: a Suitable Case for Treatment*, London: Conservative Political Centre.

O'Connor, J. (1973) *The Fiscal Crisis of the State*, New York: St Martin's Press.

O'Connor, J. (1984) *Accumulation Crisis*, New York: St Martin's Press.

O'Higgins, M. (1983) 'Inequality, redistribution and recession: the British Experience 1976–82', *Journal of Social Policy*, 14, 3.

O'Higgins, M. (1983) 'Rolling back the welfare state', in C. Jones and J. Stevenson (eds), *Social Policy Yearbook*.

Offe, C. (1982) 'Some contradictions of the modern welfare state', *Critical Social Policy*, 2 (2) pp. 7–16.

Offe, C. (1984) *Contradictions of the Welfare State*, London: Hutchinson.

Offe, C. and Ronge, V. (1975) 'Theses on the theory of the state', *New German Critique*, 6, pp. 139–47.

Owen, D. (1976) *In Sickness and in Health*, London: Quartet.

Panitch, L. (1986) *Working Class Politics in Crisis*, London: Verso.

Papadakis, E. and Taylor-Gooby, P. (1987) *The Private Provision of Public Welfare*, Hemel Hempstead: Harvester Wheatsheaf.

Parkinson, M. (1970) *The Labour Party and the Organisation of Secondary Education 1918–65*, London: Routledge & Kegan Paul.

Parry, N., Rustin, M. and Satyamurti, C. (eds) (1979) *Social Work, Welfare and the State*, London: Edward Arnold.

Pascall, G. (1983) 'Women and social welfare', in *Approaches to Welfare*, P. Bean and S. MacPherson (eds), London: Routledge & Kegan Paul.

Paton, C. (1992) *Competition and Planning in the NHS: the Danger of Unplanned Markets*, London: Chapman & Hall.

Peden, G. (1991) *British Economic and Social Policy*, Hemel Hempstead: Harvester Wheatsheaf.

Pelling, H. (1968) *Popular Politics and Society in Late Victorian Britain*, London: Macmillan.

Pelling, H. (1984) *The Labour Governments 1945–51*, London: Macmillan.

Pincus, H. and Minahan, A. (1973) *Social Work Practice: Model and Method*, New York: Free Press.

Pimlott, B. (1988) 'The myth of consensus', in *The Making of Britain: Echoes of Greatness*, Smith, L. (ed.), London: Macmillan and London Weekend Television.

Pimlott, B. (1993) *Harold Wilson*, London: HarperCollins.

Pinker, R. (1971) *Social Theory and Social Policy*, London: Heinemann.

Pinker, R. (1979) *Social Theory and Social Policy*, 2nd edition, London: Heinemann.

Pirie, M. and Butler, E. (1988) *The Health of Nations*, London: Adam Smith Institute.

Piven, F. and Cloward, R. (1985) *The New Class War*, New York: Pantheon Books.

Powell, J. E. (1966) *Medicine and Politics*, London: Pitman.

Powell, J. E. (1969) *Freedom and Reality*, London: Elliot Rightway Books.

Powell, J. E. (1972) *Still to Decide*, London: Elliot Rightway Books.

Powell, J. E. (n.d.) *Income Tax at 4/3 in the Pound*, London: Stacey.

Prentice, R. (1991) Interview with the author.

Prior, J. (1986) *A Balance of Power*, London: Hamish Hamilton.

Radice, G. (1991) Interview with the author.

Radice, G. and Radice, L. (1986) *Socialists in the Recession*, London: Macmillan.

Raison. T. (1990) *Tories and the Welfare State*, London: Macmillan.

Ridley, N. (1988) *The Local Right*, London: Centre for Policy Studies.

Ridley, N. (1991) *My Style of Government*, London: Hutchinson.

Reynolds, D. and Sullivan, M. (1987) *The Comprehensive Experiment*, Brighton: Falmer Press.

Riddell, P. (1983) *The Thatcher Government*, Oxford: Martin Robertson.

Robbins, Lord (1963) *Report on Higher Education*, Cmnd 2514, London: HMSO.

Robson, W. (1976) *Welfare State and Welfare Society*, London: Allen & Unwin.

Rose, R. (1989) *Ordinary People and Public Policy*, London: Sage.

Rubinstein, D. and Simon, B. (1972) *The Evolution of the Comprehensive School 1926–72*, London: Routledge & Kegan Paul.

Ruggles, P. and O'Higgins, M. (1987) 'Retrenchment and the New Right' in *Stagnation and Renewal in Social Policy*, Rein, M., Esping-Andersen, G. and Rainwater, L. (eds) Armonk, New York: M. E. Sharpe.

Rutter, M. and Madge, N. (1977) *Cycles of Disadvantage*, London: Heinemann.

Sainsbury, E. (1977) *The Personal Social Services*, London: Pitman.

Saville, J. (1957) 'The welfare state: an historical approach', *New Reasoner*, 3.

Saville, J. (1968) 'Labourism and the Labour government', in *Socialist Register*, Saville, J. and Miliband, R. (eds), London: Merlin.

Seebohm, F., Sir (1968) *Report of the Committee on Local Authority and Allied Personal Social Services*, Cmnd 3703, London: HMSO.

Seed, P. (1973) *The Expansion of Social Work in Britain*, London: Routledge & Kegan Paul.

Seldon, A. (1967) *Taxation and Welfare*, London: Institute of Economic Affairs.

Seldon, A. (1977) *Charge*, London: Temple Smith.

Seldon, A. (1981) *Wither the Welfare State*, London: Institute of Economic Affairs.

Seldon, A. (1986) *The Riddle of the Voucher*, London: Institute of Economic Affairs.

Shaw, G. B. (1893) *The Impossibilities of Anarchism*, London, Fabian Society.

Shaw, G. B. (1896) *Report on Fabian Policy*, London: Fabian Society.

Simon, B. (1974) *Education and the Labour Movement*, London: Lawrence & Wishart.

Simon, B. (1988) *Breaking the Rules*, London: Lawrence & Wishart.

Simon, B. (1991) *Education and the Social Order*, London: Lawrence & Wishart.

Sked, A. and Cook, C. (1979) *Post War Britain: a Political History*, Harmondsworth: Penguin Books.

Slack, K. (1966) *Social Administration and the Citizen*, London: Michael Joseph.

Sleeman, J. (1978) *Resources for the Welfare State*, London: Longman.

Smith, L. (ed) (1988) *The Making of Britain: Echoes of Greatness*, London: Macmillan and London Weekend Television.

Specht, H. and Vickery, A. (1978) *Integrating Social Work Methods*, London: National Institute of Social Work.

Spens, Sir. W. (1938) *Secondary Education, With Special Reference to Grammar Schools and Technical High Schools*, London: HMSO.

Steadman Jones, G. (1971) *Outcast London*, Oxford: Oxford University Press.

Stockman, D. (1985) 'The social pork barrel' *The Public Interest*, Spring.

Sullivan, M. (1984) 'The crisis in welfare?', Unpublished paper presented to School of Social Studies Colloquium, University College of Swansea.

Sullivan, M. (1987) *Sociology and Social Welfare*, London: Allen & Unwin.

Sullivan, M. (1989) *The Social Politics of Thatcherism: New Conservatism and the Welfare State*, Swansea: University of Wales.

Sullivan, M. (1990) 'Communities and social policy' in *South and West Wales Towards the Year 2000*, Jenkins, R. and Edwards, A. (eds), Llandysul: Gomer Press.

Sullivan, M. (1991) *The Labour Party and Social Reform*, Cardiff: University of Wales.

Sullivan, M. (1992) *The Politics of Social Policy*, Hemel Hempstead: Harvester Wheatsheaf.

Sullivan, M. (1994) *Modern Social Policy*, Hemel Hempstead: Harvester Wheatsheaf.

Tawney, R. H. (1952) *Equality*, London: Allen & Unwin.

Tawney, R. H. (1964) *The Radical Tradition*, Harmondsworth: Penguin Books.

Taylor-Gooby, P. (1985) *Public Opinion, Ideology and State Welfare*, London: Routledge & Kegan Paul.

Taylor-Gooby, P. (1987) *The Future of the British Welfare State*, Canterbury: University of Kent.

Taylor-Gooby, P. (1990) 'Social welfare: the unkindest cuts' in *British Social Attitudes: the Seventh Report*, Jowell, R., Witherspoon, S. and Brook, L. (eds), Aldershot: Gower.

Taylor-Gooby, P. (1991) *Social Change, Social Welfare and Social Science*, Hemel Hempstead: Harvester Wheatsheaf.

Taylor-Gooby, P. and Dale, J. (1981) *Social Theory and Social Welfare*, London: Edward Arnold.

Thane, P. (1982) *The Foundations of the Welfare State*, London: Longman.

Thane, P. (1984) 'The working class and state welfare in Britain 1800–1914', *History Journal*, 27(4).

Thatcher, M. (1968) *What's Wrong with Politics?*, London: Conservative Political Centre.

Thatcher, M. (1977) *Let Our Children Grow Tall*, London: Centre for Policy Studies.

Thatcher, M. (1979) Interview, *The Times*, 9 May.

Thatcher, M. (1993) *The Downing Street Years*, London: HarperCollins.

Therborn, G. (1984) 'The prospects of labour and the transformation of advanced capitalism', *New Left Review* 145.

Therborn, G. and Roebroek, J. (1986) 'The irreversible welfare state', *International Journal of Health Services*, 16, (3).

Timmins, N. (1995) *The Five Giants: a Biography of the Welfare State*, London: HarperCollins.

Titmuss, R. M. (1950) *Problems of Social Policy*, London: HMSO and Longman Green and Co.

Titmuss, R. M. (1958) *Essays on the Welfare State*, London: Allen & Unwin.

Titmuss, R. (1963) *Essays on the Welfare State*, London: Allen & Unwin.

Titmuss, R. M. (1968) *Commitment to Welfare*, London: Allen & Unwin.

Titmuss, R. M. (1970) *The Gift Relationship*, Harmondsworth: Penguin Books.

Townsend, P. (1974) 'The cycle of deprivation: the history of a confused thesis', in *The Cycle of Deprivation*, Thomas, J. (ed.), Birmingham: BASW Publications.

Townsend, P. (1979) *Poverty in the UK*, Harmondsworth: Penguin Books.

Townsend P. and Abel-Smith, B. (1965) *The Poor and the Poorest*, London: Bell.

Townsend, P. and Davidson, N. (1982) *Inequalities in Health*, Harmondsworth: Penguin Books.

Turner, B. (1987) *Citizenship and Capitalism: the Debate over Reformism*, London: Allen & Unwin.

University Grants Committee (1984) *Strategy Document*, London, University Grants Committee.

Vernon, P. (1957) *The Intelligence Test*, London: Allen & Unwin.

Walker, A. (1983) 'Conservative social policy: the economic consequences', in *Thatcherism and the Poor*, Bull, D. and Wilding, P. (eds), London: Child Poverty Action Group.

Walker, A. and Walker, C. (1987) *The Growing Divide*, London: Child Poverty Action Group.

Watkin, B. (1978) *The National Health Service*, London: Routledge.

Webb, B. and Webb, S. (1909) *English Poor Law Policy*, London: Allen & Unwin.

Webb, B. and Webb, S. (1948) *Our Partnership*, London: Allen & Unwin.

Webster, C. (1988) *The National Health Service Since the War*, London: Longman.

Weeks, A. (1986) *Comprehensive Schools: Past, Present and Future*, London: Methuen.

Whiteley, P. and Winyard, S. (1987) *Pressure for the Poor: the Poverty Lobby and Policy Making*, London: Methuen.

Whitney, R. (1988) *National Health Crisis: a Modern Solution*, London: Shepheard-Walwyn.

Wicks, M. (1987) *All our Future*, London: Fontana.

Willcocks, A. (1968) *The Creation of the National Health Service*, London: Routledge & Kegan Paul.

Willetts, D. (1992) *Modern Conservatism*, Harmondsworth: Penguin Books.

Williams, P. (1979) *Hugh Gaitskell*, London: Cape.

Williamson, B. (1990) *The Temper of the Times: British Society Since World War II*, Oxford: Blackwell.

Willmott, P. and Murie, A. (1988) *Polarisation and Social Housing*, London: Policy Studies Institute.

Wilson, H. (1964) Speech to Labour Party Annual Conference.

Winter, J. M. and Joslin, D. M. (1972) *R. H. Tawney's Commonplace Book*, Cambridge: Cambridge University Press.

Woolfe, W. (1975) *From Radicalism to Socialism*, New Haven: Yale University Press.

Wooton, B. (1959) *Social Science and Social Pathology*, London: Allen & Unwin.

Wright, N. (1977) *Progress in Education*, London: Croom Helm.

Young, H. (1990) *One of Us*, London: Macmillan.

Younghusband, E. (1978) *Social Work in Britain*, London: Allen & Unwin.

Index